Missing Persons

Missing Persons

Multidisciplinary Perspectives on the Disappeared

Edited by Derek Congram

Canadian Scholars' Press
Toronto

Missing Persons: Multidisciplinary Perspectives on the Disappeared
Edited by Derek Congram

First published in 2016 by
Canadian Scholars' Press Inc.
425 Adelaide Street West, Suite 200
Toronto, Ontario
M5V 3C1

www.cspi.org

Library and Archives Canada Cataloguing in Publication

Missing persons : multidisciplinary perspectives on the disappeared / edited by Derek Congram.

Includes bibliographical references and index.
Issued in print and electronic formats.
ISBN 978-1-55130-930-9 (paperback).--ISBN 978-1-55130-931-6 (pdf).--ISBN 978-1-55130-932-3 (epub)

1. Missing persons. I. Congram, Derek, 1974-, author, editor

HV6762.A3M58 2016   363.2'336   C2016-901989-6   C2016-901990-X

Text and cover design by Peggy & Co. Design Inc.
Cover image: Ilbusca

16 17 18 19 20   5 4 3 2 1

*This book is dedicated to the families
of missing persons and to
Clyde Collins Snow (1928–2014),
a man who taught so many of us how
to work to bring a measure of peace to these families.*

Contents

Foreword

Professor Emeritus Dr. Mark Skinner

As the following pages so movingly attest, there are many meanings to the phrase "missing person." Each of us who strives to recover the remains of individuals and provide identities to concerned families and communities works within spheres of knowledge whose limitations are made evident by the extraordinary variety of contexts in which persons are considered "missing," ranging from natural disasters to enforced disappearances and even museum bones from involuntary sources. It is a disturbing realization that many children are still unaccounted for in what were residential schools for First Nations in Canada, and that descendants still grieve for missing grandparents in many countries.

Uniting all the extraordinarily interesting and often touching narratives in this volume is a sense of compassion—a conviction that accounting for the missing is deeply worth doing. When in casual conversation one remarks that they work on mass graves or do forensics, a common reaction is "How can you do that; doesn't it upset you?" A glib response along the lines of familiarity, doing the right thing, or the fascination of solving a puzzle is an easy deflection. Unexpressed, and perhaps not even known by the individual investigator, is a deep involvement with the persona of the missing, wanting them to matter again, not to be forgotten, and that by engaging in a search for the missing we reassure ourselves that someone would do the same for us, that indeed we have a "shared humanity." The editor and authors in this volume have worked globally on the issue of missing persons, but even more striking is the historical depth of their searches, going back to persons missing from conflicts half a century or more old. There is an inheritance of fear in the descendants and relations of persons still missing when perpetrators, whether individuals or governments, remain unpunished. The breadth and depth of experience contained within this volume is an unparalleled testament to the years of commitment by the editor and authors to resolving historic and emergent challenges of missing persons. As I write these words, a terrible earthquake has just occurred in Nepal and a human smuggling ship overfull with migrant families has foundered in the Mediterranean. There is a small measure of comfort in knowing that individuals like those who have authored these pages, and those who come after, will embrace the task of finding and identifying the missing.

Dr. Mark Skinner
Professor Emeritus, University of York
June 2015

Foreword

Dr. Marie Wilson

I am standing in a field of heartache and possibility. It is a hot July day on the outskirts of town in rural Saskatchewan in western Canada. The weathering teddy bears hanging from the white wooden fencing are the most visible markers of the spot; that, and the sheer lonely isolation of the field. This is the burial ground of the Regina Industrial School. I am overwhelmed with the same devastating feelings and questions that any human being would have: what if the children lying in this field were mine? What if they were my grandchildren, nieces, nephews, or neighbours? What if they were the children of my ancestors? What if this had happened to me? What if the beloved little ones in my life had been taken away by government agents, or by the police, or by church officials, with a promise of the good education they would receive, only to end their shortened lives in an abandoned burial ground, location overrun, graves unmarked, names and causes of death a riddle yet to be solved, if ever, from scattered fragments of documentation in government and church archives?

Both these questions and the location itself are most haunting by their familiarity. As a Commissioner of the historic Truth and Reconciliation Commission of Canada (TRC), this is not the first gravesite for Indigenous schoolchildren that I have visited. Over the past six years the TRC has heard from almost 7,000 former students of the so-called Indian Residential Schools. Many among them told us they were also speaking for those who could not speak for themselves ... those they had seen die, and those they had known to have died, as schoolmates, as friends, and as siblings.

Almost 150,000 Indigenous children—First Nations, Inuit, and Metis—spent their childhoods in Canada's residential schools, often against the will of their parents and nations. Former students brought a collective court action against the government and the churches that ran the schools. It led to a massive out-of-court settlement, with an obligation on the Canadian government to create this country's first ever Truth and Reconciliation Commission, the first in the world to focus on harms caused specifically to children of a particular ethnicity.

The most definitive of all those harms was death itself, although today we cannot yet say for certain how many children died. We know of over 3,000 who perished at the schools. At least double that number is suspected, in addition to the many that the records show were sent home, or sent to Indian hospitals in the final stages of illness to die there.

These deaths, this complete and utter disregard for the well-being of children, found its root in the same attitudes that enabled the schools to exist in the first place: a belief that Indigenous peoples were inferior, a belief that their cultures should, could, and would be extinguished. Most of the bodies of deceased children were never sent back to their home communities. Instead they were buried at the schools, in cemeteries that have long since been abandoned and forgotten. Their families often had no opportunity to say goodbye. In some cases, children were buried before their parents were even told of their passing. Many parents had no idea where their children were buried. Many of these same questions remain unanswered today ... some families have no idea what became of their children, sisters, brothers, aunties, or uncles.

As part of its core research, the TRC initiated the first national effort ever undertaken to record the names of all the students who died at the schools, or as a result of them, and to locate their often-unmarked graves. To this end, the Commission employed a dedicated team of six researchers led by TRC archaeologist Alex Maass, the author of the first chapter in this volume. Her team worked against time to review thousands of late-arriving and sometimes-incomplete government documents and visit disappearing cemeteries from one end of the country to the other. The result is Canada's first National Residential School Student Death Register. Her chapter discusses this new research and details its results. Although the TRC's research is just a beginning and much remains to be done throughout Canada to find and care for these Missing Children, this work is a substantial and important start.

I think about the wisdom of those who crafted our TRC mandate. It calls for reconciliation as an ongoing individual and collective process involving survivors, churches, the government, and the people of Canada. It creates a legal obligation and a moral expectation that we will all do something towards repairing the many things broken by the schools, among them trust, respect, dignity, opportunity, identity, humanity, and in thousands of cases, life itself. I think of this with great hope as I consider the sacred reconciliation work that is currently underway between local communities, church representatives, and various levels of government to restore the names of these children, to reconnect them with family, to protect the burial grounds where they lie, and to reconsecrate their lives as beloved and remembered.

The great potential is in this: those who would rarely, if ever, have found themselves in the same rooms for common purpose in the past—Indigenous people and more recent settlers—are now working together, for the sake of the children, in the name of justice, and in the spirit of reconciliation.

Such collaborative efforts in Canada, through the courage of the survivors who created this Commission and who have been at the heart of our work, have enormous potential in the wider world, where so many have also been lost or disappeared through a wide range of circumstances. But only if, now that we know the truth of what happened in Canadian residential schools, Canada makes it a national priority to keep up the momentum created by the Commission and to live up to the spirit of ongoing reconciliation.

This means supporting the actions the TRC has called for, including finding and identifying the rest of the Missing Children, recording them in the National Residential School Student Death Register, and honouring their families' wishes for determining and commemorating their final resting places. Only then might we serve as an example and an inspiration to other parts of the world.

As all of this is just beginning to take hold in Canada, I remain standing in this countrywide field of heartache and possibility. I acknowledge and honour the value of this book, of the particular and varied expertise that is already at work, with its potential to further deepen our collective understanding of so much that has happened here and elsewhere, and that is still needed to uphold the lives of those who have been lost.

Dr. Marie Wilson
Commissioner, Truth and Reconciliation Commission of Canada
July 2015

Acknowledgements

In July of 1999, I was a frustrated foreign graduate student completing course-work in a subject that few had heard of, was working long hours at an upstart cafe, and was stressed about my increasing student debt. A Peruvian forensic anthropologist (Jose Pablo Baraybar), who worked for the United Nations International Criminal Tribunal for the former Yugoslavia, offered me a position as an intern (and I was recommended to him by a sympathetic course director, Professor Margaret Cox). I put on my only suit, boarded a plane for some unknown destination (airport code SJJ), hauling all of my goods in a hockey bag. I ended up in Bosnia (my hockey bag wouldn't arrive until several days later), sweating nervously as an ex-British soldier drove me in a white, unmarked Land Rover to a mortuary. It was 4:30 in the afternoon and I assumed that work would be winding up for the day. Baraybar came out to the entrance of the mortuary, greeted me hastily, expressed surprise at the formality of my attire, and instructed me to change into hospital scrubs. Appropriately dressed, he handed me a portion of someone's semi-fleshed pelvis, and shockingly nonchalantly said: "Here, clean this off so we can age this person." A British scenes-of-crime officer (Barrie Fitzgerald), who had a master of science degree in forensic archaeology, called me to a table and gently walked me through the process.

Fifteen years later I am still being guided by and learning from those around me (many of whom contributed to this book)—those whose training, experience, and interpretive acuity are different from and in so many ways superior to my own. I owe these people so much for their kindness, insight, patience, guidance, and encouragement. One colleague chose not to contribute to the book because she disagreed with the premise of the chapter I proposed to her. After some thought, and at her kind suggestion, I rephrased the premise and invited another author that she proposed to me; the latter colleague agreed. It is professional kindness such as this—when one does not share a perspective but helps anyway—that inspires me.

Mark F. Skinner, my doctoral supervisor and a founding father of forensic archaeology and anthropology in Canada, was always kind and encouraging. His repeated (to me) phrase of "unfit for publication in its current form" was always received and appreciated in a positive critical spirit.

Thomas D. Holland and friends at the Central Identification Laboratory of the Joint POW/MIA Accounting Command (now rebranded as the Defense POW/MIA Accounting Agency) have been kind and inspirational. Their lab was an incredibly stimulating intellectual and professional oasis amidst the sometimes socio-political torrent that is the recovery and identification of missing US personnel from past conflicts.

I was editing chapters of the book while working with the Argentine Forensic Anthropology Team in Tbilisi, Georgia (on behalf of the International Committee of the Red Cross). Team members (friends) kindly helped me with some translation from Spanish for Chapter 5.

I also acknowledge the very helpful comments of four anonymous reviewers.

Many thanks to the staff at Canadian Scholars' Press for encouraging the creation of this book, and particular thanks/apologies to copy editor Emma Johnson.

Thank you also to the Global Justice Lab at the Munk School of Global Affairs, University of Toronto.

My wife Ariana (friend, family, coach, colleague, and collaborator) and children are tremendous supporters. Ariana, by her example, reminds me of the critical importance of curiosity and creativity, and also that empathy is the root of what we do and an excellent measure of professionalism. Sophia, our seven-year-old daughter, keeps me thinking critically ("Do we have two hearts? Because I can feel one in my neck." "No, what you feel is a carotid artery, which carries blood from your heart to what is clearly a hard-working brain"). Her questions serve as excellent preparation for cross-examination in court by people who are generally more than 120 cm in height and much more intimidating (though not necessarily more clever). Thomas, our five-year-old, while reminding me to take regular breaks from the computer, taxes my editorial abilities as he works at learning his third language.

During the writing and editing of this book I was continually conscious about what I was asking of the multinational contributors—taking time away from their critical work to contribute to a small publication in Canada—and this weighed on my conscience. I am indebted to them for their commitment of time and energy. My hope, naturally, is that their words will inspire and enlighten others in the work of finding, identifying, and returning the remains of missing persons to their families and, ultimately, deterring future disappearances.

Introduction

Missing Persons and Those Who Seek Them: Questions of Perspective and Place

Derek Congram (University of Toronto)

For about 30 minutes when I was five years old I was a missing person. I had been with my parents and sister in the two-line Toronto subway system. I was holding my father's hand when a train pulled into the station and stopped at the platform alongside us, as we walked towards the stairs to transfer to the other line. Foreign but excited to be in the Big Smoke, as Toronto is known, I was confident that I had this new place figured out. The subway doors opened, people squeezed out, I broke free of my father's hand and moved quickly onto the train as the doors closed just behind me. Turning around, I could see my father's panicked eyes through the glass window in the door and barely made out his words as he yelled at me to stay on the train and go to the end of the line, whatever that meant. In that instant I knew the terror of what it was to be not only lost in a very foreign place, but also moving helplessly away from where I wanted—no, needed—to be.

The busy subway car was full and it was clear to everyone just what had happened. An elderly pair of women snatched me up and tried to calm me down, offering me a mint. To all these onlookers, I was not missing. But if you asked me, my parents, or my sister, I was gone and it was not at all clear when or where we would see each other again. At the final stop, my aged minders escorted me out of the car as I continued to sob and refuse their well-meaning but ineffective consolation. The next thing I remember is standing on that same platform with my family and an unimpressed police officer.

I barely thought about this event growing up, despite researching and working on the search for and the identification of missing people for the last 15 years. However, recently I have started to reflect back upon my very brief and, in hindsight, relatively banal experience as a missing person. This reflection is due in large part to my own young children (aged five and seven), who are prone to deciding suddenly and independently where they need to go and when. My personal realization of *potential* loss has made me much more aware of the impact that loved ones gone missing has on individuals, families, and societies.

The term *missing person* is a complex construct that covers a broad range of scenarios. It can include the very brief separation of a child from his or her family or the deliberate, unannounced, and unnoticed migration of a person to a new city. Tragically, and perhaps most often, a person goes missing unwillingly. We read about it all the time in the news. In 2014, a group of 43 student teachers were detained by the police in Mexico and, despite informant testimony about their killing and burial, they have not been found—alive or dead (Goldman, 2015). Although "missing" and "disappeared" are sometimes used interchangeably, there is often an important connotation with the latter: that being absent is a result of force against the will of a person.

On March 8, 2014, Malaysia Airlines Flight MH370 disappeared with 239 people on board. More than 24 countries have been involved in the ongoing search for the plane, its passengers, and its crew. One man, whose family was on the plane, exclaimed to the press, "How can I believe that my family is gone?" (CBC, 2014). The man's reaction highlights the challenge for families of the missing to believe what others assume: that the missing are dead. Other cases take place over a longer and sometimes never-ending time period, such as the continuing search for Richard Marlow, a nine-year-old boy who went missing from his home in Etobicoke, Canada, in 1944. His sister, who is now almost 90 years old, is still looking for him (McDiarmid, 2014).

Those who never existed and those who lived and died a long time ago can be considered missing. Leveraging the emotional impact of missing persons, a pro-life organization used the theme to include aborted fetuses among the "disappeared" (Figure 0.1).

The location of many missing persons is known, but is known by those who do not recognize (actively or passively) the significance of it. This applies to thousands of sets of usually unidentified (at the individual level) skeletal remains that are boxed or shelved in museum and university storerooms. There are also those whose remains are routinely stared at while on display or handled by people who, like me, studied osteology. Many of these victims were sometimes "kidnapped" (albeit post-mortem) by scientists for study and seemingly perpetual "curation." In some instances, the families, communities, and ancestors of these victims have successfully demanded their return. Such demands triggered important legislation in the United States in the form of the Native American Graves Protection and Repatriation Act (1990), which has dramatically changed the way

FIGURE 0.1   **A Right-to-Life advertisement suggesting that aborted fetuses are among those who should be considered missing persons.**
Source: Niagara Region Right to Life, printed by permission

that archaeologists and biological anthropologists interact with Native Americans/First Nations peoples. Tellingly, the URL "www.repatriation.ca" is owned by a Canadian First Nations group whose mission is to bring "home the remains of our ancestors, grave materials and ancient Haida treasures from museums and private collections around the world" (Skidegate Repatriation & Cultural Committee, n.d.). Adam Rosenblatt, in his recent book about international forensic work *Digging for the Disappeared*, also draws a comparison between the recent, criminal dead and the past enforced disappearance of Native American remains (2015).

Millions of others go missing during armed conflict. This includes combatants and civilians; some of the latter are inadvertent casualties, but there are also those who are the objects of targeted killings. The numbers of missing civilians from very recent conflicts are astounding: between 250,000 and 1 million in Iraq; 50,000 in Syria; and 26,000 in Mexico (*Al Jazeera*, 2015; Congram, Sterenberg, & Finegan, forthcoming; Euronews, 2013). It is disturbing that these reported numbers are so neatly rounded, a phenomena that inspired Polish poet Wisława Szymborska to remark that: "History counts its skeletons in round numbers. A thousand and one remains a thousand, as though the one had never existed" (in Forche, 1993, p. 459). The 1,001st victim of enforced disappearance is twice victimized. Szymborska was reflecting upon the atrocities of the Second World War, but her words have been used repeatedly to refer to events in the former Yugoslavia, Rwanda, Argentina, and Iraq (e.g., Stover and Shigekane, 2002; Hinman, 2006), despite all of the animated but empty retorts of "never again."

The International Committee of the Red Cross is active in dozens of countries helping governments find and identify persons missing from conflict, mass fatality incidents, and undocumented migration. Their work is critical in part because governments are the perpetrators of most civilian deaths and disappearances (Human Security Report, 2013). Problematically, governments also bear the legal responsibility for resolving cases of missing persons. The United States Defense POW/MIA Accounting Agency (or DPAA, formerly—until January 2015—called the Joint POW/MIA Accounting Command) employs almost 500 people and spends hundreds of millions of dollars annually in the search for tens of thousands of personnel missing from past American conflicts. As part of this endeavour, the DPAA runs the world's largest forensic anthropology laboratory (National Public Radio, 2014).

In 1980, the United Nations formed the Working Group on Enforced or Involuntary Disappearances, which works with governments to help relatives ascertain the fate and whereabouts of their disappeared family members. The Working Group's efforts are rooted in the 1992 United Nations General Assembly Declaration on the Protection of All Persons from Enforced Disappearance (UN Resolution 47/133), which entered into force in 2010 and has been ratified by 42 countries (United Nations Treaty Collection, 2014).

There is an increasing awareness of the problem of missing persons in all its forms. Hundreds of millions of dollars are dedicated to preventing, combatting, and resolving disappearances, and there is an overall global decrease of political armed conflict (Human Security Report Project, 2013; Pinker, 2011), which is the context in which most of the missing disappear. Yet the pain of those who suffer such loss is not lessened by any of these facts, and the phenomenon of missing persons sadly persists on a global scale.

Book Overview

This volume is a response to a growing but still limited public consciousness of the breadth of the problem of persons missing due to armed conflict, repressive regimes, criminal behaviour, mass fatality incidents, structural violence, and the legacy of racist colonial policies towards Indigenous persons and minority populations. Organizations such as the United Nations, the International Committee of the Red Cross, law enforcement agencies, and non-governmental organizations dedicate themselves year-round to the unending challenge of the missing in different contexts. The list of countries that are the focus of investigations include not only those engrossed in open conflict and lawlessness, but also stable, pacific democracies such as Spain and Canada.

To be missing almost always means that one is missed by someone else. This volume centres its attention on the people who seek others. The volume explores how scientists, law-enforcement agents, and researchers who work to find the missing serve and relate to those who miss. Due to the large scope of those who can be considered "missing," this book is focused on the people whose absence may be considered or is believed to be the result of criminal acts. However, even this restriction includes a diverse set of scenarios, as you will see from the outset. This book has 14 chapters that are loosely divided into two non-mutually exclusive sections: Contexts and Perspectives (Chapters 1 through 6) and Methods Used towards Finding and Identifying the Missing (Chapters 7 through 14). These sections cover a variety of social and scientific subjects that are inherent parts of the phenomena and resolution of disappeared persons.

Section One: Contexts and Perspectives

The volume opens with a discussion of a particular group of missing First Nations persons in Canada: those who died in or disappeared from state-run/sponsored residential schools. This subject will resonate with people in other countries, particularly the United States where, for example, researchers have been exhuming and identifying juvenile boys who died in state reform schools and whose bodies were buried in anonymous graves outside those institutions (Kimmerle, 2014). The origin of the problem in Canada goes back directly to the 19th century, but can be said to have started with the arrival of colonial-minded Europeans in North America. In Chapter 1, Alex Maass, former member of a Truth and Reconciliation Commission into abuse and deaths at the schools, discusses the current socio-political issues surrounding how Canada as a country has and continues to struggle with racist, colonial policies and attitudes towards First Nations people. She also explores how victim communities are responding to the disappearance of their members as a result of forced relocation, neglect, and/or abuse and death. The dead are seldom memorialized in a traditional sense because they were buried in what have become unmarked—one might say hidden—graves outside the institutions in which they died. Many of these institutions are no longer standing and only faint traces of the buildings still exist (e.g., Dielissen, 2012). One of the most remarkable things in her chapter is the use of the term "survivor," a term almost all of us would never associate with school. This is not a euphemism; to survive was a real, objective concern for many students, and many did not manage.

Chapter 2 presents the experience of finding and identifying the missing from two viewpoints: victim families and those who do the identification work. The context, however, is very different from the preceding chapter: victims of genocide in Bosnia and Herzegovina. Cultural anthropologist Sarah Wagner's ethnography and forensic pathologist Rifat Kešetović's testimony introduce us to victim families and explore how they understand and interact with the scientists who adapted state-of-the-art technology to find, identify, and repatriate the postwar missing.

Chapter 3 significantly broadens the discussion. The International Committee of the Red Cross operates globally, advising, building capacity, and partnering with governments to support families of missing persons. Shuala Drawdy and Cheryl Katzmarzyk help us understand the complications—with infrastructure, law, culture, and resources—that make their support critical in so many countries, particularly those that are more susceptible to mass disaster and mass fatalities. The authors trace the origins of systematic efforts to locate and identify missing persons in Latin America and show how, in particular, the Argentine Forensic Anthropology Team has influenced the globalization of these efforts.

In Chapter 4, social anthropologist Francisco Ferrándiz and journalist Emilio Silva Barrera tell us about a much lesser-known context of the missing: Spain. More commonly thought of as a sunny, cultural mecca, the authors introduce us to the political and legal wrangling that surround the controversial issue of revisiting and remembering a violent past. Ferrándiz and Silva Barrera eloquently make the case that missing persons in Spain are a product of transnational human rights discourses, reminding us that the missing there and in any country are the potential problem and solution for us all.

Psychologist Mónica Esmeralda Pinzón González takes us to Guatemala in Chapter 5 where she examines psychosocial issues from the perspective of Indigenous families of victims in Guatemala: how does one experience and manage *not knowing* the whereabouts of a loved one? Her research with Indigenous communities that were terrorized by military violence gives us amazing insight into how certain groups understand the violent loss of family and rupture of community. Her data is presented here for the first time in English and is a tremendous example of how those who aim to help families of the missing must connect directly with them on their terms, in order to hear their story as they wish to tell it.

The last chapter in this section, Chapter 6, brings us back to Canada and another tension that was produced in part by colonial policies. Janet Young explores the concept of museum skeletons as missing persons. The chapter demonstrates how different stakeholders negotiate the policies and processes of repatriation of First Nations remains to their native communities. Young adeptly spells out how different groups can have very different conceptions about who is "missing" and how these divergent viewpoints can address the products of past (and ongoing) structural violence.

Section Two: Methods Used towards Finding and Identifying the Missing

The chapters in Section Two look more closely at *how* scientists, researchers, and other experts work to find and identify the missing and detail several case studies that exemplify these efforts. Chapter 7 provides a logical beginning by Michael Dolski, an historian who works for the US Defense POW/MIA Accounting Agency. Dolski's work involves two forms of investigation. First, he ties together multiple lines of evidence including oral accounts, archives, and military maps to hone in on possible battlefield burial locations of US service members who died in combat. Then, working in reverse from those who find themselves analyzing accidentally discovered remains, Dolski tries to deduce who is buried in marked graves of "unknown" soldiers at a military cemetery in Hawai'i. Dolski demonstrates in detail how the missing are often much closer than we suppose, and that with the right combination of will, dedication, and deduction, naming the "unknown" can be productive. Critically, however, Dolski also explores at length why the United States government dedicates such an extraordinary amount of resources to searching for its missing military personnel from past conflicts.

In Chapter 8, Vedrana Mladina, a psychologist formerly at the International Criminal Court, talks about two critical areas that have received little attention in similar literature. The first relates to how and when witnesses of serious crimes, such as forced disappearance, should be interviewed. The risk of causing further harm to vulnerable survivors is great and ought to be a primary consideration in the investigation of missing persons, particularly in the context of armed conflict and gross human rights violations. This subject leads naturally into the negative psychological effects that investigations can have on those asking the questions or performing the work of finding missing persons.

Chapters 9 and 10 explore how criminals navigate their geographic environment and how criminal investigators use geographic tools to track them down. *Geographic profiling* is an approach that identifies and analyzes serial crimes—theft, rape, murder, or kidnappings (Rossmo, 2000). Rossmo was among those who raised an early alarm about the possibility of a serial killer being responsible for the disappearance of sex-trade workers and drug addicts in Vancouver's East End in the 1990s and early 2000s. Robert William Pickton was convicted of seven murders in 2007, although evidence existed of other victims, including a confession by Pickton to killing 49 women (CTV News, 2007). In Chapter 9, Samantha Lundrigan, a criminal psychologist, reviews the use of spatial analysis and geographic profiling to understand perpetrator behaviour to find both perpetrators (deliberately "missing") and the disposal sites of their murder victims. Chapter 10 is a collaboration between two forensic anthropologists and a geographer. Using Geographic Information Science and an ecological approach, Derek Congram, Arthur Green, and Hugh Tuller advocate for a new direction in the location of victim burial sites in armed conflict contexts, a method that can be critical when eyewitnesses cease to be reliable in the discovery of graves of the missing.

Chapter 11 is about a more recognizable context to most: contemporary missing persons in peacetime. Royal Canadian Mounted Police Inspector Carole Bird was the Officer in Charge of the National Centre for Missing Persons and Unidentified Remains. She discusses the government's new initiative to address the diverse scenarios of those who go missing in Canada. Bird also explores the related issue of identifying human remains discovered throughout Canada. There is an acknowledgement here that the narrow scope and traditional provincial jurisdiction of investigating the missing is often ineffective because the missing migrate—willingly or unwillingly—across provincial, and sometimes national, borders. Although Bird does not state it, she demonstrates that the development of larger-scope, national institutions such as the one that she worked for can help not only solve disappearances, but also work to resolve structural shortcomings in the way we approach the problem. This in turn could lead to the detection of structural problems that produce the inequities that determine who is more likely to be murdered and go missing. In Canada, the most obvious such group is Indigenous women (see Chapters 1 and 5 in this volume). We hope that organizations that are not solely reactive, but which draw on contemporary research and inspire innovative approaches to the missing, will result in more equitable protection against disappearance.

The next two chapters are collaborations between biological and cultural anthropologists. In Chapter 12, Robin Reineke and Bruce Anderson speak of their experience finding and identifying the remains of those who die attempting to cross illegally from Mexico into Arizona. Their chapter adroitly demonstrates why and how cross-disciplinary collaboration is required to solve the mysteries of unidentified remains of socially marginalized persons. These victims generally "disappear" voluntarily, attempting to migrate anonymously into the US, but criminal acts and harsh environments often prevent their success and result in their involuntary disappearance. In Chapter 13, Ariana Fernández Muñoz and Derek Congram draw on their experience working in Iraq, Spain, and the former Yugoslavia to discuss how cultural material (such as objects and clothing) can be critical evidence that identifies individuals as members of a specific group, and also how they can elucidate the circumstances of a person's death. These objects, tangible, tactile, and often recognizable to families, are sometimes the only evidence that exists of who a person was and how they lived out their final moments. The authors make recommendations for sorting and analyzing material evidence in the context of mass graves.

The final chapter, Chapter 14 by Laurel Clegg, is a case study of young men who left their homes in central Canada to fight in France during the First World War. This case pushes the temporal limits of those who we can scientifically identify on an individual level, and also addresses the political and economic challenges of attempting to do so. Despite these limits, as Clegg demonstrates, the tools do exist, and it is the creativity and will of those who search (and those who send them) that differentiate the cases of those lost from those found.

This volume is a challenging exploration of social and scientific questions that people all around the world face; questions that probe what it means to be missing and how to deal with it. Context is essential to answering these questions, and this volume not only demonstrates different technical and cultural approaches to multiple situations, but also accentuates many similarities among seemingly distinct cases. A single book could be devoted to each method or section within this book. The aim, however, is to introduce readers to the linkages that unite victims, families, academics, scientists, law-enforcement officers, bureaucrats, policy-makers, and civil society in a social problem that affects us all, directly or indirectly. By way of this volume, the authors also hope to inspire further research, development, discussion, and applied efforts towards finding the missing, exploring the various forms of reparation that we owe to their families and communities, and working to prevent people from going missing at all.

This book benefits from having contributions from those who work for governments, including police and military institutions, without being a government publication. I have challenged these authors to be frank and present their work critically. Necessarily, their employers have vetted their chapters, as there are valid concerns about privacy and professional discretion that had to be considered, but it is clear that what you read here presents an honest and sincere representation of these peoples' experiences. Critically, we also hear the voices of families of the disappeared. In most cases, their voices and stories are relayed to us by others. To an extent this is necessary because of the tremendous geographic, contextual, disciplinary, and linguistic range that this volume covers. In cases where the individual missing are named, their families have granted the authors permission to write their stories.

Overall, this book illustrates how one problem—albeit in different forms—is caused, perceived, experienced, and resolved around the world. Methods applied to missing persons cases must always be cognizant of specific situations and provide context-specific solutions, but you will find throughout this volume recurring themes that show how much one situation resembles the next. These echoes remind us why the missing in one place affect us all.

References

Al Jazeera. (2015, August 7). "Almost quarter of a million people" dead in Syria war. Retrieved from www.aljazeera.com/news/2015/08/quarter-million-people-dead-syria-war-150807093941704.html.

CBC. (2014, March 22). *The National*. News broadcast. Canadian Broadcasting Corporation.

Congram, D., Sterenberg, J., & Finegan, O. (forthcoming). Continuing challenges for forensic archaeology and anthropology in Iraq. In S. Blau & D. H. Ubelaker (eds.), *Handbook of forensic anthropology and archaeology, 2nd Ed.* Walnut Creek, CA: Left Coast Press.

CTV News. (2007, January 22). *Crown says Pickton confessed to killing 49.* Retrieved from www.ctvnews.ca/crown-says-pickton-confessed-to-killing-49-1.225554.

Dielissen, S. (2012). *Teaching a school to talk; Archaeology of the Queen Victoria Jubilee Home for Indian Children.* Unpublished master of arts thesis, Simon Fraser University.

Etxeberría Gabilondo, F. (2012). Exhumaciones contemporáneas en España: Las fosas comunes de la Guerra Civil. *Boletín Galego de Medicina Legal e Forense, 18,* 13–28.

Euronews. (2013, October 30). *Finding the millions of missing people across the world.* Retrieved from www.euronews.com/2013/10/30/finding-the-millions-of-missing-people-across-the-world/.

Forche, C. (1993). *Against forgetting: Twentieth century poetry of witness.* New York, NY: W. W. Norton.

Goldman, F. (2015, June 8). The missing forty-three: The government's case collapses. *The New Yorker.* Retrieved from www.newyorker.com/news/news-desk/the-missing-forty-three-the-governments-case-collapses.

Hinman, K. (2006, December 6). CSI: Iraq goes to court. *Riverfront Times.* Retrieved from www.riverfronttimes.com/2006-12-06/news/csi-iraq-goes-to-court/full/.

Human Security Report Project. (2013). *Human security report 2014: The decline in global violence: Evidence, explanation, and contestation.* Vancouver: Human Security Press.

Kimmerle, E. H. (2014). Forensic anthropology in long-term investigations: 100 cold years. *Annals of Anthropological Practice, 38*(1), 7–21.

McDiarmid, J. (2014, March 1). Seventy years missing. Still missed. *Toronto Star*, p. A3.

National Public Radio and ProPublica. (2014). *Grave science.* Retrieved from apps.npr.org/grave-science/.

Pinker, S. (2011). *The better angels of our nature.* New York, NY: Viking.

Rosenblatt, A. (2015). *Digging for the disappeared.* Stanford, CA: Stanford University Press, Ca.

Rossmo, D. K. (2000). *Geographic profiling.* Boca Raton, FL: CRC Press.

Skidegate Repatriation & Cultural Committee. (n.d.). Retrieved from www.repatriation.ca.

Stover, E., & Shigekane, R. (2002). The missing in the aftermath of war: When do the needs of victims' families and international war crimes tribunals clash? *International Review of the Red Cross, 84*(848), 845–866.

United Nations Treaty Collection. (2014). *International convention for the protection of all persons from enforced disappearance.* Retrieved from treaties.un.org/Pages/ViewDetails.aspx?src=TREATY&mtdsg_no=IV-16&chapter=4&lang=en.

Contexts and Perspectives

Chapter 1

Perspectives on the Missing: Residential Schools for Aboriginal Children in Canada

Alex Maass (Truth and Reconciliation Commission of Canada, former/Aboriginal Affairs and Northern Development Canada, current)

Introduction

For more than 100 years the Canadian government pursued a policy of residential schooling for Aboriginal children in cooperation with the Catholic and Protestant churches. The 1996 Canadian Royal Commission on Aboriginal Peoples (RCAP, 1996) and various other reports and inquiries have documented the emotional, physical, and sexual abuse that many children experienced during their school years. Beginning in the mid-1990s, thousands of former students took legal action against the churches that ran the schools and the federal government that funded them. These civil lawsuits sought compensation for the injuries that individuals had sustained, and for loss of language and culture. They were the basis of several large class-action suits that were resolved in 2007 with the signing of the Indian Residential Schools Settlement Agreement (IRSSA, 2007), the largest class-action settlement in Canadian history. The Agreement, which was implemented under Canadian court supervision, is intended to begin repairing the harms caused by the residential school system. In addition to providing compensation to former students for the loss of language and culture, Schedule N of the Agreement (IRSSA, 2007) established the Indian Residential School Truth and Reconciliation Commission of Canada (TRC), with a budget of $60 million and a five-year term.[1] This chapter examines the research undertaken by the Truth and Reconciliation Commission of Canada into student deaths, and the identification of the many unmarked graves and disappearing cemeteries in which these children are buried.

Objectives of the Truth and Reconciliation Commission of Canada

The Commission's principle goals were twofold:

1. To reveal to Canadians the complex truth about the history and the ongoing legacy of the church-run residential schools, in a manner that fully documents the individual and collective harms perpetrated against Aboriginal peoples, and honours the resiliency and courage of former students, their families, and communities; and

2. To guide and inspire a process of truth and healing, leading toward reconciliation within Aboriginal families, and between Aboriginal peoples and non-Aboriginal communities, churches, governments, and Canadians generally. The process will work to renew relationships on a basis of inclusion, mutual understanding, and respect. (TRC, 2012, p. 1–2)

By 1867 the churches had already established a small number of boarding schools for Aboriginal students, primarily in the eastern part of the country. As European settlement moved westward in the 1870s, Roman Catholic and Protestant missionaries established missions and small boarding schools across the prairies and into British Columbia. The mid-west saw the first government-funded, church-administered schools open in 1883. Fifty years later there were in excess of 70 Indian Residential Schools (IRS) representing every region of the country (Milloy, 1999). Some were situated on reserves or later in urban areas, but most were in remote locations often far from the home communities of the Aboriginal children who attended them. To date, a total of 139 residential schools have been recognized under the Settlement Agreement (IRSSA, 2007). However, these were not the only residential schools that Aboriginal students attended in Canada. Religious and charitable institutions operated additional schools without federal government support. Many Aboriginal children attended federal-government day schools, where the goal of education was also to further the assimilation of Aboriginal people. The designation of the particular schools provided for under the Indian Residential Schools Settlement Agreement continues to be a matter of controversy and legal action.

It is estimated that some 150,000 Aboriginal children were sent to these schools before the last one closed in the mid-1990s (AANDC, 2008). The schools were funded on a per capita system and were intended to be partially self-supporting. This meant that, until the 1950s, the children were taught reading, writing, and arithmetic in the morning and in the afternoon the boys worked the farmland on which the school buildings were often situated, tending crops and livestock, while the girls performed domestic duties, such as cooking and cleaning the school buildings. The conditions could be extremely difficult; early church buildings were inadequately equipped for their function, and while the government subsequently provided purpose-built accommodations, the schools were always underfunded, particularly during the war years. As a result, disease was widespread and death rates were high (Milloy, 1999).

The government policy of assimilation through education was intended to "civilize and Christianize" Aboriginal children, and this could be best accomplished by separating children from the influence of their parents. The schools were intentionally designed to undermine Aboriginal culture: for many children the language of instruction was foreign and there was a conscious policy of punishment for speaking their mother tongue as a means to force the children to learn English or French. Students were given new names and sometimes simply referred to by a number, and were dressed in European clothes and fed unfamiliar food. Corporal punishment was commonly used in the schools, whereas it was rarely employed in most Aboriginal cultures. Many children ran away, sometimes with tragic results. Over the last 20 years it has come to light that many children were subjected to physical and sexual abuse in the schools. Although parents often raised their concerns with both church and government officials, they were not permitted to have any direct involvement in the running of the schools. Legally the children were wards of the state. This disruption in Aboriginal family life had a profound and ongoing impact on Aboriginal peoples and their communities. It was not until 1969 that the federal government ended its partnership arrangement with the churches and slowly began to close the schools.

Missing Children Project

Large numbers of the Aboriginal children who were sent to residential schools never returned to their home communities because they went missing, or died while they were in attendance at the schools.[2] Often their parents and families were not informed of their disappearance or death and the fate of one or more family members remains unresolved even today for some Aboriginal families.

The fate of these children, who have come to be known as the Missing Children, was the focus of a series of research projects conducted by the TRC, with work beginning in July 2009.

Working within the limits of the Indian Residential School Settlement Agreement, the Missing Children research project collaborated with the Parties to the agreement, particularly with Aboriginal organizations, Survivors,[3] and community members, to document the fate of those children who never returned to their home communities. The project was intended to produce as complete a record as possible of the children who had gone missing or died while in attendance at a residential school and the cause of their deaths. Finally, it set out to identify and locate the many small cemeteries and unmarked burial sites associated with the 139 recognized residential schools in the system, where it is likely that these children were buried (IRSSA, 2007).

The Missing Children Working Group

The Missing Children Working Group was established in response to a question tabled in the House of Commons by Gary Merasty, the Liberal Member of Parliament for Desnethé/Missinippi/Churchill River, on April 24, 2007:

> ... [the schools] were set up to assimilate a people against their will.
> They were places of disease, hunger, overcrowding and despair.
> Many children died. In 1914 a departmental official said "fifty per
> cent of the children who passed through these schools did not live
> to benefit from the education which they had received therein."[4]
> Yet, nothing was done.... Mr. Speaker, above all else, I stand for
> these children, many of whom buried their friends, families and
> siblings at these schools.... Will the Prime Minister commit to the
> repatriation of the bodies and an apology to the residential school
> survivors? (House of Commons Debates, 2007)

In response, James Prentice, the Minister of Indian Affairs and Northern Development and Federal Interlocutor for Métis and Non-Status Indians, as well as Minister responsible for the Office of Indian Residential Schools Resolution Canada, responded: "We will get to the bottom of the disappeared children. The Truth and Reconciliation Commission will hear much about that. I have instructed our officials to look into that and to work with Oblate records of the churches to get to the bottom of this issue, and this sad chapter in our history" (House of Commons Debates, 2007).

Gary Merasty had raised the issue in response to a growing awareness in the press about persistent reports by former IRS students of high death rates at the schools. Among Survivors, the death of immediate relatives and more distant family members over generations was understood as the most painful unresolved impact of the school experience. John Milloy was among the first to document the high rates of death in his history of the schools *A National Crime: The Canadian Government and the Residential School System, 1879–1986* (Milloy, 1999). Three years earlier James R. Miller had produced the first comprehensive study of the history of Aboriginal education, tracing the foundations of residential schooling to seventeenth-century New France (Miller, 1996).

Despite this growing consciousness, the mandate of the Truth and Reconciliation Commission made no specific mention of the need to investigate this aspect of the IRS experience, other than requiring the Commission "to create as complete an historical record as possible of the IRS system and legacy" (Terms of Reference, Schedule N, IRSSA, 2007). Subsequent to Gary Merasty's question, Mr. Robert Watts, Interim Executive Director for the Truth and Reconciliation Commission, was charged with establishing a Working Group to examine the issue and explore options for further research.

The Working Group was made up of representatives from major national Aboriginal organizations, a national organization representing former students of Indian Residential Schools, the churches, and the federal government. Its membership included representatives from the Assembly of First Nations, Inuit Tapiriit Kanatami, the Métis National Council, the National Residential School Survivor's Society, the Department of Aboriginal Affairs and Northern Development Canada, Library and Archives Canada, and Catholic and Protestant Church representatives and church archivists. The Working Group's primary objective was to make recommendations for further research to the Commission.

The Working Group met on a regular basis throughout the summer and fall of 2007 and the winter of 2008. They also engaged Dr. John Milloy, who had been the chief researcher for the 1996 Canadian Royal Commission on Aboriginal Peoples on issues pertaining to the history of Indian Residential Schools, and was the author of the previously mentioned history of the schools (1999).

Working Group Recommendations

The Working Group identified the key questions and priorities that governed the research objectives of the Missing Children research project. They emphasized the need for the research to be comprehensive, professional, timely, and sensitive to the needs and concerns of Survivors and their families. They also recommended that information derived from the collection of historical documents, personal statements, and ground truthing[5] be used to form the basis of a series of research projects intended to answer the questions:

1. Who and how many IRS students died?
2. What did IRS students die from?
3. Where are IRS students buried?
4. Who went missing? (WGMC&UB, 2008)

In response to their four key questions, the Working Group proposed four distinct research projects, three of which were to be completed in preparation for the Commission's report; the fourth project was expected to run through the Commission's five-year mandate. The four projects were to:

1. Conduct a statistical survey to achieve a precise estimate of student enrolment, including rates of death and disease.
2. Conduct a study on IRS Operational Policies and Custodial Care to review administrative policies pertaining to death, illness, and disappearances of IRS students, and contrast it with the actual experience of the students as gleaned from personal reminiscences and historical records.
3. Conduct a study of unmarked burials and options for commemoration to identify the location of cemeteries and gravesites in which IRS students are buried. The project would collaborate with communities to identify options for commemoration, ceremony, and further community-based research.
4. Conduct specific case research. The Commission, in collaboration with its partner organizations, was to help individual family members to locate information regarding students who may have died or gone missing while in the care of an IRS. Where possible, this would include locating the students' burial locations. Research would be undertaken as required throughout the five years of the Commission's mandate.

The Commissioners adopted these recommendations in February 2008. The Working Group emphasized the importance of addressing the questions in the context of the larger historical experience of Indian Residential Schools because the impact, for many families, of school deaths was the most significant aspect of IRS history. The Canadian government's mandate, enforced through legislation after 1920, required Aboriginal parents to send their children to residential schools many miles from their homes, and was seen as the crux of its assimilationist policies.[6]

Commission's Response to Working Group Recommendations

In response to the recommendations, the Commission undertook research to:

- Collect information from the churches and federal government departments involved in the operation of the schools related to deaths, funeral records, cemeteries, and burial locations.
- Collect information during the statement-taking process, which specifically asked Survivors for information about deaths, causes, runaways, and burials.
- Work with provincial agencies such as the Offices of the Chief Coroners and Medical Examiners and Vital Statistics to identify records that may relate to IRS deaths.
- Conduct a review of archival documents and provincial archaeological site inventories, including maps and aerial photos within the vicinity of the former schools, to inform a ground search for cemeteries and unmarked graves in association with the schools.
- Conduct a limited ground search (ground truthing) of a selected number of known or suspected burial sites to verify documentary and oral information obtained from the sources listed above on cemetery and unmarked burial locations.

Almost four years into its five-year mandate, the Commission was still in the process of collecting documents from the Parties to the Settlement Agreement, the churches, and the federal government departments involved with the schools. This process was slower and more expensive than anticipated. The federal government first provided access to substantial numbers of documents in the fall of 2011 through an Aboriginal Affairs and Northern Development Canada (AANDC)[7] departmental online database. Over the rest of 2011 and throughout 2012 more records were added to the database until it comprised almost one million documents.[8] Additional documents were sent directly to the Commission as other departments began to search their records.

The AANDC database contained documents that had been compiled in the late 1990s from records at Library and Archives Canada and various church archives. These documents had been collected for the purposes of settling alternate dispute resolution claims brought by former residential school students. Although it contained many relevant documents, the database had never been designed to collect documents related to school deaths. As a result, where the database contained documentation related to school deaths (e.g., required principal reports upon the death of a student, death certificates, cemetery plot maps), these had been collected in a random fashion and had not been coded to allow for relevant key word queries. The Commission ultimately sought some of these documents through provincial Coroners' offices. Allowing for these restrictions, project researchers systematically reviewed tens of thousands of selected documents from this database and recorded student deaths in every province and territory for almost every school in the system. Once this data had been compiled, a statistical analysis was conducted to determine rates of disease and death for individual schools in various regions of the country and a national register of student deaths was created.

A complementary health study was conducted to examine operational policies and custodial care in the schools. The purpose was to understand the regulatory regime of the schools with respect to the care of children, including the provision of health services, policies on discipline, runaways, deaths, and burials, as well as compliance with these regulations. The study examined the degree to which school administrators, church and departmental officials, and the government in general were aware of the prevalence of disease and deaths. This aspect of the research focused on the history of health care policy and causes of deaths, including the rampant spread of tuberculosis and related diseases.

The third aspect of the research conducted by the Commission involved a study identifying the presence of cemeteries and gravesites associated with the schools in which former students were likely to be buried. Historical maps, archival documents, archaeological site inventories, and oral testimony were used to identify potential cemetery or gravesite locations. Researchers compiled archival and historical documentation in a cemetery register showing the location and status of all known school cemeteries for which any information was available. Subsequently, data that was collected during site visits was added. In consultation with Aboriginal communities, archaeologists visited 20 of these sites to ascertain their exact location, current condition, and record any disturbance. The research team recorded school cemeteries in most provinces and territories and visited sites from Inuvik, Northwest Territories, to Shubenacadie, Nova Scotia, and many regions in between, including Alberta, British Columbia, Ontario, Quebec, and Saskatchewan. As the number of recorded deaths increased it became clear that many IRS students were buried in unidentified graves in every region of the country and many more burial sites remained to be located. It was also clear that such a large task would require more resources than the Commission had available to dedicate to this work.

As noted above, the Working Group anticipated that the Commission would receive requests for information from Survivors wanting information about individual family members who had died or gone missing after being taken away to school. In these cases the Working Group recommended that efforts be made to identify the details of the case with results of this research released to the family, subject to applicable privacy legislation.

Prior to the fall of 2011, when the Commission first gained access to substantial numbers of government documents, it had generally not been possible to track individual IRS students or confirm IRS enrolment with the documentation available. Additionally, privacy issues were thought to complicate the process and the Commission's legal counsel recommended that these requests be referred to the National Centre for Truth and Reconciliation once it was established. However, as the Parties to the Settlement Agreement produced more documents it became possible—in a small number of cases—to answer questions from individuals regarding missing relatives. The number of these requests increased with greater public awareness of the project.

Results of Research

Document Review and Statistical Survey: How Many Children Died?

The collected data was compiled in the Commission's National Residential School Student Death Register. The resultant database is as complete a record as has been produced to date of children who died at the schools, and includes all collected information pertaining to their deaths: individual student names, date of death, and cause when known (including those who died as a result of disease, fire, drowning, or running away), dates of admission and discharge, and burial locations. Over 4,100 deaths were documented and recorded in the combined register of students deaths, however a realistic number is likely closer to 6,000.[9]

The related cemetery database contains information about the location and condition of cemeteries in association with many schools.

The research also found that some children went missing in the system when they were transferred from the schools to tuberculosis sanatoriums, Indian hospitals, foster homes, or other institutions without their parents' knowledge. Some of these children died and were buried near the hospitals, again without notification to their parents. Unfortunately, resolving such disappearances would have required in-depth tracing of individual students as they transited the school system, which the Commission would ultimately not have the time or documentation to properly pursue.

Estimates for the large numbers of children who died at the schools were being openly discussed in the media long before the Commission began its systematic research of the documents. The argument for these very large numbers was based on the miscalculation of an early quote in which Duncan Campbell Scott, Deputy Superintendent of the Department of Indian Affairs from 1913 to 1932, stated that half the students in attendance at the schools in the early days of the system had not survived. Subsequently, this statement was used to calculate the number of deaths based on the entire estimated population of students who had attended the schools over their 100-year history. The numbers were so regularly overstated in the press that reliable sources began to accept the inflated numbers as fact without any evidential basis.[10] When the TRC released much smaller numbers—with the caveat that the research was incomplete and the numbers likely low—these inflated numbers continued to be quoted; it seemed the more realistic numbers were not sufficiently dramatic for the press, even though they were shockingly high for particular schools in the early years of the system.

Unfortunately, despite the concerted efforts of the Commission, it was unlikely that a completely accurate count of the number of children who died at the schools would be possible during the Commission's operational mandate. This was in part because the records spanned more than 100 years and they were, unsurprisingly, incomplete. For some periods or particular schools, records do not appear to have survived at all. In addition, the Commission had still not received all the documents that were in the government's possession and available in their archives, and it was not likely to receive them before the end of its mandate.

Nevertheless, despite the incompleteness of the records, some of the early government documents that have survived recorded school deaths in great detail. This indicates that the number of deaths occurring in some schools and their causes were well understood at the time. Particularly during the interwar years, there appear to have been fewer efforts made to record school deaths in an aggregated way, and they stopped being reported at all in the Annual Reports of the Department of Indian and Northern Affairs (DIAND) after 1915, although they had been regularly reported in the department's annual reports before that year (DIAND, 1865–1975).

The available documents revealed that for certain schools the death rate, especially during the rise of epidemic diseases at end of the 1890s, was as high as 25 percent according to the government's own records at the time (DIAND, n.d.). Between 1904 and 1914, Dr. Peter Bryce acted as Chief Medical Officer for the Departments of the Interior and Indian Affairs. He began a strenuous campaign to address the health crisis in the schools with particular attention to tuberculosis, but much of his efforts met with bureaucratic resistance. His 1907 report documented high rates of infection and shocking conditions in the schools, supported by statistics revealing death rates for 15 schools in Manitoba, Alberta, and Saskatchewan. The rate for all students and all deaths ranged between 11 percent and 40 percent, with an average of 24 percent (DIAND, 1907).

By 1909, Dr. Lafferty, Medical Officer for Alberta, had reached the same conclusion as Bryce (DIAND, 1909a). Ultimately, however, the main reason for the rejection of the approach suggested by medical officers like Lafferty and Bryce was a financial one. In a March 10, 1910, memorandum, Duncan Campbell Scott, noted that "[i]t will be obvious at once that Dr. Bryce's recommendations while they may be scientific are quite inapplicable to the system under which these schools are conducted" (Scott, 1910). Although some changes were made, at least on paper, regarding stricter admission policies and minimal standards for medical examination prior to admission, their impacts were rather limited (Sproule-Jones, 1996). Little had improved when 15 years later Scott noted that "[t]he cost of adopting an extensive system for the suppression of tuberculosis amongst the Indians would undoubtedly be very great, but until it becomes possible to remove the existing financial handicap, we cannot hope to take the radical steps necessary toward the elimination of tuberculosis" (DIAND, 1927a, p. 10). Therefore, it was not until the 1940s that medical advances, along with increased financial capacity and the political will to institute better medical screening practices, began making a difference in the health of Aboriginal students.

A complete file review of all documents was not a realistic goal due to the late and incomplete production of documents by the Parties and the limited resources available to the Commission to carry out a review of millions of documents. It was, nevertheless, possible for the Commission to isolate patterns and make general statements about infection rates and rates and causes of death.

As previously noted, more than 4,100 student deaths have been documented. Due to the nature of the documents, many of these children remained unnamed in the records, either because only aggregated numbers were provided in the documents, or the document in question provided an account of a child's death but failed to provide the child's name. In these cases a careful examination and comparison of all records from the same school and for the same school year was conducted, allowing researchers to avoid duplication.

Research Conducted by the Offices of the Chief Coroners and Medical Examiners of Canada

Assistance with documentation also came from quarters outside of the Parties to the IRS Settlement Agreement. At the 2012 Intergovernmental Conference of the Chief Coroners and Chief Medical Examiners of Canada, officials in all provinces and territories of the country passed a unanimous resolution to support the Missing Children project and where possible to assist the Commission in identifying residential school deaths in their records. At the 2013 meeting the Commission was invited to attend and review the research accomplished to date. Prior to that time Commission researchers had been in contact with the various Chief Coroners offices across the country and many were generous with their time and offers of assistance. In most cases, as a starting point for their record searches, the Commission provided each office with the results of the Commission's research, namely a record of residential school deaths for their province or territory. As a result, the various offices were able to assist with a review of their records, resulting in additional information about previously unknown deaths and further details about known deaths. This was particularly helpful for deaths that had occurred in the latter years of the schools' operations where a coroner's investigation had taken place. Unfortunately, a coroner's investigation had not been conducted for most of the recorded deaths in the Commission's growing database.[11]

Continued Research by the National Centre for Truth and Reconciliation

Accurate numbers for total enrolment and total deaths at the schools, which operated for over 100 years in most parts of the country, may never be fully tallied. However, continued research beyond the mandate of the Commission will likely achieve a more complete account than is currently possible. A national research centre, provided for in the Commission's mandate, will allow researchers and individual Survivors to pursue further inquiry with the ongoing provision of new documents to the collection. As previously noted, the digitizing and processing of documents in the record collection of Library and Archives Canada, the federal government's agency tasked with the responsibility to provide the relevant documents, was still ongoing by June 2015, the Commission's (extended) closing date. The task of receiving new, incoming documents will continue at the newly formed National Centre for Truth and Reconciliation, established at the University of Manitoba. The total number of documents to be produced by the Parties to the Settlement Agreement is as yet unconfirmed, but is estimated to be close to 3 million (NCTR, 2015).

Cemetery and Unmarked Burials Study: Where Are the Children Buried?

Mrs. Annie Gaetz wrote on behalf of the Red Deer City Archives in 1970 to the Department of Indian Affairs to ask for the names of 12 children who died of scarlet fever at the Red Deer Industrial School and who were buried "in a little plot by the river, southeast of the brick school." In 1970, one rough wooden cross was standing. Mrs. Gaetz lived in the area when the school was in operation and notes that sometime between 1919 and 1925 there were nicely made wooden crosses painted white with the names of the deceased inscribed on them standing by each grave. She concludes, "I trust you will not consider this too much trouble. It seems too bad for the things of the past to be forgotten" (Gaetz in DIAND, 1970). Mrs. Gaetz could not have known, when she wrote her letter, just *how much* trouble, time, and effort would be required for subsequent generations of former students of the Red Deer school to rediscover those missing names, nor did she understand the work entailed in relocating and marking the little Red Deer cemetery after it had almost entirely disappeared from the surface of the landscape many years later (Red Deer Advocate, 2011).

The Cemetery and Unmarked Burials Study was designed to answer the third question posed by the Working Group—"where are the children buried?"—and working with Aboriginal communities, organizations, and individual Survivors was the third component of the Commission's research. Even today, many families lack information about the burial locations of relatives who died at the schools. Therefore, the primary purpose of this aspect of the research was to identify and record cemeteries and unmarked gravesites throughout the country associated with the 139 residential schools where the many children who had not survived their education were buried.

The research relied on oral testimony obtained through the Commission's statement-taking activities and archival documentation collected from the Parties to the Settlement Agreement, including site maps, drawings, letters, and, to a lesser extent, parish registries. Potential gravesite locations were identified using these varied sources prior to visiting sites. Commission staff consulted with local First Nations communities before visiting any site or proceeding with mapping and photographing. Finally, Commission archaeologists visited a small number of burial sites (20) in person and used standard field survey methods to inspect the ground surface and document possible burial locations. Sites were surveyed to ascertain the conditions and disturbance subsequent to school closures and archaeologists spoke with local First Nations members for information on school burial practices.

Research Methods: Some Challenges

There continued to be challenges with document collection, particularly with the quality of school site plans, which were historically generated by the Department of Public Works. These often contain information about cemeteries on school grounds. However, when such plans were present in the AANDC database, the initial reproduction was often so poor that they were illegible. Parish records, which often record deaths, are generally kept in local churches near the former school sites. These are another important source of burial information that is not generally available in the TRC document collection. Finally, provincial archaeology branch inventories are a useful source of information, as they often have records of historic cemeteries, including some former Indian Residential School sites. TRC researchers were able to access these inventories in some provinces, but greater use could be made of this resource. Current problems related to land ownership, jurisdiction, and site access impeded investigation. Much more could be done at provincial facilities to discover ownership and jurisdiction as they relate to IRS cemeteries.

Most IRS cemeteries were informal and unregistered or were established prior to modern provincial legislation for the regulation of cemeteries. Current information regarding land ownership is essential as a starting point before any initiatives can be undertaken towards the protection of IRS cemeteries, whether under the relevant provincial cemetery acts or corresponding heritage legislation.

As a result of these limitations, the task of identifying both marked and unmarked burial sites in association with Indian Residential Schools across Canada required the creative application of a variety of research methods ranging from standard archival file review to taking statements from family members and Survivors to community consultation and ground truthing.

Relevant maps, site plans, diagrams, graphics, land descriptions, and associated letters and memos in government and church records were reviewed. Relevant information was recorded in a purpose-designed cemetery database and a brief summary was written based on information in the document. The document collection was further searched using keywords such as "cemeter*," "grave*", and "burial." Over 500 entries were recorded in the cemetery database. In this way a record of residential school cemeteries began to emerge.

Where no cemetery records were found for particular schools in the documents produced for the Commission, priorities were set for relevant archival files at Library and Archives Canada and records were identified and reviewed online. Provincial archaeological inventories were searched in British Columbia, Ontario, the Northwest Territories, and Alberta for relevant historic cemetery sites, recorded residential school sites, and/or historic Aboriginal gravesites situated in proximity to known Indian Residential Schools. These were mapped in relation to the nearest school.

In addition, modern cemetery and ancestry websites were consulted for the locations of historic cemeteries in the vicinity of known Indian Residential Schools. Cemeteries on Aboriginal reserves and within municipal districts located near a residential school were also mapped. This was done to identify contemporaneous cemeteries or burial grounds to account for the burials of those students who were buried in nearby cemeteries on reserve or in town, rather than at the school.

Historic maps and aerial photography collections (ortho-maps) were searched in areas with residential schools to identify ground features that might indicate informal cemeteries or unmarked burials. Anglican, Presbyterian, and United Church archives were accessed to help locate cemeteries for denomination-specific schools. Finally, where no information could be located for specific schools, a review was conducted of secondary source materials, newspapers, newsletters, and church publications.

Statement and Informant Information
Specific interview questions were drafted for TRC statement takers that pertained to school deaths, cemeteries, burials, and unmarked graves. TRC statement takers were instructed to consistently ask these questions, usually towards the end of the interview process. To facilitate statements that included relevant identifying information, interviewers were asked to indicate in their notes if the statement included a reference to deaths or burials so researchers could easily find and recall them later in the TRC document database. Appropriate protocols for interviewers on issues of death and burials were reviewed with the statement takers and monitored throughout the statement-gathering process. Subsequently, Missing Children project researchers conducted a full review of all oral information (audio recordings and transcripts) obtained from former students and residents living near the schools. Relevant information was recorded and cited, taking into account the school and noting this in the cemetery database.

Site Assessments and Ground Search

Researchers with the Commission carried out 20 site visits for the purpose of establishing the location and condition of a representative sample of burial locations. The rationale for carrying out this work was twofold. First, the Commission learned about many unmarked burial places through Survivor testimonies and from informants, yet there was often little or no archival documentation of these places. Therefore, site visits targeted unmarked gravesites and/or the most disturbed cemetery sites. These were frequently the places that former students told the Commission about at public gatherings and events.

Second, it would be difficult to report on these important places without first-hand knowledge gained through direct inspection and ground truthing. Site visits would establish the current conditions and record the exact location and state of disturbance, particularly for unmarked graves, which in many cases was otherwise unknown. Site visits in six regions were planned—the Maritimes, Quebec/Ontario, Manitoba/Saskatchewan, Alberta, British Columbia, and the North—for trips ranging between two and four days each.

Cemetery Database, Reconnaissance, and Mapping

The primary research goal was to collect information about where children who died in the schools are buried. Collected data was entered into a centralized database for long-term storage and archiving at the National Centre for Truth and Reconciliation. To date, researchers have identified records of, or information about, 54 cemeteries and burial sites throughout the country, containing both marked and unmarked graves from the 139 recognized residential schools. This number is likely to increase as research continues. Information about the history and condition of each cemetery was recorded and entered into the database. Many of these sites are in a state of neglect, while others have almost disappeared from the landscape.

A well-funded national field program to include a ground search informed by archival research and carried out in close consultation with the concerned Aboriginal communities would be needed to complete the task of identifying the many small, unmarked IRS cemeteries and unmarked graves across the country. Initiatives are needed, in consultation with Aboriginal communities and heritage conservation specialists, to protect, preserve, and restore these cemeteries to their former condition and to identify unmarked graves; these sites are under ongoing threat of redevelopment.

Burial Policy and Practice

A brief overview of the burial policy and practices of the Department of Indian Affairs is discussed below. Common practice was to bury children in cemeteries on the school grounds. It was not unusual for school site plans to include provisions for a cemetery, so that one could be laid out at the time the school was constructed. In fact, research has shown that dimensions for the later cemeteries are consistent on the site plans from one end of the country to the other, indicating that even the size of the allotment had been given consideration in advance.

Ongoing discussion and debate at national and international levels has more recently begun to frame the Indian Residential School experience in the context of physical as well as cultural genocide (Mundorff, 2009; Woolford, 2013). The media frequently refers to "mass graves" when discussing unmarked IRS cemeteries. However, it should be noted that IRS burials are not mass graves as they are generally understood, for example, in the context of modern-day genocide. While the deaths of Aboriginal children were not, in the majority, treated in ways that their parents would have considered culturally appropriate, the deaths at residential schools appear to have been followed by funeral services, albeit conducted in the Christian tradition, and burial in cemeteries laid out in a systematic fashion. Although time and resources limited the TRC research, no evidence of mass graves was found.

In the course of this research, however, it became apparent that children were buried in a variety of locales. There was no consistent policy regarding place of burial or transportation of remains other than financial consideration. The Department-generated reporting forms used to record deaths—and there were several versions used throughout the history of the schools—never included information about place of burial (DIAND, 1941a). Although Indian Affairs generally attempted to avoid the costs of shipping remains long distances, there are numerous exceptions to this policy. However, generally speaking, children were buried near the schools, whether in a school cemetery, a cemetery on a nearby reserve, in a local church graveyard, or even in a municipal cemetery.

In the early years of the system, churches often built schools as a component of a mission settlement; children dying at these early mission schools were buried in the mission churchyard or in a larger nearby cemetery that served the whole community. Other schools were built near reserves, in part to facilitate recruitment. Due to the proximity of their families, children's remains could be sent home or collected by their parents and taken back to the reserve for burial (DIAND, 1895). In the case of the school on the Sechelt reserve in British Columbia, the parish records for 1873 described the Benediction of the Seashell (*sic*)

Cemetery for this purpose by the Vicar, "which the Sechelt have prepared and suitably enclosed about two hundred paces to the east of their church at Chatledge" (Dawe, 1979).

The practice of burying children in nearby cemeteries, rather than on the school grounds, was evident in Inuvik when Commission researchers visited in June 2011; it was possible, for example, to match deaths of students at Stringer Hall School recorded in the Anglican parish records with the corresponding headstones at the local municipal cemetery (Anglican Diocese of the Arctic, 2011). The practice was also evident at the Indian Brook reserve, near the Shubenacadie IRS, when Commission researchers visited the reserve in October 2011. Although the earliest parish burial records burned in a church fire some years before, it was nevertheless still possible to observe the headstones of residential school students buried in the cemetery there (Maass, 2011).

The Shubenacadie school, however, was the only one in the Maritimes and served a large catchment area, so many children would have arrived from some distance. A Survivor at the Atlantic TRC national event relayed how her father had been sent as a young soldier on leave during the Second World War to collect the body of his sister at the school and take her back to a more distant reserve where their parents could bury her (Anonymous, 2011). Other examples in the document collection for this school discuss the transport of children's remains from the hospital in Halifax to their home communities. In April 1931, Mary Cuhue's body was sent to her mother's house in Hantsport for burial (DIAND, 1931) and, a few years later in 1934, Anna Bernard's body was sent to Salmon River where her mother was living (DIAND, 1934). As the school had only opened in 1930, this would suggest that at least during this early period the school had no cemetery to receive the children's remains.

Several other examples of the transport of children's bodies are notable exceptions to the rule (DIAND, 1927b, 1966; GNWT, 1966). In 1966, following the sudden death of David Neacappo at the Shingwauk residential school, the Department of Indian Affairs and Northern Development paid to ship his body to Timmins, Ontario, and then by air to his home in Fort George, Quebec, a distance of 1,600 kilometres; they also paid the costs for his three brothers to accompany his body, despite the existence of a long-established school cemetery at the Shingwauk school. His three brothers travelled from as far away as Toronto and Sudbury to accompany the body home (DIAND, 1966).

Despite these examples, in general children were buried at the schools because the Department deemed the cost of sending their bodies long distances for burial in their home community prohibitive. In 1938, a mother requested that the body of her son, who was dying of tubercular meningitis at the school in Spanish, Ontario, be sent to her in Cornwall, Ontario, for burial (DIAND, 1938b). The response from Indian Affairs to the school was this: "I have to point out that it is not the practice of the Department to send bodies of Indians by rail excepting under very exceptional circumstances. Bodies so shipped have to be properly prepared by the undertakers for transshipment under the laws of the province, and the expense of a long journey such as this would entail an expenditure, which the Department does not feel warranted in authorizing" (DIAND, 1938a). The boy's body was buried at Spanish in the Catholic cemetery near the school (Shanahan, 2004, p. 96).

Two weeks after the girls' school in Spanish, Ontario, opened in 1913, a group of students were taken out for a picnic, travelling by boat up the Spanish River. The boat capsized and two girls, Anna Lahache from Kahnawake and Jennie Robertson from Garden River, drowned (DIAND, 1913a). The school officials stated that they buried Jennie at the school after being unable to reach her mother within four days (DIAND, 1913b). However, Anna's body was not actually recovered until a week after the incident. While her mother requested that her body be returned home for burial, it was decided that it was too badly decomposed and the cost too high to ship her body home (DIAND, 1913c).

Funeral Costs

Normally funeral costs were a charge against the school administrative expenses. In a letter from the Port Alberni IRS in British Columbia in 1941, Principal Scott requested the Department cover burial costs because the child died in hospital (DIAND, 1941b). The Department agreed to do so for this reason only, but stated that transportation costs would have to be borne by the school if the principal wished to return the body to the home reserve.

At the height of the influenza epidemic in 1918, Principal Woodsworth of the Red Deer Industrial School was overwhelmed by sick students and staff. "[W]ithout an isolation ward the dead, the dying, the sick, and the convalescent were all together" and he found it was impossible to bury the dead. Therefore, he had the undertaker from Red Deer "take charge and bury the bodies" at a cost of $30 each, for an approximate total cost of $130. Woodsworth wrote to ask the Department to partially cover the costs and they agreed, perhaps because he had been frugal in his expenditures: "I instructed the undertaker to be as careful as possible in his charges, so he gave them a burial as near as possible to that of a pauper. They are buried two in a grave" (DIAND, 1918).

Burial Practices

Christian burial practices were often in conflict with those of the local Aboriginal community. In many Aboriginal cultures burial sites are powerful places, which may be potentially dangerous for children. In 1895, after the death of Mabel Cree at the St. John's Home, adjacent to the Old Sun IRS, the child's body was taken to the house of her parents on the nearby reserve so "the noise of the mourning" could be kept away from the Home premises. When the Assistant Superintendent at the Home attempted to lead a funeral procession of schoolchildren—boys and girls, two by two—to Mabel's gravesite for a funeral service, several Blackfoot men and women who saw them passing rushed out of a nearby house "and shouted at us and would not allow us to go to the grave" (DIAND, 1895).

Morgan Baillargeon discusses both traditional and modern-day adaptations of Cree burial practices (Baillargeon, 2004). There is an important distinction between traditional burial practices under normal circumstances, where burial sites can be dangerous places and lost spirits sometimes roam, and the more common practices at the schools, in which large numbers of children who died as the result of epidemic disease or some other tragedy are buried together in a single location by Christian staff, usually priests, who generally understood little about the cultural practices of those concerned. In this context, Aboriginal children's spirits are believed to roam because there has not been a proper ceremonial process to help them on their journey—they remain unresolved decades later, still needing to be brought home and properly acknowledged, fed, and feasted by their relatives.

Commemoration and Cemetery Restoration

Many previously marked cemeteries visited by TRC researchers had been lost or had fallen into disrepair. With the advent of designated TRC commemoration funding, some Aboriginal communities have been able to initiate cemetery restoration projects, and these have been undertaken in all parts of the country (AANDC, 2013).

The Chapleau Cree community of northern Ontario received commemoration and restoration funding from the Commission after a preliminary reconnaissance survey by TRC archaeologists confirmed an estimated 40 graves at the site. The Chapleau Cree First Nation had long been aware of the abandoned and neglected graveyard of the St. John's Indian Residential School in Chapleau and their own researchers had compiled a list of individuals who were likely buried there.

In the summer of 2013, with assistance from the Ontario Provincial Police Search and Rescue Unit and arranged with the help of the Ontario Coroner's office, unmarked graves at the St. John's IRS cemetery were identified and marked once more. The site was cleared of brush (Figure 1.1 shows the cemetery in 2012 before the restoration in 2013), fenced, and a commemoration ceremony was held to honour the children buried there. Nishnawbe Aski Nation Deputy Grand Chief Alvin Fiddler, Chapleau Cree First Nation Chief Keeter Corston, and First Nation community members took part. At the ceremony, Deputy Grand Chief Fiddler said: "It is critical that the unmarked burial sites of these and all residential school children be found and the remains be put to rest in an appropriate and respectful manner.... The identification and acknowledgement of these and other unmarked gravesites are a sad but very important part of the healing process to help First Nations overcome the devastating legacy of the Indian Residential School system" (Wawatay News staff, 2013). Like the St. John's IRS cemetery, with few exceptions, school cemeteries were informal, unregistered, and had no legal status. There were, therefore, few protections to prevent previously marked cemeteries from being "decommissioned" by school authorities when the school was moved, or when the land was sold after the school closed. This was the case with the unmarked burial ground at the Muscowequan IRS (Lestock, Saskatchewan), now located on the Muscowequan reserve. The Muscowequan cemetery came to light some years later when the Department of Indian Affairs was laying down drain tile for construction upgrades on the reserve. Although the construction was subsequently halted, many graves were disturbed at this time (DIAND, 1993).

While historic examples of "decommissioning" school cemeteries exist, there have also been attempts specifically by the United Church of Canada to work with their Aboriginal members in local congregations near their former school sites to find and honour the descendant families of the deceased students; a notable example is the Red Deer Industrial School (Red Deer Advocate, 2011).

Although the majority of residential school graves are unmarked, Figure 1.2 shows a rare marked grave in a well-maintained Oblate cemetery in British Columbia. The grave is of a young girl, a student at St. Mary's IRS, who died in 1938 at the age of eight. In the photograph it is possible to discern the child's name and age inscribed by hand in the wet cement. The edges of this homemade headstone have been inset with children's marbles.

FIGURE 1.1   St. John's Indian Residential School Cemetery in Chapleau, Ontario, in 2012, before restoration. Note the Indian Affairs–issued tin grave marker on the right of the photograph.
Photo credit: A. Maass

Conclusion

Given its limited time frame, the Commission was unlikely to produce a complete record of deaths and burial places within the duration of its mandate. Much more work remains to be done; many future avenues will open up as more archival and historic material is received by the National Centre for Truth and Reconciliation. The Commission has started this essential investigation and the mechanisms are now in place for the work to continue as those resources become available.

Canada is the most recent among a number of countries to have embarked on transitional justice initiatives to address past historical wrongs. Countries such as Argentina, Cambodia, East Timor, Ghana, Guatemala, Nicaragua, Peru, Sierra Leone, and South Africa, among others, have used similar mechanisms to come to terms with violent or traumatic historical events. However, the Canadian TRC differs from most of these in several important ways. It is one of the few that does not follow a change in political regime or upheaval, and while most commissions have addressed injustices that have occurred in the near past and over a relatively short time period, the Canadian effort covers a much broader

FIGURE 1.2   Child's headstone inset with marbles, Oblates of Mary Immaculate Cemetery at St. Mary's IRS in Mission, British Columbia.

Photo credit: Marina La Salle and Rich Hutchings, printed by permission

historical period. For these reasons, it is likely that other colonial countries with Indigenous populations and a similar history of assimilationist residential schooling, such as Australia, New Zealand, and the United States, will follow the Canadian Truth and Reconciliation process with interest.

Research and Policy Recommendations

Student Deaths

Data collection relating to deaths and burial sites face common problems in historical analysis, including a lack of primary documentation, aggregated data that is difficult to disaggregate to the level at which it would be useful, and the issue of racial stereotyping embedded in older archival and policy documents. In keeping with the Missing Children Working Group recommendations and under the auspices of the National Centre for Truth and Reconciliation, additional research should focus on acquiring missing admission and enrolment records at the individual school level. This research will enable more detailed analyses of trends and more fully ascertain accurate rates of disease and death.

Cemeteries and Unmarked Burials

A complete examination of (particularly late-arriving) documents in the TRC collection should be conducted for all schools within the IRS system to discover further locations of cemeteries and unmarked burial sites. A national field program, conducted in all regions of the country and in consultation with all affected Aboriginal communities, is required to complete the task of identifying IRS cemeteries and unmarked graves. Particular attention is needed to identify those burial grounds on private lands, and others in danger of disturbance. Initiatives are needed, in consultation with Aboriginal communities and heritage conservation specialists, to restore cemetery sites to their former state of repair and to protect and preserve those cemeteries and gravesites that are currently unmarked.

Individuals and Families

Easy access to death records and cemetery data must be provided to enable individuals, descendant families, and Aboriginal communities to research missing relatives and potential burial sites, particularly once further cemeteries are located. Descendant families may need assistance to research missing relatives in the collections at the National Centre for Truth and Reconciliation. The Centre should have trained staff available to assist with individual case research.

Descendant families in particular have a right to know where their individual relatives are buried and to memorialize those sites for their personal and public significance. These are important sites that Canadians, both Aboriginal and non-Aboriginal, have a need to commemorate because they are places that serve as memorials and as sites of conscience that provide an opportunity for society at large to come to terms with the legacy of the schools. TRC statement gatherers frequently heard from intergenerational Survivors that they had been tasked by older relatives with finding their "missing children," the lost relatives of previous generations. In some cases multiple relatives had gone missing as families sent their children to the same schools over several generations. For these families, reconciliation means learning where their dead relatives are buried and knowing that these burial places are respected and honoured in culturally meaningful ways.

Notes

1. The Commission's mandate was extended for one year to June 2015. The completed final report was released in December 2015.

2. Many children "went missing" in the system because they were sent to school and were subsequently transferred to sanatoriums, Indian hospitals, foster homes, or other institutions and were "lost track of" by authorities; as a result their families may never have known their fate.

3. "Survivors" is the term many former IRS students use to refer to themselves and is the term the Commission also adopted, although not all former students prefer this term, some arguing that they have done more than simply survive.

4. Gary Merasty is quoting Duncan Campbell Scott, Deputy Superintendent of the Department of Indian Affairs from 1913 to 1932, found in *Indian Affairs 1867–1912, in Canada and its Provinces* (volume 7, edited by A. Shortt & A. G. Doughty, University of Edinburgh Press, 1913), pp. 615.

5. In this context, ground truthing is the process used to determine the causes of patterns revealed by remote sensing or by analyzing aerial photography.

6. In 1920 the Indian Act of 1885 was amended so that children aged 6 to 15 could be forcibly removed from their families if they were not sent to the schools willingly.

7. As of November 2015, the Canadian government has changed the name of the department from Aboriginal Affairs and Northern Development Canada to Indigenous and Northern Affairs Canada.

8. Subsequently a court reference in January 2013 (*Fontaine v. Canada [Attorney General]*, 2013 ONSC 684), determined that the federal government, while not obliged to turn over its originals, was required *to compile all relevant documents in an organized manner* for review by the Commission rather than, as it had been doing, simply providing access to previously collected records in the AANDC claims database. The alternative, Canada had suggested, was to allow access to the archives at Library and Archives Canada (LAC) in Ottawa for the Commission's researchers. As there may be as many as 3 million relevant documents at LAC, this was a huge unbudgeted expense for the Commission. Once LAC finally began the process of digitizing and compiling the documents in their possession, the task soon became the largest undertaking of its kind in the history of the institution and one they were still engaged in after the Commission's official mandate had ended in June 2015.

9. Commissioner Marie Wilson, during a speech and presentation of the Executive Summary of the TRC Final Report. TRC Closing Ceremonies, June 2, 2015, Ottawa, Canada (*Maclean's*, 2015).

    The Commission uses a smaller number of confirmed deaths in its Summary report than the one quoted here. The discrepancy is due to different methods of tallying. In addition to named deaths recorded on the register, the research included records of unnamed deaths, and deaths that occurred subsequent to student discharge from the schools. Tuberculosis—the primary cause of death at the schools—was slow to develop and could take months and even years to reach its final stage. Many children were discharged once they showed signs of the disease and died at home or in TB hospitals after leaving the schools. Thus, student deaths occurring within two years of discharge were included in the greater count. Dr. Peter Bryce used a similar reasoning in his own counts based on evidence that the infection rate in the schools he visited was close to 80 percent (DIAND, 1909b; Robinson, 2008, p.106).

10. The inflated numbers are based on an often-quoted statement by Duncan Campbell Scott, who in 1914 said, "It cannot be gainsaid that *in the early days of school administration in the territories, while the problem was still a new one,* the system was open to criticism…. It is quite within the mark to say that fifty percent of the children who passed through these schools did not live to benefit from the education which they had received therein" (Shortt & Doughty, 1914, p. 615, my emphasis).

11. In addition, in late 2013 the British Columbia Vital Statistics Agency released over 4,000 documents, including death certificates for Aboriginal children aged 4 to 19 who died in British Columbia from 1917–1956. Without further research it will not be possible to determine how many of these records pertain to residential school students (see Walker, 2014).

References

Aboriginal Affairs and Northern Development Canada (AANDC). (2008). Prime Minister Stephen Harper, Statement of apology to former students of Indian Residential Schools, 11 June 2008. Retrieved from www.aadnc-aandc.gc.ca/eng/1100100015644/1100100015649.

Aboriginal Affairs and Northern Development Canada (AANDC). (2013). Commemoration 2012–2013—project descriptions. Retrieved from www.aadnc-aandc.gc.ca/eng/1370974253896/1370974471675.

Anglican Diocese of the Arctic. (2011). Church of the Ascension, Anglican parish records on file at 194 Mackenzie Rd., Inuvik, NT. Accessed by the author, June 2011.

Anonymous. (2011, October 29). Intergenerational survivor, in discussion with Alex Maass. Truth and Reconciliation Commission of Canada event, Halifax, Nova Scotia.

Baillargeon, M. G. F. (2004). *Walking among birds of fire: Nehiyaw beliefs concerning death, mourning, and feasting with the dead*. Unpublished PhD dissertation, Department of Classics and Religious Studies, University of Ottawa.

Dawe, H. (1979, April 11). 106th anniversary of blessing of Indian Church and Cemetery on Trail Bay. *The Peninsula Times* (SEC-001052). Ottawa, ON: Library and Archives Canada.

Department of Indian Affairs and Northern Development (DIAND). (1865–1975). *Annual reports of the Department of Indian and Northern Affairs*. Ottawa, ON: Library and Archives Canada.

Department of Indian Affairs and Northern Development (DIAND). (1895). *Letter, Assistant Superintendent of the St. John's Home, Old Sun IRS*. RG10, Volume 3928, File 117,004-1 (OLD-008066, p. 1-4). Ottawa, ON: Library and Archives Canada.

Department of Indian Affairs and Northern Development (DIAND). (1907). *Report on the Indian schools of Manitoba and the Northwest Territories, Bryce to Pedley*. RG10, Volume 4037, File 317,021. Ottawa, ON: Library and Archives Canada.

Department of Indian Affairs and Northern Development (DIAND). (1909a). *Letter, J. D. Lafferty.* RG10, Volume 3957, File 140,754-1. Ottawa, ON: Library and Archives Canada.

Department of Indian Affairs and Northern Development (DIAND). (1909b). *Report on the examination for tuberculosis of two hundred and forty-three schoolchildren in Alberta, Bryce to Pedley.* RG10, Volume 3957, File 140,754-1. Ottawa, ON: Library and Archives Canada.

Department of Indian Affairs and Northern Development (DIAND). (1913a). *Letter, N. Dugas to Dear Sir, August 25, 1913.* RG10, Volume 6217, file 471-1, Pt. 1, story no 1.1.jpg. Ottawa, ON: Library and Archives Canada.

Department of Indian Affairs and Northern Development (DIAND). (1913b). *Letter, N. Dugas to the Secretary, Indian Affairs, September 2, 1913.* RG10, Volume 6217, file 471-1, Pt. 1, story no 1.1.6.jpg. Ottawa, ON: Library and Archives Canada.

Department of Indian Affairs and Northern Development (DIAND). (1913c). *Letter, N. Dugas to J.D. McLean, August 28, 1913.* RG10, Volume 6217, file 471-1, Pt. 1, story no 1.1.7.jpg. Ottawa, ON: Library and Archives Canada.

Department of Indian Affairs and Northern Development (DIAND). (1918). *Letter to the Department, Principal Woodsworth, Red Deer Industrial School.* RG10, Volume 3921, File 116, 818-1B, (reel C-10162) (EDM-000956). Ottawa, ON: Library and Archives Canada.

Department of Indian Affairs and Northern Development (DIAND). (1927a). *Annual report for the year ended March 31, 1926, Dominion of Canada.* Ottawa, ON: Library and Archives Canada.

Department of Indian Affairs and Northern Development (DIAND). (1927b). RG10, Volume 6426, File 888-1, Pt. 2 (GRG-001631). Ottawa, ON: Library and Archives Canada.

Department of Indian Affairs and Northern Development (DIAND). (1931). *Letter.* RG10, Volume 6058, File 265-13, Pt. 2 (SRS-001311). Ottawa, ON: Library and Archives Canada.

Department of Indian Affairs and Northern Development (DIAND). (1934). *Letter.* RG10, Volume 6058, File 265-13, Pt. 1 (SRS-004882). Ottawa, ON: Library and Archives Canada.

Department of Indian Affairs and Northern Development (DIAND). (1938a). *Letter, R. A. Hoey to Howitt, August 23, 1938.* RG10, Volume 6219, file 471-13, Pt. 2, story no. 2.2.jpg. Ottawa, ON: Library and Archives Canada.

Department of Indian Affairs and Northern Development (DIAND). (1938b). *Letter, J. Howitt to the Secretary, Indian Affairs, August 20, 1938.* RG10, Volume 6219, File 471-13, Pt. 2, story no. 2.1.jpg. Ottawa, ON: Library and Archives Canada.

Department of Indian Affairs and Northern Development (DIAND). (1941a). *Kuper Island Industrial School—Death of Pupils, 1935–1941.* File 885-23, Pt. 1, Cowichan Agency - F.A. 10-17 Perm. Volume 6457, Reel C-8779 (KUP-230171-0001). Ottawa, ON: Library and Archives Canada.

Department of Indian Affairs and Northern Development (DIAND). (1941b). *Table, Principal Scott, Port Alberni IRS.* RG10, Volume 6436, File 877-23, Pt. 1, (ABR-001547). Ottawa, ON: Library and Archives Canada.

Department of Indian Affairs and Northern Development (DIAND). (1966). *Letter to parents regarding the death of their son.* RG10, Volume 1, File 493/25-13-001, (SWK-001351-0001). Ottawa, ON: Library and Archives Canada.

Department of Indian Affairs and Northern Development (DIAND). (1970). *Letter from Gaetz, A. to DIAND.* RG10, Volume 7, File 701/25-1, Control #H71-316, (NCA-015265-0003). Ottawa, ON: Library and Archives Canada.

Department of Indian Affairs and Northern Development (DIAND). (1993). *Report to Department of Indian Affairs and Northern Development, 23 March 1993.* RG10, Resolution Sector—IRS Historical Files Collection—Ottawa Muscowequan Box 23, File 28, report. Ottawa, ON: Library and Archives Canada.

Department of Indian Affairs and Northern Development (DIAND). (n.d.). *Statistics on discharges and deaths since the opening of industrial schools to December, 1898.* RG10, Volume 3964, File 149,874. Ottawa, ON: Library and Archives Canada.

Government of Northwest Territories (GNWT). (1966). *Report*. File 630-105/12-1,2,3, Pt. 1, Akaitcho Hall, 1966–1968, Archival Box 229-2, Archival Acc. G-1979-003 (AHU-001528). Yellowknife, NT: Government of Northwest Territories Archives.

House of Commons Debates. (2007). *Official Report (Hansard)*, Volume 141, Number 139, 1st Session, 39th Parliament, Tuesday, April 24, 2007.

Indian Residential School Settlement Agreement (IRSSA). (2007). Indian Residential Schools Settlement—Official court website. Retrieved from www.residentialschoolsettlement.ca/.

Maass, A. (2011). Author's field notes for October 25, 2011. On file at the Truth and Reconciliation Commission of Canada, Winnipeg, Manitoba.

Maclean's. (2015, June 2). For the record: Justice Murray Sinclair on residential schools. Retrieved from www.macleans.ca/politics/for-the-record-justice-murray-sinclair-on-residential-schools/.

Miller, J. R. (1996). *Shingwauk's vision: A history of Native residential schools*. Toronto, ON: University of Toronto Press, 1996.

Milloy, J. (1999). *A national crime: The Canadian government and the residential school system, 1879–1986*. Winnipeg, MB: University of Manitoba Press.

Mundorff, K. (2009). Other peoples' children: A textual and contextual interpretation of the Genocide Convention, Article 2(e). *Harvard Journal of International Law, 50*(1), 61–128.

National Centre for Truth and Reconciliation (NCTR). (2015). About the collection. Retrieved from umanitoba.ca/centres/nctr/collection.html.

Red Deer Advocate. (2011, June 28). *Ceremony to mark transfer of wooden headboards*.

Robinson, M. M. (2008). *Dying to learn: Infectious disease and death among the children in Southern Alberta's Indian Residential Schools, 1889–1920*. Unpublished master of arts thesis, Laurentian University.

Royal Commission on Aboriginal Peoples (RCAP). (1996). Volumes 1–17. Ottawa, ON: Government of Canada.

Scott, D. C. (1910, March 10). Memorandum from D. C. Scott, Department of Indian and Northern Affairs. NAC, DIA, Black Series, RG10, Volume 3957, File 1407S4-1. Ottawa, ON: Library and Archives Canada.

Shanahan, D. F. (2004). *The Jesuit residential school at Spanish: "More than mere talent."* Toronto, ON: William Lonc for the Canadian Institute of Jesuit Studies.

Shortt, A., & Doughty, A. G. (eds.). (1914). *Indian Affairs, 1867–1912: Canada and its provinces*, vol. VII. (Archive edition). Toronto, ON: Brook and Company.

Sproule-Jones, M. (1996). Crusading for the forgotten: Dr. Peter Bryce, public health, and prairie Native residential schools. *Canadian Bulletin of Medical History 13*(2), 199–224.

Truth and Reconciliation Commission of Canada (TRC). (2012). *Interim report*. Retrieved from www.myrobust.com/websites/trcinstitution/File/Interim%20report%20English%20electronic.pdf.

Walker, C. (2014, January 7). New documents may shed light on residential school deaths. *CBC News*. Retrieved from www.cbc.ca/news/aboriginal/new-documents-may-shed-light-on-residential-school-deaths-1.2487015.

Wawatay News staff. (2013, August 22). Chapleau hosts ceremony for unmarked graves. *Wawatay News*, volume 40, no. 33. Retrieved from www.wawataynews.ca/home/chapleau-hosts-ceremony-unmarked-graves.

Woolford, A. (2013). Nodal repair and networks of destruction: Residential schools, colonial genocide and redress in Canada. *Settler Colonial Studies, 3*(1), 61–77.

Working Group on Missing Children and Unmarked Burials (WGMC&UB). (2008, February 21). Missing children and unmarked burials research recommendations. On file at the Truth and Reconciliation Commission of Canada archives.

Related Sources

Indian Residential Schools Settlement, Official Court Website: www.residentialschoolsettlement.ca/

National Research Centre for Truth and Reconciliation: umanitoba.ca/centres/nctr/

Reconciliation Canada: reconciliationcanada.ca/

Truth and Reconciliation Commission of Canada: www.trc.ca/

Chapter 2

Absent Bodies, Absent Knowledge: The Forensic Work of Identifying Srebrenica's Missing and the Social Experiences of Families

Sarah Wagner (George Washington University)
Rifat Kešetović (University of Tuzla)

To sit on the hillside along the far western edge of the Srebrenica-Potočari Memorial and Cemetery in 2015 and take in the expanse below, with its almost 7,000 uniform white tombstones, is to behold the work of forensic science in countering the annihilating effects of genocide. Srebrenica, Bosnia and Herzegovina, is often referred to as the worst atrocity to occur in Europe since the Second World War. The intensity and scale of violence that took place from July 11 to July 19, 1995, set it apart from other events, sustained campaigns of ethnic violence, during the three-and-a-half-year war that ravaged the people and land of Bosnia and Herzegovina from 1992 to 1995 (Nettelfield & Wagner, 2014, pp. 8–17).

It was there at the United Nations "safe area" of Srebrenica that the Army of Republika Srpska (Vojske Republike Srpske or VRS) overran the enclave where some tens of thousands of Bosniak (Bosnian Muslim) refugees had taken shelter, forcibly expelling 25,000 women, children, and elderly, and killing over 8,000 men and boys (Honig & Both, 1997; Rohde, 1997; Wagner, 2008, pp. 21–57). In the aftermath of the war, Srebrenica has become synonymous not only with mass killing but also mass graves. The majority of the genocide victims were executed in large groups, their bodies buried in primary gravesites, to which the perpetrators later returned, robbing and dispersing their contents into what became a vast network of secondary mass graves, trenches full of commingled and partial skeletal remains (Vennemeyer, 2012).

FIGURE 2.1   **Temporary grave markers at the Srebrenica-Potočari Memorial and Cemetery, March 2004.**

Photo credit: S. Wagner

The memorial centre and especially its cemetery have come to represent a kind of triumph—scientific, political, and social—over the wilful destruction of human life. Yet the almost picturesque view of the thousands of marble *nišani* (headstones) erected in the cemetery belies the extraordinary task of reassembling the bodies so brutally violated in death and disposition; their uniformity and order mask the complexities of that process for the forensic scientific personnel

FIGURE 2.2   **Ten years after the first collective burials at the Srebrenica-Potočari Memorial and Cemetery, July 2013.**

Photo credit: S. Wagner

dedicated to identifying victims' remains and, more importantly, for the surviving families of the missing who have had to navigate the uncharted waters of the often fragmented recovery and return of their loved ones.

In this chapter, we take stock of the identification process that has spanned the past 19 years and, in doing so, examine the fundamental concept of a missing person and the act of identification from both a scientific and social perspective. Although exceptional in much of its circumstances, Srebrenica offers insight into the complex nature of mass fatality identification efforts more generally, exposing the interplay between techno-scientific resources and expertise and the hopes, fears, and, above all, needs of families of the missing. We argue that identification efforts must be informed by those needs, and that trust in the process and especially its results depends on families' participation throughout. In charting the course of the Srebrenica cases, we also illustrate how the identification process itself is a social as much as a scientific endeavour, where changes in forensic practice and families' experiences of engagement with recovery and identification efforts are mutually constituting—one cannot be understood apart from the other. Finally, we address the looming question of what the future holds, namely for families for whom remains may never be recovered or identified. In short, how does the scientific process anticipate its close, and how do families respond to the possibility that their loved one may remain indefinitely missing?

A Note on Structure

This chapter is structured as both an exchange about and reflection on the Srebrenica identification process. Given our respective disciplinary framings as a forensic pathologist (Rifat Kešetović) and a social anthropologist (Sarah Wagner), we are struck by different milestones and challenges, different contingencies, influences, and responses to the work of recovering and identifying Srebrenica's missing. In canvassing the social and scientific sides of this process, we begin with the more abstract phenomenon of a "missing person," recalling a conversation the two of us had over 10 years ago, when the efforts to identify and return remains to surviving kin had begun to meet with significant success. We then shift focus to concrete data, the results of the identification efforts to date, to provide a backdrop to the chapter's two major sections: an account of how the scientific practice evolved over time (Rifat Kešetović's "retrospective" from the first-hand knowledge gained as the person directly responsible for determining an identification with the Srebrenica cases), followed by an analysis of the social experiences and communal responses to the identifications over the past two decades (Sarah Wagner's ethnographic exploration of time, memory, and absence among the families of the missing).

Missing Person (Sarah Wagner)

In 2004, we sat down to an interview. During the course of the conversation, I asked Rifat about the identification process, and he responded by first reflecting on what the very term, "missing person," meant, as he perceived it. I recall being struck by the powerful sentiment he captured when he noted the unsatisfactory nature of absence—not just absent bodies, but absent knowledge—because it mirrored so much of what I have heard and observed conducting research among the families of the missing, in particular among members of the Tuzla-based organization, the Women of Srebrenica (Udruženje Žene Srebrenice). Rifat explained:

> We all know that it is a very difficult expression a "missing person."
> Not just the expression, the feeling that someone is missing. It is

clear to all of us that a person cannot go missing, simply that a person has his own fate. It is clear to us that after so many years that person is probably dead. But for me it is also an understandable feeling of the family that it is not satisfactory—for them it is not a satisfactory knowledge that their missing relative is probably dead somewhere. (Wagner, 2008, p. 7)

In 2015, over 10 years later, we continued our conversation. I asked him, "What for you still holds true with this statement? What, if anything, has changed with the passage of time?" Rifat responded:

Of course I cannot know the opinion of all the families, but I have the impression that little if anything has changed regarding what I described in 2004. Even after 20 years, families want the remains of their loved ones found; indeed, in some cases, for some among them, that wish has only intensified. As a human being, I can only imagine that agony. I have the impression that with the passage of time and the delay in finding new graves the feeling of hopelessness among these people returns once again. For those of us in the profession, it remains only the task of continually reviewing the mortuary, which we now maintain, trying to ensure in the very least that we do not miss a case that has not yet been identified. Along those same lines, the Institute for Missing Persons (Institut za nestale osobe), the state court, and the International Commission on Missing Persons also invest additional efforts into locating mass graves, which have not yet been discovered.

Results of the Srebrenica Identification Process

As the cemetery in the Srebrenica-Potočari Memorial makes manifest, the results have been significant, with over 80 percent of the Srebrenica victims identified to date.[1] Those results stem from an extraordinary intervention of local and international forensic expertise, much of it concentrated in one particular institution, the Podrinje Identification Project (PIP). Under the auspices of the International Commission on Missing Persons (ICMP), the PIP was established on January 1, 1999, as the forensic facility responsible for the Srebrenica July 1995–related cases. Many of the missing persons were in fact displaced persons from throughout the area of the Drina Valley (Podrinje), who took shelter in the UN "safe area" of Srebrenica, and, therefore, to capture this broader population, the project adopted its name from the wider region. In June 2010 the PIP was transferred to local authorities, specifically the Tuzla Municipality, with extended support from ICMP, employing one senior anthropologist, two osteologists, and Dr. Rifat Kešetović as its supervisor. Since its establishment, PIP has processed thousands of the Srebrenica cases, from relatively complete to highly partial sets of remains.

During that period of time, over 17,500 sets of remains have been exhumed related to the crimes in Srebrenica in July 1995 and their victims. Depending on the type of grave (primary, secondary, a disturbed primary grave, or remains from a surface site), those sets represented complete bodies, nearly complete bodies, body parts, or mixed body parts. The complex circumstances of recovery thus required us to take enough bone samples for DNA analysis to distinguish unassociated bones. To date, we have received 6,809 unique DNA profiles. Many of the recovered sets of remains, however, were composed of isolated small bones, fragments of bones, or mixed small parts of the skeleton, where DNA analysis mostly failed; these remains therefore have ended up designated for the collective ossuary, which will be located in the Srebrenica-Potočari Memorial and Cemetery. We have officially identified 6,507 persons, and 302 cases await families to sign off on the identification of incomplete remains.

In accordance with postwar practice, the official identification of the Srebrenica missing (as is the case with all missing persons within the postwar context in Bosnia) depends on the acceptance of that identification by the designated primary next of kin.[2] In this regard, the scientific process depends on its social recognition. Without the family's consent, the identification cannot proceed towards the next logical step in the care for the missing, now identified, individual; rather than being buried, for example within the cemetery at the memorial centre, the remains continue to be stored in the PIP's mortuary facility, until the point at which the family consents to accept the identification and decides on a burial location. Delays in families' decisions to accept the news of identification often mirror the effects of the Srebrenica crimes: some wait in hopes for additional remains to be recovered from related secondary mass gravesites; others await the possibility for relatives living abroad (themselves displaced by the conflict) to return to Bosnia to take part in the burial; and still others, much smaller in number, are simply not ready to bury at all.

A Retrospective on the Forensic Work of Identifying Srebrenica's Missing (Rifat Kešetović)

The work of locating, exhuming, and identifying the Srebrenica victims began almost as soon as the war in Bosnia and Herzegovina ended. Just a few months after the signing of the Dayton Peace Agreement on December 14, 1995, the first team of experts from Finland appointed by the United Nations recovered the remains of 52 Srebrenica victims from surface areas in the locality of Mratinci, near the village of Kamenica. They began anthropological analysis of the remains at the facilities of the Institute of Forensic Medicine at the Clinical Center in Tuzla. For those of us employed at the Institute at that time, it was our first encounter with the fields of physical anthropology and forensic odontology. Even then it was clear that an enormous task lay before us: recovering and identifying the vast number of the Srebrenica "missing." An expert team from the International Criminal Tribunal for the former Yugoslavia (ICTY) in The Hague completed the initial exhumations from first primary and later secondary mass graves, and by the end of 1998 the body bags with mortal remains already numbered in the thousands. Since the experts from ICTY were working solely on the forensic analysis of the remains, the actual identification process became our responsibility. At the end of the summer in 1996, a local team of forensic specialists also began and would later continue to exhume remains from surface sites in the wider region of Pobuđe, as well as in other areas located on the route taken by the column of men fleeing the Srebrenica enclave in July 1995 as they tried to reach territory under the control of the Army of Bosnia and Herzegovina.[3]

By 1996, Physicians for Human Rights (PHR) and a division of the Office of the High Representative in Bosnia and Herzegovina became involved in the forensic work, including coordinating efforts with local forensic specialists, the commissions for the recovery of missing persons, and the competent courts associated with the identification of the exhumed remains. The International Committee of the Red Cross (ICRC) had itself already compiled a list of missing persons on the basis of family declarations (Stover & Shikegane, 2000; Vollen, 2001; Wagner, 2008, pp. 91–92). One of the most important tasks for PHR was collecting antemortem data about the biological profile of the missing and establishing a database. Employed with PHR at that time, I took part in designing the antemortem questionnaire. The first samples for mitochondrial DNA analysis (mtDNA, which is inherited exclusively from the mother) were sent through PHR to the United States and the United Kingdom. At that time as well, under the auspices of PHR, the first team of case managers was formed; they maintained the identification/missing persons–related documentation and collected blood samples from relatives of the missing for specific cases.

From a professional and scientific approach, albeit at the beginning of the efforts, one can say that there existed an organized and systematic approach to the problem of identification. Here, I obviously stress the formation of the antemortem database and the early use of mtDNA analysis and later nuclear DNA. Unfortunately, the state of Bosnia and Herzegovina, even then, did not recognize the need and the timing to establish a specialized scientific institution that could take control of the identification process. Furthermore, an attempt at massive identification through classical or traditional methods was, for me, not an alternative from a professional standpoint. By 2001, when the ICMP officially started its large-scale DNA testing identification program, only 51 cases had been identified through such means; this stands in contrast to other regions in Bosnia and Herzegovina, where it would be revealed later that there were large numbers of misidentifications. In the case of Srebrenica, even today, not a single one of the "classical" (i.e., through traditional methodology) identifications has been disproved. From the perspective of the families of the missing, this was a painful period, the five to six years after the war, with the extremely slow and inefficient resolution of the fate of their missing. But it was probably in that same time that the incentive arose to move towards the pioneering attempt of over-arching DNA analysis, begun in 2001 by ICMP. The year preceding this attempt was the most crucial for us, because we first needed to convince families to give blood for analysis. This required a series of campaigns, meetings, round table discussions, and contacts with the associations of the missing, as families were still skeptical about the scientific process and the fate of their loved ones, even with the passage of time.

This period, or rather the period of the formation of the Podrinje Identification Project, can be marked as the beginning of the systematic resolution of problems on a scientific basis, with the preceding time employing only classical methods of identification. It should be noted that with victims from Srebrenica there are a number of instances in which traditional methods of identification, including forensic anthropology, are useful and an indispensable part of the overall process: for example, distinguishing between childless siblings, resolving commingling in a small population, and verifying a DNA match or re-association (Yazedjian & Kešetović, 2008). But, in conditions of mass fatalities like Srebrenica, the classical method alone is not the method of choice, because there is a large probability for error. In the project "Book of Photos," which was realized with ICRC, we established that the probability of error was up to 30 percent when using traditional methods (Kešetović et al., 2010).

Because this was a pioneering venture, we had to resolve a series of technical as well as moral dilemmas. The principle of direct participation of families in the identification process proved to be a critical means for resolving the moral concerns. These dilemmas basically consisted of several simple questions: Is it necessary to inform the family if even one bone is found? Should families bury incomplete, identified remains, or wait until the other missing body parts are found? What should be done if other missing parts are found after the burial? How should personal genetic information be protected? What is the proper course of action in cases when misattributed paternity is revealed, and so on? Questions that fall within the realm of the right of families to know and to decide were determined as exclusively theirs to answer, with the remaining questions addressed through ICMP's standard operating procedures.

When it comes to technical matters, probably the most important challenge was the large number of brothers among the Srebrenica missing, and the extreme disarticulation and commingling of remains arising from the disturbance (i.e., robbing) of the primary mass graves as perpetrators attempted to hide the traces of the crimes. The question of the identities of missing brothers, to which DNA analysis alone cannot offer an answer, was resolved through a combination of traditional anthropological methods and the participation of families in recognizing articles of clothing and personal possessions, as well as through antemortem data they might provide. Alongside the resolution of identity, the re-association of disarticulated skeletal remains is another benefit of DNA analysis. Re-association, since parts of skeletons were found in different graves (in some extreme examples, the remains of one individual was found in four or five mass graves), yields information about the interconnections between primary and secondary mass graves. DNA analysis has been the key to revealing those interconnections: "One particular mass grave assemblage consisted of two disturbed primary gravesites and 14 related secondary graves distributed over 30 square kilometers. The disturbance of the graves resulted in some 400 bodies being divided among two or more graves. This type of DNA matching among scattered body parts has made DNA a primary method to confirm links between grave sites" (Sarkin et al., 2014). In the end, the process of resolving the Srebrenica cases has been one of continual adaptation and development, and of lessons learned from the challenging circumstances of the secondary mass graves, the extent of commingling and disarticulation of victim bodies, and the families' painful reckoning with the fact of their loved ones' deaths. While DNA analysis has proven the most powerful tool, its success depended on families' trust in the scientific process and the results it yielded.

Social Experience of the Identification Process: Time, Memory, and the Missing (Sarah Wagner)

Years ago, when I first began doing fieldwork in Srebrenica, I visited an older woman in her home. It was 2003, and she lived in a part of the city where just a handful of Bosniak displaced persons had returned to their pre-war homes. I was not alone—I had come to the house with a Dutch nurse who worked on a project to support returnees and elderly members of the community, monitoring their health. I was her interpreter.

It was late in the day and we were tired. As I recall, we did not have much energy for the meeting. The elderly woman herself had seemed fatigued, almost withdrawn. It was not that she resented our appearance at her doorstep, but there was a despondence about her that effused grief. After the nurse had made her inquiries into the woman's general state of health, I asked a few questions about her return to Srebrenica in hopes of breaking the awkward silence that had enveloped us.

Despite her rebuilt home and her decision to take up residence once again in Srebrenica, little seemed to have assuaged the grief that hung so palpably in this woman's home. While my memory of our encounter has faded into a cluster of blurred scenes, there is one thing that stands out in sharp relief—a sound. I can still feel (even more than hear) the metronomic tick of the clock that hung on the wall. Each tick seemed to pierce the air anew, an oppressive insistence of time passing, moving forward, in a space that seemed transfixed by sorrow.

I cannot help but wonder if this impression emerged from the noise itself—in contrast to the silence that weighed down on us in that room at that moment—or whether it formed in my mind because of another jarring sensory element. The clock hung between two framed photos. In one of the pictures the woman and her husband sat surrounded by their immediate family—their two sons, their daughter-in-law, and a grandchild. The other picture was a snapshot of her elder son with his wife, a strikingly handsome couple, beaming at the camera, as they sat at some café or restaurant in Sarajevo.

Raising a single thin finger in the air before her, the woman explained to us, "*Ja sam sama*" (I am alone). Both sons were killed at the fall of Srebrenica, the younger separated from her by the Army of Republika Srpska at the United Nations peacekeepers' compound in the nearby village of Potočari. Her husband had survived the genocide but died four years later in 1999. Her daughter-in-law and grandchild had left the country and were living abroad. Indeed, she was alone.

Perhaps more than any other conversation I had during those first few months of research among Srebrenica survivors, that space, the noise of the clock, and the sight of those photos made clear to me the interconnections among absence, time, and memory that run throughout the social experience of missing persons and efforts to resolve their fate. Three themes emerge from those interconnections. The first is the instrumentality of recollection in the recovery and identification process, where memory exists as a site of knowledge production. The focus here is on individual recollection, which evokes an intuitive and phenomenological conception of time. Second are the effects of time in the identification process, where collective experience often shapes how individuals respond to the past and plan for the future. In contrast to the more phenomenological notion of time being "lived and acted," this second aspect reveals the shared and coercive force of collective experience. Finally, the example of Srebrenica exposes time as both threat and burden in the context of missing person identification efforts in post-conflict societies, spotlighting the race between time passing and the work of resolving absence and returning remains to surviving kin. The realms are thoroughly interconnected, elements within the broader social experience of reconciling absent bodies and absent knowledge with present conditions and future expectations.

As purposeful acts of recollection, memory plays an important role in the context of missing persons when perpetrator testimony helps to uncover Srebrenica's mass graves. But such instances are limited, as, unfortunately, the contentious politics of postwar redress have meant that very few individuals from among the perpetrators have come forward with information about the crimes and the dispositions of the victims' remains. When they do, the effect is profound, with many of the mass graves containing hundreds of sets of mortal remains. The instrumentality of recollection in this context is thus overtly political, a fact underscored by how, more often than not, these memories are silenced or withheld by the perpetrators. Withholding knowledge—specific recollections of the crimes and their locations—becomes a means of denying their existence and, by extension, the existence of the victims themselves.

In contrast to the purposeful act of recalling gravesites, there is the work of memory within the identification process itself—that is, when families' recollections play a role in "recognizing" the missing person. Obviously, the identification efforts have succeeded in large part because of DNA technology. But, like any line of forensic evidence, DNA never operates alone, and, indeed, as detailed above, the complexity of the Srebrenica cases often requires additional data to determine individual identity. In some instances, families' recollections may assist in the process.

Take, for example, the case of two missing brothers, close in age, both killed in the genocide. Suppose neither had married, nor had had children, and so DNA testing (here nuclear DNA analysis) could only determine that the recovered remains were those of two brothers.

The genetic profiles could not distinguish the two sets of skeletal remains as belonging to one or the other sibling. The forensic specialists would then turn to other forms of evidence. Since, in the case of the Podrinje victims in Srebrenica, there were no dental records available for comparison, other antemortem data became especially important—for example, what the surviving kin could recall about the missing person's physical characteristics, previous trauma, what he was wearing at the time of separation, and so on. To make instrumental their recollections—to assist the process—relatives had to relive the experience of separation, recalling the minute details of the missing person. For many of the Srebrenica survivors, the effort to recollect was an especially harrowing experience, one that transported the family member back to the moment of final separation, when she last glimpsed her loved one.

But what happens when that mental movement falters and images or information elude? In fact, sometimes memory fails entirely, as recollections are disfigured with the passage of time, and the surviving kin feels the terrible weight of guilt when she cannot recall the images or provide specific details that might help recover her husband's remains. "It's been nine years, not nine months," a young widow angrily insisted as she struggled to remember the details of her husband's clothing the very last time she saw him, with her mother-in-law and father-in-law seated in the same room during the antemortem data collection interview. Unable to activate the memory-image with sufficient clarity or force, she felt implicated in her missing loved one's prolonged absence. To appreciate the social import of these kinds of recollections, it is useful to think about the nature of individual memory, how recollections themselves survive or change with the passage of time. Here, phenomenologists of the past century help trace the intuitive, lived experience of memory at work—what Paul Ricoeur in *Time and Narrative*, drawing on Husserl, calls "the past that can no longer be described as the comet's tail of the present—that is, all our memories that no longer have a foothold [...] in the present" (1988, p. 31).

In its biting reminder of memory's fragility, the young woman's remark also invokes the second theme related to absence, time, and memory—that is, the effects of time within the identification process, where collective experience often shapes how individuals respond to the past and plan for the future. The argument is simple: while surviving kin make the highly personalized decisions regarding how to participate in the identification process and how to care for identified remains, they invariably do so as part of a larger community of mourners (Rosenblatt, 2010). Their decisions are shaped by what has come before them, what they see around them, and where and when others have placed their trust and chosen to act. Srebrenica provides a particularly vivid example of the effects of time on collective experience and therefore collective action within its community of mourners. Over the past 19 years, the families of the Srebrenica missing have travelled a long and circuitous path along a continuum of reckoning with absence: from the hope that their fathers, brothers, sons, and husbands had survived the horrors of July 1995 to the fear that they had not; from a sense of resignation that there would be no ready answers, to the expectation that DNA would at long last identify their loved one's remains; from the anger and fear that those remains, though identifiable, would be incomplete, to the acceptance that they might have to wait for the discovery of additional graves and additional exhumations; and finally to the hope that someday soon they will be able to bury those returned and named remains in the collective cemetery at the Srebrenica-Potočari Memorial.

For many it has been an exhausting, unjust journey. Its twists and turns rebuke easy notions of closure that too often arise when we laud the redemptive work of science in post-conflict societies. Along that journey the contours of activism and resistance are thrown into relief. There was a time when many Srebrenica families refused to provide blood samples, when relatives recoiled in anger at case managers who came to them with the news of only a few scant bones to bury, and when they were surprised to learn that the coffin they recently interred at the memorial centre would have to dug up to re-examine, replace, or remove skeletal remains already inside. The community experienced these shifts in practice as a collective, and their responses, as one case manager explained to me, became almost cyclical and organic. Once one horror, one lingering effect of the genocide was overcome, along came the next. The journey was (and is) especially arduous for families whose missing have been recovered piecemeal—that is, the thousands of partial remains exhumed from Srebrenica's web of secondary mass graves. The state of those remains has exacerbated the already fragmented process of ministering bodies so violated in death and in posthumous disposition. Under normal conditions, funerary rituals work to contain and transform the contaminating presence of the corpse. They tend the spirits of the bereaved. Émile Durkheim tells us that ceremonies of mourning have the effect of "bringing individuals together, putting them into closer contact, making them participate in the same state of the soul.... The group feels its strength gradually return; it begins to hope and to live again. Mourning is left behind, thanks to mourning itself" (2001, p. 299).

Srebrenica's secondary mass graves, however, ensure that mourning persists, and the direct effects of time on families' decisions and on their improvisations of ritual become apparent. Contrary to social and religious prescriptions of how to care for the dead, many of the Srebrenica families, especially during the mid-2000s, decided to hold off on burying partial remains with the hope that imminent excavations would unearth more bones. This is still true for some 200 cases of the already identified.

In June 2013 I watched as one family made that very decision. Two brothers had come to the Podrinje Identification Project facility in Tuzla to speak with Dr. Rifat Kešetović about the possibility of accepting the identification and burying their father. They were reluctant. Dr. Kešetović explained to them that no new graves had been discovered that were associated with the site where their father's partial remains had been recovered—nothing for the past two years. And in all likelihood, he said gently, there would be no other graves. But still the two men decided to wait: even so many years later, they were not yet ready to bury their father, or at least such a partial, fragmented remainder of the man.

The example of the two brothers, and their painful deliberations that day, raises the third and final point about the social experience of missing persons and the identification process: the notion of time as both threat and burden. There are competing clocks at work within identification efforts. On the one hand, money and political will are finite, and the forensic personnel are under immense pressure to "produce" results (i.e., identifications). On the other hand, relatives, especially parents, fear their own time will run out before remains are identified, and they will not live to partake in the postponed burial.

President of the Women of Srebrenica Hajra Ćatić is one of those people who still awaits the recovery and identification of her missing son, Nino Ćatić, 19 years later. In an interview for the newspaper *Oslobođenje* in July 2014, she explained what she would now wish for. The twisted logic of genocide has forced upon her a ghastly resignation:

If I had the choice, I would choose that Nino is in some mass grave because it will someday be exhumed. I just fear that they will never find him. That is killing me.

I know how it is for every mother who buries her child, but waiting is even worse. We all are just living for the return of [our loved ones'] mortal remains, so that we can bury them and we can have a place where we can recite the *Fatiha*. (Oslobođenje, 2014)

FIGURE 2.3   The memorial stone's inscription of "8372 …" hints at the perceived incompleteness in tabulating Srebrenica's missing.

Photo credit: S. Wagner

Hajra fears she will not live to see the day they recover her son. This sentiment is shared by those who still await news of their missing relatives from the staff at the Podrinje Identification Project.

Nor is the dread of going to one's grave before being able to bury a missing loved one exclusive to the Srebrenica families. It exists for thousands of surviving kin in former Yugoslavia, where some 12,000 individuals remain missing as a result of the wars of succession in the 1990s.[4] Despite the extraordinary resources and efforts expended to recover and identify the missing from those conflicts, there is a recognition among forensic personnel and most families that the task of identifying and returning all of the missing will never be complete—that there will always be some number among them whose remains will never be recovered, or if recovered, may never be identified.

One of the most prominent memorial stones in the Srebrenica-Potočari Memorial and Cemetery captures this same sense of incompleteness. It lists the number of missing as 8,372, followed tellingly by an ellipsis. Just as the memorial centre and state officials acknowledge that there will likely never be a definitive number of the Srebrenica victims, so too do others tacitly acknowledge that there will come a time when the work of forensic science in recovering and identifying Srebrenica's missing will come to a close. Material constraints—waning budgets and redirected resources—alongside the dwindling number of remains being exhumed or recovered may accelerate that end, despite the enduring advocacy of individuals and family associations.

Conclusion

If the memorial centre and the collective cemetery in Potočari are any indication, the forensic efforts of the past two decades have been extraordinarily successful. That success becomes even clearer in light of the challenging circumstances resulting from the crimes of July 1995. Both the living and the dead were torn asunder and dispersed by the genocide. For the dead, the majority of the victims' physical remains were scattered among the web of primary and secondary mass graves in eastern Bosnia. For the living, thousands of surviving families were permanently displaced and sought refuge abroad, becoming scattered across the globe. To identify Srebrenica's missing has therefore required exceptional interventions in reuniting the living and the dead: locating gravesites, exhuming their contents, and reassembling and reattaching individual names to remains, including by collecting blood samples from relatives who live outside Bosnia and Herzegovina.

As we have underscored throughout this chapter, the successful fruition of these efforts would not have been possible without the participation of the families of the missing. From the beginning, the most mobilized among them, individuals such as Hajra Ćatić and the members of the Women of Srebrenica, pushed for "truth and justice" (*istina i pravda*) in the form of the return of their loved ones' remains. Local and international forensic personnel understood the central role such families would play in helping to disseminate knowledge and encourage participation in the blood collection campaigns, and that such participation presented the only viable and just means for resolving the myriad moral dilemmas introduced by the genocide's legacy of mass graves and partial bodies. Finally, the families' collective experience of encountering news of identification and making decisions about burial illustrates that the process, though driven by exacting science, is nevertheless an inherently social one. As the efforts gradually draw down, that collective experience will also have to include the painful recognition that some missing will always remain missing. Fortunately, the Srebrenica-Potočari Memorial and Cemetery has already anticipated this last wound: families and religious leaders decided years ago that tombstones would be placed for all victims, even in cases when no remains have been recovered. Their souls will be tended alongside the other victims, identified and buried in the same space.

Notes

1. As of September 29, 2014, the combined forensic efforts of the International Criminal Tribunal for the former Yugoslavia, the International Commission on Missing Persons (ICMP), the Podrinje Identification Project, and the local Federal Commission for Missing Persons, which was eventually subsumed into the Missing Persons Institute of Bosnia and Herzegovina, have succeeded in identifying over 6,922 Srebrenica missing. For figures on reference samples collected and remains identified, see the ICMP's online inquiry which provides updated statistics for missing persons in Bosnia and Herzegovina per municipality of disappearance: www.icmp.int/fdmsweb/index.php?w=intro&1=en.

2. The primacy of a missing person's surviving kin embedded in the identification process also appears in postwar legislation around the issue. The Bosnian Parliamentary Assembly adopted a Missing Persons Law in 2004 (BiH Official Gazette 50/2004) designed to protect families of the missing by explicitly establishing their "right to know" what happened to their missing relatives and the whereabouts of their remains. Translated into several languages, the law is available on the ICMP website: www.ic-mp.org/?resources=law-on-missing-persons-bih.

3. In an organized column, 10,000 to 15,000 men and boys fled on foot out of the enclave beginning in the evening of July 11, 1995, heading towards Tuzla and territory controlled by the Army of Bosnia and Herzegovina's 2nd Corps. An estimated 6,000 of those men and boys were captured and killed by the VRS. See David Rohde's detailed chronicle of the flight in *Endgame* (1997).

4. An estimated 40,000 individuals were reported missing at the end of the conflicts in the Western Balkans.

References

Durkheim, É. (2001). *The elementary forms of religious life*. (C. Cosman, Trans.). New York, NY: Oxford University Press.

Honig, J. W., & Both, N. (1997). *Srebrenica: Record of a war crime*. New York, NY: Penguin Books.

International Commission on Missing Persons. (2013). *Law on Missing Persons*. Retrieved from www.ic-mp.org/?resources=law-on-missing-persons-bih.

Kešetović, R., Yazedjian, L., Vučetić, D., Kurtalić, E., Šabanović, Z., Rizvić, A., & Parsons, T. J. (2010). *The Podrinje identification project: A dedicated mortuary facility for the missing from Srebrenica*. Presented at the American Academy of Forensic Sciences 62nd Annual Meeting, Seattle, Washington.

Nettelfield, L. J., & Wagner, S. E. (2014). *Srebrenica in the aftermath of genocide*. New York, NY: Cambridge University Press.

Oslobođenje. (2014, July 8). *Haira, majka Nihada Ćatić a koji je molio za pomoć Srebrenici*. Retrieved from www.oslobodjenje.ba/vijesti/bih/hajra-majka-nihada-catica-koji-je-molio-za-pomoc-srebrenici-gubim-nadu-da-cu-ikada-pronaci-sina.

Ricoeur, P. (1988). *Time and narrative. Vol. 3*. (K. MacLaughlin & D. Pellauer, Trans.). Chicago, IL: University of Chicago Press.

Rohde, D. (1997). *Endgame: The betrayal and fall of Srebrenica, Europe's worst massacre since World War II*. New York, NY: Farrar, Straus and Giroux.

Rosenblatt, A. (2010). International forensic investigations and the human rights of the dead. *Human Rights Quarterly, 32*(4), 921–950.

Sarkin, J., Nettelfield, L., Matthews, M., & Kosalka, R. (2014). *Bosnia and Herzegovina missing persons from the armed conflicts of the 1990s: A stocktaking.* Sarajevo: International Commission on Missing Persons.

Stover, E., & Shikegane, R. (2000). The missing in the aftermath of war: When do the needs of victims' families and international war crimes tribunals clash? *International Review of the Red Cross, 48,* 845–866.

Vennemeyer, M. (2012). *An analysis of linkages between robbed primary graves and secondary graves related to Srebrenica missing.* Presentation at the Alpe-Adria-Pannonia International Meeting on Forensic Medicine, May 31–June 2, Sarajevo.

Vollen, L. (2001). All that remains: Identifying the victims of the Srebrenica massacre. *Cambridge Quarterly of Healthcare Ethics, 10*(3), 336–340.

Wagner, S. (2008). *To know where he lies: DNA technology and the search for Srebrenica's missing.* Berkeley: University of California Press.

Yazedjian, L., & Kešetović, J. E. (2008). The application of traditional anthropological methods in a large-scale DNA led identification system. In B. Adams & J. Byrd (eds.), *Recovery, analysis, and identification of commingled human remains* (pp. 271–284). Totowa, NJ & London, UK: Humana.

Related Sources

Institute for Research of Crimes against Humanity and International Law: www.institut-genocid.unsa.ba

Srebrenica-Potočari Memorial and Cemetery: www.potocarimc.org/

Youth Initiative for Human Rights, Mapping Genocide project: www.srebrenica-mappinggenocide.com/en-m/

Chapter 3

The Missing Files: The Experience of the International Committee of the Red Cross[1]

Shuala M. Drawdy and Cheryl Katzmarzyk
(International Committee of the Red Cross)

Introduction

According to the mission statement for the International Committee of the Red
Cross (ICRC), it is

> an impartial, neutral, and independent organization whose exclu-
> sively humanitarian mission is to protect the lives and dignity of
> victims of armed conflict and other situations of violence and to
> provide them with assistance. The ICRC also endeavours to prevent
> suffering by promoting and strengthening humanitarian law and
> universal humanitarian principles. Established in 1863, the ICRC is
> at the origin of the Geneva Conventions and the International Red
> Cross and Red Crescent Movement. It directs and coordinates the
> international activities conducted by the Movement in armed con-
> flicts and other situations of violence. (ICRC, n.d.)

In 2002, the ICRC began looking at ways of increasing efforts to assist the missing
and their families. The aim was first to review all methods of preventing disappearances, of processing cases of missing persons and of assisting their families,
then to agree on common practices in this area and move the issue further up
the international agenda. Following an international conference of governmental

and non-governmental experts (held in Geneva, February 19–20, 2003), the 28th International Conference of the Red Cross and Red Crescent adopted the Agenda for Humanitarian Action on December 6, 2003, which sets out clear objectives for states and the International Red Cross and Red Crescent Movement. Among these objectives was the creation in 2003 of Forensic Services within the Assistance Division of the ICRC.

At the outset, the Forensic Services' main activities focused largely on programs to assist in resolving the fate of post-conflict missing persons. Catalyzed by the December 2004 Asian Tsunami and other natural disasters, the International Red Cross and Red Crescent Movement designated the ICRC in 2008 as the lead agency within the Movement on issues related to the management of the dead and forensic science. In 2010, the ICRC determined to help address the vast humanitarian needs associated with migration, including issues related to deceased migrants. Today, the ICRC Forensic Services serves as a reference worldwide in the application of forensic science to promoting humanitarian principles, ethics, and law, and forensic practice to meet the needs of victims.

The initiatives and activities of the Forensic Services are in line with fulfilling vital obligations under international humanitarian law. Significant elements of the four Geneva Conventions of 1949 and their first and second Additional Protocols of 1977, which guide Forensic Services, include obligations to search for the dead, maintain the dignity of the dead and their gravesites (non-despoliation), identify the dead, and return remains to their country of origin. Also included are the obligations to note locations of graves, ensure access to the families of the deceased, and clarify the fate of missing persons to fulfill the families' right to know. The ICRC Forensic Services also respects guiding principles under international human rights law, most notably those enshrined in the International Covenant on Civil and Political Rights of 1966.

At the time of writing, the ICRC Forensic Services works in over 50 operational contexts with 30 staff members worldwide, working either in their home countries or abroad. The Forensic Services' staff hail from all parts of the world: 18 from Latin America (Argentina, Chile, Colombia, Guatemala, Mexico, and Peru); six from Europe (Austria, Cyprus, France, Germany, Greece, and Ireland); four from North America (Canada and the US); and two from Africa (Kenya and South Africa). Likewise, the Forensic Services' staff represent diverse professional forensic backgrounds: 18 from anthropology; five from medicine; two from archaeology; three from odontology; one from criminalistics; and one from a coroner's office. The Forensic Services are assisted by an external Forensic Advisory Board consisting of forensic professionals from around the world and a network of external forensic consultants.

The Evolution of Humanitarian Forensic Action

The first large-scale application of forensic science to address questions of international law is often cited as that applied to the 1940 massacre of over 25,000 Polish officers and elites in the Katyn Forest, in which accountability was the main objective (Debons, Fleury, & Pitteloud, 2009). But it was not until the 1980s in Latin America that forensic science was systematically and sustainably applied to investigations of war crimes and crimes against humanity. While these investigations did, and still do, include a justice component, they also seek to identify victims and provide answers to their families. The 1990s saw further expansion of the systematic application of forensic science to investigate violations of international law, with the International Criminal Tribunal for the former Yugoslavia (ICTY) and the International Criminal Tribunal for Rwanda (ICTR).

While the forensic investigations of the ICTR were limited in both scope and scale, the ICTY's investigations involved the excavation and examination of thousands of victims of the armed conflicts in the former Yugoslavia, most notably in Bosnia and Herzegovina and Kosovo. This brought the concept of international forensic investigations to the world stage, sparking interest in both the general public and the forensic science world alike. More importantly, however, it brought a striking blow to Europe and the rest of the Western developed world when genocide and the plight of victims of armed conflict were revealed in their backyard, issues that the West did not expect a recurrence of following the atrocities of the Second World War.

Most of these investigations, however, contained a primary mandate of judicial investigation for the purposes of accountability. It was not until 2003, with the ICRC's Missing initiative, that the concept of international forensic investigations purely for humanitarian purposes became truly conceivable. Contrary to investigations aimed at judicial proceedings, the ICRC's humanitarian forensic action centres solely on the dignified handling and professional management of the dead, as well as bringing answers to families to clarify the fate of missing persons.

The scope and scale of forensic investigations grounded in international law instruments today is still largely tied to its origins. As mentioned, Latin America has a rich history of applying forensic science to investigations of systematic political killings and, as a result, this work has inspired a large number of individuals to follow a forensic science career path. For these reasons, as well as increased international interest from many organizations including the ICRC, investigations in Latin America have expanded throughout the region and include conflict-related missing persons (e.g., Argentina, Peru), active conflict situations (e.g., Colombia), urban violence (e.g., Brazil), and migration (e.g., Mexico).

Europe has also seen an expansion of forensic investigations beyond the Balkans, most notably in countries that experienced armed conflict in the 1990s, such as the Republic of Georgia, where approximately 2,000 people remain missing after the conflicts in Abkhazia and South Ossetia. In Spain, investigations of tens of thousands of illegal killings during the 1936–39 Civil War were largely suppressed by the Franco dictatorship for four decades. Since 2000, grassroots organizations have been actively investigating and exhuming victim remains (Mason, 2012). Likewise, the Committee on Missing Persons in Cyprus (CMP) only began systematic work in 2006 on the victims of intercommunal violence from 1963–64 and fighting following the Turkish invasion in 1974.

Africa and Asia, on the other hand, have been slower to initiate large-scale missing persons projects. In addition, the diversity of the two continents can be viewed through varied cultural traditions, religious practices, and local languages, both within and between borders. Likewise, levels of development across the two continents are highly variable, which contributes to the availability of social and political space in which to address the missing persons issue. Unlike the Americas, many countries in Africa and Asia still lack a strong capacity in forensic science, and the array of forensic sciences practised is limited. Unlike Europe, conflicts in Africa and Asia have received less media coverage and attention in Western states, where most aid agencies and human rights organizations are based. It is also worth noting that the time elapsed since the end of hostilities could be an important factor. In almost all countries of the world that have experienced large-scale armed violence, the issue of persons having gone missing as a result of the violence is often sensitive. Likewise, countries immediately coming out of a conflict period commonly see the need for infrastructure rebuilding as more crucial to peace and stability than issues more directly associated with the past conflict. Therefore, in many instances it may simply be a matter of time before the missing persons problem is addressed, as can be observed now with South Korea and Vietnam. Finally, as an extremely disaster-prone region with the highest population density rates in the world, the large numbers of disaster dead in Asia may simply overshadow the dead from armed conflicts.

It also bears mentioning that experience has shown, at least to the authors, that Western concepts of legal and humanitarian obligations are not similarly understood outside the West. This is not to say that non-Western cultures do not recognize or respect legal and humanitarian obligations, but merely that interpretations of fulfilling legal and humanitarian obligations vary.

The Approach of the ICRC

The ICRC's exclusively humanitarian mission puts the victims and their families, rather than judicial investigations, at the centre of forensic endeavours. With this approach, the ICRC encourages relevant authorities to take action to resolve cases of missing persons and supports local practitioners to develop their human identification capacity and work towards forensic best practices in areas such as developing national policies and standard operating procedures, as well as implementing data management strategies.

In addition, the ICRC's broad understanding of missing persons allows it to address the multitude of needs associated with missing persons files, rather than being strictly confined to cases for which judicial proceedings are applicable. Therefore, missing persons can include family members separated from each other and for whom information on whereabouts are unknown, or even individuals who are known to have perished from natural circumstances but for which the whereabouts of the remains are unknown by the family. This more inclusive approach allows for a comprehensive response to the thousands of missing persons cases worldwide, such as the more than 68,000 people who remain missing in Colombia or the more than 16,000 individuals unaccounted for in Sri Lanka (ICRC, 2014).

The Scope of ICRC Forensic Activities in Relation to the Dead

In order to appropriately and comprehensively address forensic issues associated with missing persons, the ICRC provides support for both case resolution as well as prevention. Capacity to address day-to-day forensic casework, usually involving the examination of recently dead bodies primarily for the purposes of establishing cause and manner of death, is generally sound in many countries with established forensic infrastructures. However, in countries without forensic anthropology and archaeology capacity (still a majority of countries in the world), local practitioners are often unfamiliar with the techniques and skills required to scientifically search for, recover, analyze, and identify large numbers of human remains in different states of decomposition. In addition, while information about the identity of unknown remains (i.e., antemortem data) may be available or obtainable, the location of buried remains may be unknown. Absent or inadequate human identification capacity can significantly slow or irreparably damage chances of identifying human remains and results in further victimization for next of kin awaiting the remains of their loved ones. The ICRC supports

FIGURE 3.1   Participants of the ICRC's National Course on the Management of the Dead in Emergencies, Disasters and Catastrophes held in Peshawar, Pakistan, recovering human remains (life-size latex props) after a mock bomb blast field exercise, March 2015.

Source: International Committee of the Red Cross, printed by permission

local authorities and forensic practitioners in the establishment and growth of human identification initiatives by providing professional advice, training, and other capacity-building efforts (Figure 3.1).

Likewise, centralized systems, standardized procedures, and adherence to best practices are crucial to ensuring the appropriate handling of human remains in the context of established forensic infrastructures. Deficiencies of centralization and standardization often result in the lack of any composite knowledge about the handling of human remains and a weak system that cannot learn from its own mistakes. This could then lead to several damaging consequences, including but not limited to: unidentified remains being buried without any record whatsoever of their location; unidentified remains ending up in places other than recognized places of burial; inconsistent types of recovery and post-mortem data being recorded, depending upon the usual practices and skill level of any individual practitioner; no centralized (and therefore searchable) repository of recovery and post-mortem data that would be useful if antemortem data becomes available; and the permanent loss of recovery and post-mortem data should individual files become lost or get destroyed. The ICRC assists local forensic infrastructures moving towards centralization, standardization, and best practices by providing advice, assisting in the development of strategies and standard operating procedures (SOPs), promoting best practices and professional accountability through quality assurance and control measures, and the distribution and/or development of professional forensic tools.

In an effort to prevent deceased individuals from becoming missing persons, especially in emergency circumstances and/or when proper (forensic) infrastructures are compromised or inadequate, it may become necessary to involve the use of first responders in the handling of the dead or to provide emergency forensic advice and support to authorities. These needs are typical immediately following disasters and during times of active conflict or other armed violence (including in the handling of deaths in displacement camps or in custody), but also occur in other similar circumstances. The core objective is to mitigate potential damage by ensuring that basic practices are carried out in the documentation and handling of remains and by preventing mismanagement that can result in significant, if not permanent and irreparable, mistakes until forensic infrastructures are capable of taking over operations and implementing complete and thorough forensic investigations.

The ICRC promotes the dignified handling and professional management of the dead in compromised circumstances, and, when requested, provides advice, support, and technical assistance. The ICRC also provides training to first responders in the collection of the deceased, advising and supporting overwhelmed forensic systems in the management of unexpected numbers of dead bodies, and distributing emergency forensic materials. The desired impact of these activities is the dignified handling of remains for the sake of surviving families and communities and the eventual implementation of forensic best practices due to the temporary implementation of damage-control measures. It is also hoped that adequate and appropriate emergency response will help to prevent the deceased from becoming missing persons. It is in this last realm of ICRC forensic work in relation to the dead that activities have expanded most in Africa and Asia.

With ongoing conflicts, natural disasters, and the spread of infectious diseases, there is no dearth of human remains in need of dignified handling and professional management in Africa. However, many African nations lack the forensic and related infrastructures to appropriately deal with these remains. Thus, in many countries first responders are called upon, particularly in the recovery of remains and their transport to designated facilities. The ICRC provides training, advice, and support in a number of African countries, often in partnership with national Red Cross and Red Crescent societies.

Similarly, as the most disaster prone and most densely populated region on earth, countries throughout Asia often face staggering numbers of human remains in need of dignified handling and professional management where exist-ing forensic infrastructures often cannot cope. In a number of Asian countries the ICRC supports local authorities and forensic practitioners in: developing human remains management strategies (often with agencies of disaster management preparedness and response); comprehensive local and contextualized guide-lines on the management of remains that clearly outline responsibilities of all concerned actors, including first responders; training strategies and initiatives; and equipment procurement and preparedness.

While the ICRC's involvement in such initiatives is still relatively new and evolving, it has quickly learned that disaster response will often fall short of needs if strategies are not structurally comprehensive in their approach. That is, all strategies should promote ownership of responsibilities by all concerned actors and address all facets of the response, including legal, logistic, and technical issues. Training of first responders alone may result in wasted training efforts if those trained are not legally authorized to act as first responders. Likewise, perfect handling of remains by first responders will help ensure the dignity of the dead but may not prevent the dead from becoming missing persons if adequate identification capacity is lacking by those actors to whom the remains are released. Finally, stocks of required equipment become useless if those who need the materials cannot obtain them due to obstacles in the supply chain. For these reasons, the ICRC seeks a fully integrated approach from the highest level of authority down to those in action on the ground.

Promoting Sustainability

Apart from its regular strategies, programs, and activities, the ICRC Foren-sic Services promotes local sustainability whenever possible. This approach is grounded upon a firm belief that local ownership (i.e., accepting responsibility) coupled with local capacity (i.e., sufficient knowledge, skills, and abilities) is key to sustainably addressing local problems with local solutions. This approach, however, requires a healthy dose of patience.

In a number of contexts around the world, international forensic actors have loaned their expertise by helping to address forensic needs associated with missing persons cases. This assistance has been crucial to expediently resolving a number of missing persons cases. When this approach is applied in isolation, however, questions of sustainability arise.

In most contexts in which there are a large number of missing persons, such as large-scale armed conflicts or disasters, initiatives to locate, recover, analyze, and identify remains are long-term endeavours lasting years or, more commonly, decades. At the outset of these initiatives, it is sometimes easier to gather crucial information about remains (e.g., grave locations, possible identities, and associated antemortem data), which assists in rapid resolution to cases. However, as time passes, information becomes scant and the identification process slows. Unfortunately, this often coincides with the exit period of international assistance (see also Challenges, discussed below). If sustainable local mechanisms and capacity have not been built, then local authorities and practitioners are left without the necessary infrastructure, skills, and guidance to tackle the identification process when it becomes most difficult.

Likewise, it is imperative that all forensic investigations operate within a legitimate legal framework. While international organizations may sometimes be granted jurisdiction based on their mandate, such as the work of the tribunals for the former Yugoslavia and Rwanda, more commonly than not forensic investigations would only be recognized as legal and valid within the relevant domestic legal framework. As such, the involvement of local actors authorized to carry out investigations is imperative. Promoting local capacity from the outset ensures that these actors have the necessary skills to continue high-quality professional investigations after international assistance is no longer available.

Perhaps the most well-known and successful efforts to establish local forensic capacity to address the remains of conflict-related missing persons are those from Latin America. Following the restoration of democracy to Argentina in 1984, a group of forensic scientists from the American Association for the Advancement of Science (AAAS) travelled to Argentina to assist with clarifying the fate of the disappeared. Dr. Clyde Snow, a world-renowned American forensic anthropologist and member of the AAAS delegation, helped set up and train the Argentine Forensic Anthropology Team (EAAF). The EAAF still operates today to continue clarifying the fate of thousands of disappeared Argentinians, and also works in countries around the world to assist local practitioners in forensic investigations of missing persons and establish local capacity (EAAF, n.d.).

The Committee on Missing Persons in Cyprus (CMP) also serves as a model of best practice in establishing sustainable local capacity. In 2006, a bi-communal team of Greek and Turkish Cypriot archaeologists and anthropologists was established to clarify the fate of the roughly 2,000 Cypriots missing as a result of armed conflict from 1963–64 and again in 1974. The EAAF was instrumental in helping to establish this team, upon recommendation from the ICRC (CMP, n.d.). Lauding these local teams and others, the ICRC promotes a long-term sustainable local approach whenever possible.

A Multidisciplinary Approach

In all cases of missing persons, but especially in relation to post-conflict missing persons, the ICRC tries to take a multidisciplinary approach whenever possible. Specifically, the ICRC approaches the issue of missing persons not only in terms of handling human remains, but also views the problem from the perspective of the families of the missing. In this regard, the ICRC carries out needs assessments, taking an integrated approach to gauge the administrative, legal, economic, psychosocial, and other needs of families. Based on assessment results, the ICRC then formulates a plan to address each set of needs, a process called "accompaniment" (ICRC, 2013).

ICRC accompaniment programs vary from context to context, not only dependent upon the assessed needs, but also upon local factors. For example, local availability and capacity of expertise (e.g., psychosocial support providers) greatly affects the scope and scale of viable support programs. Likewise, local regulations and legislation associated with having a missing family member are highly variable from place to place and therefore require a contextualized approach to addressing families' legal and administrative needs. Socio-economic needs also tend to vary greatly, influenced not only by the overall socio-economic character of a country but also the cross-sections of society that represent the families of missing persons. For example, families of conflict-related missing persons often suffer from the loss of the family breadwinner, particularly if the conflict is international in nature and a large number of missing persons are combatants. In such cases, women-headed households may represent the largest demographic in need of socio-economic support. Natural disasters, on the other hand, tend to be less discriminatory about victims. Finally, cultural and religious influences can have a great impact upon strategies to address the needs of families and therefore contribute significantly to the acceptance and implementation of accompaniment procedures.

In relation to human remains, families should be incorporated into the forensic investigation process whenever possible and wherever feasible. Families should be well informed of the legal and scientific procedures associated with the forensic process through a clear communication strategy. Likewise, they should have a right to participate in forensic activities within the confines of the law and respecting legal and logistic practicalities such as scene security. Similarly, forensic practice should be fully transparent throughout the investigation process. Involvement of families helps to build trust and establish the legitimacy of the operations, not only for the families themselves but also for communities and civil society as a whole (Tidball-Binz, 2012).

Challenges to Addressing the Missing Persons Issue

Despite international legal obligations upon states, the road to resolving cases of missing persons is often a bumpy one. This can be due to a number of factors. The most obvious and commonly pervasive resistance to addressing missing persons revolves around the often politically sensitive nature of the issue. Particularly in post-conflict periods, authorities from both sides of a conflict may be sensitive about actions condoned by their respective parties that may be brought to light with forensic investigations. Even in situations where forensic investigations are deemed to be entirely humanitarian in nature with no intent to tie judicial proceedings with investigations, political sensitivities can bring about challenges to addressing missing persons. In highly sensitive situations, issues of safety and security for forensic practitioners and other investigators can also be an important concern. Natural disaster–related missing persons can even present political sensitivities if inadequate responses or conditions that contributed to the scale of the disaster are exposed.

Cultural and religious considerations can also present unique challenges. Some religions view post-mortem examination as desecration of human remains, even for skeletal remains (Carpenter, Tait, & Quadrelli, 2014). This is especially true when tissue samples are to be extracted for testing purposes (e.g., DNA). For example, Islamic principles prohibit the removal of parts from a body, which many Muslims understand to encompass the collection of samples for testing purposes. This presents obvious challenges to the scientific process of identification. Likewise, some religions or cultures promote immediate burial or cremation of remains. In these situations, delicate discussions and compromises must take place with families who still maintain their right to know the fate and whereabouts of their loved ones. In these situations, it is often helpful to engage in transparent dialogue with religious and other community leaders to promote community buy-in, which in and of itself can present its own unique challenges, especially when local authorities are considered non-representative of the interests of communities or foreign intervention is offered and/or requested by a government.

Gaps in the legal framework of a country can present obstacles towards ensuring that the best interests of missing persons and their families are addressed. For example, many families of missing persons refuse to accept a death certificate, often believing, or at least hoping, that their missing loved ones are still alive. This, however, results in challenges for families in addressing issues of estate and inheritance, remarriage, military or public pension claims, etc. In this instance, the ICRC promotes the implementation of a certificate of absence to assist with addressing administrative issues without touching upon whether the missing person is alive or dead.

A lack of legislation on the protection of personal (including genetic) data can also present a host of ethical dilemmas. Without physical and social information about missing persons, as well as information on the circumstances of their disappearance (i.e., antemortem data, or AMD), identifying their remains becomes impossible. However, this personal data of the deceased, as well as the personal data of their family members and any witnesses noted during AMD collection interviews, should be strictly protected through legislation to ensure that the information remains confidential and serves only the purpose for which it was collected. This should be based on a clear understanding of individual wishes on transmissibility of the information as outlined in the statement of consent. Not doing so could result in negative consequences, even including the targeting of families and witnesses for sensitive information conveyed about circumstances of disappearance (e.g., suspected perpetrators, war crimes). Genetic data collected from the remains of missing persons and their family members for purposes of DNA kinship matching must be similarly protected and serve only the purpose for which they were collected to avoid, for example, unauthorized genetic research for either scientific or legal purposes. Without clear and comprehensive data protection legislation in place, the benefits of promoting the collection of such data must be weighed against the potential consequences of its misuse.

Establishing forensic specialist capacity, particularly for scientific identification, can also pose a challenge for local capacity and long-term sustainability. Many countries, particularly in Africa and Asia, do not have specialized forensic training for pathology or simply do not have archaeological or anthropological expertise for expert recovery and analysis, among other forensic specialties. Moreover, the forensic science specialty may not exist or be legally recognized as part of the system. Options vary from support for formal international accreditation of individuals, requiring long-term and substantial investment, to informal and/or ad hoc training of lesser knowledge and perhaps quality. In some countries, it remains one of the greatest challenges.

Finally, funding is a ubiquitous challenge. Given that programs to address missing persons issues tend to be large-scale and long-term, funding must be secured not only for project initiation, but also to ensure sustainability. In post-conflict rebuilding periods government funding can be slight for missing persons work, due to the need to direct available monies for other recovery and development efforts. When funding comes from external sources, donor fatigue can come into play, especially when significant time has elapsed since the onset of funding initiatives and new emergencies arise requiring redirection of donations.

Summary

From the first systematic application of forensic science to investigate missing persons in the 1980s to the present day, humanitarian forensic action continues to evolve and expand in both scope and scale. While conflict-related missing persons investigations continue throughout Latin America and Europe, Africa and Asia have seen the greatest expansion in relation to disaster dead, and efforts today focus not only on resolution of missing persons cases, but also prevention.

Despite this, challenges remain to adequately addressing missing persons cases. The often politically sensitive nature of such investigations can result in delays or stagnation of the process. Inadequate legal frameworks including lack of legislation on protection of personal data can pose questions related to jurisdiction and ethical responsibilities in data collection. Cultural and religious constraints can pose unique hurdles that must be delicately negotiated. Building sustainable forensic capacity can be variously successful. Identifying sources of funding and coping with donor fatigue can require added administrative and bureaucratic layers to the investigation process.

To this end, the ICRC provides advice and support to governmental authorities and local practitioners in addressing the above challenges for the prevention and resolution of missing persons cases. Taking a multidisciplinary approach, the ICRC focuses on the exclusively humanitarian objective of the identification of remains and their return to families, at the same time addressing the unique socio-economic, legal, administrative, and psychosocial needs of families of missing persons. Throughout its efforts, the ICRC promotes local ownership and local capacity as the key to sustainably addressing local problems with local solutions.

Note

1.   The views, opinions, and assertions expressed herein are those of the individual authors, and are not to be construed to represent those of the International Committee of the Red Cross.

References

Argentine Forensic Anthropology Team (EAAF). (n.d.). The Argentine Forensic Anthropology Team (*Equipo Argentino de Antropología Forense*). Retrieved from eaaf.typepad.com/founding_of_ eaaf/. Accessed December 23, 2014.

Carpenter, B., Tait, G., & Quadrelli, C. (2014). The body in grief: Death investigations, objections to autopsy, and the religious and cultural "other." *Religions, 5*, 165–178.

Committee on Missing Persons in Cyrus (CMP). (n.d.). Committee on missing persons in Cyprus. Retrieved from www.cmp-cyprus.org/.

Debons, D., Fleury, A., & Pitteloud, J-F. (eds.). (2009). *Katyn and Switzerland: Forensic investigations and investigators in humanitarian crises, 1920–2007.* Geneva, Switzerland: Georg.

(n.d.) Internation Committee of the Red Cross (ICRC). Mission Statement. Retrieved from www.icrc.org/eng/resources/documents/misc/icrc-mission-190608.htm.

International Committee of the Red Cross (ICRC). (2013). *Accompanying the families of missing persons: A practical handbook.* Geneva, Switzerland: ICRC.

International Committee of the Red Cross (ICRC). (2014, October 27). *Missing persons must not be forgotten.* Retrieved from www.icrc.org/eng/resources/documents/news-release/2014/ 08-28-day-disappeared-missing.htm.

Mason, P. (2012, December 18). Amid scars of past conflict Spanish far right grows. *BBC News.* Retrieved from www.bbc.com/news/world-20773516.

Tidball-Binz, M. (2012). Global forensic science and the search for the dead and missing from armed conflict: The perspective of the International Committee of the Red Cross. In D. Ubelaker (ed.), *Forensic science: Current issues, future practices* (pp. 337–365). Chichester, UK: Wiley-Blackwell.

Related Sources

Argentine Forensic Anthropology Team (EAAF): www.eaaf.org

Forensic Anthropology Foundation of Guatemala (FAFG): www.fafg.org/

International Commission on Missing Persons (ICMP): www.ic-mp.org

International Committee of the Red Cross (ICRC): www.icrc.org

International Committee of the Red Cross. (2003). *ICRC report: The missing and their families.* Geneva, Switzerland: ICRC. Retrieved from www.icrc.org/eng/resources/documents/ report/5jahr8.htm.

Joyce, C., & Stover, E. (1992). *Witnesses from the grave: The stories bones tell.* New York, NY: Ballantine Books.

Petrig, A. (2009). The war dead and their gravesites. *International Review of the Red Cross, 874*, 341–369.

Physicians for Human Rights (PHR), International Forensic Program: physiciansforhumanrights.org/ justice-forensic-science/ifp/

Chapter 4

From Mass Graves to Human Rights: The Discovery of Forced Disappearances in Contemporary Spain[1]

Francisco Ferrándiz (Spanish National Research Council/Consejo Superior de Investigaciones Científicas)
Emilio Silva Barrera (Association for the Recovery of Historical Memory/Asociación para la Recuperación de la Memoria Histórica)

This chapter consists of two contributions on the situation of persons missing in Spain from the 1936–39 Civil War and postwar dictatorship until 1975. The first section is by Francisco Ferrándiz about his ethnography of victim exhumations in the context of transnational human rights discourses. The second section is by Emilio Silva Barrera and discusses the most recent legal events that help frame the (in)action of the Spanish state relative to international influence.

Part 1 (Francisco Ferrándiz)

The Social Life of Rights

The most recent trends in the anthropology of human rights include concepts such as the "social life of rights" in order to get past the difficulties resulting from the proliferation and fragmentation of discourses and associated practices, and the multiplication of social and state actors who use legislation and rhetoric linked to human rights to mobilize different kinds of political and economic agendas. It is also quite relevant that the social life of rights is being used to go beyond the obsolete debate between the "universalism" and "relativism" of human rights that has dominated the discipline for decades. Thus, Richard Wilson makes the point that, considering the fragmentary and plural nature—as well as the ideological promiscuity—of contemporary discourse regarding rights, anthropology should pay more attention to "the performative dimensions of human rights, the dynamics of social mobilization, and the changes in attitude of elite and non-elitist groups toward the concepts of 'rights' and 'justice' both within and outside of the legal system" (2006, p. 77). Jane Cowan states that we must construct theoretical mechanisms that will allow us to determine how rights are simultaneously liberating and limiting, without losing sight of the fact that their social practice goes far beyond legal technicalities and produces new subjectivities, relations, identities, and cultures (2006, pp. 9–10). According to Cowan, constructing these mechanisms is indispensable in the framework of the expansion of the "culture of human rights"—a structuring discourse that conditions the way the world is perceived and which has flourished since the end of the 20th century. In fact, one of the correlates to the increasing use of the language of rights in negotiations among diverse social and institutional groups is the parallel process of the vernacularization of rights, a term used to desig-nate the local uses of and changes to universal concepts (Cowan, 2006, p. 10). Sally E. Merry discusses the importance of analyzing cosmopolitan and popular practices and perceptions of rights jointly, mapping out the diversity of social actors (knowledge brokers) who participate in translating between one sphere and the other in a back-and-forth movement, from the global arena downward and from the local sphere upward (2006, p. 38). Wilson points out that once this dynamism is demonstrated, many anthropologists who work in the field question the predominance of "legalistic, instrumental, and technocratic" approaches to human rights, as well as positivist interpretations of knowledge and history that fail to consider such crucial aspects as victim and perpetrator subjectivity, the origins, causes, and consequences of the violence that infringes rights, and the controversies surrounding the meaning and mobilization of rights; all of these areas are extraordinarily interesting to anthropologists (2006, p. 80).

In this chapter, I will start by exploring how certain actions criminal-ized by international criminal law and set forth in prestigious international conventions—especially forced disappearances, protection from which formally became a universal right in 2007—are being *downloaded* and *re-translated* by different groups in Spain today. This is taking place within a controversial process of building a culture of rights regarding the victims of rearguard rebel army violence during the Spanish Civil War and, later, the victims of repressive Franco-regime violence. When using the term *legal download*, we refer to the different ways and channels for moving and translating international criminal legislation to national or local contexts, within contexts that demand different kinds of rights. I am also referring, more literally, to the new possibilities of access to this legislation and to the agencies and organizations that establish and promote it by means of new communications and knowledge technologies. These new technologies make it possible to consult and file documents with a single click of the mouse, at a very low or zero economic cost, and almost in real time.[2]

My main hypothesis is that Spanish Judge Baltasar Garzón's polemical October 16, 2008, judicial indictment of leading figures of the former Franco government, together with the entire intricate legal battle deriving from it, was a turning point in how the repressive Franco regime's legacy was perceived, especially by the social and political left wing. The aftermath of this indictment is leading to the formulation and demand of new kinds of rights for the victims of the Franco regime within the framework of universal justice. In this sense, the movement to recover historical memory that began in 2000 with the exhumation of the losing side's graves,[3] and which has been underway for 15 years, is becoming a social movement against the broader impunity of the Franco regime that has larger claims, and where the application of universal justice to the Spanish case is viewed as indispensable.[4] Thus, it is important to emphasize that once concepts, conventions, or legal cases originating in international criminal law are downloaded to the agenda of associations, media discourse, or legal and political reasoning, the more specific legal blocking that can happen—appeals, writs of prohibition, or charges—in no way slow down the social life of rights, but rather become part of them.

I will now briefly analyze the birth of forced disappearances as a universal crime, as well as the divergences between different cultures that exist in the Spanish legal system, following some of the positions taken up regarding Garzón's indictment. Then I will discuss the path this legal downloading is taking in the cultures of groups outside of the legal system, for example, in academia, in the media, and especially in the associations for the recovery of historical memory.[5] This chapter defends the relevance of not only the legal but also the extralegal use of the concept of *disappearance* in the Spanish case. In order to argue that this concept is relevant, I will use the example of mass graves, mainstays of a terror machine meant to sow uncertainty about the final resting places and identities of people who were kidnapped or jailed and later shot, a terror machine whose efficacy is clear even today in the difficulty in identifying the bodies that are disinterred. Apart from the legal disappearances, as we will see in this discussion, there are also historical and social disappearances, and each of these refer to a different experience, reasoning, and sphere of action. In this context, three rituals of reappearance in the public sphere for the *fusilados* (people executed by shooting) are discussed—exhumations, the return of the remains to the relatives, and demonstrations against impunity—that illustrate the trajectory from mass graves to demanding rights.

Legal Ins and Outs

The International Convention for the Protection of All People from Forced Disappearances was adopted by the General Assembly of the United Nations in New York in 2006, and corroborated by 53 countries in Paris on February 6, 2007. It definitively and universally classified the crime in the framework of crimes against humanity. Spain signed the Convention on September 27, 2007, and ratified it on September 24, 2009. Despite its limitations and the legal limbos that it does not resolve, this Convention received the support of organizations such as Amnesty International, Human Rights Watch, and the International Lawyers' Commission (Chinchón, 2008, pp. 15–17). The story of how this crime is articulated in international humanitarian law is long and complicated, full of legal and diplomatic ins and outs, and can be found in a growing number of technical texts.[6] I will only look at some of the most important milestones here. The Convention is the result of numerous initiatives by governments and civil society, and of the development of jurisprudence in different institutions. It began when the Inter-American Court of Human Rights of the Organization of American States constructed the first legal instruments for prosecuting this crime in the 1970s, and pronounced the first sentences condemning it at the end of the 1980s. In parallel, the UN Commission of Human Rights needed to react to complaints that had been coming from Chile since the mid-70s, and in 1980 the Commission decided to establish the Working Group on Enforced or Involuntary Disappearances (WGEID). In this context—and until they were definitively classified as crimes against humanity in 2007, more than 25 years after the Working Group was created—forced disappearances have gradually emerged as a compound crime against humanity that involves the violation of different human rights. For example, disappearance is a permanent crime that is protracted each day that the person is missing; it has no statute of limitations (it can only be identified as this crime once it is solved), and its victims are legally defenseless. One of the places where the classification of this crime originated was in the lawsuits brought to court for abuses committed by Latin American dictatorships.

The Spanish case soon put the efficacy and the limits of this new universal legal instrument to the test. It is important to note that, in 2003, the WGEID had included Spain among the countries with open cases of forced disappearances, specifically in relation to two anti-Franco guerrilla member cases from 1947 and 1949, reported by the Association for the Recovery of Historical Memory (ARMH)[7] in August 2002, and a third case of a guerrilla that dates from 1950. In all three cases, the members were presumably kidnapped by the Guardia Civil, the Spanish military police.[8] The 2009 WGEID Report showed that the Spanish government was informed of a fourth disappearance, the case of Abel Ballart Sans, who was last seen in March 1946 at the Portant (Vall de Aran) military headquarters. The Spanish government's response to the WGEID was, in each case, that the 1977 Amnesty Law declared the crimes they were denouncing lapsed, closing the door to any kind of investigation.

On the other hand, soon after signing the aforementioned UN Convention, the Spanish government published "Law 52/2007, December 26, recognizing and extending the rights and establishing measures in favour of those who suffered persecution or violence during the Civil War and the dictatorship," in the *Boletín Oficial del Estado* (Official Government Bulletin) (2007). This law, known as the Law of Historic Memory (Ley de la Memoria Histórica, 52/2007), was passed after tough parliamentary debates and media controversies, during which there were accusations of sectarianism, partisanship, irresponsibility, and *guerracivilismo*.[9] The law tiptoed over the category of missing persons in Articles 11 to 14, but there is no express mention of the important, recently signed UN Convention. Article 11 barely mentions that victims' descendants will be "assisted" in "activities of inquiry, location, and identification of persons who disappeared violently during the Civil War or during the following political repression and whose fate is unknown" (Ley de la Memoria Histórica, 2007). In fact, the 2009 WGEID report A/HRC/13/31 specifically states that in responding to criticisms of the law by the Working Group, the Spanish Government argues that "the purpose" of Law 52/2007 "is not to categorize and sanction the crime of forced disappearance, but rather to promote measures that can contribute to a knowledge of history and facilitate democratic memory, all within the framework of a spirit of reconciliation" (United Nations Human Rights Council, 2009, p. 103).

Law 52/2007 also declared the illegitimacy—but not the nullity—of the Civil War and Franco courts and of the sentences passed (Article 3), and only briefly considered the mortuary monument Valley of the Fallen (Article 16). As a result of all these shortcomings, the groups who focus on recovering the historical memory of the losing side in the struggle, from family associations to nation-wide NGOs, found the law very unsatisfactory.[10] Once they realized the lukewarm reception many of their demands would receive in this law, some associations sought other openings for their demands, channelling them through the national judicial system and their legal advisors. Starting on December 14, 2006, different associations brought lawsuits to the Central Court of Justice Number 5 of the National Court, presided by Baltasar Garzón. They asked him to declare himself competent to investigate and judge alleged crimes of illegal detention "mainly due to the existence of a systematic and preconceived plan to eliminate political opponents by means of multiple deaths, torture, exile, and forced disappearances (illegal detentions) of people starting in 1936, during the Civil War years, and during the following postwar years, produced at different geographical locations in the Spanish territory" (Garzón, 2008a, p. 3, author translation). When Judge Baltasar Garzón declared himself competent to process the case for alleged crimes of illegal detention in the framework of crimes against humanity, there was an intense but short-lived whirlwind—barely four weeks long—in which legal technicalities were mixed with political controversies and a significant media storm. He registered a total of 114,266 cases that had taken place between July 1936 and December 1951.

The legal whirlwind began with the October 16, 2008, indictment. Judge Garzón took into account that there had been serious violations of rights during the Civil War and the Franco dictatorship that could be considered to be crimes against humanity. He maintained that, in the context of a crime against high offices of the nation, the procedure of forced disappearances—proceeding from war edicts, summary court martials, and other elements in the repressive structure of government after 1945—was systematically used to obstruct the identification of victims and to prevent justice from taking place right up to the present. Garzón appealed to Article 607 bis of the Spanish Penal Code, introduced in the year 2003, which deals with the enduring validity of crimes against humanity in accordance with international law. He also appealed to the 1998 Statute of the International Criminal Court, and to other precedents such as the Nuremberg Statute (1945) and certain decisions by the European Court of Human Rights, that disappearances should be included under the legal definition of permanent crimes of illegal detention without accounting for the victim's whereabouts, which is equivalent to forced disappearance (2008a, pp. 17–20; 2008b, p. 10–21). In the appeal Chief Prosecutor Javier Zaragoza made to Garzón's indictment (2008), he pointed out that, from a legal point of view, the authority to investigate alleged forced disappearances was not appropriate, referring to the 1977 Amnesty Law and to the fact that "it is publicly known and notorious that the victims were executed at that time and, consequently, we are manifestly dealing with a crime of assassination, a situation which ended the illicit situation of deprivation of freedom." He stated that it is also clear that the "possible authors of this crime of rebellion" are dead and that the legal judgments chosen by Garzón do not exist in the Penal Code in Spain (Zaragoza, 2008, pp. 2–3).

Zaragoza argued that the Law of Historic Memory sufficiently satisfied the demands of the victims in the framework of reparative justice. He also argued that, in any case, "the legal judgment of the events denounced as crimes against humanity is not applicable to this case, because the written normative corpus and customary law that constitute international penal legality did not exist at the moment the acts were committed," so that, in the legal legislation presently in force, these would be lapsed crimes (2008, pp. 21–22). Finally, the prosecutor strongly asserted that, 70 years after the fact, Garzón was incorrect to consider each disappeared person alive and illegally detained as long as no body had been produced, which stretched the inexistence of the statute of limitations for possible pending penal responsibilities. He particularly questioned this because there were, in fact, "registered declarations of death for many of the victims of reprisals in the war and in the post-war period" (pp. 30–31). Zaragoza judged these events not as forced disappearances in the most recent international legal interpretation, but rather as common crimes that would be under the jurisdiction of territorial courts (pp. 33; 40); this astonished some associations.

After some dizzying weeks and procedural difficulties, once the National Audience Penal Court's (*Sala de lo Penal de la Audiencia Nacional,* an internal appeal court) decision to close the case was clear and the deaths of those alleged by Garzón to be responsible for the alleged killings had been certified. Garzón responded. In his extensive writ of prohibition on November 18, 2008, Garzón based his argument more specifically on the UN Convention on Enforced Disappearances and on the 2005 Resolution of the Parliamentary Assembly of the European Council on the same subject (2008b, p. 42–46). He also called attention to the seriousness of other crimes against humanity committed during the Franco dictatorship that could still be considered within the statute of limitations. Specifically, he referred to the crimes documented by Dr. Vallejo Nágera's Office of Psychological Research and the crimes related to the so-called "lost children of the Franco regime," particularly in the cases of guardianship and stolen children resulting from an organized system that made minors disappear (Vinyes, 2002; Vinyes, Armengou, & Belis, 2002). This new focus allowed him, on one hand, to differentiate between deceased (but not registered) missing persons and living missing persons (Garzón, 2008b, 81), and, on the other hand, to establish parallels with the case of Argentina and the jurisprudence generated there (p. 73; see also Marre, 2009).

There are several recent events that should be mentioned. One is the admission by the Supreme Court of the complaint by Manos Limpias and the Falange Española de las JONS—two ultra-right-wing organizations—against Garzón for a breach of trust. The charge against Garzón triggered protest in his defence

FIGURE 4.1   **People protesting in front of the Spanish Supreme Court in January 2012, in defence of Judge Baltasar Garzón, demanding judicial investigation into disappearances from the Spanish Civil War.**

Photo credit: Óscar Rodríguez, volunteer photographer with ARMH, printed by permission

(Figure 4.1), and a judge acquitted him in February 2012. Another is the presentation in Argentina of a criminal complaint "for the commission of crimes of genocide and/or crimes against humanity that took place in Spain during the period between July 17, 1939, and June 17, 1977." Garzón petitioned to be moved to the International Criminal Court as Advisor on May 11 of the same year—with the ARMH immediately calling him the last exile of the Franco regime and the first of the 21st century.[11]

Beyond the Law

Was Garzón, as journalist Javier Pradera said, on a "drug-induced trip to the heart of darkness of the Civil War" (2008b, p. 12)? The case's passage through the court system was ephemeral and convulsive. Independent of the legal path I have described and of its evident difficulties—made particularly explicit in the National Court—in attempting to translate universal crimes from a plurality of legal cultures in both the national and transnational spheres, the transcendence of Garzón's indictment beyond its legal aspects must not be underestimated. He applied notions such as "crimes against humanity" and "forced

disappearances" to the Spanish context, using a legal argument based on international humanitarian law. As a result of this indictment, Prosecutor Zaragoza's
response, the later writ of prohibition, and the debates that have followed the
Supreme Court's prosecution of Garzón for applying legal terms outside of his
jurisdiction, a direct download route has been established—a re-translation of
certain concepts from international humanitarian law to the Spanish case, with its
polemics and nuances. This downloading has been a turning point not only in the
national and international tone of the debate and in the discourse of the associations and groups of families of people who suffered reprisals, but also in the
depth and structure of their demands for investigation and redress. In this section
I will discuss the social, political, and symbolic effects deriving from Garzón's
indictment and from the permeation—probably irreversible but always subject
to transformation—of the concept of "forced disappearances" in contemporary
Spanish political culture, referring to certain victims of the Franco regime. In
other words, I will discuss what Wilson calls the social life of rights (2006).

Without trying to be exhaustive, it is relevant to point out that the term *missing
person*, far from being a neologism inherited from Latin American dictatorships
and from international humanitarian law and then implanted in Spain out of
context and with no scientific rigour, actually has precedents in Spain, even with
reference to the Civil War itself. In the *Boletín Oficial del Estado* (*BOE*) Number
27 from November 11, 1936, published in Burgos and valid for the territory under
his control, Francisco Franco signed Decree 67 (*BOE*, 1936a). In this decree's
preamble it was argued that a situation as exceptional as a war requires a process
for "the registration of absences, disappearances, or deaths." The missing persons
would be moved to the category of "assumed dead" five years after being registered (p. 154). As a result of this decree, a process was begun for the "registration
of the dead or missing" in the Civil Registry (published in the November 13 *BOE*
[1936b, p. 176]), including instructions to prepare the lists of all the known data
on the circumstances of disappearance and giving them a legal status equivalent
to "absent."[12] The newspaper for municipal administration and justice from July
12, 1939, which circulated throughout all the towns of Spain, included the Order
of May 17, 1939 (*BOE*, 1939). The Order extended the previously cited decree to
promote the exemption or reduction of municipal taxes applied to "inhumations,
exhumations, and transfer of corpses of the barberie roja (Red, or communist,
barbarity), or who had died in the frontlines or as a consequence of disease or
wounds acquired during the military operations" (p. 138).

The Causa General (General Lawsuit) was a large-scale legal procedure that
took its inquiries to all the municipalities of the country, created by decree on
April 26, 1940. Entrusted to the Supreme Court Public Prosecutor's office, it used

the term "missing persons" in Estado Número 1 (a section of the Causa General) as an administrative and legal category, defined as "list of people residing in this municipality who were violently killed or who disappeared and are believed to have been assassinated during the red domination," requesting the exact "date of death or disappearance" (Casanova, 2002, pp. 30–31; see also Ledesma, 2005). The provincial reports of National Security Headquarters also refer to these missing people, along with other categories such as *fusilados* (shot), *fugitivos* (fugitives), *desterrados* (exiles), and *sancionados* (punished people). And a quick look at the newspapers from this period shows that the term has been in use in Spain since at least the Civil War. Evidently, these uses of the notion of *missing* are much earlier than their application to the repressive practices of Latin American dictatorships in the 70s and 80s, their emergence in international law, the establishment of universal jurisprudence, and, of course, their contemporary use in the case of the rearguard repression of the rebel army and later of the Franco regime. But they are a testimony to the relevance and antiquity of the *local* use of this concept in reference to the Civil War.[13]

In short, the term is in no way foreign to the Spanish case since at least the Civil War. What is new is the way it has become generalized in the last decade to talk about people who were shot. Also new are the consequences that may derive from its contemporary anchoring in legal categories defined by international penal law and crimes against humanity, as we have seen. In this sense, it is important to specify that Garzón was not the first to import the concept into the Spanish context, but he was the person who managed to popularize an informed translation of the term's new expression in international penal law to the Spanish case, and who codified it in his indictment. He popularized it intentionally, though without anticipating the political, legal, media, and social controversy that the indictment would unleash both in Spain and elsewhere. Even so, it is evident that the events linked to the Garzón affair have been the main catalyst for the massive eruption of the notion of forced disappearances in Spanish political, legal, media, and association discourse, together with its associated resonances and transnational iconographies (Ferrándiz & Baer, 2008). However, the notion of the missing person—which is still diffuse—was present right from the beginning of the most recent cycle of exhumations of mass graves, which most analysts place in the year 2000 (Ferrándiz, 2009a). For example, just a few days before the well-known disinterment in Priaranza del Bierzo in October 2000, which was, for many, the founding moment of the most recent phase of exhumations in Spain (Figure 4.2), author Emilio Silva Barrera wrote an article titled "Mi abuelo también fue un desaparecido (My grandfather was a missing person, too)" (*La Crónica de León*, October 8, 2000, in Silva, 2005), specifically

FIGURE 4.2   **A plaque marking the location of the first scientifically excavated mass grave from the Spanish Civil War. It reads, "This ditch was, for 64 years, [the site of] a mass grave of thirteen civilian republicans, victims of the Francoist repression. Its exhumation, the 21st of October 2000, broke the silence about the thousands of disappeared persons and resulted in the birth of the Association for the Recovery of Historical Memory. Their dignity and their tragedy must be part of our memory."**

Photo credit: Óscar Rodríguez, volunteer photographer with ARMH, printed by permission

seeking resonance with other disappearances such as those in Argentina or Chile. As we have already noted, in August 2002 the Association for the Recovery of Historical Memory (ARMH) turned to the United Nations Working Group on Enforced or Involuntary Disappearances, which is under the Commission on Human Rights, with the intention of "internationalizing the problem" and "showing that forced disappearance was a method of political persecution used by the Franco authorities in a continuous way, not 'collateral damage' of the Civil War" (Silva, 2005, p. 118). At that time, however, they were informed that the UN had a hard time investigating cases of disappearances previous to its founding in 1945, and only two of the reported cases were accepted (Silva, 2005, pp. 113–118).

As in the Silva case described, there are numerous examples of how this concept of enforced disappearance has been used by the many associations for the recovery of historical memory right from the start, although their co-awareness of legal and symbolic kinship with other cases of political violence in other parts of the world has grown and become more sophisticated over time. In this sense, we can talk about a process of intensification of the discursive presence of forced disappearances in the case of the Civil War and the postwar period, insofar as the associations have taken up the strategic importance of the concept and have placed it at the centre of their political and legal claims. They are also aware of the transnational legal, political, and symbolic capital that it carries. They have used these aspects to give new visibility to the *fusilados* and *paseados*[14]: by placing them under the umbrella of *missing persons*, they went, fundamentally, from being a home-grown product of the Franco repression to being part of a much broader category that has been transnationalized and legally sanctioned by international penal law in the context of crimes against humanity. This legal and symbolic transition from *fusilado* (shot) to *desaparecido* (disappeared) provides the associations with new and powerful tools to continue the fight for their memory and redress, under the umbrella of human rights, and for denouncing the hypocrisy of a state that signs international conventions against forced disappearances but does not apply them to its own recent history.

There is another, more recent example that is directly related to the Garzón case. The collective of associations that channelled accusations of disappearances to Garzón in the National Court, following their legal advisors' guidance and stimulated by the legal arguments in reports of prestigious organizations such as Amnesty International (2005; 2006a; 2006b; 2008a; 2008b), made it clear that a boomerang effect strategy (i.e., putting pressure on the state and on the Department of Justice to act by raising the case to international law) was necessary. It was clear even in the name of the group: Plataforma por las Victimas de las Desapariciones Forzadas del Franquismo (Platform for the Victims of Forced Disappearances in the Franco Regime, or PVDFF; see memoriadesaparecidos. blogspot.com/), as well as in how the crimes reported to the Central Court of Justice Number 5 were categorized. On December 27, 2008, a delegation from the collective (which also included Amnesty International and other NGOs) met again with the UN Working Group on Enforced and Involuntary Disappearances. After the collective was dissolved due to internal discrepancies when Garzón was served the writ of prohibition, the concept was eliminated from its new name: Coordinadora de Colectivos de Víctimas del Franquismo (Coordinator of the Groups of Victims of the Franco Regime), but was in no way eliminated from its objectives, as this new association declared itself heir to the PVDFF's efforts and objectives.[15]

There is no doubt that the missing persons of the Franco regime have proliferated in public discourse and have had a great mobilizing capacity. This category of victims also correlates in a quite dizzying way with transnational issues of crimes against humanity, filling the repressive machinery of the rebel army and later the dictatorship with borrowed meaning while outlining a potential soft but increasingly prestigious legal apparatus for anchoring the demands of the victims of the Franco regime and their descendants. Faced with these issues, some intellectuals and editorial journalists have begun to present an incipient debate to set the boundaries of (or strangle) the semantic field of this term and to question the potentially promiscuous, inexact, and nonsensical use of the category in the Spanish case. In some cases, the criticisms refer directly to Garzón's (supposedly inappropriate) use of this concept. These criticisms are not only from a technical point of view,[16] but also because he contributed to the consolidation of what we could call *social jurisprudence*, that is, the process by which a legal term captures the political mind of certain social groups unusually quickly and takes a tenacious hold on public discourse that did not previously contain or accommodate this term. This process gives meaning and transnational projection to repressive experiences that were often interpreted in national, autonomic, and even local terms. There are different kinds of objections to identifying shooting victims and *paseados* with missing persons, and they require a nuanced analysis; here, I will only discuss some examples of the controversies in left-wing politics.[17] Globally, monitoring the communications media shows that right-wing politicians and media consider this identification to be very unusual, confused, ill-intentioned, and totally lacking any basis, although the term has also become part of their vocabulary and they are, doubtless, contributing new angles to the debate.

On one hand, historians such as Julián Casanova, who hold that the government should create a National Commission of Missing Persons for victims of the political violence during the Civil War and Franco dictatorship, have argued that the category of missing persons is confusing and should only be applied to the "clandestine" victims of the so-called "hot terror" of the first months of the struggle and those who were not added to the civil registers by the Franco death bureaucracy (Casanova, 2008). In his opinion piece, Casanova (2008) calculates the number of early victims who could legitimately be included in this category to be around 30,000; we could call these people "historiographic missing persons." Historiographically speaking, Casanova maintains, shootings that are documented or registered in archives would not produce missing persons but rather another type of victim. This would be true even if the deaths are the result of court martial of questionable legitimacy and full of "anomalies and falsifications regarding the causes of death," and also even if access to archives is slow or restricted and they are, in some cases, deteriorated or destroyed. Another historian, Santos Juliá, goes one step further to emphasize the legal impracticality and procedural absurdity committed by Garzón when he tried to use the concept of forced disappearances in a Spanish context, agreeing with the appeal of Chief Prosecutor Javier Zaragoza and the writ of prohibition (Juliá, 2008).

Other influential journalists such as Javier Pradera reject upfront the categorization of "missing persons," which he considers to be an inexact and deceitful copy of Latin American experience, which is still the paradigmatic reference. He prefers vernacular terms that are more rooted in Spanish experience and perception, terms such as *paseado* or *fusilado*.[18] "La guerra que no cesa (The never-ending war)" (Pradera, 2008a) ironically already foreshadowed Pradera's disgust with the idea of the *desaparecido*, anachronistically substituting the vernacular *paseados*, projected retrospectively from contemporary Latin American dictatorships back to 1936 Spain. In "Un mal viaje de ida y vuelta (A bad trip there and back again)" (Pradera, 2008c), Pradera questioned the Spanish transition to Latin America, and he asked for caution with continuing the "false parallelisms" between the two shores of the Atlantic that imported the concept of missing persons to refer to the *paseados* of the Civil War. He also insisted that care must be taken with transferring the category of kidnapped children to the "children of dead, jailed or exiled republicans, who had been given up for adoption." In his most recent column on the subject, "Paseos y tumbas (Walks and graves)" (Pradera, 2010), he finally refines the differentiation, contrasting the cold and secret extermination of missing persons, due to fear of international condemnation, with the *paseados*, the result of a "savage repression of quasi-public dimensions" deriving from hate and intolerance. This relativist fear of the alleged denaturalization of the Franco regime victims because of the historical experience of missing persons in South American dictatorships does, in fact, have a basis in reality. It is evident that arrested missing persons in this area are not equivalent to the *fusilados* of the Franco dictatorship, just as the mechanisms for making people disappear are not the same, despite the similar sinister result (Gatti, 2008). They are not immediately and automatically translatable and it is, therefore, necessary to differentiate historically, socially, legally, and even symbolically between the two forms of political terror, as well as looking for ways that nuanced parallels can be established. But does this mean that they cannot be part of a similar legal structure? Once the boundaries of each kind of repression have been defined (e.g., the kinds of violence they generate, the bureaucracies of silence and of death they generate, the different contexts of political interpretation, the different kinds of repressive violence) it seems legitimate to propose that these historical experiences, with their specificities, could be integrated into the same kind of transnational crime without confusing them. To argue the opposite would be to argue that a crime set forth in international conventions can only be legitimately applied to the social context in which the first steps towards its classification had been taken.

Other intellectuals, such as Reyes Mate, while remaining cautious about a use of these terms that is not nuanced, have openly defended the relevance of "forced disappearance" in specific cases such as that of Federico García Lorca, especially after an unsuccessful exhumation attempt (Mate, 2009). According to the way he theorizes this complex concept of political repression, it was precisely the failure of the search for his grave that has put him squarely into the category of missing persons. Because Lorca is the missing person who "best represents the enduring validity of political crime," the absence of the body "is the same as saying that Lorca will now be more present than before in the critical consciousness of the Spanish people" (Mate, 2009). For Mate, forced disappearance, as a "technique of forgetting," perfects the criminal killings conducted by the Nazis in concentration camps. A forced disappearance is more than an assassination. It expresses the political will to leave no trace in order to make the memory work of future generations impossible, turning the victims into ghosts. The present-day nature of the disappearances—permanent, with no statute of limitations—turns them into basic agents of the "contemporaneousness of that which is anachronistic," because our present time continues to be the time of disappearance. The missing ghost of Lorca, with the possibility of finding his body lost (for the moment), "will always be a court of history pronouncing a sentence" against the Franco regime (Mate, 2009).

If we accept that the concept of disappearance, with its nuances and different manifestations, has an heuristic and interpretative potential which, with its symbolism and its capacity to represent political violence, goes far beyond its strict legal application in the framework of universal justice, we are able to ask new kinds of questions. We are also able to establish new forms of parallelism or exceptionality in relation to experiences of repression in other parts of the world, not only in cases that are close to us historically and culturally, but in others that are slowly being assimilated to the legal classification in international law. For example, what kind of machinery for making people disappear (Calveiro, 1998; Gatti, 2008) is expressed by the scattering of mass graves throughout the Spanish geography, in comparison to the machinery that caused the arrested missing persons of Latin America, or the disappearances related to the dirty war against the Islamic Salvation Front in Algeria, or the ethnic cleansing in Bosnia? In the Spanish context, to what degree can mass graves be considered nodes of disappearance, or black holes of Franco regime repression, meant to bewilder, misinform, and interrupt mourning (Ferrándiz, 2009b; Robben, 2000)? With respect to some historians' objections, would the existence of court martials or death certificates in archives that were off-limits for decades (and are hard to get into even today) cancel out the personal, family, local, and political experience of the *fusilados* or *paseados* as missing persons?

The legal concept of forced disappearance, with its by-products of crimes against humanity, imprescriptibility, and the permanence of the crime, is in Spain to stay, although it is evident that the debate over how it fits and applies to the Spanish case is very important and should be kept alive, as long as it leads to greater knowledge of the consequences of the political repression linked to the Civil War, and not to a dead end. But beyond the historiographic or legal terminology regarding its relevance or nuances, forced disappearance is rooted in Spain as a category of political and symbolic action with a great capacity for social and media mobilization, as we will see in the following section. The conceptual positions regarding the adequacy of the term or its limits in the Spanish case are enormously interesting: on one hand, they can contribute to a better understanding of the characteristics of rearguard repression during the Civil War and the postwar period; on the other, they are an axis for establishing correlations between different forms of political barbarism in different places around the world and in different historical contexts. As I have already suggested, this means following the path of the intense, and often contradictory, social life of human rights that authors such as Wilson (2006) and Cowan (2006) refer to, as well as understanding how different forms of human rights violations in different locations around the world are interwoven with emerging or consolidated legal concepts in international law.

In summary, present-day controversies regarding the existence or inexistence of missing persons from the Civil War have two particularly notable aspects. On one hand, organizations and judges can, by means of the legally constituted concept of forced disappearance, download international human rights legislation in order to try to resolve, or at least point out, certain legal and legislative contradictions in the contemporary management of Franco regime repression during the war and the postwar period (Jiménez Villarejo, 2010). On the other hand, once the information has been obtained and processed, if the national authorities respond in a way that the civil organizations feel is inadequate, these organizations can raise their cases to the next higher authority (the boomerang effect), trying to force the authorities to confront prestigious international agencies and communications media. In any case, beyond political fluctuations, academic debates, legal blockages, and media scandals, the concept of forced disappearance has already triumphed in the country's mind as a new symbolic anchoring point for the *fusilados* or *paseados* who were victims of the rebel troops and the Franco dictatorship.

After the Garzón case, the concept of Spanish missing persons has taken root in the public arena and become social, political, and media common sense, even in the spheres that are least favourable to it; it has even been supported in a well-known *New York Times* editorial (An Injustice in Spain, 2008). This concept, despite its still diffuse outlines and despite the critiques already formulated and the ones that are yet to come, has connected so deeply with the so-called "movement for the recovery of historical memory" that these concepts and processes are already inextricable from the Spanish case. The social life of the missing may be the key connection between the Franco regime victims and an emerging form of low-intensity transnational citizenship[19] linked to the expansion of human rights discourse and practice which will, by making it possible to weave analogies and mark differences with other historical experiences in other parts of the world, irreversibly add the case of the Spanish Civil War and the dictatorship of Francisco Franco to the universal catalogue of massive violations of human rights.

Part 2 (Emilio Silva Barrera)

Historical Memory in Spain: The End of Silence, the Beginning of Justice

When the dictator Francisco Franco died on November 20, 1975, the elites who had seized enormous and exclusive privileges under his regime built into their model of democracy the necessary preservation of the political, economic, and social conquests they had achieved thanks to the regime's corruption. That is why, during the first democratic elections, parties that sought the return of the republic and a clean break that would impede the survival of Francoist structures in state power were not allowed to participate. Parties such as the Republican Left, which had enjoyed significant political representation during the previous democratic period, were not legalized until after elections in June 1977.

With the approval of the Amnesty Law (October 14, 1977) and the Constitution, which characterized Spain as a parliamentary monarchy (in a referendum on December 6, 1978), the accounts and versions of the dictatorship's past were settled. At least, that is what the regime's elites wanted, since their political project was to preserve their influence in the democracy to which they had arrived with an enormous head start and with representatives of their social class well positioned in both major political parties; both parties, though they had different discourses regarding the dictatorship, have never promoted any legislation that would undermine the privileges of those who had supported Franco.

This operation included the cover-up of the dictatorship's crimes, the exclusion of discussions of uncomfortable issues from the recent past, and the perpetuation, by inertia, of the idea in the collective imagination that the Second Republic (1931–39, which the Franco dictatorship ended) was a convulsive period, full of violence and devoid of social progress.

The very choice of the word "transition" to define the political period that followed Franco's death effaces the fact that Spain had previously enjoyed another democratic period. During the Second Republic, democratic elections were held with universal suffrage (men and women), different ideologies had alternated in power, and there were constitutional guarantees. It was in those years that Spain took its first steps in democracy, but the Francoist elites who were driving the post-dictatorship process preferred not to speak of the *recovery* of democracy, thus creating the illusion that Spain's first recognition of public freedoms was brought about thanks to the restoration of the monarchy.

Juan Gelman, the Argentine poet, once said that as soon as the dictatorship ends, the organizers of oblivion swoop in. The case of Spain was no exception in this regard. Once iron-clad impunity, memory loss, silence, and the mechanisms of fear had been firmly established, it seemed like the political project consisted mainly of sitting back and waiting for biology to do the job of erasing the memory of the dictatorship's crimes—waiting for the death of witnesses and victims of Francoist repression, and hoping that history would look on the dictatorship period with benevolent eyes, just as the people who have governed during our recovered democracy have done.

But there is one thing that a society can never escape from, no matter how hard and fast it runs: its own past. In the year 2000, in a small town in northwest Spain, 13 men were scientifically exhumed from a mass grave into which they had been thrown after being "disappeared" on October 16, 1936. It was a place where no armies had ever faced each other in battle; all there ever was in this part of Spain was repression, carried out by those who supported the *coup d'état* initiated by General Franco. The exhumation of their grave 63 years later represented a little hole in forgetting of the dictatorship's crimes and marked a turning point in the pathological relationship that Spanish society has with its traumatic past.

On April 14, 2010, Darío Rivas, the son of a Republican mayor who had been disappeared by Francoist repression, presented a complaint before a court of law in Buenos Aires, Argentina, which requested the application of the principle of universal justice in order to open up an investigation into the crimes committed during General Franco's dictatorship. Next to Darío, in the meeting at which the court case was announced, stood the Nobel Peace Prize laureate Adolfo Pérez Esquivel; Nora Cortiñas, the founder of the Argentine Mothers of the Plaza de Mayo; and many representatives of Argentina's human rights movements.

This court case was the result of victims of the Francoist dictatorship becoming empowered as a consequence of the exhumations of mass graves. The denunciations of forced disappearances that were made before Spanish courts and international organizations, and the doors closed by the members of the Spanish oligarchy who enjoy impunity, led the Association for the Recovery of Historical Memory to promote the initiation of this case.

Spain has been one of the primary international engines of universal justice. In November 1998, when Judge Baltasar Garzón issued an arrest warrant for the Chilean dictator Augusto Pinochet, who was in London at the time, Spanish justice occupied the vanguard in the struggle to globalize justice. The most important judicial organs of the country (e.g., the Supreme Court, the Constitutional Court) recognized the jurisdiction of Garzón's National Court to prosecute crimes against humanity, even those that were committed thousands of miles away from Spain.

But those very same state agencies have slammed the door shut on any investigation into the crimes of the Francoist dictatorship. When, on October 16, 2008, the same judge declared that he had jurisdiction to investigate the crimes of the Francoist dictatorship, the regime's elites, who still exercise enormous power and influence over political and judicial matters, pulled out all the stops in order to preserve their own impunity.

Nevertheless, the victims of the Francoist dictatorship continue their struggle to put an end to impunity and oblivion. In September 2013, two representatives of the United Nations Working Group on Enforced or Involuntary Disappearances made an official visit to Spain. This group answers to the United Nations' High Commission on Human Rights. For a week they travelled around to different cities in Spain, interviewed members of the government, representatives of political parties, historical memory associations, anthropologists, forensic scientists, historians, and numerous victims.

Six months later, the UN's Special Rapporteur on the promotion of truth, justice, reparation, and guarantees of non-recurrence, Pablo de Greiff, also made an official visit to Spain. He spent nine days in the country and, at a press conference before departing, he affirmed that Spain must judge Francoist repression, that the argument used by the judiciary to justify not doing so—the 1977 Amnesty Law—had no validity given the gravity of the alleged crimes. He also stated that he had noticed an enormous divide between the victims of the dictatorship and the government.

By the summer of 2015, both UN agencies published separate reports in which they harshly criticized the Spanish state's inaction with regard to providing reparations to the victims of the Franco dictatorship. The Working Group on Forced or Involuntary Disappearances included the following in its list of recommendations (United Nations Human Rights Council, 2014, pp. 16–18):

- Act with appropriate urgency and speed to investigate forced disappearances, as stipulated in the Declaration on the Protection of All Persons from Enforced Disappearance, and comply with other related international obligations. Urgency and speed are essential given the advanced age of many of the family members and witnesses who were the last to see the victims before they were disappeared during the Civil War and subsequent dictatorship.
- Ratify the Convention on the Non-Applicability of Statutory Limitations to War Crimes and Crimes against Humanity.
- Incorporate forced disappearance into the penal code as a distinct crime, following the definition that can be found in the UN Declaration. Establish appropriate sentences for the crime, which take into account its extreme gravity.
- Explicitly stipulate that the freestanding crime of forced disappearance has no statute of limitations, or, taking into account current rules in Spain about statute of limitations for permanent crimes, ensure that the judiciary counts the beginning of the statute of limitations from the moment in which the forced disappearance is terminated (i.e., once the person is found alive, or his or her remains are found, or his or her identity is restored).
- Adopt the necessary legislative measures to ensure that cases of forced disappearance can be tried by jurisdictions of competent common law, and not by any other special jurisdiction, in particular, by military jurisdiction.
- Officially investigate and try all forced disappearances, in accordance with international obligations, in an exhaustive and impartial manner and with no regard to the time that has passed since the initiation of the crimes.
- Adopt all necessary legislative and judicial measures to ensure that forced disappearances cannot be covered by any amnesty, and, in particular, completely vacate the judicial interpretation that has been given to the 1977 Amnesty Law.

The Working Group urged Spain's government to present a plan within 90 days for the implementation of the recommendations to address forced disappearances during the Civil War and the Francoist dictatorship, but the deadline passed and Spain's executive branch made no such presentation.

In his report as the Special Rapporteur on the promotion of truth, justice, reparation, and guarantees of non-recurrence, Pablo de Greiff denounced the Spanish state's failure to fulfill its obligations to the victims of the Francoist dictatorship. He also repeated his earlier observation of the large gap between the positions of most State institutions and the victims and associations with whom de Greiff had spoken. Civil society and, in particular, organizations of victims and family members (especially the grandchildren of victims) are those who have promoted initiatives aimed at promoting truth, justice, reparations, and guarantees that these atrocities will never happen again. There is a profound commitment among victims, families, and associations, who strive to keep alive the voices and reclamations of the victims; this is in stark contrast to the inertia of the state, which refuses to listen to them.

The Special Rapporteur noted that, in his meetings with various representatives of the government, the officials framed the discussions in this way: "Either we all agree that we are fully reconciled, or the only alternative is the resurgence of underlying hatreds, which would entail too high a risk" (de Greiff, 2014, p. 19). In the Rapporteur's opinion, this position does not do justice to the progress made during Spain's process of democratization. He underscores the fact that, considering the solidity of Spain's institutions and the lack of risks for the stability of the country's democratic order, he finds it particularly surprising that more hasn't been done to support the rights of so many victims. In his 2014 report, de Greiff had the following recommendations, which fit into several groups:

Non-recurrence (pp. 5–10):

- Systematize the initiatives regarding Francoist symbols and monuments, in accordance with the current legislation, promoting differentiated interventions, as well as contextualization and "resignification" of the symbols and monuments when removing them is not recommended.
- Implement the recommendations formulated by the Committee of Experts for the Future of the Valley of the Fallen in its report from 2011, in particular with regard to the "resignification" of the site, research and outreach programs, and restoration and conservation, including maintaining the dignity of the cemetery and the respectful safekeeping of the remains of all the persons interred there.
- Strengthen training programs for civil servants, including the judiciary and security forces, with regards to human rights. Incorporate material related to the history of the Civil War and Francoism in line with the national curriculum, including the study of the state institutions' serious violations of human rights and humanitarian law during this period, as a measure of education, sensitization, and in order to promote guarantees of non-recurrence. Centre this study on the rights of all the victims.

Truth (pp. 10–13):

- Promote the establishment of truth by urgently attending to the demands of the victims and establishing some mechanism to make official and resolve the excessive fragmentation that characterizes the construction of memory in Spain. Re-establish or increase the available resources for this matter.

Justice (pp. 14–16):

- Identify appropriate mechanisms to nullify sentences that were given out in violation of the most basic principles of law and due process during the Civil War and the Franco regime. Comparative studies with the experiences of other countries that have faced similar challenges, including many European countries, could be most beneficial.
- Explore alternatives, and nullify the dispositions of the 1977 Amnesty Law that impede access to justice and investigations into the grave violations of human rights committed during the Civil War and Francoist regime.
- Promote greater awareness of the international obligations with regard to access to justice, the right to truth, and the guarantees of due process; give adequate institutional expression to these obligations.
- Guarantee the collaboration of Spanish justice with foreign judicial proceedings, and take action against the weakening of universal jurisdiction being carried out by Spanish tribunals.

Reparations (pp. 16–18):

- Broaden the recognition and coverage of reparation programs so that they include all categories of victims that might have been excluded from existent programs. Take measures to attend to requests related to the restitution of properties and documents that were expropriated from individuals. Make a stronger effort to establish measures of reparation that are symbolic rather than material.
- Broaden existing studies about the violation of human rights of women, and develop initiatives of reparation and of special recognition of the harm suffered by women as a consequence of the Civil War and Francoism, including sexual violence, aggression, humiliation, and discrimination as a form of punishment because of women's real or imagined affiliations, or those of their families or partners.

FIGURE 4.3   **Members of the Association for the Recovery of Historical Memory excavating a Civil War mass grave at Joarilla de las Matas, Spain.**

Photo credit: Óscar Rodríguez, volunteer photographer with ARMH, printed by permission

These two reports (de Greiff, 2014; United Nations Human Rights Council, 2014) from the UN's High Commission for Human Rights offer compelling support to the victims of the Francoist dictatorship, yet the response of the government continues to be the same passivity that it has maintained for decades.

In the meantime, victims continue filing complaints before Argentine courts. There, Judge María Servini de Cubría has opened a case and has issued an international arrest warrant for 11 leaders and torturers of the dictatorship, among them the former ministers Rodolfo Martín Villa and José Utrera Molina. For the families of the disappeared the difficult fight continues, but in the 15 years that have gone by since the first scientifically exhumed mass grave, many things have been revealed that the political elites had swept under the rug of an alleged reconciliation. The most recent exhumations performed by the Association for the Recovery of Historical Memory (ARMH) have been made possible thanks to donations provided by Elogit, a Norwegian trade union of electricians. The Association's skeletal analysis laboratory in Ponferrada was going to close due to a lack of resources in 2014; however, ARMH was recently awarded the Alba-Puffin Award, a prize that recognizes work in defence of human rights given by the Abraham Lincoln Brigade Archives based in New York City. Thanks to the prize associated with this award, ARMH will be able to remain operational for at least two more years (Figure 4.3).

Spain is an example of impunity existing in a country where there are adequate economic, political, and legal resources to take on the challenge of justice that the victims of serious human rights violations are demanding. It is paradoxical that the country with the highest number of common graves of disappeared people after Cambodia is part of the European Union, and yet neither European nor Spanish institutions do anything to resolve this issue. The 113,226 men and women who were assassinated and thrown in those mass graves await the end of silence that might finally signify the beginning of justice.

Notes

1. A version of the first section of this chapter was originally published in Spanish as: Ferrándiz, F. (2010). De las fosas comunes a los derechos humanos: El descubrimiento de las desapariciones forzadas en la España contemporánea. *Revista de Antropología Social, 19,* 161–189.

2. Future reflection on the inverse process, that is, *uploading,* the influence that governments, institutions, and different groups in civil society could have on the transformations of universal justice due to local demands or rights, is also necessary. In the case of Spanish missing persons, this upward movement is still very limited, but there can be no doubt about the influence of missing persons in the Latin American dictatorships on the consolidation of the universal category of forced disappearances.

3. This movement is neither unique nor original, but rather a recent episode in a long history of open and clandestine initiatives, within Spain and in exile, that date from the time of the defeat and the instalment of the Franco regime. See Ferrándiz, 2005, p. 114.

4. On the double game in the case of Pinochet that is, on one hand, the field of *globalized justice* and, on the other, the field of Chilean *popular sovereignty,* see Golob, 2002a and 2002b. If we follow Golob's analysis, there are clear parallels, as well as divergences, in how transnational schema of justice and local political and legal agendas are interwoven, both in the case of Pinochet and in the case of the victims of the Franco regime.

5. Due to the limits of space and the complexity of this issue, I can only briefly discuss one important aspect of this whole process: the actions that right-wing and ultra-right-wing political groups are carrying out in Spain in reaction to the expansion and assumed increase in the stories of defeat in the Civil War and their associated public policies. These include everything from blocking measures of redress in parliament and publishing revisionist books to organizing exhumations of Republican mass graves, as in the case of the mine in the town of Camuñas, Toledo, in January 2010. Regarding the contemporary role of the mass graves in the Republican repression, see, for example, Ledesma, 2003.

6. For a bibliography of legal texts on this issue, see Chinchón, 2008.

7. Asociación para la Recuperación de la Memoria Histórica.

8. See Chinchón, 2008, p. 53, and the section regarding Spain (pp. 53–54) in the 2004 United Nations document *Los derechos civiles y políticos, en particular las cuestiones relacionadas con las desapariciones y las ejecuciones* sumarias (daccess-dds-ny.un.org/doc/UNDOC/GEN/ G04/103/99/PDF/G0410399.pdf?OpenElement).

9. This term refers to discourses and practices anchored in Civil War frameworks.

10. See Martín Pallín and Escudero Alday (2008) for a detailed analysis of the potential and the limitations of the moral and legal aspects of Law 52/2007.

11.   Carlos Slepoy, the Argentinian lawyer who represents family members of Spanish missing persons, has made especially interesting declarations. He states that the complaint lodged in Argentina also attempted to demonstrate that "universal justice is not a colonial weapon" and that it can flow, as in this instance, from the ex-colony to the ex-metropolis (El polvorín, 2010, p. 21).

12.   For more on *Decree of Missing Persons Number 67*, the procedures of "concealing genocide" by falsifying the register, and the fact that, today, many people are still not registered despite the "avalanche of registrations at the end of the seventies and beginning of the eighties," see Espinosa, 2002, pp. 103–114.

13.   I would like to thank Javier Rodrigo and José Luis Ledesma for their valuable insight regarding the historical aspects of the term in Spain.

14.   "Taken for a walk," the term used in the Civil War to refer to those who were shot in the rearguard, is still used today to refer to the victims of the shootings.

15.   As Layla Renshaw (2010, p. 52) has pointed out, it is important to differentiate between the use of "missing persons" in public discourse and the linguistic patterns in more local and rural spheres, where "missing person" is not yet the most common term for referring to the people who are in mass graves. However, given the term's growing use in the public sphere today, it is possible to hypothesize that its extension to the activists and family members who are farthest from the urban movements is only a matter of time and, very probably, will be a generational change.

16.   See, for example, the October 20, 2008, Appeal by the Chief Public Prosecutor of the National Courts, Javier-Alberto Zaragoza, against Garzón's decree.

17.   Since it is impossible to discuss all the media products and political debates on this subject here, I will focus mainly on the media considered to be "left-wing." To consider the impact on the social, political, and media right-wing, see the articles following the Garzón case and its legal, social, and political derivations in *La Razón*, the *ABC*, *El Mundo*, and *La Gaceta*.

18.   On the other hand, comparisons between the Spanish cases and the Latin American dictatorships are inevitable, occur in many spheres, and are not necessarily simplifications or caricatures. Regarding the "Argentinization" of the Spanish model of impunity and the demand for legal consequences for political crimes, see the interesting opinion article by Ricard Vinyes, "La impunidad y la doncella" (2010).

19.   *Low-intensity citizenship* is associated with thin rights derived from the progressive implantation of soft law, as in the case of human rights (Fox, 2005, pp. 191–194). Regarding the impact of the transnationalization processes of victimization on identity, belonging, and national citizenship, see also Golob, 2002a.

References

Amnesty International. (2005). *España: Poner fin al silencio y a la injusticia: La deuda pendiente con las víctimas de la Guerra Civil española y del régimen franquista*. Madrid: Sección española de Amnistía Internacional.

Amnesty International. (2006a). *Víctimas de la Guerra Civil y el Franquismo: El desastre de los archivos, la privatización de la verdad*. Madrid: Sección española de Amnistía Internacional.

Amnesty International. (2006b). *Víctimas de la Guerra Civil y el Franquismo: No hay derecho. Preocupaciones sobre el Proyecto de Ley de Derechos de las víctimas de la Guerra Civil y el Franquismo*. Madrid: Sección española de Amnistía Internacional.

Amnesty International. (2008a). *España: La obligación de investigar los crímenes del pasado y garantizar los derechos de las víctimas de desaparición forzada durante la Guerra Civil y el Franquismo*. Madrid: Sección española de Amnistía Internacional.

Amnesty International. (2008b). *España: Ejercer la jurisdiccón para acabar con la impunidad.* Madrid: Sección española de Amnistía Internacional.

An Injustice in Spain [Editorial]. (2008, April 9). *New York Times,* p. A26. Retrieved from www.nytimes.com/2010/04/09/opinion/09fri2.html?_r=0.

Boletín Oficial del Estado. (1936a). Decreto número 67, 11 de noviembre de 1936. Número 27, p. 154. Burgos: Government of Spain.

Boletín Oficial del Estado. (1936b). Disposición en cumplimiento del Decreto número sesenta y siete y oída la Comisión de Justicia, 13 de noviembre de 1936. Número 29, p. 176. Burgos: Government of Spain.

Boletín Oficial del Estado. (1939). Ley de 16 de Mayo de 1939 facultando a los Ayuntamientos para dispensar o reducir las exacciones municipales que gravan las inhumaciones, exhumaciones, y traslados de cadáveres víctimas de la barbarie roja muerta en el frente, 17 de mayo de 1939. Número 137, pp. 2687–2688. Madrid: Government of Spain.

Boletín Oficial del Estado. (2007). Ley 52/2007, de 26 de diciembre, por la que se reconocen y amplían derechos y se establecen medidas en favor de quienes padecieron persecución o violencia durante la guerra civil y la dictadura, 27 de diciembre de 2007. Número 310, pp. 53410–53416. Madrid: Government of Spain.

Calveiro, P. (1998). *Poder y desaparición: Los campos de concentración en Argentina.* Buenos Aires: Colihue.

Casanova, J. (2002). Una dictadura de cuarenta años. In J. Casanova (ed.), *Morir, matar, sobrevivir: La violencia en la dictadura de Franco* (pp. 1–50). Barcelona: Crítica.

Casanova, J. (2008, July 10). Desaparecidos. *El País.* Retrieved from elpais.com/diario/2008/07/10/opinión/1215640805_850215.html.

Cowan, J. K. (2006). Culture and rights after *Culture and Rights. American Anthropologist, 108*(1), 9–24.

Chinchón, J. (2008). La convención internacional para la protección de todas las personas contra las desapariciones forzadas: Nunca es tarde si la dicha es ¿buena? Examen general y perspectivas en España tras la aprobación de la "Ley de Memoria Histórica." *Foro (Nueva Época), 7,* 13–55.

de Greiff, P. (2014). Report of the Special Rapporteur on the promotion of truth, justice, reparation and guarantees of non-recurrence: Mission to Spain. Retrieved from daccess-dds-ny.un.org/doc/UNDOC/GEN/G14/090/52/PDF/G1409052.pdf?OpenElement.

El polvorín. (2010, April 9). Las víctimas de Franco apelan a la justicia argentina. *El polvorín* [blog]. Retrieved from elpolvorin.over-blog.es/article-las-victimas-de-franco-apelan-a-la-justicia-argentina-48320636.html.

Espinosa, F. (2002). Julio de 1936: Golpe militar y plan de exterminio. In J. Casanova (ed.), *Morir, matar, sobrevivir: La violencia en la dictadura de Franco* (pp. 51–119). Barcelona: Crítica.

Ferrándiz, F. (2005). La memoria de los vencidos de la Guerra Civil: El impacto de las exhumaciones de fosas comunes en la España contemporánea. In J. M. Valcuende & S. Narotzky (eds.), *Las políticas de la memoria en los sistemas democráticos: Poder, cultura y mercado* (pp. 109–132). Seville: ASANA.

Ferrándiz, F. (2009a). Fosas comunes, paisajes del Terror. *Revista de Dialectología y Tradiciones Populares, LXIV*(1), 61–94.

Ferrándiz, F. (2009b). Exhumaciones y relatos de la derrota en la España actual. *Jerónimo Zurita, 84,* 135–162.

Ferrándiz, F. (2010). De las fosas comunes a los derechos humanos: El descubrimiento de las desapariciones forzadas en la España contemporánea. *Revista de Antropología Social, 19,* 161–189.

Ferrándiz, F., & Baer, A. (2008). Digital memory: The visual recording of mass grave exhumations in contemporary Spain. *Forum Qualitative Sozialforschung/Forum:Qualitative Social Research, 9*(3), Art. 35.

Fox, J. (2005). Unpacking "transnational citizenship." *Annual Review of Political Science, 8,* 171–201.

Garzón, B. (2008a). *Auto, Diligencias previas (proc. abreviado) 399/2006V* (16-10-2008). Madrid: Juzgado Central de Instrucción n 5, Audiencia Nacional.

Garzón, B. (2008b). *Auto, Sumario (proc. ordinario) 53/2008e* (18-11-2008). Madrid: Juzgado Central de Instrucción n 5, Audiencia Nacional.

Gatti, G. (2008). *El detenido-desaparecido. Narrativas posibles para una catástrofe de la identidad.* Montevideo: Trilce.

Golob, S. (2002a). "Forced to be free": Globalized justice, pacted democracy, and the Pinochet case. *Democratization, 9*(2), 21–42.

Golob, S. (2002b). The Pinochet case: "Forced to be free abroad and at home." *Democratization, 9*(4), 25–57.

Jiménez Villarejo, C. (2010). Prólogo. In B. Garzón, *Garzón contra el franquismo: Los autos íntegros del juez sobre los crímenes de la dictadura* (pp. 9–14). Madrid: Diario Público.

Juliá, S. (ed.). (2008, February 10). Una personalidad autoritaria. *El País Domingo.* Retrieved from elpais.com/diario/2008/02/10/domingo/1202617832_850215.html.

Ledesma, J. L. (2003). *Los días de llamas de la revolución: Violencia y política en la retaguardia republicana de Zaragoza durante la Guerra Civil.* Zaragoza: Institución Fernando el Católico.

Ledesma, J. L. (2005). La "Causa General": Fuente sobre la violencia, la Guerra Civil (y el franquismo). *Spagna Contemporánea, 28*(XIV), 203–220.

Ley de la Memoria Histórica. (2007). *Ley 52/2007 de 26 de Diciembre.* Ministerio de Justicia, Government of Spain.

Marre, D. (2009). Los silencios de la adopción en España. *Revista de Antropología Social, 18,* 97–126.

Martín Pallín, J. A., & Escudero Alday, R. (eds.) (2008). *Derecho y memoria histórica.* Madrid: Trotta.

Mate, R. (2009, December 27). Lorca, un desaparecido. *El País.* Retrieved from elpais.com/diario/2009/12/27/opinión/1261868405_850215.html.

Merry, S. E. (2006). Transnational human rights and local activism: Mapping the middle. *American Anthropologist, 108*(1), 38–51.

Pradera, J. (2008a, September 7). La guerra que no cesa. *El País Domingo.* Retrieved from: elpais.com/diario/2008/09/07/domingo/1220758233_850215.html.

Pradera, J. (2008b, November 23). Un viaje aluncinógeno. *El País Domingo.* Retrieved from: elpais.com/diario/2008/11/23/domingo/1227414634_850215.html.

Pradera, J. (2008c, December 3). Un mal viaje de ida y vuelta. *El País.* Retrieved from: elpais.com/diario/2009/12/03/espana/1228258815_850215.html.

Pradera, J. (2010, January 10). Paseos y tumbas. *El País Domingo.* Retrieved from: elpais.com/diario/2010/01/10/domingo/1263097835_850215.html.

Renshaw, L. (2010). Missing bodies near-at-hand: The dissonant memory and dormant graves of the Spanish Civil War. In M. Bille, F. Hastrup, & T. Flohr (eds.), *An anthropology of absence: Materializations of trascendence and loss* (pp. 45–61). London, UK: Springer.

Robben, A. C. G. M. (2000). State terror in the Netherworld: Disappearance and reburial in Argentina. In J. A. Sluka (ed.), *Death squad: The anthropology of state terror* (pp. 91–113). Philadelphia, PA: University of Pennsylvania Press.

Silva, E. (2005). *Las fosas de Franco: Crónica de un desagravio.* Madrid: Temas de Hoy.

United Nations. (2004, January 21). Civil and political rights, including the questions of: Disappearances and summary executions. *Report of the Working Group on Enforced or Involuntary Disappearances.* United Nations Economic and Social Council, document E/CN 4/2004/58.

United Nations Human Rights Council. (2009). *Report of the Working Group on Enforced or Involuntary Disappearances*. Retrieved from www2.ohchr.org/english/bodies/hrcouncil/docs/13session/A-HRC-13-31.pdf.

United Nations Human Rights Council. (2014). *Report of the working group on enforced or involuntary disappearances*: Addendum, mission to Spain. Retrieved from ap.ohchr.org/documents/dpage_e.aspx?si=A/HRC/27/49/Add.1.

Vinyes, R. (2002). *Irredentas: Las presas políticas y sus hijos en las cárceles franquistas*. Madrid: Temas de Hoy.

Vinyes, R. (2010, May 2). La impunidad y la doncella. *Público*. Retrieved from blogs.publico.es/dominiopublico/1990/la-impunidad-y-la-doncella/.

Vinyes, R., Armengou, M., & Belis, R. (2002). *Los niños perdidos del franquismo*. Barcelona: Plaza y Janés.

Wilson, R. A. (2006). Afterword to "Anthropology and human fights in a new key": The social life of human rights. *American Anthropologist, 108*(1), 77–83.

Zaragoza, J. A. (2008). *Recurso a las diligencias previas 399/2006 del Juzgado Central de Instrucción nº 5 (actualmente sumario 53/08)*. Madrid: Fiscalía de la Audiencia Nacional.

Related Sources

Association for the Recovery of Historical Memory: memoriahistorica.org.es

Ferrándiz, F. (2014). *El Pasado bajo tierra: Exhumaciones contemoráneas de la Guerra Civil*. Barcelona: Anthopos/SigloXXI.

Ferrándiz, F., & Robben, A. C. G. M. (2014). *Necropolitics: Mass graves and exhumations in the age of human rights*. Philadelphia, PA: University of Pennsylvania Press.

Jerez-Farrán, C., & Amago, S. (eds.). (2010). *Unearthing Franco's legacy*. Notre Dame, IN: University of Notre Dame Press.

Las Políticas de la Memoria: www.politicasdelamemoria.org

Chapter 5

Psychosocial Perspectives on the Enforced Disappearance of Indigenous Peoples in Guatemala

Mónica Esmeralda Pinzón González[1] (Universidad de San Carlos de Guatemala)

This chapter begins with a brief introduction on Maya ancestral history and the colonial and post-colonial history of Guatemala. This is followed by an account of the Maya cosmo-vision of life and death to better understand the repression and enforced disappearance that occurred during the last half of the 20th century. The chapter concludes with a brief discussion on Indigenous peoples' perspectives in the face of enforced disappearance.

Guatemalan Ancestral, Historical, Political, and Social Context

Historically, Indigenous peoples have been guardians, not owners, of mother earth, whom they see as the giver of life. They co-exist with rivers, lakes, mountains, volcanoes, animals, forests, and plants (both for food and medicine), and at the same time safeguard their life-giving breath. The cosmogonic character of Guatemalan Indigenous peoples is made up of thoughts, feelings, living, understanding, the way we act in our surroundings, and respect for all living things in the universe. This philosophy is supreme and acquires importance in social interactions, and thus in day-to-day life. The Indigenous population believes that each object (e.g., minerals, household items such as pots and grinding stones) has energy, and therefore also has life. Anthropologically, it is said that artifacts are a part of culture's vital geography (Guitart, 2011). Maya objects are filled with substantial symbolism that signifies love, memories, and ancestral legends, which are handed down through rituals from generation to generation. For Maya Indigenous people, everything is part of a whole, and when something is not respected or is altered, everything else becomes unbalanced, requiring spiritual rituals of apology to re-establish balance and harmony.

Ardón (2012) has detailed the principles that govern Maya belief and culture. These include principles of duality, processuality, complementarity, respect, consensus, participation, contribution, and listening. *Duality* does not mean antagonism, rather two components constituting a whole in a complementary way: life and death, day and night, etc. These opposites form a whole, a duality that gives the universe life. *Processuality* refers to life as a journey of learning: nothing is finite and perfect. This principle fosters an attitude of flexibility in the face of new changes. Complementarity goes hand-in-hand with duality, and is most manifest in the union of man and woman, because the couple is a reflection of the sun and moon. The principle of *respect* emphasizes one's position as a part of the whole. Being disrespectful affects not only the person who is being disrespected, but also the community and, therefore, oneself. From this principle derives the sense of reparation, particularly when an action is intentional. *Consensus* creates multiple complementary opinions through dialogue and active participation from everyone in order to weigh the good of the collective against the individual. The principle of *participation* signifies that each family and community member should contribute their ideas, because community actions should take into account the needs and interests of all members. The sense of responsibility and collective responsibility inspires the principle of contribution. *Contribution* might be a material, an idea, or advice given as a response to a need. Contributions are not judged by quantity or quality, but by the willingness to make them. For example (and relevant to this chapter), expressing condolences when someone dies is not expressed by words, but instead by accompanying the mourners and demonstrating a collective solidarity. Finally, the principle of *listening* is based on the notion that everything is unfinished. Listening allows one to obtain more information and facilitates group consultation. This principle promotes awareness, dialogue, analysis, and negotiation on any topic of interest to the group.

These principles apply to all things that have life, including the universe. These principles are part of Maya identity: beliefs, rites, legends, customs, ancestral knowledge, language, clothing, food, art, and technology. Regional or group cultural identity and collective practice are based upon these things.

Maya Concepts of Time and Space

For the Maya, time goes well beyond the measuring of space, cycles, and periods, and goes well beyond the passing of life too: time is cyclical and can be seen as a spiral. Time determines the creation of spaces and moments for spiritual rites, and it is understood to be one of the manifestations of the cosmos/universe that creates life: fertilization, gestation, birth, and human development. In the cycles of existence, there are seasonal changes marked by equinox and solstice. These guide agricultural activities or the preservation of natural resources for the survival of the collective.

For the Indigenous people of Guatemala, death is seen not as the end of life, but rather the beginning of something new. The spirit does not necessarily go to heaven or hell but rather it stays as a duplicate of life in the same space; that is, cosmologically speaking, the dead share the same space with the living. These spirits can be invoked or called upon for help. The dead continue working on the same activities that they did when they were alive. Hence, work instruments such as pots, machetes, or hats are deliberately placed with the body during death rites so that the person/spirit can continue working in their next life.

From generation to generation, the Maya refer to the owners of hills, valleys, and mountains. It is the spirits that take care of these places. That is why they are called "The Guardians," and are referred to as "Grandpa" or "Grandma" by the younger generation. It is believed that if one enters a hill or valley without permission, the spirit can cause that person to get lost until he or she asks forgiveness. Only then will they be shown the way.

The Ahab calendar, or solar calendar, records the movement of the earth around the sun, and it has 365 days. The sacred Ahab calendar is also called the agricultural calendar, and is associated with masculinity as embodied by the sun and maize (corn). The Cholq´ij, or lunar calendar, is linked to the moon's orbit around the earth. The sacred Cholq´ij calendar has 260 days and is associated with femininity, directed by Grandmother Ixmukané (Grandmother Moon). It is through her that the nine-month pregnancy period is counted out; hence, when Maya women are pregnant, they say they are filled with the moon.

Oral traditions passed on through grandfathers and grandmothers tell that Maya ancestors arrived and settled in Mesoamerica around 5,125 years ago. Díaz and Rodgers (1993) describe early Maya society as hierarchically organized, with power and authority to lead the community given to governors or rulers, monarchs, *caciques* (chiefs), spiritual guides, merchants, and warriors. The social system accommodated the principles of collectivity, reciprocity, and balance, and these principles were the basis on which this power was built. The relationship with mother earth centred around food and human protection.

Maya Death Rites

The death rites of the Guatemalan Indigenous peoples are diverse, and follow the ethnic tradition of the person who leads them. These leaders are called *spiritual guides* and exist among all Indigenous groups. Generally speaking, the dead person is dressed in their newest clothes and, if possible, with his or her work tools. As mentioned previously, the inclusion of tools is important because in the "return to life," as death is called, it is believed that to die is to live again, and the deceased might need his or her tools to continue working in their new life. The family focuses on raising the *jaleb* ("spirit," in the Kiche language) of the deceased. According to Barone et al. (2012), there is a wake and a funeral procession in the community that reflects the cause of death. For the dead to be able to rest, a *kamalbe* ("spiritual guide," in the Kiche language) helps the *jaleb* to the other life so he or she will not bother the family.

Brief History of Colonial and Post-colonial Socio-politics in Guatemala

In 1492, America was "discovered" by Christopher Columbus, and 32 years later the Spanish invaded the territory of the Maya. Pedro de Alvarado, the so-called Conqueror of Mexico, was sent to Guatemala by Hernan Cortez. When the Spanish settled, they set in motion massive changes in the social structure of the native inhabitants. Indigenous Guatemalans were subjected to cruel, inhumane abuse and slavery, justified by racist Spanish policies. Since this time, violence against the Maya has been enacted and legitimized through battles and massacres, culminating in the first documented genocide in Guatemalan history during the 1960–96 Civil War.

It is important to recognize that native Guatemalans resisted Spanish colonization. Nevertheless, the Spanish invaders divided up the land, taking the most fertile for themselves and forcing the native peoples to work it without pay. Some Indigenous families received communal lands, but they were generally unsuitable for planting and producing good harvests. New organizational structures were introduced, such as *cofradias* (or confraternities, Catholic organizations designed to promote Christianity) and municipalities. Despite many socio-political systems imposed by the Spanish, collectivity and lineal recognition of power among elders has persisted among the Indigenous Maya. Elders maintain a direct link with their ancestors through the rites and symbols of their cosmogony.

On September 15, 1821, a group of *Criollos* (people of Spanish ancestry born in Guatemala) met with the Spanish authorities demanding that power be handed to them (Martínez Pelaez, 2009). This is commonly known as the Independence Era. Independence was granted and liberal and conservative political parties created. The Indigenous people of Guatemala, however, were not considered citizens, but slaves. For this reason, September 15 does not commemorate independence for the Indigenous peoples in Guatemala.

The year 1931, the beginning of the dictatorship of Jorge Ubico y Castañeda, marks a "before and after" period of slavery in Guatemala, an institutionalization of racial subjugation. Legislation such as the road law, vagrancy law, and law of flight (*ley de fugas*) were instituted, which effectively formalized and legitimized forced Indigenous labour (McCreary, 1983). In September 1938, the post of "military commissioner" was created through ministerial agreement. Commissioners were locals who spoke the language of the region where they lived and would, during the internal armed conflict to come, direct the "security" forces of the Guatemalan state in their operations of forced disappearance and torture.

The so-called Revolution Era began in 1944, forcing the resignation of Ubico. Juan José Arévalo was elected president in 1944, followed by Jacobo Árbenz in 1950. In 1954, there was a counter-revolution supported by the United States that led to the overthrow of the revolutionary government (Gordon, 1971). Carlos Castillo Armas led the coup and proclaimed himself president, only to be assassinated three years later in 1957. In 1960, the leftist "Revolutionary Movement 13th November" (MR13 in Spanish) rose up in the Sierra de Las Minas mountains, near the city of Zacapa, against the military dictator Miguel Ydígoras Fuentes. This group was later joined by other guerrilla organizations against the government and military, which led to 36 years of internal armed conflict.

During this period of conflict, Indigenous communities would be razed and inhabitants were tortured, massacred, or "disappeared" (i.e., were victims of enforced disappearance). Throughout the conflict, sexual violence was directed against women of mixed ancestry (*mestizas*), and particularly against Indigenous females of all ages (Commission for Historical Clarification, 1999). Sexual violence was not excessively used by any particular military group, but rather was a systematic tactic of domination and humiliation. This sexual violence left in its wake a psychosocial aftershock that would remain silent, and which greatly affected the collectivity of Indigenous people. The women who were raped not only experienced high levels of post-traumatic stress, but they were seen as having transgressed cultural bonds, inadvertently transmitting fear and desolation to new generations.

In addition, elders and leaders (male and female) were targeted by the military, which greatly affected cultural tradition and the ways in which the Indigenous people solved their problems in accordance with the teachings of their ancestors. In other words, this directed persecution disrupted not only the lives of individuals, but also Indigenous community, cosmogony, and ritual.

Crops, houses, and cultural property were destroyed, leaving in the wake of military assaults a mortal cultural injury. The effects of the attacks were particularly traumatic given that recovery from the destruction of each of these things requires the collective support of brothers, sisters, and fellow community members, many of whom were now gone. Planting, for example, is communal and requires many days of mutual collaboration. It is not just an act and product in itself, but rather a collective activity. It is the same with cultural goods, handed down from generation to generation. There is a commitment embedded in these objects and they cannot simply be replaced by other, similar objects. Similarly, housing is a symbol of cooperation and support, because all community members provide for the well-being of each family. The arrival and occupation of Europeans in Guatemala can be characterized as a continuing but shifting suppression by colonizers, who institutionalized racist attitudes, culminating in genocide of Indigenous peoples.

Documenting Recent Genocide in Guatemala

On December 29, 1996, peace accords were signed in Guatemala mandating the fulfillment of two projects:

1. Recovery of Historical Memory (Recuperación de la Memoria Histórica, or REMHI) was a documentation project carried out by Monsignor Gerardi[2] of the Catholic Church in 1998. Gerardi, along with catechists, compiled and documented eyewitness accounts of the crimes perpetrated against the Guatemalan population. The report, *Guatemala: Nunca Más* (*Guatemala: Never Again* [Catholic Institute for International Relations, 1999]) has been published in several languages, including English.

2. The Commission for Historical Clarification (Comisión para la Esclarecimiento Histórico, or CEH) was established in 1994 as a result of the Accord of Oslo between the Government of the Republic of Guatemala and the Guatemalan National Revolutionary Unity.

The CEH recorded 42,275 victims of 61,648 acts of violence and human rights violations. Sexual crimes accounted for 2.38 percent of the total number of crimes committed. Only a small proportion of the 1,465 reported cases of sexual violence could be investigated by the Commission, because of a limited mandate and the fear many witnesses had of giving testimony (Guatemala, memoria del silencio, 1999). Up to 85 percent of these crimes were committed by the military, 99 percent were against women, and 89 percent were against Indigenous Maya women. Of the crimes documented by CEH, 38 percent were arbitrary executions, followed by torture (19 percent), enforced disappearances (10 percent), and rape (2 percent) (Guatemala, memoria del silencio, 1999).

On May 10, 2013, former General and President of Guatemala Efraín Ríos Montt was convicted of genocide and crimes against humanity by the First Criminal Trial Court, on the charges of planning and carrying out orders for the extermination of Indigenous people. Ríos Montt was sentenced to 80 years in prison: 50 years for genocide, and 30 years for crimes against humanity (Malkin, 2013).

Indigenous Guatemalans and Enforced Disappearance

The internal armed conflict destroyed the framework of Indigenous relationships and death rites, given that the first to be sought out and killed were ancestral leaders. This left the Indigenous people without trusted authority figures. More than just terrorize the Indigenous population, this genocidal strategy dismantled Maya cosmogonic systems.

What happened to the death rites of families of missing persons? Given the extreme stress due to the conflict and a focus on survival, families were simply unable to fulfill the funerary customs dictated by their culture. Worse still, in the absence of a body, customary rituals simply cannot be performed. Families of the missing are therefore suffering because, in their minds, the missing are angry, sad, or feel like abandoned animals, and this impedes their spiritual well-being.

Suazo (2002, p. 16) points out that the words "dead" and "deceased" are words borrowed from Latin. One refers to the person who no longer has a social life (*defunctus*) and the other refers to one who has reached an end. Both words are foreign to Maya ways of thinking about the dead, since for them the dead never end their social lives, nor do the Maya believe that those who have died cease to exist. Suazo (2002) also states that, for the "Western world," death represents a cold place filled with ghosts, whereas for the Maya it is a dimension filled with life and warmth. Death takes you to a dimension similar to that of life; reality is duplicated on the other side.

In the ritual language of the Achí people, the words *spirit* or *soul* are used to refer to any dead person in spirit form. These words can be heard, for example, when a missing person's body is found and exhumed from a clandestine cemetery 30 years after having disappeared. In this cultural framework there is a relationship between the living and dead, and there are existing ties between the ancestor, the deceased, and those who are in spirit form. With regard to Maya cosmo-vision, death is not the end of life; it is a new beginning. People live with more than one deity (understood as ancestral energies that connect a person with his or her forebears), who communicate or manifest themselves through nature: animals, wind, rain, volcanoes, fog, hills, and dreams. There are many signs in nature and in objects that allow us to predict or communicate something that is about to happen. There are certain bodily sensations (cramps, tremors), natural phenomena, meetings with animals, etc., that can be interpreted as good or bad auguries depending on how each is felt. Due to the absence of a victim's body as a result of the armed conflict in Guatemala, relatives use dreams as a means to communicate with those who are not present.

The Meaning of Dreams in Maya Culture[3]

Dreams are not unique to any social class, gender, or ethnicity. However, they present themselves differently depending on the person, the context, and the culture in which they occur. They have different meanings and interpretations.

Through dreams, the Maya are able to communicate with the victims of forced disappearance from the conflict. This does not mean that it is not important, however, to find their bodies. Since one does not know where a person was murdered, they also do not know where the person's spirit is. As mentioned previously, place and form of death are critical to helping the spirit on his or her way to a new life.

According to Maya culture there are many types of dreams. What follows is an explanation of different kinds of dreams, as documented during research by the author in 2007 during efforts to help Indigenous women who are relatives of victims of enforced disappearance (Figure 5.1).

FIGURE 5.1   The author (facing camera) speaking with a group of Maya Achí Indigenous women.
Photo credit: Mónica Pinzón González

Dreams as News or Warning

These dreams are harbingers of events to come and are not aimed at the person who has them, but they can have implications for the community. Cabrera (2004) recalls that before a massacre in Xaman, an ethnic Mam female leader who was wounded dreamt that "they were running in the mountains because the soldiers had come and were shooting at them. After the massacre she again dreamt that [the soldiers] were killing cows and sharing the meat amongst the people, but she attributes a meaning to this dream: 'I believe they were not cows but people, because that is what happened during the massacre'" (p. 151).

An interesting element of this type of dream is the interpretation given to it by relatives. For dreams to have meaning, they need to be interpreted from existing symbolism and cultural elements. The preceding passage shows that there are two levels of interpretation of dreams; these are outlined below:

1. When family members or relatives have these dreams, they interpret them without the help of outsiders, using symbolic elements that they know and are in their cultural context.

2. Some dreams require a higher level of interpretation and may need specialized reading. In these instances, relatives seek traditional figures who, among other things, can perform divination, which brings news or a warning about some problem.

It is not surprising then that after a Maya woman has a dream, it is interpreted and important action is taken that relates directly to who had the dream and to whom the dream is directed. It is important to remember that the dreams of Maya are not necessarily direct personal messages, but might involve other community members.

The Achí Maya culture demonstrates a particular way of relating with the dead; they try not to bother the spirit because the spirit will continue to scold, watch, or guide the behaviour of the living: "They are more alive than us, they scream, they cry" (Suazo, 2002, p. 89). Pichinao (1998, p. 268) also reports how premonitions come about through dreams, citing two examples from cultures other than the Maya:

1. In Judeo-Christianity, the prophet Moses, King David, and others interpreted dreams as a mode of divine communication or premonition.
2. Two types of commonly occurring dreams were documented among the Chilean Mapuche people: a vague warning of a situation where the individual will lose control, and an explicit warning of what will happen that needs no interpretation.

Through symbolic elements, dreams tell us about something that is going to happen to the dreamer or a member of his or her family. For cultures such as the Mapuche, for example, a dream involving the loss of a personal item of clothing, an animal, or a loved one is a premonition of death.

Dreams as Messengers of Meaning

According to Maya spiritual guides, dreams are also messengers of meaning in their lives. Upon the occurrence of such a dream, their lives take a different path. When a peasant Maya presents their dreams they are interpreted, decisions are made based on the interpretation, behaviour is guided, and their lives take important turns. In this way dreams are understood as messengers of meaning or understanding. In the words of Cabrera (2004, p. 45): "Dreams activate our memory as a process that reconstructs and gives meaning to the experiences we have lived."

Dreams as Links and Means of Communication

Within the cosmo-vision of the Maya population and *mestizas* of Guatemala, the study of dreams as channels of communication between the dead and the living is of vital importance. Dreams as a mode of communication fulfill a social role embedded in the interpretation of symbols, which are subject to multiple meanings. In Maya Achí culture, when they dream of their dead, those who dream are very careful not to disturb the dead who speak: "They talk to us because they want us to do something, they are telling us how they feel, they are more alive than we are and they can bring us harm if we do not treat them well" (author interview, No. 1).

Dreams That Signify and Confirm Death

Through dreams, a missing person tells the living person about his or her condition through existing symbols, which the living are sometimes able to recognize by themselves, or at times may need the help of spiritual guides to interpret. In this context of systematic political violence, the dreams of children of victims can take on special meaning. One woman, whose husband had disappeared, talked about how her daughter's dream helped them realize that her husband was, in fact, dead: "I told the old man [elder] about my daughter's dream of her father. 'Oh, poor man,' he replied, 'he's dead; he died and was buried with the others, they all died'" (author interview, No. 4).

Another case was that of a midwife who was only able to speak Achí. She reported that after dreaming about her husband, she sought the opinion of an *ajmesa* or *sajorin* (spiritual guide): "I told the man my dream, he told me to look no further, 'don't look for him anymore because he has gone to the other world'" (author interview, No. 5). This woman, after leaving the guide, stopped looking for her husband and began to accept her husband's death.

Another woman, who had been searching for her husband for up to a year and had been having many dreams of him, also sought the advice of a guide to know the whereabouts of her husband: "[I searched until] I had gone to the men who divine. 'No ma'am, not anymore, your husband is no longer here, he is dead.' 'And where will I go to look for him?' 'No' is all he could tell me, that he [the husband] is already dead. Where else was I to look for him? 'No, he told me, stop looking'" (author interview, No. 2). As in the previous case, this woman receives confirmation from the *sajorin* that her husband is dead, and she is told to stop looking for him as if he were alive. Despite this, she did not, in the end, believe him about the death, and so the guide instructed her to pay attention to the dreams of her children. The woman recounts what happened next: "Ten days later my daughter told me that she had a dream, 'the procession was coming and there were a lot of people, and the Lord was carrying his cross,' she told me, 'but there were so many people!' 'Oh, my dear little daughter,' I said, 'your father is no longer with us, no more, he is no longer with us,' and I went again to see the old man [spiritual guide]" (author interview, No. 2).

Of the seven women who were interviewed, one was the mother of an only child who had disappeared. For her, a dream about her son was more than clear, and she discovered its meaning on her own: "'Mom,' he said, 'here's your hat.' He said to me, 'I came as quickly as I could ...' My poor baby had arrived. 'Hey, hey!' he said to me, 'I'm leaving, Mom, I'm going down there,' he said to me, 'your hat ...' 'Goodbye,' he said to me, 'I'm leaving Mom.' That is how he spoke to me ... that is how he told me" (author interview, No. 1). This dream shows how a mother, through dreams, transitions her son from being alive to being dead. In the dream, he himself tells her that he has left.

Another important dream was related in the seventh interview, a dream recounted to a *sajorin*: "I had a dream, one where [my husband] entered the house after returning from the field and I didn't have anything prepared. He was very thirsty so I gave him some water and he told me to take good care of the children" (author interview, No. 7). This woman understood that her husband was already dead. When she visited the spiritual guide, it was only to relate her husband's death and his instruction to care for the children.

Dreams That Guide the Search for Graves

Some women from one of the focus groups shared how they were able to find their deceased relatives because the missing told the women, through their dreams, where they were buried. One of the women shared her dream: "Before the exhumation I dreamt of my deceased, he was dressed in coarse cotton, the way the old people dress. He was wearing a hat, and with the hat he showed me where to find him. He was near a ditch with white-coloured stones, and then I woke up" (author focus group, No. 2). The woman said that the following day, an excavation to find the grave was carried out near a hill all day long, but they found nothing. It was not until the psychosocial team asked about her dream that she remembered, and shared her dream with the psychologist and the other women present. The search began in the place that she had dreamt about, and when they began digging, they found her husband's remains in the ditch, just as she had dreamt.

In a personal interview, a Maya spiritual guide called *aji'ij* described a time when locals were unable to find the burial place of missing people, but dreams provided consolation:

> We began to search with some of the relatives. For two nights we searched, but found nothing. The place is beautiful, in the end it's a place filled with energy and I suppose that in the past it was a ceremonial altar, a ceremonial place, where all would gather. First, [the missing] appeared by fire, there were five missing relatives who appeared, and they told us not to worry, that they were all right, that they were in a more peaceful and much better place; all that they had suffered was nothing compared to how they were now living. So, where are they? Here with us, but in another space, another dimension. Many times this is difficult for people to understand … well, all that they have shared with us, all that we believe, I have shared with the women who were searching.
>
> The three women who were there told me: "Ah that's why I dreamt, for example, that he told me to open the door and asked me for some water. When I gave it to him, he said, 'Thanks, now I can go in peace, don't worry anymore, I will continue watching over the children; I know the children are grown up, but you must live your life, do what you have to do, I am no longer here as I used to be and how we used to live, but I'm always looking after you.'" This put her at ease, she let out all her sorrow. She cried a lot and she told me this, she said that it felt good and even though we haven't found the remains, it's not a problem, because she knows he's going to be okay. (author interview, No. 1)

We can see through these accounts that people, especially women who have searched for their loved ones through excavations, need a space to share their day-to-day life filled with symbolism and meaning. This is what the Maya dream interpreters call the "half-life." Those who work in the psychosocial field are not always aware of the cultural knowledge that is needed to understand this vital dynamic. However, as we have seen, the deceased are able to show where their spirit can be found.

Accepting Death after the Dreams

It is essential to observe in these interviews the effects of consultation with traditional figures (diviners and spiritual guides), and how after speaking with these figures each woman makes a decision that changes her way of living and helps her accept death, despite not having retrieved the body of her loved one. Teresa, for example, after going to the spiritual guide, performed religious rites as if the person were dead, despite not having the body: "Yes, we have had a requiem for him. After seven years, fourteen years I … still pray. He is up there … and with the 14th anniversary [of his death] coming up, my children dreamt of him. You see? He is dead" (author interview, No. 2). In another example, a mother of a missing person takes religious actions so that her son may rest: "because I keep chickens, well, I killed a chicken. Oh, my poor son" (author interview, No. 1). (Death rituals may differ in the offering that is given, depending on whether or not the person is the mother or the wife of the missing.)

Antonia held a traditional Maya ceremony for her husband so that his spirit would stop crying, wherever he was: "I gave him a *Kotzi* [an offering of flowers or Maya ceremony] and I wished he were in a cemetery, but I go to the cemetery on Monday and Thursday and I light a candle for him, my poor husband, God knows where his body is" (author interview, No. 6). After accepting the death of her husband, one woman named Juana engaged in rites that were appeasing to the ancestors: "I looked for someone who conducts offerings so that he could call the spirit and help him walk with the ancestor. That is the custom, even though we didn't see even a piece of his body. But since he really is dead, one has to go back to work" (author interview, No. 4). For others, like Candelaria, coming to terms with the death involved other family members: "My family was with me for the first year, the second year, my family has helped me over the years" (author interview, No. 5).

The five testimonies above reflect the acceptance of the death of those who are missing, how the interpretation of dreams—often by way of a spiritual guide—help with that acceptance, and the various religious and customary rites that are taken following acceptance of death. These actions are taken by the women in order to give peace to the spirit of their dead, wherever they may be.

Conclusion

Enforced disappearance constitutes a form of psychosocial torture that is particularly acute for Indigenous families in Guatemala, due to the fact that it destroys the social structure of the family and the community. For the family of a disappeared person, this torture causes a sense of hopelessness, anguish, hostility, and impotence, preventing them from controlling the normal trajectory of their own lives. For Indigenous communities the absence of a body impedes normal mortuary rituals. For the Maya of Guatemala, these rituals are necessary for the transcendence of the dead and in order to re-establish community and communication between the living and the dead.

Indigenous families seek out spiritual guides to help confront enforced disappearance; the guide can connect with the energy of the missing person and determine if he or she is dead or alive. Sometimes, however, the guides are unable to ascertain if the disappeared is dead, and at times they are more alive than the living. That is why it might be difficult to find concrete answers, except when the spirit of the missing person appears through fire and dreams to speak to his or her relatives. These communications, directed at families but sometimes mediated or interpreted by guides, permit the survivors to accept the transition of the missing, perform the appropriate rites, and continue with their lives.

Acknowledgements

The author wishes to thank Clement Martin Casimiro for his generous assistance with translation of this text from Spanish to English.

Notes

1. The author belongs to the Maya Kaqchikel ethnic group, and is a psychologist and a Maya spiritual guide. Much of the information on Maya culture and ancestry in this article is based upon personal and community knowledge handed down orally.

2. Monsignor Gerardi was murdered two days after the release of the REMHI report.

3. The text that follows discusses research conducted by the author of this chapter in 2007 on the dreams of Maya Achí with relation to disappeared persons, victims of the internal armed conflict in Guatemala. Primary data was collected through participant observation, in-depth interviews, two focus groups, informal and group dialogue, and workshops. Eight Maya Achí women between 50 and 80 years of age were interviewed in depth. All of the women had been searching for missing husbands who had been killed by the military. To protect the identity of research participants, their real names are not used and interviews were assigned a number in the order that they occurred.

References

Ardón, A. (2012). *Diseño curso de formación a formadoras mujeres lideresas para la paz y seguridad.* Guatemala: Sinergía Noj.

Barone, P., Chávez, C., Pol Morales, F., & Morales Pantó, E. (2012). *¿Yab'il xane K'oqil? ¿Enfermedades o Consecuencias? Seis psicopatologías identificadas y tratadas por los terapeutas Maya'ib' K'iche'ib.* El Quiché, Guatemala: Asociación Médicos Descalzos.

Cabrera Pérez-Armiñán, M. L. (1997). Los sueños entre los mayas campesinos. *Revista de Estudios Interétnicos,* No. 7. Guatemala: Instituto de Estudios Interétnicos, Universidad de San Carlos de Guatemala.

Cabrera Pérez-Armiñán, M. L. (2004). *Violencia e impunidad en comunidades mayas de Guatemala La Masacre de Xaman.* Unpublished PhD thesis, Facultad de Ciencias Políticas y Sociología, Universidad Complutense de Madrid. Retrieved from biblioteca.ucm.es/tesis/cps/ucm-t28075.pdf.

Catholic Institute for International Relations (Latin American Bureau) & Proyecto Interdiocesano Recuperación de la Memoria Histórica (Guatemala). (1999). *Guatemala, never again!* (Abridged English ed.). Maryknoll, NY: CIIR (Latin American Bureau).

Commission for Historical Clarification. (1999). *Guatemala memory of silence: Report of the Commission for Historical Clarification—Conclusions and recommendations.* Retrieved from www.aaas.org/sites/default/files/migrate/uploads/mos_en.pdf.

Díaz, G., & Rodgers, A. (1993). *The Codex Borgia: A full-color restoration of the ancient Mexican manuscript.* New York, NY: Dover Publications.

Gordon, M. (1971). A case history of U.S. subversion: Guatemala, 1954. *Science & Society, 35*(2), 129–155.

Guatemala, memoria del silencio. 1999. Comisión para el Esclarecimiento Histórico. Guatemala: Oficina de Servicios para Proyectos de las Naciones Unidas (UNOPS). Retrieved from biblio3.url.edu.gt/Libros/memoria_del_silencio/.

Guitart, M. E. (2011). Una interpretación de la psicología cultural: Aplicaciones practices y principios teóricos. *Suma Psicológica, 18*(2). Retrieved from www.scielo.org.co/scielo.php?pid=S0121-43812011000200006&script=sci_arttext.

Malkin, E. (2013, May 10). Former leader of Guatemala is guilty of genocide against Mayan group. *International New York Times.* Retrieved from www.nytimes.com/2013/05/11/world/americas/gen-efrain-rios-montt-of-guatemala-guilty-of-genocide.html?pagewanted=all&_r=0.

Martínez Pelaez, S. (2009). *La Patria del Criollo: An interpretation of colonial Guatemala.* Durham, NC: Duke University Press.

McCreary, D. (1983). Debt servitude in rural Guatemala. *The Hispanic American Historical Review, 63*(4), 735–759.

Pichinao, J. (1998). Sueños y premoniciones relacionados con el hecho represivo: descripción y significado simbólico. In T. Durán Pérez, R. Bacic Herzfeld, & P. Pérez Sales (eds.), *Muerte y Desaparición Forzada en la Araucanía: Una Aproximación Étnica* (Chapter 14). Santiago, Chile: Ediciones LOM Ltda. Retrieved from www.derechos.org/koago/x/mapuches.

Pinzón González, M. (2007). Los sueños como afrontamientos culturales en mujeres Maya Achí y búsqueda de desaparecidos en procesos de exhumación Guatemala. Unpublished field research.

Suazo, F. (2002). *La Cultura Maya ante la Muerte: Dano y Duelo en la Comunidad Achí de Rabinal.* Programa de Naciones Unidas para el Desarrollo. Guatemala: Editores Siglo Veintiuno.

Related Sources

Navarro García, S., Pérez-Sales, P., & Fernández-Liria, A. (2010). Exhumation processes in fourteen countries in Latin America. *Journal for Social Action in Counseling and Psychology, 2*(2), 48–83. Retrieved from www.psysr.org/jsacp/garcia-v2n2-10_48-81.pdf.

Sanford, V. (2003). *Buried secrets: Truth and human rights in Guatemala.* New York, NY: Palgrave MacMillan.

Weld, K. (2014). *Paper cadavers: The archives of dictatorship in Guatemala.* Durham, NC: Duke University Press.

Chapter 6

Collection, Curation, Repatriation: Exploring the Concept of Museum Skeletal Populations as Missing Persons

Janet Young (Canadian Museum of History)

Introduction

Anthropology museums frequently curate human remains. In North America, many of these collections, a product of centuries-old collecting and curating practices, include Native American remains and objects. In the past, the acquisition of these human remains was often justified as scientific exploration and preservation (Fforde, 2004; Page, 2011; Powell, Garza, & Hendricks, 1993; Raines, 1992; Rose, Green, & Green, 1996; Urry, 1989). The insensitivity of this approach, perhaps prevalent at the time, may forever be linked to current institutions and by extrapolation their employees and activities. But life is not static and, in Canada, as early as 1979, steps were taken by the Canadian Association for Physical Anthropology to address public concern over the study of human remains (Cybulski, Ossenberg, & Wade, 1979; Cybulski, 2011). This non-legislated, internally motivated push for change exemplified the determination of the field to transform itself. Today, with continued changing sensitivities and societal norms, many institutions that draw on anthropological expertise have implemented protocols restricting the collection, use, and display of human remains (for examples see British Museum, 2011; Canadian Museum of History, 2007; National Museum of Ireland, 2006). Many have also instituted policies to govern the repatriation of these collections to identified descendants and/or descendant groups (for examples see Canadian Museum of History, 2001; National Museum of Natural History, 2012; National Museum of the American Indian, 2014; Royal Ontario Museum, 2009). The Canadian Museum of History (CMH), an established institution for over 150 years, is one of those that has changed and adapted to evolving societal and cultural standards.

At first glance, conceptualizing human remains collections as missing persons seems incompatible with mainstream definitions. A missing person, someone whose whereabouts are unknown (Government of Canada, 2014; Native Women's Association of Canada, 2014), is alive when they disappear, they have names, identities, and their absence is noted in day-to-day life. In contrast, skeletal populations in museum collections represent individuals long dead, usually anonymous to modern society, and often not missed in day-to-day life by descendants who may not be aware of their existence (Raines, 1992).

These differences in the individual's state, living versus dead, and identity, known versus unknown, mark the greatest divergence between modern and archaeological cases. However, these points hinge on basic philosophies of death and the individual. Often, in Western society, the individual once dead is objectified and loses their personhood. This change is reflected in definitions such as the corpse, cadaver, remains, skeleton, and body (Jenkins, 2011). As an example, according to the Government of Canada's website *Canada's Missing* (2014), remains of unknown individuals are not categorized as missing persons or even unidentified persons but as unidentified remains.

In contrast to this objectification, the philosophical perspective of some Native American groups emphasizes the continuation of the person as a complete entity even into death and highlights a multi-generational obligation to respect and protect these individuals, their state of personhood, and their well-being, allowing them to continue their journey into death and peace (Ayau & Tengan, 2002; Dongoske, 1996; Gulliford, 1996; Jenkins, 2011; Mihesuah, 1996; Minhorn, 1996; Riding, 1996). With this perspective in mind, considering human skeletal remains as missing persons becomes more tenable and parallels between modern cases and archaeological collections can be identified. These parallels appear to concentrate on the primary actors and their actions (Figure 6.1): the missing (archaeological human remains in museum collections/missing persons), the seekers (family/friends/community groups), and the facilitators (those who search, learn, identify, locate, repatriate); and one goal, to return people home, or repatriate, from the Latin *repatriatus*, to go home again (Merriam-Webster, 2014b).

Using this primary actor/action model to contrast elements of modern missing persons cases and the collection, curation, and repatriation of human remains at the CMH, this chapter will explore the concept of archaeological human skeletal populations as missing persons.

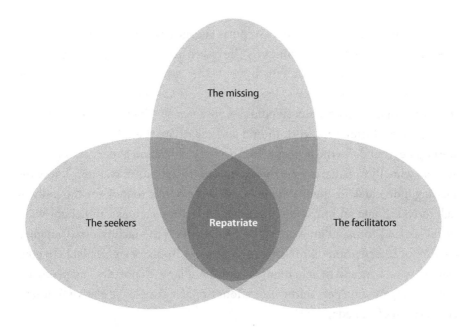

FIGURE 6.1   Primary actor/action model.

The Modern Context

The Missing

A missing person can be defined as "anyone reported to police or by police as someone whose whereabouts are unknown, whatever the circumstances of their disappearance, and they are considered missing until located" (Government of Canada, 2014). Categories of missing persons include those who are lost (wish to be found), have voluntarily gone missing (freedom of will and control over their actions), and have involuntarily gone missing (under the influence of another person) (Quad Cities Missing Persons Network, 2014).

The Seekers and Facilitators

Family, friends, colleagues, and/or acquaintances are those who note the absence of an individual and seek their whereabouts. Their search usually begins with the filing of a missing persons report with local police (Government of Canada, 2014; National Centre for Policing Excellence, 2005; Native Women's Association of

Canada, 2014; Pfeiffer, 2006). These reports engage law enforcement and initiate mechanisms to search for the missing. The police become facilitators—someone who helps bring about an outcome by providing assistance (Merriam-Webster, 2014a)—conducting interviews, completing background research, identifying key data, investigating leads, etc. (Pfeiffer, 2006; see also Chapter 11, this volume). Though these facilitators work to find and repatriate the missing they are not the engines that drive the process. This primary obligation appears to fall to the seekers who, in Canada, are encouraged to notify all those who may know the missing individual, to engage the media and the public to look for the individual, to coordinate and promote awareness activities such as candlelight vigils or rallies, and to maintain a constant dialogue with the facilitators (Canadian Centre for Information on Missing Adults, 2013). Toolkits are available to educate these seekers and to help them become familiar with policies and protocols surrounding missing persons investigations (for an example see Native Women's Association of Canada, 2014).

The Museum Context

The journey of human remains from their original resting place to museum collections (Figure 6.2) began with the individual and the community from which they derive. Community is a broad term with no temporal restrictions and may include family and friends, but for archaeological remains *community* often refers to First Peoples' descendant communities.

The individual was physically separated from the community in death and deposition and, with temporal distancing, their remains became a passive participant in a journey that was activated by collectors and driven by a museum apparatus. As such, these individuals, represented by their physical remains, were collected, acquired, curated, and will possibly be repatriated. The community, now many generations removed from the decedent, becomes a primary driver in initiating a search for these lost members of their groups. They identify and experience the loss of the individual even if it is beyond immediate memory. These seekers are driven by a sense of responsibility to seek out missing individuals and become their advocates (Fforde, 2004; Hubert & Fforde, 2002). Their efforts are focused on retrieving their ancestors, liberating them, and returning them to the community (Dongoske, 1996; Minhorn, 1996).

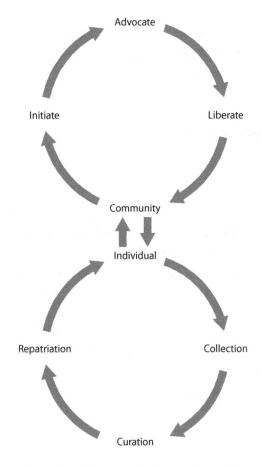

FIGURE 6.2   **The interacting paths of the community (past and present) and the individual represented by their physical remains.**

The Seekers

Those who seek archaeological human remains in museum settings are usually First Peoples' descendant groups who originate from communities within the vicinity of the decedent's original place of burial. These groups may believe that their ancestor's remains are in a museum collection or they may just be concerned that there might be remains in a collection based on the known history of collecting practices of many museums. In either case, the seekers' primary goal is to find those who may be missing and bring them home. At the CMH, this means engaging the museum through its corporate policies (human remains and repatriation) and initiating a search of their collections. If remains are found that fit the criteria of the missing, i.e., collected from a defined geographic location, the seekers will often advocate for their ancestors based on traditional roles and responsibilities. This may include negotiating a memorandum of understanding delineating procedures relevant to the remains, or initiating a repatriation request.

The Missing and Facilitators

Collection

For the purposes of this discussion, the collecting of human remains is defined as the practice of physically removing individuals from where they were laid to rest, died, or were subsequently disturbed by natural forces (e.g., floods) or faunal/human intervention. Human skeletal collections are largely a product of excavations (fieldwork, including rescue projects) or surface collecting. Approximately 70 percent of CMH's physical anthropology holdings were collected during fieldwork, mainly by museum staff. The remainder of the collection was donated or purchased. Of the human remains in the CMH collections, 95 percent were accessioned into the collection prior to 1980 and approximately 85 percent of current holdings are Native American.

Acquisition

The collection of archaeological material does not guarantee its inclusion in the National Collection at the CMH. All material, including human remains, goes through an acquisitions process that ensures all required documentation and authorizations are in place. The current acquisition process engages members from many museum divisions, including research, conservation, and collections, and amongst other priorities guarantees that all considered material is legally obtained. Acquisition protocols have developed over the decades and are stricter now than in the past. Notwithstanding, all human remains have to be accepted into the National Collection by an authorizing body. Once acquisitions are approved, collections are assigned accession numbers and all items within the accession lot are given catalogue numbers in preparation for their curation.

Human remains are still excavated and studied by CMH staff, but only with permission of representative groups including designated governments and descendent populations. These remains are not routinely accessioned into the National Collection but are usually returned for reburial once an analysis is completed.

Curation

The CMH has curated human remains since the 1870s. These individuals have been housed in many buildings over the years. Currently, they are held in drawers in cabinets in a temperature- and humidity-controlled room and access to them is restricted to authorized personnel, approved researchers, and identified descendant groups.

Following CMH's human remains policy, the skeletal populations "are held solely for the purposes of scholarly research by qualified professionals who have been properly trained to handle and study human skeletal remains" (Canadian Museum of History, 2007, p. 1). Every researcher interested in accessing the remains has to provide a detailed proposal along with their curriculum vitae and any relevant letters of support (e.g., students require letters of support from their supervisors). These documents are reviewed for validity and ethics and, if sufficient, are approved by the authorizing curator. Most of the human remains housed at CMH are available for research. However, some collections are restricted and require written permissions from descendant groups prior to accessing them. These permissions are pursued through formal channels with the CMH acting as conduit between the requesting researcher and the First Peoples' representatives.

Repatriation

Repatriation in Canada is not governed by legislation such as the Native American Graves Protection and Repatriation Act in the United States, but is handled case by case under the policies and procedures of affected institutions (see Young, 2010, for further discussion). The repatriation of the skeletal populations from the CMH has been ongoing since 1995. In response to early First Peoples' requests and based on the recommendations of the Assembly of First Nations and the Canadian Museums Association Task Force on Museums and First Peoples, a repatriation policy was developed for CMH and approved by its Board of Trustees in 2001. The policy, which encourages a cooperative, non-adversarial approach (Cybulski, 2011), stipulates the conditions in which human remains and burial objects are to be repatriated. Things that are considered include "the historical relationship of the requestor to the human remains or objects concerned" and "competing claims to the material" (Canadian Museum of History, 2001, p. 3).

The process of repatriating human remains from the National Collection at CMH is complex (see Figure 6.3), with multiple phases, levels of engagement, and

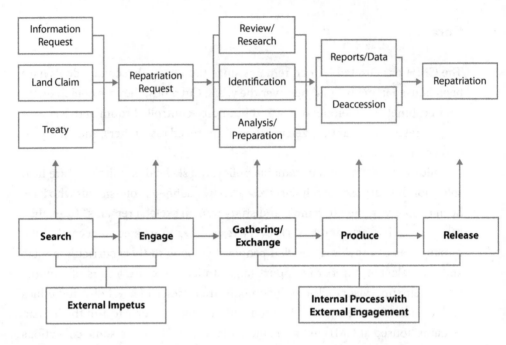

FIGURE 6.3   Human remains repatriation process at the Canadian Museum of History.

processes. This complexity, a product of various levels of internal and external approvals and consensus, produces unique repatriation experiences tailored to each of the requesting communities.

Search

The repatriation process at the CMH is triggered by searches for specific human remains initiated by a requesting group, the seekers. Mechanisms to engage the process include information requests, or land claim and treaty preparations. Once information is requested, the CMH will conduct a preliminary review of its collections to identify any relevant human remains and burial goods. Searches of archaeological collections are usually geographically delineated, since archaeological collections are not always identified by cultural affiliation, or, due to limited information, cannot be related to a single descendant group. A broad summary of the initial review is provided to the requesting community.

Engage

Once a group is provided with a summary of relevant CMH holdings, they can request the release of the remains through an official repatriation request. As stipulated in CMH's repatriation policy, repatriation requests must be received in writing and originate from Aboriginal individuals or governments, in the context

FIGURE 6.4   **Representatives of the Anishinabeg Nation (left) meet with CMH staff (right) to present a repatriation request written on beaver skin.**
Source: Canadian Museum of History, photographer Steven Darby, IMG2002-0209

of comprehensive land claims or self-government negotiations. These requests are usually received in letter form. However, requests have been received in other formats: for example, in 2002 representatives of the Anishinabeg Nation came to the museum to present CMH with a prepared beaver skin on which was inscribed, in Algonquian, the repatriation request (Figure 6.4). Once received, a request engages the facilitators and the system in which they work. However, sometimes there are no relevant holdings, and sometimes groups choose not to officially ask for the return of their ancestors.

Gather/Exchange

Upon receipt of a repatriation request, facilitators review the documentation related to the relevant collections and consult all archival sources. Efforts are made to verify a direct ancestral-descendant relationship between the requesting group and the remains. Information gathered from background research, analysis of related artifacts, and identification of temporal context advises the decision on the appropriateness of repatriating the remains. Often the community requesting the remains is only one of several descendant groups who could submit such a claim. In these cases of overlap, the CMH identifies all possible known descendant groups and asks them to put in writing whether they affirm

or reject repatriation to the requesting community. If groups reject the legitimacy of the repatriation, the requesting group is required to negotiate directly
with those groups and provide the CMH proof that the disagreement has been
resolved prior to a repatriation moving to fruition.

Concurrent to the exchange between CMH and the requesting group, a detailed
inventory, analysis, and visual documentation of the remains is conducted. The
human remains curated at CMH are officially a part of the National Collection.
As such, CMH staff have an obligation to maximize the biological information
compiled from the remains and archive this information for future generations
of researchers. This data capture is based solely on non-destructive techniques.
Once a repatriation request is received, any destructive analysis, such as radio-
carbon dating, diet identification through stable isotopes, or DNA sequencing
requires written permission from the requesting group. To date, there has been
only one example of DNA being used to confirm the connection of remains to
a descendant group prior to repatriation, and this testing was approved by the
requesting group. There have been no examples where individual identity has
been sought through DNA testing of the archaeological populations.

Produce

Through the gathering and exchange process, data are generated and reports are
produced. This information serves a number of purposes, including the preparation of archival resources and the production of subject reports. The reports
are provided to the requesting community to assist in their preparations for
the release of the human remains and associated burial objects. The reports are
also needed to inform the CMH's Board of Trustees, who has the sole authority
to deaccession or release material from the National Collection. It is only after
deaccessioning that human remains and their associated burial objects are available for release to the designated community.

Release

Once human remains are deaccessioned they are no longer part of the National
Collection, and are no longer available for study by external researchers unless
explicit permissions are sought by the researcher from the representative group.
The remains are maintained in the collections area until the requesting group is
able to receive them and methods for the preparation and release of the remains
are in place. These preparations are completed at the discretion of the requesting
group and could take anywhere from a few weeks to many years.

The role of the facilitators in the release of the human remains to their communities varies and is dependent on the preferences of the requesting group.

There are examples in which CMH staff are asked to wrap the remains for transport, transport the remains, place the remains back in the earth, and participate in all ceremonies and feasts. There are also times when they are asked not to participate at all, but simply to provide a restricted area for the community to prepare the remains. No matter what role these facilitators play and what requests are made of the CMH, great care is taken to try and accommodate all the wishes of descendant communities. To date, 15 human remains repatriations have been successfully completed.

Discussion

The CMH has curated human remains for over 100 years. These collections have been the cornerstone of many research projects including master's and PhD theses. Their collection, acquisition, and curation have offered an opportunity to learn about the past from those who lived in the past. Though the practices that developed these collections are inconsistent with current protocols, it must still be acknowledged that these archaeological populations have been an important scientific resource. From improving our understanding of adaptation, mobility, growth and development, activity patterns, diet, health, and disease, to opening windows on population dynamics, the peopling of the New World, and gene flow patterns, we continue to learn from these individuals who probably could never have grasped the depth of their contributions.

Despite this scientific viewpoint, the sense of violation that many First Peoples' groups have surrounding the removal of their ancestors cannot be dismissed. As such, today a balance is sought between the obligations to past, present, and future generations. Part of this balance includes the return of individuals to their descendant communities. It is in this repatriation process that key players are brought together, key players whose roles find correlates in some modern missing person scenarios.

Contemporary missing persons can be broadly grouped as lost, voluntarily missing, and involuntarily missing. Of these categories, the involuntarily missing provide most of the equivalents to archaeological cases where a third party collected the individuals from their resting places. Through this lens and beneath the umbrella categories of the missing, the seekers, and the facilitators, comparisons can be drawn between modern and archaeological cases.

Archaeological human remains do not fit the standard definitions of missing persons based primarily on two points: the individuals within these collections are long dead and, due to this temporal distance, their individual identity is unknown. However, if we adopt the perspective of some First Peoples, i.e., that skeletal populations represent active individuals known to them through lineage (Raines, 1992), then we can explore the relevancy of categorizing museum human remains collections as missing persons.

In contemporary cases, the missing are not only defined by their relationships with those who seek them, but also by their individual, socially established, and known identities. Their individuality is exerted through their physical form, but in archaeological cases, the physical remains lack the animation and interaction that establishes individuality in the world. Their identities become defined solely by their descendants, who may have a spiritual connection to the individual but, as their surrogates, cannot substantially relate the individual to the external world. Viewed from an analytic standpoint, the identities of the remains become a cultural construct, a representation of all those who have come before—an embodiment of a people. While their loss is felt keenly by their descendant groups, these missing persons become defined to the outside world by their seekers. As such, there are two fundamental differences between modern missing persons and archaeological human skeletal collections. First, while modern missing persons are able to define their own identity, archaeological remains lack that ability. Second, in modern cases missing persons are absent physically but their identities are known, while human remains in museums are present physically but unknown individually. These fundamental differences emphasize the importance of perspective when defining museum collections. To museum facilitators, the physical remains are present but their identities and relationships are missing. To descendent groups, the individual ancestors may be known spiritually but their physical remains are missing. Therefore, the former perspective may include the use of the term "unidentified remains," as employed by *Canada's Missing*, or "human remains collections" as employed by the museum, while the latter perspective may perceive the collections as "missing persons" being sought.

Despite this difference in perspective, the actors that surround both archaeological and contemporary missing are very similar in goal and action. In both instances, the seekers experience a sense of loss and violation due to the third-party removal of the individual. These feelings provide the impetus for the seekers to initiate the search for the missing, engage the facilitators and systems that are in place to assist them, and act as the engines that drive and maintain efforts surrounding the search and return of those they seek, for justice and closure (Thornton, 2002). The facilitators work within defined systems to assist the search, provide information and support, and maintain a continued dialogue with the seekers, with the goal of eventually repatriating the missing.

Conclusion

I do not presume to understand the emotions felt by those seeking the missing, whether they are modern or archaeological. If this aspect of the discussion were explored further, there would probably be more similarities than differences surrounding the people and scenarios involved. Instead, this paper explored, through the experience of the CMH, the possibility of using the descriptor of "missing persons" for archaeological human skeletal populations in a museum setting. Through this exercise it was discovered that the use of the term "missing person" for museum collections of human remains is not exact, and that the contextual similarities that promote such a cross-disciplinary usage of the term lie in the actors that surround these skeletal populations, their perspectives, and the goal of repatriation, and not specifically in the populations themselves. However, those who define personhood broadly might find resonance in a link between modern missing persons and the remains of their ancestors, which might lie in museum collections.

References

Ayau, E., & Tengan, T. (2002). Ka huaka'i o nā 'Ōiwi: The journey home. In C. Fforde, J. Hubert, & P. Turnbull (eds.), *The dead and their possessions: Repatriation in principle, policy and practice* (pp. 171–189). New York, NY: Routledge Taylor & Francis Group.

British Museum. (2011). *The British Museum policy on human remains*. Retrieved from www.britishmuseum.org/PDF/Human%20Remains%206%20Oct%202006.pdf.

Canadian Centre for Information on Missing Adults. (2013). *Assisting in the search for your missing loved one*. Retrieved from missingpersonsinformation.ca/resources/.

Canadian Museum of History. (2001). *Repatriation policy*. Retrieved from www.historymuseum.ca/wp-content/uploads/2015/09/REPATRIATION-POLICY.pdf.

Canadian Museum of History. (2007). *Human remains policy*. Retrieved from cmcwiis071/PublicContent/Policies/policies-e/202-e.pdf.

Cybulski, J. (2011). Canada. In N. Marquez-Grant & L. Fibiger (eds.), *The Routledge handbook of archaeological human remains and legislation: An international guide to laws and practice in the excavation and treatment of archaeological human remains* (pp. 525–530). New York, NY: Routledge Taylor & Francis Group.

Cybulski, J., Ossenberg, N., & Wade, W. (1979). Statement on the excavation, treatment, analysis and disposition of human skeletal remains from archaeological sites in Canada. *Canadian Review of Physical Anthropology, 1*(1), 32–36.

Dongoske, K. (1996). The Native American Graves Protection and Repatriation Act: A new beginning, not the end, for osteological analysis—a Hopi perspective. *American Indian Quarterly, 20*(2), 287–296.

Fforde, C. (2004). *Collecting the dead: Archaeology and the reburial issue*. London, UK: Gerald Duckworth & Co. Ltd.

Government of Canada. (2014). *Canada's missing.* Retrieved from www.canadasmissing.ca/index-eng.htm.

Gulliford, A. (1996). Bones of contention: The repatriation of Native American human remains. *The Public Historian, 18*(4), 119–143.

Hubert, J., & Fforde, C. (2002). Introduction: The reburial issue in the twenty-first century. In C. Fforde, J. Hubert, & P. Turnbull (eds.), *The dead and their possessions: Repatriation in principle, policy and practice* (pp. 1–16). New York, NY: Routledge Taylor & Francis Group.

Jenkins, T. (2011). *Contesting human remains in museum collections: The crisis of cultural authority.* New York, NY: Routledge Taylor & Francis Group.

Merriam-Webster Online. (2014a). Facilitator. Retrieved from www.merriam-webster.com/dictionary/facilitator.

Merriam-Webster Online. (2014b). Repatriate. Retrieved from www.merriam-webster.com/dictionary/repatriate.

Mihesuah, D. (1996). American Indians, anthropologists, pothunters, and repatriation: Ethical, religious, and political differences. *American Indian Quarterly, 20*(2), 229–237.

Minhorn, A. (1996). *Human remains should be reburied.* Retrieved from www.asd5.org/cms/lib4/WAO1001311/centricity/Domain/629/Human%20Remains%20Should%20Be%20Reburied.pdf.

National Centre for Policing Excellence (NCPE). (2005). *Guidance on the management, recording and investigation of missing persons.* Retrieved from www.gpdg.co.uk/pact_old/pdf/MissingPersonsInteractive.pdf.

National Museum of Ireland. (2006). *Policy on human remains.* Retrieved from www.museum.ie/NationalMuseumIreland/media/Corporate-Information/Policies%20and%20Guidelines/Policy-Human-Remains-Final.pdf.

National Museum of Natural History (Smithsonian Institution). (2012). *Guidelines and procedures for repatriation.* Retrieved from anthropology.si.edu/repatriation/pdf/NMNH%20Repatriation%20Guidelines%20and%20Procedures%202012.pdf.

National Museum of the American Indian (Smithsonian Institution). (2014). *Repatriation policy.* Retrieved from nmai.si.edu/sites/1/files/pdf/repatriation/NMAI-Repatriation Policy-2014.pdf.

Native Women's Association of Canada. (2014). Toolkit: Navigating the missing persons process. Retrieved from www.nwac.ca/sites/default/files/imce/NWAC_2B_Toolkit_e.pdf.

Page, K. (2011). *The significance of human remains in museum collections: Implications for collections management.* Unpublished master of arts thesis, History and Social Studies Education Department, The State University of New York. Retrieved from digitalcommons.buffalostate.edu/history_theses/1/

Pfeiffer, J. (2006). *Missing persons in Saskatchewan: Police policy and practice.* Retrieved from www.justice.gov.sk.ca/adx/aspx/adxGetMedia.aspx?DocID=3025,104,81,1,Documents&MediaID=ac6662c8-6ecc-4979-bc47-.70c005fd273e&Filename=JEFF+PFEIFER+REPORT+ON+Missing+Persons+-+Police+Policy+and+Practice+-+Final+Report.pdf.

Powell, S., Garza, C., & Hendricks, A. (1993). Ethics and ownership of the past: The reburial and repatriation controversy. *Archaeological Method and Theory, 5,* 1–42.

Quad Cities Missing Persons Network. (2014). What is the definition of "missing people"? Retrieved from www.qcmpn.com/definition-of-a-missing-person.html.

Raines, J. (1992). One is missing: Native American Graves Protection and Repatriation Act; an overview and analysis. *American Indian Law Review, 17*(2), 639–664.

Riding, J. (1996). Repatriation: A Pawnee's perspective. *American Indian Quarterly, (20)*2, 238–250.

Rose, J., Green, T., & Green, V. (1996). NAGPRA is forever: Osteology and the repatriation of skeletons. *Annual Review of Anthropology, 25,* 81–103.

Royal Ontario Museum. (2009). *Board policy: Repatriation of human remains of the Aboriginal Peoples of Canada*. Retrieved from www.rom.on.ca/sites/default/files/imce/hrrepatriationtrev2012.pdf.

Thornton, R. (2002). Repatriation as healing the wounds of the trauma of history: Cases of Native Americans in the United States of America. In C. Fforde, J. Hubert, & P. Turnbull (eds.), *The dead and their possessions: Repatriation in principle, policy and practice* (pp. 17–24). New York, NY: Routledge Taylor & Francis Group.

Urry, J. (1989). Headhunters and body-snatchers. *Anthropology Today, 5*(5), 11–13.

Young, J. L. (2010). Responsive repatriation: Human remains management at a Canadian national museum. *Anthropology News, 51*, 9–12.

Related Sources

Hanna, M. G. (2005). The changing legal and ethical context of archaeological practice in Canada with special reference to the repatriation of human remains. *Journal of Museum Ethnography, 17*, 141–151.

Kakaliouras, A. M. (2012). An anthropology of repatriation: Contemporary physical anthropological and Native American ontologies of practice. *Current Anthropology, 53*(S5), S210–S221.

Peers, L. (2004). Repatriation: A gain for science? *Anthropology Today, 20*(6), 3–4.

Methods Used towards Finding and Identifying the Missing

Chapter 7

When *X* Doesn't Mark the Spot: Historical Investigation and Identifying Remains from the Korean War

Michael R. Dolski (Defense POW/MIA Accounting Agency, U.S. Department of Defense)

Accounting for the Military Dead[1]

On a bright, sunny day in the middle of December 2013, dozens of people came together for a funeral near Leesville, a small town in western Louisiana. These individuals included relatives of the deceased, the mayor of the town, a state representative, the commander of a nearby U.S. Army facility, members of the Patriot Guard organization, and local media figures.[2] This group sought to honour Jerry Pat Craig, a "True American Hero" who was killed in action (*PFC Jerry P. Craig*, n.d.; *MIA Korean War veteran*, 2014). Although only recently identified, Private First Class (Pfc) Jerry Craig died 63 years before this interment.

This chapter explains the process of identifying Jerry Craig's remains. It was not preordained that American society would allocate an immense amount of effort and resources to the mission of recovering and sending home the remains of fallen service personnel such as Pfc Craig. Therefore, in order to discuss "how" the identification happened, it is necessary to devote some time to addressing "why" it occurred in the first place. Thus, this chapter will explore the intertwining of American national identity, commemoration, and accounting efforts linked to the remains of deceased service personnel. In the process, the argument presented herein will also demonstrate the particular ways in which historical analysis has helped the US accounting effort.

The Frozen Chosin and a Missing American

The Chosin Reservoir is a large man-made body of water high in the mountains of North Korea, approximately 110 km south of the border with China.[3] Those factual details, however, fail to convey the awesome and chilling implications of that name, as any veteran of the November–December 1950 battles in the area can readily attest. With air temperatures dipping to 35–40°C below zero, freezing to death presented a constant threat to forces engaged in combat in that terrible period (Appleman, 1990, p. xi). As Hospital Corpsman Third Class William Davis advised, "You had to eat fast because everything was turning cold" (in Knox, 1985, p. 471). As if weather was not enough, soldiers had to contend with extremely rugged terrain, usually nothing more than a lone line of communication for supply (assuming any was available), and, of course, the murderous intent of enemy forces. Private First Class Fred Davidson captured all of the misery by exclaiming, "There was always a hill to climb and it was always cold! ... When it snowed it was cold. When the sun shone it was cold. When we marched north it was cold. When we marched south it was cold. And I was tired. I'd been in combat since August 2 [four months at that point]. I was tired and damned near ready to give up the ghost" (in Knox, 1985, p. 475).

By late 1950, United Nations (UN) forces moved towards what seemed an end to the Korean War. Major fighting had erupted months earlier in June as North Korea's military rushed in a torrent through the poorly prepared defences of its southern neighbour. After holding on to a chunk in the southeast of the peninsula called the Pusan Perimeter (Figure 7.1), UN forces reversed the tide, liberated the south, and then invaded the north. The hoped-for conclusion to this war was the reunification of the Korean peninsula under the aegis of the US-backed South Korea. As part of the general advance conducted by UN forces that fall, the U.S. Army's X Corps held responsibility for northeastern Korea. This corps included U.S. Marines, U.S. Army units, attached air and navy components, and large South Korean contingents. Due to the ranging operational area, and with changing orders forcing frequent reorientations, the components of this corps were spread far and wide in the rush to the Yalu River, the boundary separating China from Korea. The U.S. 1st Marine Division formed one component of this drive, leading the way towards the Chosin Reservoir. Upon reaching that landmark in November 1950, the 1st Marine Division split, with the 7th Marine Regiment going westwards, the 5th Marine Regiment going eastwards, and the 1st Marine Regiment covering the areas left behind. Yet with a change of operational intent calling for a new general direction of advance (west instead of north), the 5th Marine Regiment shifted to the west side of the reservoir. To

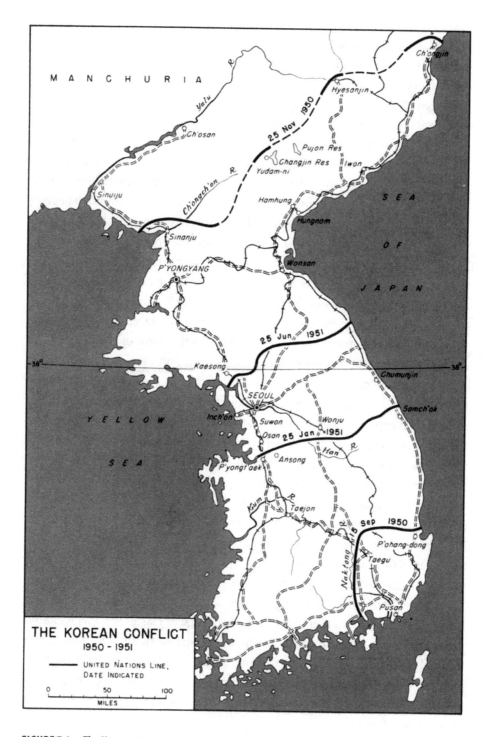

FIGURE 7.1   The Korean War major battle phases, June 1950–July 1951.

Source: Map courtesy of the U.S. Army, *American Military History*, chapter 25, "The Korean War, 1950–1953." Retrieved from www.history.army.mil/books/AMH/AMH-25.htm.

fill its place, a hastily composed unit, the 31st Regimental Combat Team (RCT), quickly moved most of its scattered parts to the eastern shore of the reservoir in late November (Mossman, 1990, pp. 84–88) (Figure 7.2).

The 31st RCT, commanded by Colonel Allan MacLean, came together as an expedient—it was a unit created to solve the problem of covering a key piece of terrain. Little planning or forethought went into its creation, its pell-mell deployment, or its support. Rather, the unit was rushed to its target area in a precipitate manner, which left it fragmented into non-supporting fighting positions by November 27, 1950, the night that the Chinese Communist Forces (CCF) began a major offensive in the Chosin area (Appleman, 1990, pp. 75–86; Gugeler, 1987, pp. 54–56). This offensive marked yet another transition in the Korean War as the Chinese now intervened in massive numbers, which pushed the battle southward for the remainder of the war (Spurr, 1988).[4] Unfortunately for the UN forces, all of the components of the 31st RCT did not come together in time to face the CCF onslaught. The soldiers in this unit faced repeated assaults by overwhelming numbers of enemy forces from the night of November 27 to December 2 and, in the process, they suffered near annihilation.

This fragmented and spread-out force endured heavy losses while successively consolidating into more compact and (it was hoped) defensible positions. This isolated unit experienced the initial shock of unexpected battle, lost key leaders like Colonel MacLean, and coped with the harsh environment as supplies quickly dwindled. In an unenviable situation, by December 1 the acting commander, Lieutenant Colonel Don Carlos Faith, Jr., opted to attempt a breakout. He hoped to take his beleaguered soldiers back to the relative safety of friendly lines in the south. With but a single road south, the enemy knew when and where to strike. The result of the escape attempt was horrendous losses, total confusion, disarticulation of the retreating forces, and a daylong ordeal that ended with the main column halted miles from friendly lines (*Action report*, n.d.; Appleman, 1990; Blumenson, 2001; Gray, 1993; Gugeler, 1987). Some survivors managed to reach the main defensive position in the area, the village of Hagaru-ri, which alerted forces there of the column's disintegration. The next morning, December 2, one intrepid officer led a small group to hunt for survivors, managing to bring back a reported 319 soldiers (Montross & Canzona, 1957/1990, p. 245). Additional remnants of the task force continued to trickle into the Hagaru-ri perimeter over the next few days.

Any attempt to determine the fates of, or account for, those missing from the battle east of the Chosin is fraught with problems. The RCT's disintegration ensured an incomplete after-action analysis due, in some part, to the destruction of records prior to the breakout attempt. As one veteran of the battle indicated,

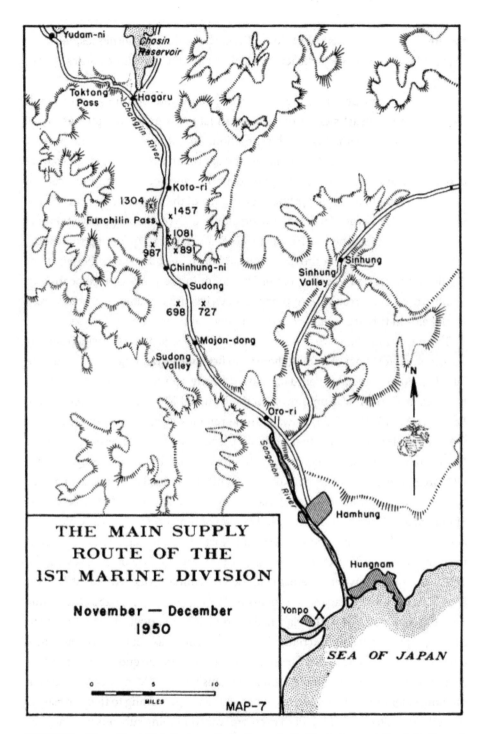

FIGURE 7.2   Disposition of U.S. Marine units leading up to the Chosin Reservoir (top left of image) prior to the Chinese offensive.

Source: Lynn Montross and Nicholas A. Canzona, *U.S. Marine Operations in Korea, 1950–1953, v. 3: The Chosin Reservoir Campaign* (Washington, DC: GPO, 1957; Austin, TX: R. J. Speights, 1990). Retrieved from www.koreanwar.org/html/korean_war_maps_results_navy.html?id=82.

this unit's "heroic demise, with loss of records and many witnesses, left only scattered survivors to reconstruct the tragic saga of the east shore battles" (Gray, 1993, p. 38).

Historian Roy Appleman suggested that somewhere around 3,000 US soldiers went to the east side of the Chosin in late November (Appleman, 1987, pp. 300–301). Following his rough estimation, 385 soldiers were fit and present for duty in Hagaru-ri after the breakout, and approximately 1,500 casualties were evacuated from Hagaru-ri, leaving about 1,000 captured or dead in uncertain locations (Appleman, 1990, pp. 300–304). Some of the Hagaru-ri evacuees were individuals killed in action during the breakout, with bodies shipped to temporary cemeteries in Koto-ri or Hungnam (*U.S. dead*, n.d.).[5] Following this battle, UN forces retreated from the Chosin Reservoir region. By December 23, all of the fleeing units had left the port of Hungnam in the process of relocating to South Korea. As a result, temporary cemeteries and remains scattered across battlefields in this area were left to the mercies of the enemy and nature.

There are more than 800 casualties from the east side of the Chosin Reservoir unaccounted for today, meaning there is no firm understanding of their ultimate fate. U.S. Army officials eventually buried nearly 70 reported recoveries from this area as Korean War unknowns in the National Memorial Cemetery of the Pacific (NMCP), Honolulu, Hawaii. These remains were recovered during the Operation Glory exchange that took place after the armistice. From August 31 to November 9, 1954, in accordance with provisions in the armistice agreement, UN forces, the CCF, and North Korea exchanged war dead at Munsan-ni, South Korea (*Historical summary*, 1954). As part of this exchange, UN forces received Shipment 24, Roster 4-1, which included a set of remains marked as "Unknown" and labelled "2724" that the Chinese and North Koreans reportedly recovered from an isolated burial on the eastern side of the Chosin Reservoir (Harvey, 1954).[6] Officials shipped this set of remains to the U.S. Military's Central Identification Unit (CIU) in Kokura, Japan, for processing (*Unknown X-15724*, n.d.). During this period, personnel at the CIU relabelled the remains, eventually designating them as "X-15724."[7] Relabelling and renumbering of remains was a common occurrence, despite the obvious potential for confusion or error. In the end, processing officials appointed each set of unidentified remains with an "X" number, indicating unknown identity, and compiled a set of documents pertaining to their investigation efforts (called an X-file). Perhaps there was something subconscious at play, akin to the creation of a treasure map: maybe one day, in the future, somebody would discover what identity lay hidden below this particular X.

United Nations forces received the shipment that contained X-15724 on September 14, 1954. This transfer included 25 sets of remains reportedly recovered from isolated burials east of the Chosin Reservoir. The CIU verified name associations or otherwise identified 12 of these remains. Processing resulted in the classification of an additional nine sets of remains as "Mongoloid" or "Korean national." The CIU sent the final four sets of these remains, including X-15724, as unknowns to the NMCP (Harvey, 1954). The remains identified from this group consisted of U.S. Army soldiers primarily from the 1st Battalion, 32nd Infantry Regiment, or the 3rd Battalion, 31st Infantry Regiment. These battalions, along with other artillery units, regimental formations, and some U.S. Air Force and U.S. Marine Corps Tactical Air Control Parties formed the 31st RCT (Appleman, 1987, pp. 10, 342–344).

At the time of the battle, Private First Class Jerry Pat Craig was assigned to Headquarters Company, 1st Battalion, 32nd Infantry Regiment. His superior officers reported him Missing in Action (MIA) effective December 2, 1950. Craig, who had enlisted only eight months prior, was a few weeks short of his 18th birthday when he went missing. This young man was barely over 150 lbs at the time and stood just over 6 feet tall (*Individual Deceased Personnel File*, n.d.). With heavy losses incurred during the battles along the eastern shore of the Chosin Reservoir, accompanied by the destruction of most unit records, the casualty accounting for these events largely took place after the fact. Because of this confusing situation, commanding officers designated many of the individuals that did not report present for duty by December 2 or 3, or even as late as December 16, as missing effective December 2. When UN forces evacuated the region, Craig's superiors still did not know his whereabouts. Several years later, without any further information, Jerry Craig's fate remained undetermined. Unfortunately, this was an all-too-common outcome for American (as well as Allied) forces fighting through the harsh and chaotic maelstrom of combat in North Korea during late 1950. The enemy did not report Pfc Craig as a prisoner of war and he did not return with the transfer of prisoners in 1953. He was also not conclusively associated with any of the remains turned over during Operation Glory in 1954. With little more to work with, a Board of Officers approved the "Findings of Nonrecoverability of Remains" for him on January 16, 1956 (*Individual Deceased Personnel File*, n.d.). It seemed likely that Jerry Craig would be another unaccounted for casualty of war—just one more name to chalk up as a missing person, without details on his presumed death or even a body for his family to mourn.

Meanwhile, the CIU in Kokura received more than 300 sets of remains reportedly recovered from the overall area in which Craig was last seen. Officials at the CIU determined that X-15724 belonged to a Caucasian male between 18 and 20 years of age with an estimated height of 6 feet, 1.25 inches. Fingerprints

FIGURE 7.3   Disinterment of a set of unknown remains from the National Memorial Cemetery of the Pacific (NMCP), Honolulu, Hawaii.

Source: Image courtesy of the U.S. Department of Defense, Defense POW/MIA Accounting Agency. Retrieved from www.dpaa.mil/NewsStories/MediaGallery.aspx?igphoto=2001317251.
Photo by: SSft La'Shanette Garrett

were unobtainable due to the deteriorated state of the remains, which were also not accompanied by any clothing or personal effects. Unknown X-15724 demonstrated "evidence of [a] missile wound, right side of skull" (*Unknown X-15724*, n.d.).

Despite some promising clues about X-15724's identity, on October 12, 1955, a Board of Officers determined that the set of remains was unidentifiable. The classification of X-15724 as unidentifiable developed after "manually comparing data on subject remains with unresolved casualties without effecting a conclusive association" (*Unknown X-15724*, n.d.). Battlefield trauma, such as a gunshot wound to the head, is seldom a distinguishing characteristic in the midst of a major war. Similarly, most of those lost in late 1950 were young, white males of average stature and health. Dental records provided suggestive, and at times distinctive, details, but they were incomplete, recorded using a variety of protocols, and only represented one potential means for narrowing down possibilities to a definitive identity. The CIU officials handled more than 4,000 sets of remains turned over through Operation Glory, along with thousands more recovered by

UN forces during or immediately after the war. Further complicating matters, there were problems related to the provenance of the remains turned over during Operation Glory. While the communist forces reported recovery locations, attempted identifications raised questions about this potential clue. Recovery location for the remains could suggest a limited number of casualty associations to consider as a match for a given set of remains. Yet enough anomalies appeared on the whole to warrant caution about the reliability of this information.[8] With such a workload, in the face of incomplete records, and examining remains in varied states of completeness and decomposition, it is remarkable that the CIU staff identified as many individuals as it did. In this case, however, the possibilities were exhausted and they sent X-15724 to the NMCP in 1956 for burial as a Korean War unknown.

That does not end the story for X-15724. In July 2013 cemetery staff at the NMCP disinterred X-15724. The remains had become the focus of a new investigation—a new effort to resolve the fates of missing service personnel. As the result of detailed historical research, an argument emerged that linked X-15724 to a pool of potential candidates, all unresolved individuals from the Chosin battles. Upon disinterment, the remains became the subject of forensic analysis that included odontological comparisons of antemortem dental records for each individual and the dental remains present, as well as an anthropological comparison that assessed age, stature, ancestry, and any distinguishing features (including ante- and peri-mortem trauma).

This round of analysis depended heavily on advances in scientific processes and technology. However, certain developments in these disciplines proved of little utility for this case. For a variety of reasons, seldom has a useful DNA profile been developed from remains processed through Operation Glory and the CIU. Instead, another recent development proved vital. This approach uses antemortem chest radiographs taken at induction into the military to screen for tuberculosis, superimposes the imaged skeletal elements with present-day radiographs taken of the remains, and analyzes that product to look for points of concordance and discordance (Stephan et al., 2014). Historical research, thus, created a pool of potential candidates for association with a set of remains. With a convincing argument in place, military authorities consented to disinter the remains for forensic analysis. Eventually, laboratory staff would compare the results against the pool of associated casualties. One individual came up as a match: Pfc Jerry Pat Craig. Converging lines of evidence and argumentation proved the case, including historical/circumstantial, dental, anthropological, and the chest radiograph comparison. No single line of evidence worked on its own; however, all other lines depended upon the array of limited names generated through historical research. In November 2013, X-15724 was identified as Jerry Craig. The U.S. military sent his remains home for interment at the Central Louisiana Military Cemetery on December 19, 2013, over 60 years after his death (*MIA Korean War veteran*, 2014).

Although this was a relatively inexpensive and undramatic recovery and identification, the highly charged actions of disturbing, examining, and testing these remains raises several questions. What motivated this action in the first place? Why exhume remains properly laid to rest and, in the act, potentially reawaken long-dormant feelings tied to the traumas of a wartime loss? In short, why did the US government feel compelled to disinter these remains?

Public Sphere, National Identity, and Warfare

The first caveat to this question is one that warns away from oversimplifying actors and their actions. The US government was, and is, a highly fragmented actor, which is particularly evident in the mission of accounting for missing service members. The government is also hardly the lone force, or even at times the most significant. Nevertheless, as a powerful influence on the process of shaping national identity, its role in defining the national story is of paramount concern. The accounting effort is an integral part of refining and adjusting that national story. As Benedict Anderson persuasively argued in his famous 1991 book, *Imagined Communities*, national entities consist of communities of people drawn together through shared understandings of their past, present, and future. These fictive relationships with countless others depend quite substantially on framing the past in mutually agreeable ways. These understandings, as Anderson demonstrated, developed freely in environments of public interaction enhanced through emergent communications technology (Anderson, 1991, pp. 6, 11, 23; see also Halbwachs, 1992). This concept drew from theories of interaction in a "public sphere" advanced by Jürgen Habermas (Habermas, 1991). Anderson, however, left it for others to determine *what* these communities deemed of utmost significance to their national past and present identities.

Many historians have provided intellectual grist for this mill in the two decades since. Michael Kammen presented answers by exploring some of the most prevalent stories told about the national past. Significantly, Kammen also discussed, at some length, the many actors involved in making meaning out of that past. He described ways in which common narratives evolved over time through a dynamic process of advancing and refining these understandings in a collective setting (Kammen, 1991, pp. 3–13, 572–587, 645–701; see also Bodnar,

1992, and Gillis, 1994). Historian Kurt Piehler narrowed the focus by exploring the specific topic of war commemoration. In the act, he demonstrated a uniquely American way of remembering wars past through pluralistic interaction, again in the public sphere. As Piehler argued, one theme of these stories that has become increasingly evident over time is the collective experiences of common soldiers (Piehler, 1995/2004, pp. xiii–xiv, 1–9).

While addressing the democratization of American collective remembrance, Piehler's work also spoke to some of the *themes* advanced concerning military actions. Overall, Americans tend to focus on wars as common experiences expressive of collective ideals such as the concern for freedom, fair play, and the worth of the individual. With this setting in mind, one can ascertain the social as well as personal significance of current accounting efforts for missing service personnel. These heroes of democracy, as they are often characterized, serve as exemplars for American ideals, even in the supposedly rare instances when the nation deviates from its "right" path, as suggested in interpretations of the Vietnam War. Thus, these champions of the American way deserve accolades upon return home, even if society often fails to attend to serious or long-term needs of veterans, as suggested by Finkel (2013). Of course, such laudations were oriented more intently towards those sacrificed in military ventures. Stories linked to the hailed return of the dead serve also as instructions on how and why to mourn. They also offer the opportunity for a celebration of the nation that gave rise to people worthy of public mourning in the first place (Sledge, 2005, pp. 8–29). Yet the pressing question lingers of what to do concerning those consumed by war—both those who don't leave behind a body to mourn and those who grieve for such a loss. The accounting mission arose as the official effort to address that issue.

Accounting History

America's present accounting mission was borne out of the Vietnam War, although there were certainly efforts to recover, identify, and return the dead prior to that conflict. Drew Gilpin Faust (2008) has recently demonstrated just such a dynamic dating back to the Civil War, and Lisa Budreau (2010) explored a similar topic with regard to the First World War. One distinctive American approach to war commemoration and treatment of the dead arose following the latter conflict. While countries such as Germany, France, or the United Kingdom left the remains of their far more numerous losses lying *in situ* or nearby, American officials inaugurated a recovery and repatriation program. Families of those killed largely opted for this course and, as a result, through enormous effort and expense, tens of thousands of sets of remains from the First World War were shipped back to the US (Budreau, 2010, pp. 15–36).

Even with the Second World War and the Korean War added for consideration, certain characteristics of the American approach to the dead helped foster a present-day accounting effort. In each war, the effort to locate, recover, identify, repatriate (for the majority), and inter the remains comprised a short-term, limited, challenging, yet defined project. At a certain point in each case, officials declared an end to the accounting effort. This attempted conclusion left many individuals in a nebulous state as missing, presumed dead, or body not found, but no longer the object of official concern. Families and loved ones often found that difficult to accept, but with limited options available, they had to find a way to move on with life. Margaret Burger, as one example, conducted a letter-writing campaign to find details concerning the disappearance of her Korean War MIA son, Pfc Elmer V. Burger. When one addressee did not respond in a timely manner, Mrs. Burger would write that person a follow-up while also turning to another potential source of information. Her activities continued throughout the 1950s, as one military or political official after another sadly repeated what little there was to know: Pfc Burger was last seen on December 1, 1950, during the withdrawal from the Chosin Reservoir area. By 1957, Mrs. Burger was still urging recipients of her letters to "please answer as soon as you *can* for we are just living from day to day hoping" (Burger, 1957; emphasis in original). Unfortunately, that hope for anything more would pass unfulfilled.

With such a raw emotional context in mind, it is worth considering official actions. Two major changes took place that ultimately shaped the accounting mission into what it is today. The first is more germane to the issues addressed in this chapter: concurrent return of the dead that emerged with the Korean War. The second, concerning Vietnam, applies to the US government's accounting activities overall. With this latter conflict, the accounting mission has lingered to the present, extending well beyond previous temporal boundaries for such activities.

To provide a proper explanation of the first change—regarding Korea—one must turn, however, to the Second World War. The Second World War was a massive conflagration that involved fighting and dying across the globe. As a result, US resources were stretched thin, particularly among the widely dispersed islands of the Pacific Area of Operation or in the extremely challenging terrain of the China-Burma-India Zone. Fighting a world war with finite resources required some difficult choices that complicated recovery activities. Graves registration units were often under strength, supplied with poorly trained personnel, faced with a herculean task, and were usually treated as an afterthought by operational planners. The resultant complications hindered efforts to recover the remains of those eventually deemed recoverable out of the nearly 400,000 American lives lost in this globe-spanning fight. Aside from finding remains, attempted identification of those recovered was also made more problematic due to wartime exigencies and postwar constraints. Setting aside major identification activities until after the cessation of hostilities, as was the policy for that war, necessarily meant that critical biological information decayed with time and circumstantial information eroded with witness memories. The postwar project was enormous: one official history says 280,000 sets of remains were recovered, with 171,000 of those repatriated for final burial in the United States (Steere & Boardman, 1957, pp. v–vi). More than 9,000 "sets" of remains existed as unidentifiable after the conclusion of this effort. Accounting activities for this war were further disrupted by the outbreak of the Korean War, but they nonetheless came to a close in the 1950s with more than 70,000 individuals left missing but presumed dead. Despite these problems, upon the outbreak of formal hostilities in Korea in June 1950, US forces took with them many Second World War operating protocols and expectations—as well as many of the same systemic defects.

When major conflict erupted on the Korean peninsula on June 25, 1950, US President Harry Truman quickly opted to resist what his administration characterized as communist aggression. He called for a United Nations resolution condemning the incursion of North Korean forces into South Korean territory. Such a resolution proved forthcoming, resulting in the UN Command that would direct the fight against communist forces in Korea. Truman also authorized deployment of US forces and drew on those closest at hand—the occupation troops in Japan—who landed in South Korea beginning July 1, 1950 (Appleman, 1960/2000, pp. 19–100). Although in name a UN Command, the US contingent was the largest of foreign forces. As a result, the US commander was dually tasked as leader of the national as well as the collective units engaged in the fight. These US forces deployed in a chaotic state and the see-saw battles of the first year exacerbated an extremely confused battlefield situation.

Drawing initially on Second World War approaches to combat losses, the operating practice in Korea involved collecting and then burying the dead in an array of temporary cemeteries. The presumptions motivating this approach were: 1) most American families would demand repatriation of remains; 2) wartime conditions prevented immediate transfer of the remains home; and 3) the general outline would follow the Second World War where, setbacks aside, the result was forward progress over time, ending in total victory and control of the battlefields (thus permitting thorough postwar recovery efforts). The latter two assumptions were mistaken. Military families began calling for concurrent return of the dead almost immediately upon the outbreak of hostilities. When the head of the U.S. Eighth Army, the major ground force element in Korea, died in a jeep accident in December 1950, officials quickly shipped his body back to the United States for burial. The uproar over this glaring example of preferential treatment pushed military leaders to act on a plan loosely considered before. Now, as individuals died and their bodies came to collection points, rather than bury them in temporary cemeteries they would be subject to identification efforts and then sent home as soon as possible. The concurrent return program remains standing policy to this day. Although shaping the accounting effort today with this major change, the rest of the Korean War experience with processing the dead followed the Second World War model. Recoveries continued throughout the war and after the armistice. Identification efforts also proceeded, but in 1956 major efforts were halted. This left families of over 8,000 individuals without a body to mourn and the nation with over 800 sets of unidentifiable remains buried on US soil (Coleman, 2008; *Graves Registration Service*, 1954).

The American experience of the Vietnam War was similar, to a point. The concurrent return program continued, as did official desires to support a major wartime and initial postwar recovery/identification program that had an ultimate end point. That last part, however, was not accomplished, as the families of the still-missing refused to permit an official bookend to their suffering and anger. Historian Michael Allen (2009) has superbly analyzed these developments and there is no need for full reconsideration here. Pertinent to this discussion is the fact that the accounting effort continued much longer than the short periods permitted for the Second World War and the Korean War. In fact, it has never ended. Due to this second major change, in an odd twist of circumstances, the continued focus on unresolved losses from Vietnam has opened the door for demands made by families of missing personnel from the Second World War and the Korean War. The Central Identification Laboratory (CIL), located in Southeast Asia for most of the Vietnam War, was relocated to Hawaii (becoming CIL-HI) in 1973. It ultimately merged with another accounting organization in 2003 to become the Joint POW/MIA Accounting Command (JPAC), which forms the primary operational arm of the US accounting community today.[9]

The mission of JPAC is to "conduct global search, recovery, and laboratory operations to identify unaccounted-for Americans from past conflicts in order to support the Department of Defense's personnel accounting efforts" (Budreau, 2013). This approach is necessarily field-intensive, and it is also focused primarily on the conflict that prompted the continuance of this accounting effort: Vietnam. Nevertheless, families of the missing from other conflicts became emboldened and empowered over time to begin demanding resolution for their loved ones. Today, the command has a global scope, with missions ranging from Germany to Papua New Guinea, including South Korea as well as the countries of Southeast Asia. All of the major wars since 1941 are now represented, even as the Vietnam focus has prevailed.[10]

As in all complex stories, there are many turning points in the tale of American accounting efforts. The Korean War presented one such shift as it led to the expectation of quick return—of prisoners of war and bodies of the fallen alike—upon cessation of hostilities. In fact, as elaborated upon above, the anguish of loved ones truncated the timeframe further by raising expectations for recovery, identification, and return of remains even while the fighting continued. Although the American Graves Registration Service (AGRS) personnel did the best that they could in difficult circumstances, there were many questions left unanswered when major accounting efforts for Korea finished in 1956. One significant issue that remained and intensified with the passage of time was the clash between expectation and reality.

It would take decades, and the public-official dynamic resulting from the divisive Vietnam War, to spark widespread interest in the problem of Korean War (and Second World War) missing service personnel. As one historian argued, "It is as if it was necessary to understand the wounds of Vietnam, maybe even to heal them, before consideration could be given to the Korean War" (Edwards, 2000, p. 145). Korean War–focused service and commemoration organizations, such as The Chosin Few, did not begin forming until the 1980s. By the 1990s, in the midst of widespread Second World War commemorations, Korean War veterans and families began demanding greater acknowledgement of their sacrifices (Adams, 1994; Dolski, 2012, pp. 247–285). The year 1995 marked the dedication of the Korean War Veterans Memorial on the National Mall in Washington, DC (Korean War Veterans, 1995). Despite these official efforts to recognize Korean War service and loss, questions lingered about the missing. Vietnam would no longer hold all the attention when it came to the difficult task of finding, recovering, identifying, and returning remains long after a war's conclusion. Still, the major point of potential conflict remained: when expectation and reality do not meet, frustration quickly mounts. What, then, was the US government to do about the Korean War missing?

Locating and recovering remains in the field is extremely difficult work. Aside from fiscal constraints and personnel limitations, JPAC also must contend with diminishing returns and ever-growing expectations, as well as the uncertainties of the international environment. After all, the US is not always on good terms with countries controlling former battlegrounds. Furthermore, readers may

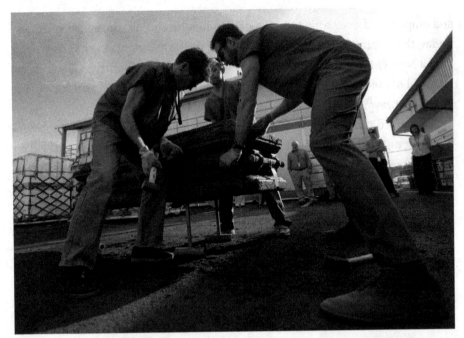

FIGURE 7.4   Opening a casket that contains a set of "unknown" remains from the Korean War.
Source: Image courtesy of the U.S. Department of Defense, Joint POW/MIA Accounting Command

recall that following these conflicts, military leaders classified remains deemed unidentifiable as unknowns, assigned them an X number, and interred them in US-controlled cemeteries. Budgetary pressures influence JPAC's operational plans and, at times, field operations in certain countries are too dangerous or prohibited entirely. Yet families for the missing of the Second World War and Korean War called for answers. With more than 9,000 sets of unidentified remains in US-controlled cemeteries either at home or abroad, JPAC turned in 2009 to a concerted disinterment program for the purposeful analysis and identification of these unknown individuals, casualties of both wars. It was time to uncover what lay behind the Xs (Figure 7.4).

The Disinterment Project

One of the unique features of the post-conflict relationship with North Korea is that the US and the UN never signed a formal peace treaty with it. Hostile relations have endured for decades. The ramifications for any effort to recover the remains of missing combatants are plainly evident. For years after signing the armistice agreement, the only steady recovery efforts took place in South Korea.

By the 1990s, however, diplomatic overtures seemed to bear fruit. The North Korean regime implemented a series of unilateral turnovers, meaning it voluntarily sent the purported remains of UN soldiers to the US for identification analysis. The largest of these turnovers took place in 1993–94, but that group of remains was so commingled (i.e., the remains of multiple persons were mixed together) that they required over two decades of analysis to sort out, an effort that continues to this day.

Aside from unilateral activity, the North Korean regime has relented to US diplomatic pressure in other ways. Beginning in 1996, a series of joint North Korea–US recovery activities took place in selected areas of the north, including several battle sites related to the Chosin Reservoir campaign. The perils of this seemingly promising development were twofold. First, the North Koreans maintained an extremely close watch on all joint activities and, in fact, only permitted recovery efforts in areas they designated in advance. With the commingling and provenance issues evident in unilateral turnovers, suspicions soon arose that they had "salted" (deliberately placed and buried) remains prior to these field activities to guarantee relatively straightforward, successful discovery. Salting potentially introduces the remains of individuals to sites other than their loss or death locations, thereby complicating efforts to use circumstantial information during identification analyses. The second major danger stemmed from the mercurial nature of North Korean–US relations. The negotiations for field missions were often tense and subject to mutual recriminations, and in 2005 this activity halted entirely. With over 8,000 unresolved cases from that conflict and in light of diminishing returns from the field in South Korea, how could the government account for so many missing?

Enter into the situation one dynamic Korean War veteran. Ronald ("Ron") Douglas Broward was born April 3, 1933, in Los Angeles, California. In 1950, he and his brother, Al, enlisted in the U.S. Marine Corps. Ron was still a minor, but as he expressed to this author, at the time nobody seemed to care (R. Broward, personal communication, April 8, 2012). Ron's posting was to the 1st Marine Regiment under the lead of famed officer Colonel Lewis "Chesty" Puller (Hoffman, 2001, p. 411–412). Ron fought in the Chosin Reservoir campaign. The 1st Marines occupied a village about 33 km south of the reservoir on the main north-south route. In holding that location, they secured the retreat passage for those forces more closely engaged around the Chosin. Ron and his unit later fought in South Korea, then—after stymieing several Chinese offensives—back northward in some hotly contested battles closer to the present-day armistice line. In this latter period, Ron lost one of his close friends, Pfc Warren Jackson Rarick (Martelle, n.d.). The loss would haunt Ron for the rest of his life, as would the profound ways his brother Al had changed as the result of combat along the western shores of the Chosin. In later life, Ron felt he had to do something regarding those Americans lost in the war and still missing. He turned to the US accounting community, bringing his own pragmatic approach to problem solving (Figure 7.5). While Ron hoped for and, on occasion, provided input regarding field activities in South Korea, with keen insight he turned his attention to another potential avenue for resolution: the remains interred as unknowns in American-held cemeteries. He thought that it was short-sighted to only look to field recoveries for identifications when these unidentified remains were resting within easy reach. Ron pushed to disinter single cases that he had researched, but he also called for a concerted approach to all of the Korean War unknowns.

Through Ron's constant and well-intentioned pressure, and in order to assist with the quickest possible resolution of unresolved casualties, JPAC's Central Identification Laboratory (herein referred to as the "laboratory") expanded the disinterment program to attempt identification of remains from these graves. Since the 1980s, JPAC and its predecessor organizations had intermittently disinterred and identified remains from America's military conflicts. This ad hoc approach to disinterment changed several times. In 1999, based on Ron's insistence, a more systematic approach emerged. The first two disinterments, however, quickly demonstrated that DNA analysis would prove of limited utility for this effort. DNA sampling of these remains did not produce reportable results, due in all likelihood to the CIU's processing efforts conducted in the 1950s, which included exposure to formaldehyde and high levels of radiation. Failed DNA extraction hampered the emergent disinterment program and progress over the next decade was slow. DNA was far from the only means of making an identification, yet with provenance and commingling both factors to consider, anthropological and odontological analyses had limitations as well.

The program continued, but permission to disinter depended upon presenting a very high probability of successful identification based on sound evidence. In the early stages this was a one-person effort that produced steady but minimal results. By 2009, a more formalized program emerged to address the disinterment and identification of these remains. This new approach (currently in effect) is holistic in scope, multidisciplinary in nature, and comprehensive. Based on analysis of historical evidence, the disinterment program staff nominate cases for consideration by the Scientific Director of the laboratory, and only those cases with a high probability to yield positive identification receive his approval.

Each case nomination appears in the form of a disinterment memorandum. These documents are the chief responsibility of a historian assigned to investigate a particular geographic area. Each historian conducts extensive research

FIGURE 7.5   **Mr. Ron Broward discussing a Korean War case at the Joint POW/MIA Accounting Command's headquarters in Hawaii.**

Source: Image courtesy of the U.S. Department of Defense, Joint POW/MIA Accounting Command

into the combat operations, casualties, identification activities, and treatment of the unidentified remains from a bounded area. As a result of this strenuous effort, he or she is better equipped to select cases that show high potential for identification. The historian develops a pool of potentially associated casualties that is both as exclusionary as possible yet as inclusive as necessary. Walking this fine line is critically important, as the remainder of the analytical process will depend upon the initial casualty pool generated by the historian. Reducing complex cases down to one potential match risks a total failure should that assumed association fail to hold true once the remains have been analyzed in the lab. The historian must employ a healthy dose of skepticism regarding evidence and analysis to avoid unduly biasing the results of an investigation. Also prior to exhumation, odontologists and anthropologists in the laboratory attempt to further reduce the potential casualty association list by excluding individuals based on dental or skeletal information in a casualty's personnel records when compared to details present in the files for the unidentified remains. In the case of X-15724, this collaborative effort helped narrow the range of possibilities from the more than 800 individuals associated with the recovery location to a pool that appeared both convincing and manageable.

After each memorandum undergoes a thorough, multi-stage review, the Scientific Director considers approval. Even after the in-depth vetting process, any approved cases still go to the JPAC Commander, the U.S. Army, the Defense Prisoner of War/Missing Personnel Office, and various other organizations for their review and consideration. All of these entities take a critical stance and look for logical fallacies or flawed work that may undermine the potential for identifying a given set of remains.

The disinterment memorandum only starts the process. Once permitted, the laboratory staff coordinates the exhumation and transportation of remains to the lab for analysis. As with the initial casework, this part of the identification process draws upon multiple lines of evidence. Odontologists, anthropologists, material evidence analysts, chest radiograph comparison specialists (when applicable), and DNA scientists all contribute to the processing of the remains. While the public often fixates on DNA for forensic analysis, all of these lines of evidence must come together to demonstrate a positive identification.[11] Many of these caskets contain commingled remains of more than one individual, which may not be evident from the available historical documentation.

The scientific techniques and tools available today far surpass those available to processing technicians 60 or 70 years ago. Yet some of those constraints that faced our forebears still linger today. The most difficult cases were deemed unidentifiable at Kokura in the 1950s, and these are the cases under consideration today. While scientific advances and a robust methodology have permitted success with the disinterment program, challenges persist. These reservations may seem like quibbling, but they bear due respect, as they can unhinge any future disinterment activity.

Nevertheless, Ron Broward had struck upon an extremely promising vein of accounting for some of the missing. Admittedly, disinterment-based resolution efforts can only form a small piece of the overall US accounting. After all, there are no unidentified remains interred in cemeteries for the Vietnam War, and for the Second World War and the Korean War the unknowns only number about 1 in 10 of the more than 80,000 designated as missing from those two conflicts.[12] Still, this is one area of activity previously unappreciated and unexplored. Why go through the difficulties and dangers of looking in the field for remains of the missing if they happen already to be in an American-controlled cemetery? Despite public and official unease over "improperly" disturbing remains, Ron's brilliant ideas and efforts have helped bring answers to more than 50 Korean War veteran families.[13] The disinterment approach will obviously only work in certain circumstances. Thus, one may wonder why, aside from the singular Ron Broward, did JPAC first focus on the Korean War for this action?

The Korean War as a Case Study

The Korean War presented a unique mix of problems and possibilities for the US accounting community. Korea was the least commemorated of the three major conflicts at the heart of the accounting mission. Yet it was to account for this war's missing that JPAC developed a new approach to identifications. There are two reasons for this. The first centres on capability. The second depends upon an element of demand. Over time, a community of interest formed that pushed the government to act differently on the matter of Korean War missing personnel.

Capability

The simplest explanation for the initial disinterment focus on Korea is that the scope of effort was manageable. In 1998, disinterment and subsequent identification of the official Vietnam War Unknown from Arlington National Cemetery closed off that route, since these were the only unidentified remains from that conflict buried in US territory (Wagner, 2013). The only two conflicts within JPAC's primary purview with unknowns to consider are the Second World War and the Korean War. There are ten times as many unknowns from the former as from the latter. The Korean War unknowns presented a challenge that seemed more manageable due to sheer numbers alone. Furthermore, the unidentified from the Second World War were buried in different cemeteries across the globe, whereas those from the Korean War were all buried in one cemetery (except for the official unknown soldier at Arlington). This cemetery, the NMCP, through a fortunate set of circumstances is only about 15 km away from the JPAC lab in Hawaii. Added to the numbers of unidentified and proximity of the remains was one more factor: the extent of the documentary record. The Korean War records are far more complete than those for the Second World War. Nowhere is this factor more evident than with personnel files and documentation of the recovery and laboratory processing for the unidentified remains.

Unidentified remains were recovered from both South Korea and North Korea. Those from South Korea stemmed from field recoveries conducted by UN forces during and after the war. The North Korean returns all came from the postwar Operation Glory, when the Chinese and North Koreans handed over approximately 4,300 sets of remains to UN forces in 1954. Over barely more than one year, from late 1954 to early 1956, processing technicians at Kokura designated nearly 2,900 sets of remains as those of American personnel, yet they were unable to identify 416 of these.

In 1956, US officials interred all of the 848 sets of unidentified remains from the Korean War (416 from the north and 432 in the south) as unknowns in the NMCP. Over the next 15 years cemetery staff interred an additional 19 unknowns accruing from field recoveries in South Korea. In 1958, US military officials arranged for the disinterment of one unknown for shipment to the east coast of the continental United States. This set of remains became the officially designated Unknown for the Korean War and now lies in Arlington National Cemetery (*Selection of World War II*, n.d.). In total, 866 unknowns remained in the NMCP by the late 1990s.[14]

Demand

Capability is only one part of the explanation for the emergence of a Korean War disinterment program. Pressure also arose from multiple sources. Sudden death, even in times of war, can produce an array of intense emotions and reactions, particularly for the family members of those killed. While somewhat platitudinous, this reorients focus here to those individuals impacted by the horrors of war. Admittedly, here we are only considering one small community: the killed service personnel (and their families) of the American military, which was relatively far more fortunate than the enemy forces and civilians caught in the path of this war. Despite that qualification, these are still more than 36,500 stories of loss and anguish for US soldiers who died in battle or "in theatre" (Department of Veterans Affairs, 2015). The point made above and returned to here is that loss becomes more difficult to bear when there is no body to mourn, and when there are no definite answers about what happened to a particular loved one (Cox & Jones, 2014, pp. 298–299). For instance, Mrs. Mary E. Kincaid went to great lengths in order to discover more information about her son, Pfc Lonnie H. Kincaid, an individual MIA since November 30, 1950. After writing to a US Senator to no avail, she turned to the Commandant of the U.S. Marine Corps, General Clifton B. Cates, to inquire "if there was no way possible for him [Lonnie] to be located and send some sort of a message to an anxious mother" (Kincaid, 1951). Documents in the records of missing personnel attest to the legal, financial, and emotional difficulties experienced by families as they struggled to overcome the loss of someone without a body to *prove* death (see also Bender, 2013, pp. 233–238, for an example from the Second World War).

The theoretical section included earlier in this chapter conveyed the idea that nations consist of imagined communities that depend upon the shared memories, beliefs, and interests of their constituents. Although Korea remained a limited war, losses in this conflict nevertheless tore apart the social fabric. Unfortunately, with regard to Korea, American society often effaced this communal gap with oblivion. Forgetting the entire affair became a way to ease the pain and discomfort over losses in a murky war with no clear end. Vietnam families, in contrast, were able to keep their pain in the public consciousness. Ever since the mid-1980s, on the other hand, American society has engaged in hagiographic veneration of the Second World War generation. These claims of both these wars on public attention combined to push Korean War families into the public sphere to call for redress of their grievances, as they felt increasingly slighted. In a sense, a community of interested parties formed to shape the historical/commemorative record, in accordance with the process of the collective shaping of the past described by historian Michael Kammen (1991, pp. 8–13).

Ron Broward, the Korean War veteran introduced above, was just one of many individuals that came together to create this community. Families of the missing also added to this community; these include Hal and Ted Barker, the founders of the Korean War Project, which runs an online database and communication forum for those interested in missing personnel affairs (www.koreanwar.org). The Barkers are examples of this dynamic, but there are others, such as John Zimmerlee, the son of a missing Korean War airman, researcher, and MIA affairs advocate (www.kpows.com/thezimmerleereports.html). These memory activists and policy proponents insert themselves into the public sphere in an attempt to shape the discourse on missing personnel. Less vocal, but more numerous, are the families of the missing that are interested in their own stories. They come together at reunions, meetings, and at annual updates to receive information provided by the government. The attitudes and desires vary amongst this diverse array of people, but all of them demand more answers.

Thus, a large, nebulous, interested "community" formed around the issue of Korean War missing personnel. Tellingly, the language of sacrifice, redemption, and national obligation suffuses this activity. At times, the discourse becomes quite heated and critical of the government's accounting efforts (and the perceived societal neglect of the topic); at others, people come together to ask, to learn, to seek understanding, and to attempt to heal. In all settings, however, there is an implicit (and, increasingly so, explicit) call for greater action and more information.

The difficult question, though, is how to address this demand. How does the government act to repay such a debt? One possible response has been provided with the creation of an accounting community. The underlying intent of this community's diverse organizations and their functions is to "account for" an individual. Of course, that term can suggest several different outcomes. The focus has lingered on biological remains: the primary means of resolving a case is to locate the remains, subject them to forensic analysis, identify them, and then send them for final disposition per the direction of next of kin. These remains can come from three general sources: recoveries in the field; unilateral turnovers from other entities (in this case, the North Korean government); or exhuming Korean War unidentified remains. With perpetual North Korean–American discord, opportunities for field recoveries seem minimal, as does the likelihood of any major turnover of remains in the near future (Keene, 2010). Thus, disinterring and identifying the Korean War unknowns presents an obvious way to address the social demand to send these casualties home to their families.

Yet certain obstacles required surmounting before this approach garnered widespread support. Officials of the accounting community had to address public unease over disturbing resting remains. Plans had to address the logistics of disinterring remains as well as shipping them home for final disposition once identified. Forensic testing efforts for this particular problem set required validation and, in this case, a major hurdle appeared concerning DNA analysis. As a result, JPAC staff developed a new process to allay concerns about specious or disrespectful disinterments. The intent was to foster belief in the ability of the government to deliver results. Although a team effort of a multidisciplinary nature, the process begins with and depends upon sound historical investigation.

History's Role in Accounting: When *X* Does Not Mark the Spot

Historical investigation is more of an art than a science. This reality, at first glance, may make history seem out of place in a laboratory setting. Searching for a professional historian in popular portrayals of forensic science (fiction), such as *Bones* or *CSI*, yields little. Despite that lacuna, there is an obvious role for history and the historian in the accounting community at large and even in the science-driven process of remains identification. The laboratory is an academic institution that promotes open inquiry, intensive research, peer review, and the challenging of interpretations—all of benefit to rigorous historical investigation. Furthermore, in regard to the disinterment effort, JPAC has employed a process that is multidisciplinary in nature. Historians working collaboratively with anthropologists and odontologists attempt to produce results in this extremely complex task. Despite the essential requirement of teamwork, of drawing on the skills and experiences of many types of individuals, the disinterment effort is heavily reliant upon the strength of historical assessments.

Historians generate lists of potentially associated casualties for comparison to sets of unidentified remains. These lists incorporate a spectrum of historical analyses. The underlying motivation is an attempt to account for the broad range of problematic factors inherent in the recovery and identification efforts that produced the unidentified remains. It is this list of candidates that anthropologists and odontologists review to make a recommendation for inclusion or exclusion as associations for a set of remains. Thus, historical analysis provides the starting point for the scientific staff. While each case is entirely dependent upon having a useful and appropriate pool of candidates for consideration, the historians' task in this effort extends even further. Assessments of the unidentified remains must also factor into case selection and pursuit. If there are too many viable candidates, cases may have a reduced likelihood to yield an identification because there might be no evidence to discriminate one from another. Alternatively, if too many complicating or uncertain factors arise in the recovery efforts (e.g., suspect witness statements) or previous identification analyses (e.g., accidental commingling of skeletal elements in the laboratory), then the historian will log these issues and recommend a suspension of the case until additional information becomes available. Historians, therefore, initiate case selection, are solely responsible for generating the initial list of potentially associated casualties, and recommend case pursuit or suspension.

The final topic to consider is the ways in which historians execute their integral role in the disinterment process and, thus, factor into the identification of missing persons. Historical investigation is a tricky affair. Historians engaged in the following process: determine their scope (e.g., geographic and temporal boundaries); conduct a secondary source review; develop a primary resource collection plan; execute, review, synthesize, and modify research plans to reflect new leads; and so on. This effort proceeds until he or she develops a comprehensive understanding of an assigned geographic area. The historian considers combat activities as well as post-combat recovery and identification attempts in the area. The resultant holistic picture fosters a deeper appreciation of the many influential factors that led to the final result of unidentified remains extant today. Historians not only look at the unresolved casualties stemming from combat, but also must consider the resolved casualties—their recovery locations, the manner in which their identifications developed, the potential for the intermingling of their remains with those left as unknowns, and also the possibility of past mistaken identifications. Deep review also promotes understanding of the many problems and pitfalls experienced by (and at times exacerbated because of) the work in the region by the American Graves Registration Service (AGRS), the military unit charged with managing the bodies of the US dead. As indicated above, unidentified remains constituted the most difficult cases for military officials in the 1940s and 1950s and, as a result, pose particular challenges to researchers in the present. More than straightforward one-to-one assessments of a lone casualty and a single set of remains, the overall context must be considered. Inaccurate or conflicting data in the historical records, commingling of remains in the field or the lab, and problematic identifications in the past all complicate the picture.

The resources for this effort are varied. Historians can build on foundations set by the AGRS in the past, as they usually documented recovery efforts and laboratory processing in ways that provide clues about potential casualty associations. Furthermore, the personnel records of these casualties often contain vital details, including prior medical or dental information or loss incident details. These records provide a starting point for the historian. To expand upon this, the astute researcher next turns to unit diaries, muster rolls and morning reports (a near-daily accounting of personnel; name depends on branch of service), after-action reports, or a variety of record trails generated by military organizations engaged in combat.

Historical assessments for the disinterment project encompass more than the combat action alone. Through a review of the AGRS activities, historians can reconstruct recovery sweeps to see from where remains originate, potentially linking remains to casualty individuals. Beyond that initial step, reviewing recovery and identification processing will reveal which persons AGRS considered or failed to consider for association with a set of remains. Mistakes happened in the past, and sometimes through simple oversight or lack of complete documentation the AGRS never reviewed a potential association. More often, however, this level of analysis reveals the many difficulties inherent in a comprehensive disinterment effort. For instance, the unknown remains often lack vital skeletal elements, such as a skull, that play a major role in forensic analysis and identification. A common approach decades ago by AGRS officials was to assess multiple sets of remains simultaneously and, in that process, a record of swapping elements amongst cases becomes apparent. Therefore, historical research must account for the vast range of possibilities on the battlefield and after, as each set of recovered remains worked its way through this system. In the end, the unknown soldiers represent those cases without sufficient identifying information, with too many potential associations, or with some stopping point that prevented identification. It is up to the historian of today to provide a convincing argument that acknowledges these issues, yet still links individuals to a set of remains.

Although this research is laborious and time-intensive, it is well worth the effort for many reasons. First, historical investigation provides information of use for multiple purposes. Although this chapter has focused on the disinterment and identification of unknowns, the research required for that activity could shape proposed field investigations and recovery missions today. It will also prove useful in communications with external entities, including families of the missing, to show just what the government is doing to attempt resolution of these cases and, when applicable, to explain what else is required for success. Second, so-called desk studies are always cheaper than acting without concerted research and analysis. After all, archival research costs pale in comparison to field activities, which require transportation, logistical arrangements, lodging, labour, and many other forms of military and diplomatic support. Third, and most significantly, historical analysis enables the accounting community to conduct its activities in a more rigorous manner. Disinterment identifications emerged through the judicious use of this research, and they have provided answers to families of the missing ever since. Historical research and analysis helps the community prioritize activities while maintaining high standards throughout the life cycle of accounting efforts. In the end, the many functions of current accounting activity are complex and fraught with challenge, and the historian can mitigate some of these problems.

Conclusion

The United States is unique in the attention it devotes to the accounting effort for missing service personnel. While other countries attend to their missing, the time, money, and importance attributed to this mission in the US far exceeds them. Explanation for this development depends upon a particular socio-politico-historical combination of capability due to resource availability, manageable scope in light of relatively limited combat casualties, and the collective demand to do something about those who, once called to fight for the nation, never returned home (Figure 7.6).

In a sense, this collective impulse exemplifies the spirit behind Calvin Coolidge's 1920 proclamation that "the nation which forgets its defenders will itself be forgotten." Coolidge evoked the debt owed by society to those forced to fight on its behalf.[15] The discourse that followed is revealing. Americans, while hardly alone in this regard, tend to fixate on the moral rectitude of their fighting forces and the causes on which they embark. This framing is best represented by the "Good War" phenomenon regarding interpretations of the Second World War that arose in the 1980s and 90s, and helps explain the dissonance between expectation and reality that provoked such discord surrounding the Vietnam War (Adams, 1994; Allen, 2009; Dolski, 2012). Historian Michael Sherry has discussed the socially militarizing impact of such proclivities and he cautions against the oversimplification and romanticization of military affairs (Sherry, 1995). Americans prefer to celebrate their warriors as champions of the (good) nation. That tendency combines with another, which Michael Kammen best described as a democratization of American collective memory (Kammen, 1991). Over time, collective remembrance activities increasingly have touted the experiences, influences, and contributions of common individuals. These two desires—celebration of the warrior and acknowledgement of the everyday person—combine in the remembrance of wars past. It is important to remember that the wars of the 20th century were largely fought by conscripts, Americans forced to fight for their nation. The resultant obligations in a democratic society, one that celebrates the worth of the individual, are understandably magnified. That combination explains the desire to laud the warrior and pay homage to his (or eventually her) service. Of course, this predilection faces stumbling blocks. Unpopular wars present one challenge, but collectively the intent to divorce the war from the warrior has permitted a disjunctive rejection of the former while embracing the latter. Even more problematic, though, is the emotionally charged issue of missing and unaccounted for personnel. The accounting mission emerged as an official effort to address a collective obligation to these missing persons and to their families

FIGURE 7.6   **The NMCP today.**
Source: Image courtesy of the U.S. Department of Defense, Joint POW/MIA Accounting Command

as well as communities. There are other impulses and ramifications of this effort, such as the intent to assure those serving in the present that if they go missing a similar effort will attend to them. In many ways, the notion of past-present-future obligation ties to this mission.

While addressing the official actions of the accounting community here, the fact is that the mission is a collective endeavour that brings together a diverse array of actors. Aside from the official entities, others drawn to this activity include families of the missing, activists, independent researchers, non-governmental organizations, for-profit institutions, foreign governments, media figures, politicians, and community leaders. The complexities of locating, recovering, and identifying the remains, and thus resolving these cases, often elude those not directly involved in these processes. The public in general tends to focus on scientific procedures, technological innovations, and the field recovery activities of the US accounting community. In the latter category, historical investigation plays a large, though often invisible, role.

The potential for historians to shape accounting efforts transcends a single area, as the disinterment program discussed above amply demonstrates. The point here is to consider the multidisciplinary nature of the identification process for missing persons. Historians can provide much-needed context for any forensic analysis or field activity. They promote overall efficiency by generating lists of potentially associated individuals that focus the attention of a finite forensic staff. The collaboration produces more rigorous cases that account for the myriad possibilities of combat and post-combat recovery efforts. This model is not bounded by combat alone and, therefore, presents interesting suggestions of a way to employ public historians in applied settings.

Admittedly, with the array of actors, interests, and agendas at play, the accounting community's activities are overtly politicized. Two decades ago, there was little evident support for a concerted disinterment program. The US accounting community was in the limelight for a series of missteps and problem-ridden actions. As a result, few felt it wise to pursue a major initiative that exhumed resting remains for attempted identification. As always, there was a risk of failure to identify exhumed remains. Moreover, another hazard emerged of uncovering problematic identifications or other actions in the past that would further undermine public trust in the accounting mission. Change required the pressure of individuals like Ron Broward and the re-establishment of confidence in the accounting community. That renewed faith earned a significant boost from a community-wide reorganization and the establishment of a science-driven identification process. The risks of failure remained, but JPAC mitigated them with a new approach, using rigorous methods relying upon a mixture of disciplines and the right personnel (including knowledgeable volunteers like Broward). Success in this venture definitely depended upon the multidisciplinary model that wedded together historical and scientific analyses. To isolate one from the other would have undermined the entire effort.

After several fits and starts, through an iterative process of attempt and adjustment, JPAC developed a comprehensive disinterment program. As a result, in 2012 one historian began reviewing the 70 cases accruing from combat activity along the east side of the Chosin Reservoir more than six decades prior. One case soon rose to the forefront as a possibility: X-15724. It seemed to offer a high likelihood for identification. A year later, following the intensive case review process, garnering approval, effecting disinterment, and conducting forensic analyses, the remains of Pfc Jerry Pat Craig were finally sent home. His niece, Anita Fields-Gold, remarked that it was "the most joyous occasion I've had in a long, long time" (in *MIA Korean War*, 2014). The desire is there. The families of these missing people want answers. Although but one small, defined route among many required for full accounting, the disinterment program provides tangible results. What better testament is there to the utility of history than the reaction of Craig's family upon his return home?

Notes

1. The author would like to thank Derek Congram for vital suggestions on earlier versions of this chapter. Additional consideration is due to Emily Wilson, Jim Rose, Sarah Wagner, and the irreplaceable Ron Broward who sadly is no longer with us. Until They Are Home.

2. The Patriot Guard is an organization that attends the funerals of fallen military personnel in order to commemorate their loss, while also dissuading public protest.

3. For ease of reading and consistency, I will use North Korea and South Korea throughout this chapter rather than current official titles (Democratic People's Republic of Korea and Republic of Korea, respectively) or generalized geographic characterizations (northern or southern Korea).

4. This intervention ensured a divided Korean peninsula. Chinese involvement stemmed from many motives, including a desire to resist Western incursions in the region, hope for the spread of Communism, the goal of maintaining traditional influence over neighbour states, and the fear of permitting a unified Korean peninsula to exist under the auspices of US protection/guidance.

5. One shipment of remains transferred south via airplane, which ushered in a spat between U.S. Army and U.S. Air Force leaders. The rest of the bodies moved southward by truck.

6. On any given day during the exchange, UN forces received multiple shipments from various locations. Isolated burial, in this usage, indicates anything other than a formal burial in a cemetery setting. Thus, it could indicate an ad hoc battlefield burial or even no burial at all and instead the discovery of unburied remains in the natural environment.

7. Designations for remains often changed as the result of processing efforts, both in the Second World War and the Korean War examples. At this point, the CIU in Kokura adopted a method of adding 13,000 to enemy transport numbers (thus changing 2,724 to 15,724) and affixing an "X" at the front to designate remains as unidentifiable.

8. An anomaly here signifies an identified individual purportedly recovered from a battlefield other than the one on which he fought—sometimes tens or even hundreds of miles apart.

9. At the time of writing, a major community-wide reorganization is taking place that will purportedly merge most relevant entities into a single institution. As a result, the Joint POW/MIA Accounting Command (JPAC) discussed herein stood down effective January 30, 2015. Its personnel and mission transferred to the new organization, the Defense POW/MIA Accounting Agency. For consistency and clarity, JPAC remains in use throughout this chapter. "POW" signifies Prisoner of War; "MIA" indicates Missing in Action.

10. There are seven unresolved military and civilian casualties from military actions following Vietnam, including Operation El Dorado Canyon (Libya, 1986), Operation Desert Storm (Iraq, 1991), and Operation Iraqi Freedom (Iraq, 2003–10).

11. While the CIL has developed an alternate technique for identification of these remains with chest radiograph comparison (when suitable antemortem evidence is available), the point argued here is that DNA comparison does not represent a panacea for the accounting community's arduous task.

12. Further caution is warranted here in the case of numbers. With commingling always a possibility, any single unknown may represent the remains of multiple individuals.

13. Many more disinterred remains are currently undergoing analysis in the CIL.

14. Since 1999, the JPAC, working in coordination with NMCP staff, has exhumed approximately 100 of these unknowns for forensic analysis and identification processing.

15. The discussion and citation of this quote is widespread. The quotation comes from Coolidge's acceptance speech for the Republican vice-presidential nomination.

References

Action report of 7th Infantry Division, from 21 November 1950 to December 1950, from Hyesanjin to Hungnam outloading. (n.d.). Records of the Adjutant General's Office, U.S. Army (Record Group 407). College Park, MD: National Archives and Records Administration.

Adams, M. (1994). *The best war ever: America and World War II.* Baltimore: Johns Hopkins University Press.

Allen, M. (2009). *Until the last man comes home: POWs, MIAs, and the unending Vietnam War.* Chapel Hill, NC: University of North Carolina Press.

Anderson, B. (1991). *Imagined communities: Reflections on the origin and spread of nationalism.* Revised edition. New York, NY: Verso.

Appleman, R. (1987). *East of Chosin: Entrapment and breakout in Korea, 1950.* College Station, TX: Texas A&M University Press.

Appleman, R. (1990). *Escaping the trap: The US Army X Corps in Northeast Korea, 1950.* College Station, TX: Texas A&M University Press.

Appleman, R. (1960/2000). *South to the Naktong, north to the Yalu (June–November 1950).* Washington, DC: US Army Center of Military History.

Bender, B. (2013). *You are not forgotten: The story of a lost WWII pilot and a twenty-first-century soldier's mission to bring him home.* New York, NY: Doubleday.

Blumenson, M. (2001). Glory and heartbreak east of the reservoir. *Army, 51*(3), 25.

Bodnar, J. (1992). *Remaking America: Public memory, commemoration, and patriotism in the twentieth century.* Princeton, NJ: Princeton University Press.

Budreau, L. (2010). *Bodies of war: World War I and the politics of commemoration in America, 1919–1933.* New York, NY: New York University Press.

Budreau, L. (2013). Joint POW/MIA accounting command. In G. Piehler (ed.), *Encyclopedia of military science* (pp. 732–733). Thousand Oaks, CA: SAGE Publications.

Burger, M. (1957, April 25). *Letter, "Service Contract" for Burger, Elmer V.* Quantico, VA: Copy in possession of US Marine Corps Service Casualty Office.

Coleman, B. (2008). Recovering the Korean War dead, 1950–1958: Graves registration, forensic anthropology, and wartime memorialization. *The Journal of Military History, 72*(1), 179–222.

Cox, M., & Jones, P. (2014). Ethical considerations in the use of DNA as a contribution toward the determination of identification in historic cases: Considerations from the Western front. *New Genetics and Society, 33*(3), 295–312.

Department of Veterans Affairs. (2015). *America's Wars.* Washington, DC: Department of Veterans Affairs, Office of Public Affairs. Retrieved from www.va.gov/opa/publications/factsheets/fs_americas_wars.pdf.

Dolski, M. (2012). *"To set free a suffering humanity": D-Day in American remembrance.* Unpublished doctoral dissertation, Temple University.

Edwards, P. (2000). *To acknowledge a war: The Korean War in American memory.* Westport, CT: Greenwood Press.

Faust, D. (2008). *The republic of suffering: Death and the American Civil War.* New York, NY: Knopf.

Finkel, D. (2013). *Thank you for your service.* New York, NY: Farrar, Straus and Giroux.

Gillis, J. (ed.) (1994). *Commemorations: The politics of national identity.* Princeton, NJ: Princeton University Press.

Graves registration service in the Korean conflict. (1954). Military History Section, US Army Forces Far East. Washington, DC: US Government Publishing Office.

Gray, J. (1993). *The Chosin Reservoir campaign. John E. Gray Papers.* Carlisle, PA: Army Heritage and Education Center.

Gugeler, R. (1987). *Combat actions in Korea.* Washington, DC: Center of Military History.

Habermas, J. (1991). *The structural transformation of the public sphere: An inquiry into a category of bourgeois society.* (T. Burger, with F. Lawrence, Trans.). Cambridge, MA: MIT Press.

Halbwachs, M. (1992). *On collective memory.* (L. Coser, Trans. & Ed.). Chicago, IL: University of Chicago Press.

Harvey, W. (1954). *Roster of bodies of military personnel and prisoners of war for delivery and reception.* National Archives and Records Administration (Record Group 92: Records of the Office of the Quartermaster General). Suitland, MD: Washington National Records Center.

Historical summary, Graves Registration Division, Korean communication zone. (1954). National Archives and Records Administration (Record Group 92: Records of the Office of the Quartermaster General). Suitland, MD: Washington National Records Center.

Hoffman, J. (2001). *Chesty: The story of Lieutenant General Lewis B. Puller, USMC.* New York, NY: Random House.

Individual Deceased Personnel File (IDPF) for Craig, Jerr P, Pfc, RA18347401. (n.d.). National Archives and Records Administration (Record Group 92: Records of the Office of the Quartermaster General). Suitland, MD: Washington National Records Center.

Kammen, M. (1991). *Mystic chords of memory: The transformation of tradition in American culture.* New York, NY: Vintage Books.

Keene, J. (2010). Bodily matters above and below ground: The treatment of American remains from the Korean War. *The Public Historian, 32*(1), 59–78.

Kincaid, M. (1951, February 5). *Letter to Clifton B. Cates, "Service Contract" for Kincaid, Lonnie H.* Quantico, VA: U.S. Marine Corps Service Casualty Office.

Knox, D. (1985). *The Korean War: Pusan to Chosin; an oral history.* New York, NY: Harcourt Brace & Company.

Korean War Veterans Memorial Advisory Board (ed.). (1995). *Korean War Veteran's Memorial.* Paducah, KY: Turner Publishing Co.

Martelle, C. (n.d.). *Able Company, 1st Battalion, 1st Marines: The story of Ron Broward; from Chosin Reservoir to Horseshoe Ridge.* Joint Base Pearl Harbor-Hickam, HI: JPAC Archives.

MIA Korean War veteran laid to rest, 63 years later. (2014, January 18). Retrieved from www.kcbd.com/story/24265358/mia-korean-war-veteran-laid-to-rest-63-years-later.

Montross, L., & Canzona, N. (1957/1990). *The Chosin Reservoir campaign, US Marine operations in Korea, 1950–1953, v. 3.* Washington, D.C.: GPO/Austin, TX: R. J. Speights.

Mossman, B. (1988). The Korean War, 1950–1953. In *American Military History* (Revised ed.; pp. 545–571). Washington, DC: Center of Military History, U.S. Army.

Mossman, B. (1990). *United States Army in the Korean War: Ebb and flow; November 1950–July 1951.* Washington, DC: Center of Military History.

PFC Jerry P. Craig, 2013, Obituary. (n.d.). Retrieved from www.labbymemorial.com/home/index.cfm/obituaries/view/fh_id/10166/id/2355272.

Piehler, G. K. (1995/2004). *Remembering war the American way.* Washington, DC: Smithsonian Institution Press.

Selection of World War II and Korean War unknowns. (n.d.). National Archives and Records Administration (Record Group 92: Records of the Office of the Quartermaster General). College Park, MD: National Archives and Records Administration.

Sherry, M. (1995). *In the shadow of war: The United States since the 1930s.* New Haven, CT: Yale University Press.

Sledge, M. (2005). *Soldier dead: How we recover, identify, bury, and honor our military fallen.* New York, NY: Columbia University Press.

Spurr, R. (1988). *Enter the dragon: China's undeclared war against the US in Korea, 1950–51.* Scranton, PA: Newmarket Press.

Steere, E., & Boardman, T. (1957). *Final disposition of World War II dead, 1945–51.* Q.M.C. Historical Studies, series II, no. 4. Washington, DC: United States Government Printing Office.

Stephan, C. N., Amidan, B., Trease, H., Guyomarc'h, P., Pulsipher, T., & Byrd, J. E. (2014). Morphometric comparison of clavicle outlines from 3D bone scans and 2D chest radiographs: A shortlisting tool to assist radiographic identification of human skeletons. *Journal of Forensic Sciences, 59*(2), 306–313.

Unknown X-15724 Operation Glory file. (n.d.). National Archives and Records Administration (Record Group 92: Records of the Office of the Quartermaster General). Suitland, MD: Washington National Records Center.

U.S. dead North Korea. (n.d.). National Archives and Records Administration (Record Group 554: Records of general headquarters, Far East Command, Supreme Commander Allied Powers, and United Nations Command). College Park, MD: National Archives and Records Administration.

Wagner, S. (2013). The making and unmaking of an unknown soldier. *Social Studies of Science, 43*(5), 631–656.

Related Sources

National Memorial Cemetery of the Pacific: www.cem.va.gov/cems/nchp/nmcp.asp

Quartermaster Corps, US Army. (2000). Operation Glory. Retrieved from www.quartermaster.army.mil/oqmg/professional_bulletin/2000/spring2000/Operation_Glory.htm.

Quintyn, C., & Wagner, S. (2009). Dismantling a national icon: Genetic testing and the tomb of the Unknowns. *Anthropology News, 50*(5), 7, 9.

Wagner, S. (2015). The quandries of partial and commingled remains: Srebrenica's missing and Korean War casualties compared. In F. Ferrándiz and A. C. G. M. Robben (eds.), *Necropolitics: Mass graves and exhumations in the age of human rights* (pp. 119–140). Philadelphia, PA: University of Pennsylvania Press.

Chapter 8

Psychosocial Aspects of Interviewing and Self-Care for Practitioners

Vedrana Mladina (Clinical Psychologist/Wellness Counsellor, NYU Abu Dhabi)

Introduction

This chapter provides basic information about the general psychosocial aspects of interviewing vulnerable and potentially traumatized individuals, the consequences this might have on the practitioners, and the ways in which these can be prevented or managed. In addition to the basic or rather universal psychosocial aspects of interviewing vulnerable individuals, special attention is given to the challenges specific to the context of missing persons (i.e., interviews with family members of victims of enforced disappearance). This information should be seen and used as an addition to numerous formal and informal interviewing techniques that are being widely used by practitioners (e.g., investigators, criminologists, victimologists, forensic anthropologists, human rights activists) and is therefore focused on specific aspects, assuming that more general interviewing skills are acquired or will be acquired through training.

The first part of the chapter focuses on the main characteristics of traumatic memories and the potential psychological and emotional consequences of recalling them. Furthermore, a brief overview of the psychosocial complexity related to the particular context of missing persons is given, highlighting the additional challenges such as complicated grief, ambiguous loss, etc. This part ends with an overview of different strategies that can be applied in order to prevent or minimize the negative effects of recalling traumatic memories. The second part of the chapter is dedicated to self-care for practitioners and explains the risks and symptoms of the two most common consequences: burnout and secondary traumatization. The chapter finishes with an overview of various preventive measures that can be applied to minimize the risk of becoming affected.

Psychosocial Aspects of Interviewing

Recalling Traumatic Events

In order to better understand why it is difficult to talk about traumatic events, it is necessary to look at the main characteristics of traumatic memory as opposed to non-traumatic memory. One of the main features of traumatic memory is that a large part of it is stored as non-verbal material—everything that can be perceived with our senses (images, sounds, smells, etc.). In other words, it is not stored as a story, but as an experience that is highly emotionally loaded. Furthermore, traumatic memories are very well preserved and resistant to any potentially contaminating influences such as time, which makes them very vivid and intense. This can be explained through the phenomenon of the so-called *flashbulb memory.*

A flashbulb memory is a detailed and vivid memory that is stored on one occasion and retained for a lifetime. Usually such memories are associated with important historical or autobiographical events. People also may form flashbulb memories of important personal events, such as hearing about the death of a family member or witnessing an unusual traumatic event such as a disaster. In each case what makes the memory special is the emotional arousal at the moment that the event was registered. Flashbulb memories are not necessarily accurate in every respect, but they demonstrate that the emotional content of an event can greatly enhance the strength of the memory formed. Flashbulb memories are thought to require the participation of the amygdala, a brain structure involved in emotional memory, and possibly other brain systems that regulate mood and alertness (Myers, 2006). Since these memories are stored as non-verbal material, they are also very difficult to verbalize, explaining some of the difficulties that affected individuals face when they are trying to recall and tell their story, no matter how motivated they are to do so. Finally, in situations when a person manages to overcome the obstacle of verbalizing the non-verbal contents of the memory, the recall itself can still result in severe negative reactions, both physically and psychologically.

On a physical level, the body is reacting to the psychological pressure caused by recalling traumatic memories through, for example, feeling restless and tense, having trouble sleeping, experiencing nightmares, and suffering from aches in different parts of the body (especially in cases of sexual assault and when physical injury was sustained during a traumatic event). These psychosomatic responses have to do with the fact that the mind and the body remember traumatic events. Being that the body and the mind are interconnected and interdependent, the emotional reactions are always accompanied by bodily reactions, and vice versa. In the case of recalling traumatic events this is even more evident because of the overwhelming feelings of fear and anxiety that had a strong physical component at the time of the traumatic event taking place (i.e., the "fight or flight" response of survival). This bodily response to threat is being relived every time the traumatic memory is refreshed. Moreover, for most trauma survivors, the constant state of alertness long after the actual danger is gone is one of its negative consequences. This state of alertness is related to the permanent hyper-sensibility of the autonomous nervous system in charge of the fight or flight reaction, among other things. Notwithstanding the discomfort such bodily reactions cause, they are much easier to accept and talk about than the emotional reactions, both on an individual and social level (in many cultures, it is much more socially accepted to talk about physical pain rather than emotional pain, which also influences an individual's approach to recognizing and accepting bodily reactions to trauma as opposed to emotional reactions to it).

Psychological, emotional reactions can be very strong and therefore difficult to manage. Feelings of anger, grief, shame, and guilt can be overwhelming and could result in strong avoidance symptoms. This can become an obstacle during an interview, even if the person is very motivated and willing to talk. They are so accustomed to avoiding any situation that might remind them of the source of the trauma that they might find it very difficult to overcome the challenge of speaking about it.

Psychosocial Aspects Specific to Family Members of Victims of Enforced Disappearance

Grief and mourning are natural, necessary reactions to death and loss. Such events require time and space, and people use culturally appropriate ceremonies such as memorials, funerals, and wakes in order to achieve closure. But the grieving process can be disrupted or even completely disabled in cases of enforced disappearance of a family member, because of the uncertainty of their whereabouts and inability to perform a farewell ceremony. Continued disbelief in the death of a loved one prevents a person from starting the normal grieving process, and there is a high risk of complicated grief.

In addition, the family of the missing person is very often confronted with inevitable administrative hurdles, such as lack of official acknowledgement of the missing person's status, and therefore they are unable to get the support that family members normally receive in cases of death. This particular kind of loss has been defined by Boss (as cited in Barakovic, Avdibegovic, & Sinanovic, 2014) as an "ambiguous loss situation stemming from not having information on whether a loved one is alive or dead, absent or present." Ambiguous loss may be accompanied by the occurrence of psychological problems such as anxiety, depression, loneliness, sadness, fear, worry, agitation, and difficult family relationships (Boss, 2010; Schaal, Elbert, & Neuner, 2009; Luster et al, 2009).

Many mental health professionals have noted that if family members choose to accept the death of the disappeared loved one, they feel that they are "killing" him or her. Or they may have fantasies about their loved ones living in some faraway place and not returning home because they are not allowed to do so, or that they might be in prison. Rather than trying to take the guilt away, it is better to acknowledge the feelings of guilt and tell the family members that they are a normal reaction. Such an approach can help a person to change from feelings of complete helplessness to having some sense of control over the situation (Blaauw & Lahteenmaki, 2002).

How to Minimize the Negative Impact of Recalling Traumatic Memories

The negative impact of recalling traumatic memories can be managed and minimized right from the very beginning of an interview, when the general framework is being established, through determining the emotional state of the person and continuing to monitor it until the end of the interview. In addition, it is very helpful to acknowledge the potential hardship of the interview and show respect and appreciation for the commitment of the person.

Once the emotional state is determined and rapport with the person is established, it is then necessary to make a clear and structured introduction of the purpose and scope of the interview, and explore the person's expectations and wishes related to the interview. This will not only provide them with certainty about what is going to happen in the process, but it will also make them feel like an equal partner in the process, taking an active part in the interview (e.g., when to take breaks, whether an accompanying person is needed to support them) rather than having everything imposed on them. This is very useful in terms of establishing good rapport, but also in terms of preventing re-traumatization and even secondary traumatization, assuming that some of the interviewees have been through distressing situations where they had no choice over what was happening to them (e.g., being held as prisoners in concentration camps). Sometimes even the interview location itself can trigger bad memories (e.g., interviewing a person who has been tortured and kept in a concentration camp in a small room without windows).

The rapport established at the very beginning in the introduction phase needs to be maintained and, if necessary, re-established multiple times throughout the interview. More or less obvious changes in a person's behaviour that are triggered by a certain question should be noted and reacted to in order to eliminate any discomfort and maintain the interview dynamic.

An emotionally neutral interview atmosphere creates a safe environment and gives the necessary support for the person to feel comfortable. At the same time it does not impose anything and therefore leaves enough space for the natural development of rapport and trust. In order to establish such a neutral atmosphere, the interviewer has to be neutral in terms of their approach, attitude, reactions to interviewee's responses, attachment to the case, etc. This means that the interviewer needs to think about and be aware of any personal challenges, such as not being comfortable discussing certain subjects, or not being able to be in control of their own reactions to certain answers that they might hear during the interview.

Bearing in mind the main characteristics of traumatic memories described above, it is important to remember that an interviewee recalling anything in general is *reconstructing* what was experienced, rather than *playing it back*. It is therefore important to reassure the person that no one expects them to remember every detail about what happened, and that they should not feel bad about having forgotten certain details, or for remembering them only vaguely. On the other hand, reconstructing an event imposes chronology, meaning that ideally everything is remembered exactly as it happened, in detail, and in chronological order. This means that the person is inevitably put back in the traumatic situation, reliving it all over again. The risk of re-traumatization is therefore very high.

Repeating questions should be generally avoided, but if it must occur, then it needs to be explained why the questions are being repeated (e.g., to clarify things, rather than to get a different answer the second time around). If none of the methods listed above seem to work and there is still a lot of resistance to the interview from the affected person, for whatever reason, this needs to be recognized and the interview should be stopped to prevent any further damage.

Prolonged pressure to continue with an interview when it is obvious that it will not yield any results could lead to secondary victimization and re-traumatization of the person without any additional gain in terms of information collection.

Finally, in addition to all of the above, it is ideal to have a psychosocial expert (e.g., psychologist, social worker, or counsellor) present at the interview to monitor the person's condition and perform crisis intervention, if necessary. This is not always possible for various reasons, mostly logistical, but it is very helpful if a psychosocial expert can advise the interviewers prior to deployment on what kind of questions to ask, how to best approach the interviewee, what special considerations to be mindful of, etc. Certainly, a general training or awareness-raising about the psychosocial aspects of interviewing is beneficial for the interviewers and important for the sake of the interviewees.

The Office of the Prosecutor of the International Criminal Court has embedded in their standard operating procedures the practice of having a psychosocial expert accompanying investigative teams when interviewing vulnerable witnesses, initially to determine if the person about to be interviewed is fit enough to go through the hardship of the interview. This is determined through the so-called "pre-interview psychosocial assessment" that is conducted prior to the actual interview. Once it is determined that the interview can take place, the psychosocial expert continues to be present throughout the interview to monitor the person's well-being and provide psychological assistance in cases of crisis. In addition to this, the investigators of the Office of the Prosecutor have been trained in the psychosocial aspects of interviewing, dealing with traumatized victims in general and victims of sexual and gender-based crimes and children in particular. Various internal protocols and guidelines related to this area are also in place to assure that vulnerable witnesses do not suffer any additional harm in the interview process.

For instance, Regulation 36(3) of the Regulations of the Office stipulates the following:

> The physical and psychological well-being of persons who are questioned by the Office and are considered vulnerable (in particular children, persons with disabilities and victims of gender and sexual crimes) shall be assessed by a psychology, psychosocial or other expert during a face-to-face interview prior to questioning. This assessment shall determine whether the person's condition at that particular time allows him or her to be questioned without risk of re-traumatisation. (International Criminal Court, 2009, p. 20)

Special Considerations for Interviews with Family Members of Victims of Enforced Disappearance

The main challenge that arises in interviews with families of victims of forced disappearance is to maintain the balance between the right of the family to know the truth about what happened to the missing family member and the obligation to do no harm to the families in the process of revealing the truth. If the purpose of the interview is to collect antemortem data that would help identify the bodies (e.g., detailed descriptions of clothing, physical characteristics, personal effects before disappearance), the decision has to be made as to whether or not the family should be made aware of the actual purpose of the data collection (that is, to compare with found unidentified human remains). Whatever decision is being made, the interviewers must feel comfortable with it.

This can be very challenging, especially when the interviewers are coming from the affected community, as was the case for an Antemortem Database Project conducted by Physicians for Human Rights in July 1997 in Bosnia related to mass graves in and around Srebrenica:

> In a focus group, Bosnian interviewers admitted that they had been afraid to fully explain the purpose of the data collection for fear of destroying the only hope that sustained Srebrenica survivors, most of whom were living in the bleakest of circumstances. Even uttering the words "identification of bodies," the interviewers worried, could ruin the fragile foundation upon which families relied for their psychological survival. The interviewers—all of whom had been affected by the recent war—wished to protect the families, and themselves, from confronting a terrible reality. As one interviewer put it, "we did not wish to be the 'messengers of doom.'"
> (Keough, Kahn, & Andrejevic, 2002, p. 73)

Furthermore, if the purpose of the interview is to disclose the circumstances of a missing person's death, special care should be taken as to how to reveal the truth. Unfortunately, circumstances are often far from ideal, and for a variety of economic and political reasons it is not possible to provide adequate assistance. Ideally, the family situation and the cultural, religious, and social context will be carefully assessed before delivering information about a death. Families should be given all information about the death of their relative. The best way is to provide as many concrete details as possible (Keough, Kahn, & Andrejevic, 2002). It should be carefully considered who should give the information, for instance, an official who has been trained for this task, such as a counsellor. The most appropriate way would be to provide the information at a place where the family feels secure, giving them time and space to react.

Self-Care for Practitioners

Who Is at Risk?

All practitioners working with victims and their families are at risk of being personally affected by the process, regardless of age, gender, experience, exposure, or other factors. There are many kinds of humanitarian agencies and many kinds of humanitarian work. Each particular context creates a particular set of sources of stress, and the risks to individual staff and the resources they use can also vary. Yet a broad range of research suggests that staff in all of these situations face common challenges.

Approximately 30 percent of the international staff of five humanitarian aid and development agencies surveyed after their return from their assignments reported significant symptoms of PTSD. High levels of burnout and distress among national and international aid staff working in Darfur and high levels of PTSD symptoms and burnout among Guatemalan aid workers have been documented. Another study found that about half of national and international staff working in Darfur reported a high level of physical and emotional stress. Fifteen percent of both national and international aid workers surveyed in Kosovo in 2000 reported high levels of depression, and 10–15 percent reported high levels of anxiety. More than 15 percent of expatriate workers also reported drinking alcohol at a dangerous level (Antares Foundation, 2012).

Notwithstanding the coping mechanisms that every individual develops and uses over time and the natural progression of resistance and resilience that comes with it, one is still at risk of being affected by their work. The combination of the constants, such as personality and personal history combined with variables such as current life circumstances, is indicative of vulnerability towards the damaging effects of work.

Burnout and Work-Related Stress

Very often burnout and work-related stress get confused, but in order to understand them better we need to take a look at the major differences between them. Stress, by and large, involves *too much:* too many pressures that demand too much of you physically and psychologically. Burnout, on the other hand, is about *not enough.* Being burned out means feeling empty, devoid of motivation, and beyond caring. People experiencing burnout often do not see any hope of positive change in their situations.

Stress is characterized by over-engagement and overreactive emotions; it produces urgency and hyperactivity, leads to loss of energy, and at times can evolve into anxiety disorders. Stress may also kill a person prematurely because of the very strong physical reaction to it (e.g., heart attack). Burnout, however, is characterized by disengagement, blunted emotions, and loss of motivation and hope, which can lead to feelings of detachment and depression, making the primary damage emotional. Looking at the characteristics of both conditions, it becomes obvious that work-related stress, if not managed in an appropriate and timely way, could eventually evolve into burnout.

Causes of burnout are not only to be found in the working environment, but also in individual lifestyles and personality traits. Work environments that restrict worker freedom or flexibility, that de-emphasize planning and efficiency for the task at hand, that lack recognition or rewards for good work, that have unclear or demanding job expectations, or that are chaotic, unstable, or high pressure all elevate the risks of developing burnout. A lifestyle consisting of too much work without finding the time to relax and socialize, trying to be too many things to too many people, taking on too many responsibilities, and not allowing others to help can be very damaging in the long run. Finally, in addition to unhealthy work environments and lifestyles, personality types that are rigid and resist change, that do not adapt to changing circumstances, and that have a rather optimistic view of life are also more prone to burnout.

For professionals investigating serious international crimes (such as enforced disappearance), where the nature of the job is to work in different parts of the world for long periods of time far away from friends and family, it is even more difficult to maintain the balance between work and private life. Even when one takes the time to socialize with loved ones, it is very often quite difficult to share work experiences, since they cannot relate to the subject and therefore only disappointment and tension is created in place of understanding and relief.

Burnout is a gradual process that occurs over an extended period of time. The signs and symptoms of burnout are subtle at first, but they get worse with time. On a physical level, warning signs and symptoms manifest through feeling tired and drained most of the time, lowered immunity, frequent headaches, back pain, muscle aches as well as change in appetite or sleeping habits. On an emotional level one can experience sense of failure and self-doubt, feeling helpless, trapped, and defeated. On a more general level loss of motivation, increasingly cynical and negative outlook, and decreased satisfaction and sense of accomplishment can also be experienced.

The physical and emotional symptoms are experienced on the inside, but there are also signs and symptoms of burnout on a behavioural level that are visible to others. Withdrawing from responsibilities, isolating oneself from others, and excessively using food, alcohol, or drugs to cope with problems are just some examples of such symptoms.

Secondary Traumatization

In addition to very common and more general risks of burnout and work-related stress, practitioners working with individual victims, families, and communities in the context of exhumations are also facing a specific risk of secondary traumatization. Repeated exposure to stories of loss, suffering, and pain over a long period of time can result in secondary traumatization. The source of trauma in this case is not personal, but acquired from another person who was personally affected. Nevertheless, the feeling is the same as if it had been experienced personally.

Such feeling and inability to distance oneself from somebody else's traumatic experience goes back to empathy and commitment being two fundamental emotional parts of this kind of work. As much as both are useful in terms of building trust and staying committed to the work even under very difficult circumstances, they can also put practitioners at risk and increase their vulnerability.

Just like burnout, secondary traumatization takes time to develop and is therefore very difficult to recognize and manage properly in time. Most of the symptoms are also very similar to those of burnout, and this is because both conditions are overwhelming and absorb the whole person. Different to burnout, though, is the source of symptoms, which in this case is very specific and comes down to prolonged and severe exposure to a number of traumatic stories. Many symptoms are also "taken over" from the traumatized individuals or groups that practitioners are dealing with, such as nightmares, flashbacks (involuntary images of traumatic events), pains and aches related to assaulted or injured parts of their bodies, feelings of emotional numbness, and an inability to talk about it with others. Again, similar to burnout, risks for developing secondary traumatization are multiple and they can be found both on a personal and situational level.

What Can Be Done to Prevent Burnout and Secondary Traumatization?

First of all, it is essential to regularly perform self-awareness checks and detect any significant changes or challenges one is facing at the time. Furthermore, being aware of ever-changing vulnerability towards the negative effects of work and acknowledging and recognizing current vulnerabilities to readjust ways of approaching work is very helpful.

In addition, it is not enough to only establish and maintain the balance between work and private life by taking time for family, friends, and loved ones, engaging in relaxing and personally fulfilling activities outside of work, and trying to keep work at work. One should also try to maintain balance at work in order to preserve energy for private life, and to be more efficient and less distracted during working hours. This means balancing between difficult and less difficult tasks, making sure that breaks are also part of the day, changing working routines to increase flexibility, etc.

In times of crisis and extraordinary pressure to accomplish certain tasks at work, it is inevitable to be out of balance and to use one's entire personal and professional capacity to overcome the crisis. However, once the crisis is over it is essential to re-establish the baseline, recuperate, and only then move on to new tasks. This might often seem impossible to achieve, but nevertheless needs to be aspired to, if even for a very short period of time.

Everyone knows best what works for them when it comes to coping with stress in general, but at times when it is evident that these particular strategies are not very effective, one should try to change their usual tactics and adjust to the challenge. This ability to adapt to changes as opposed to wasting energy and resources keeping up a routine is one of the key ways to manage stress well, and prevent burnout and secondary traumatization, among other things. Seeking professional help and support in times of high pressure and increased vulnerability is a must, and it should be seen as a sign of being responsible and professional, rather than weakness or inability to perform. Finally, one of the realities of working with victims is that the time comes when one needs to decide if it still makes sense to continue with this kind of work, by recognizing personal and professional limits, putting them into perspective, and deciding on the mutual benefit to oneself and respective beneficiaries.

Conclusion

The psychosocial aspects of interviewing vulnerable individuals, especially in the context of missing persons, are complex, both on the side of the interviewer and the interviewee. It takes a lot of personal and professional effort to succeed in this process and, at times, no matter how strong the motivation is from both sides, the interview might not yield the best results. Therefore, managing expectations on both sides from the very beginning by acknowledging the hardship of the process, by having mutual respect for each other's efforts, and by recognizing one's own limits should be the basis of every such interview.

Equally important is the awareness about the vulnerabilities and risks of the interviewers. Self-care and self-compassion should therefore be seen as signs of professionalism and responsibility towards the interviewers themselves, but also for the interviewees, protecting both sides from additional harm in an already difficult and challenging situation.

References

Antares Foundation. (2012). Managing stress in humanitarian workers: Guidelines for good practice (3rd ed.). Amsterdam, The Netherlands: Author.

Barakovic, D., Avdibegovic, E., & Sinanovic, O. (2014). Posttraumatic stress disorder in women with war missing family members. *Psychiatria Danubina, 26*(4), 340–346.

Blaauw, M., & Lahteenmaki, V. (2002). "Denial and silence" or "acknowledgement and disclosure." *IRRC, 84*(848), 767–782.

Boss, P. (2010). The trauma and complicated grief of ambiguous loss. *Pastoral Psychology, 59*(2), 137–145.

International Criminal Court. (2009). *Regulations of the Office of the Prosecutor ICC-BD/05-01-09.* Retrieved from www.icc-cpi.int/NR/rdonlyres/FFF97111-ECD6-40B5-9CDA-792BCBE1E695/280253/ECCBD050109ENG.pdf.

Keough, M. E., Kahn, S., & Andrejevic, A. (2002). Disclosing the truth: Informed participation in the antemortem database project for survivors of Srebrenica. *Health and Human Rights, 5*(1), 68–87.

Luster, T., Qin, D., Bates, L., Johnson, D., & Rana, M. (2009). The *Lost Boys* of Sudan: Coping with ambiguous loss and separation from parents. *American Journal of Orthopsychiatry, 79*(2), 203–211.

Myers, C. E. (2006). Memory loss and the brain. Retrieved from www.memorylossonline.com/glossary/flashbulbmemory.html.

Schaal, S., Elbert, T., & Neuner, F. (2009). Prolonged grief disorder and depression in widows due to the Rwandan genocide. *Omega (Westport), 59*(3), 203–219.

Related Sources

Antares Foundation: www.antaresfoundation.org

Headington Institute: www.headington-institute.org

Stress Management, Psych Central: psychcentral.com/stress

Chapter 9

A Review of Research into the Spatial Behaviour of Murderers and Implications for Investigations Involving Missing Murder Victims

Samantha Lundrigan (Anglia Ruskin University)

Introduction

When a person is reported as missing, investigators are faced with the immediate task of determining whether that person is likely to have come to harm, and in particular if they have become a victim of homicide (Newiss, 2004). Thankfully, the majority of missing persons are found or return of their own accord soon after being reported missing (Abrahams & Mungal, 1992; Newiss, 1999; Tarling & Burrows, 2004; Wade et al., 1998). However, while most missing persons return and most murder victims are found before they are missed, there are those cases where a person is missing because they have become the victim of murder. In cases where it is suspected or known that a missing person has become a victim of murder, one investigative focus is on locating the victim and recovering the body (Keppel & Weis, 1993). Locating a victim's body is vital as a source of evidence for investigators. For example, Keppel and Weis (1993) found a dramatic drop in the percentage of murder cases that were solved when information about the body recovery location was unknown (from 74 percent to 8 percent). The recovery of a victim's body can also offer a degree of closure to a victim's family (Hakkanen, Hurme, & Liukkonen, 2007).

In most murder cases the body recovery location is typically the first scene known to the police (Van Patten & Delhauer, 2007). By contrast, in cases involving a missing victim, investigators will often have no information available other than where the victim was last seen or known to be. At best, there may also be suspected locations and/or a murder scene. In the absence of a victim's body, the challenge faced by investigators is how to utilize known locational information in order to systematically prioritize geographical areas to search for a victim's body. Empirically, then, an important question is whether an unknown victim disposal location can be estimated on the basis of information relating to the victim's and, if known, the suspect's spatial knowledge and mobility patterns?

Unfortunately, despite the obvious relevance of this question to those searching for missing persons and conducting murder investigations, there has been little comprehensive examination of spatial patterns and characteristics associated with murder investigations involving missing victims. However, within the fields of environmental criminology, environmental psychology, and geographic profiling, there is a significant body of research that examines criminal spatial decision-making more generally and spatial patterns of murder more specifically that may have practical implications for this particular subset of murder. Therefore, the aim of this chapter is to review the theoretical and empirical research related to distance patterns and disposal characteristics of murder and the extent to which it may be utilized to improve body search-and-recovery methods in missing murder victim investigations.

The chapter is divided into five parts. The first part addresses previous attempts to quantify and characterize the issue of missing victims of murder. Part two examines the locational components and considerations involved in the commission of a murder. In part three, the main theoretical approaches put forward to account for offender spatial behaviour are discussed with particular attention given to how they help explain the decision-making process of murderers. Part four provides an overview of the empirical research in two relevant areas: disposal site distance patterns and characteristics of disposal sites. Finally, part five explores developments in the field of geographic profiling and considers the investigative implications of previous research to the search for a missing murder victim.

The Murdered Missing

A number of studies have attempted to calculate the proportion of missing person reports that end in homicide. In a UK study, Newiss (1999) suggested that 0.3 percent of missing person reports end in a fatal outcome, although this study did not distinguish between suicides, accidents, and homicides. In another analysis of missing person cases in the state of Washington, 20 percent of missing persons were estimated to be victims of homicide with at least 15 percent of these suspected serial murder victims (Olsen & Kamb, 2003). In another North American study, Quinet (2007) estimated that 20,000 of 100,000 missing persons in the US may be homicide victims yet to be found, with as many as 3,000 of those being serial murder victims. Newiss (2004) examined a sample of 98 UK homicide cases between 1990 and 1998 that first came to the attention of the police as missing person reports. From analysis of these cases, Newiss (2004) calculated that the average risk of a missing person report resulting in a homicide was 1:7,400. He also found that risk varied considerably according to the age and gender profile of the missing person. In relation to age, adults aged 19 to 24 years were at the highest risk of a missing person report resulting in a homicide (1:1,600), followed by 25–29 year olds (1:1,900) and children aged 5–9 (1:2,200). By contrast, children aged 10–13 and 14–18 had a significantly lower than average risk (1:13,900 and 1:24,100, respectively). In relation to gender, Newiss (2004) found that females had an overall risk of 1:4,600 of a missing person report resulting in homicide, compared to a risk of 1:13,600 for males, and that females accounted for more homicide victims in every age group. Interestingly, this is contrary to the general homicide profile, where males are disproportionately more likely to become victims (Polk, 1999). Newiss (2006) examined the risk of a cancelled missing person report resulting in a fatal outcome using data on almost 33,000 missing person cases provided by the Metropolitan Police Missing Persons Bureau, London, UK. Combining the findings of this analysis with the Newiss (2004) study, he concluded that female missing persons found dead faced a much higher risk of being victims of homicide than males. Specifically, one in four missing persons found dead aged between 14 and 24 were likely to have been the victim of homicide, and one in three aged between 25 and 29 (Newiss, 2006).

One further source of information on the extent of this issue comes from a consideration of the number of cases where an offender is tried for murder without a victim's body having been recovered. While there is no formal source of recording of such cases, DiBiase (2014) calculated that there have been 408 trials involving "no body" cases in the US since the 1930s, which equates to roughly 5 cases per year. Of these, he found that 91 percent of cases involved male defendants, 58 percent of the victims were female, 16 percent were aged under 18 (mostly children of the defendant), and 54 percent were classified as domestic violence cases (DiBiase, 2014). In England and Wales, it is estimated that around two "no body" cases per year go to trial (Grice, 2013).

While useful, these studies are limited to analysis of those cases that have come to the attention of the authorities. Official statistics cannot take into account the "missing-missing," those individuals whose disappearances remain unreported either because no one is aware of them, or alternatively no one is concerned (Quinet, 2007; Smith et al., 2005). Foster children, the homeless, sex workers, and "thrownaways"—children who have been forced out by their parents—are thought to be overrepresented in the missing-missing statistics (Quinet, 2007). The missing-missing are argued to be at particular risk of predation by serial murderers, and some research suggests that the most successful serial murderers deliberately select the unmissed as victims (Hickey, 1991). Egger (2003) suggests that approximately 75 percent of female serial murder victims are sex workers, and Mott (1999) found that unsolved serial murders were significantly more likely to have targeted vulnerable populations such as sex workers, homeless people, or children in foster care.

Having reviewed attempts to quantify the problem of the murdered missing, the following section examines the locational characteristics and considerations involved in the crime of murder. Spatial behaviour is an intentional, goal-orientated aspect of an offender's *modus operandi* and it is important to understand the critical locational decision-making points involved in a murder before we can begin to account for the processes underlying these decisions.

The Locational Logistics of Murder

There are a number of potential sites associated with a murder. Rossmo (2000) categorizes these as: the encounter site, where the offender first encounters and targets the victim; the attack site, where the first instance of criminal assault takes place; the murder site, where the victim is murdered; and finally, the disposal site, the location where the victim's body is left. All four sites can occupy the same physical space, can be separated in time and space, or can exist in any number of combinations. The specific pattern produced in a murder event can offer insight not only to the spatial decision-making of an offender but also his psychological state (Van Patten & Delhauer, 2007). When an offender encounters a victim he will make one of two spatial choices: the offender will either carry out the murder at the point of encounter, or the victim will be abducted or coerced and taken to a different location. This decision will be influenced by environmental conditions external to the offender's control, such as the presence or absence of witnesses, as well as by individual characteristics of the murderer and style of murder (Lundrigan & Canter, 2001).

Once the murder has taken place, the offender will make a decision to either leave the body as it is, conceal it in some way, or move it to another location altogether. It logically follows that the greater the efforts of an offender to conceal a victim's body, the less likely it will be discovered, and the more likely the victim will first come to the attention of authorities as a missing person. Therefore, it is useful to consider the factors that may influence an offender's decision-making at this point in the murder process. Furthermore, past research has demonstrated that of all the locations associated with a murder, the location where an offender disposes of a victim's body may be particularly helpful in understanding the offender's spatial decision-making, as it is the site where arguably the offender has the most locational control (Ressler & Shachtman, 1992; Rossmo, 2000). For example, the choice of encounter site may be influenced by the location of the victim, while the murder site may be influenced by the difficulty of constraining or transporting a live victim. Once a victim has been murdered, these constraints are no longer factors. However, an offender's decision of where to leave a victim's body may be influenced by a number of other factors, including practical considerations, their relationship with the victim, and the characteristics of the murder location.

One of the most obvious factors relates to the practicalities of the task. Put simply, the decision to move a body, as well as how far to move it, are likely to be influenced by practical considerations such as the resources available to an offender. A murderer moving a dead victim is subject to time, distance, and effort constraints, as well as a heightened level of risk. It takes time and effort to move a body any significant distance. For example, without access to a vehicle an offender is limited in how far they can transport a body (Snook, Cullen, et al., 2005). Furthermore, this is arguably the crime trip where, by being in possession of a dead body, the offender is at most risk of detection were they to be seen or stopped by police (Lundrigan & Canter, 2001; Rossmo, 2000). These practical considerations may mean that an offender will only move a victim's body if the potential benefits outweigh these considerations, or there is no choice and moving or concealing the body is in some way a necessity (e.g., the murder took place in the offender's home).

The type of murder location is also likely to influence an offender's decision regarding how to dispose of a victim's body. In particular, the extent to which an offender can be connected to a location may influence spatial decisions at this point. Murder can take place in a domain connected to the offender and/ or the victim, or can occur in a public place unconnected to either. It is logical to expect that the more connected an offender is with a murder location, the greater the motivation might be to move or conceal a victim's body. Another factor may be the relationship between the victim and offender (i.e., stranger or known relationship). For example, some research suggests that if an offender knows a victim this acts as a motivation to move and/or hide the body (Santtila et al., 2003). Other studies, however, have demonstrated that offenders who know their victims are more likely to leave the body at the crime scene (Hakkanen & Laajasalo, 2006; Salfati, 2003). These different findings may, in part, relate to the type of murder location involved.

In order to explore this further, Table 9.1 illustrates a range of possible murder scenarios varying according to victim-offender relationship and murder location type. Associated with each relationship/murder location scenario are hypothetical disposal decisions. These are based on a consideration of potential risks (in terms of apprehension and/or witnesses) and potential rewards (e.g., delayed discovery, destroying forensic evidence). As Table 9.1 shows, where there is no victim-offender relationship (i.e., they are strangers) and no offender-location connection (i.e., the murder takes place in the victim's domain or a public place), there may be less motivation to risk moving a victim's body to a separate disposal location. However, if a murder takes place in an offender's home, then the location immediately connects the offender to the crime and so either concealing or moving the body will be worth the risks involved.

Similarly, in those cases where there is a known relationship between offender and victim and the murder location, concealing or moving a victim's body may become more likely because of the connection between them. The offender may be more prepared to take the risk of moving or concealing the body in order to prevent detection for as long as possible.

TABLE 9.1   Hypothetical disposal decisions according to victim-offender relationship and murder location type

Relationship to victim	Murder location	Hypothetical disposal decision		
		In situ at murder scene	Conceal at murder scene	Separate disposal location
Stranger	Offender domain			
	Victim domain			
	Public place			
Known	Offender domain			
	Victim domain			
	Offender-victim domain			
	Public place			

In both the stranger and known-relationship scenarios, if the murder takes place in a public location, an offender's decision is likely to be influenced more by the characteristics of the public place (i.e., opportunity and risk) and how determined the offender is to delay discovery (i.e., the potential "reward"). For example, if a murder takes place in an isolated woodland, the risks involved in moving a body are low, but so too are the chances of a body being discovered quickly. By contrast, if a murder takes place in a city park, the risks associated with moving a victim's body are high, but so too are the chances of a body being discovered quickly. In reality, of course, the actual decision an offender makes in these types of scenario is likely to be further influenced by a range of factors including the style of offence (e.g., expressive [intended to communicate something] versus instrumental [intended to accomplish something]), the characteristics of the offender (e.g., mental illness or drug intoxication), and the resources available to him (e.g., access to a vehicle).

In addition to resources, relationship, and murder location type, two further factors have been found to influence the decision of where to dispose of a victim's body. The first relates to offender criminal experience—whether an offence is part of a series or not (Fox & Levin, 1994; Rossmo, 2000). Kraemer, Lord, and Heilbrun (2004) found that single homicide offenders were more likely to have the same site for initial contact, murder, and disposal, while serial offenders were more likely to use many different locations and dispose of their victims' bodies in remote locations. Another factor relates to the age of the victim. Hanfland, Keppel, and Weis (1997) found that child abduction killers were more likely to conceal victims' bodies than murderers in general, and were more likely to deliberately select separate disposal sites. Similarly, Beauregard et al. (2008) found that older victims were more likely to be left at the crime scene, while children were more likely to be transported to a different disposal location. They suggest that this may partly be due to younger victims being both more readily transportable and easier to hide.

This section has explored the logistics of murder from a locational perspective. It has also demonstrated that the circumstances of murder may influence the extent to which a victim is either concealed or moved, and begins to hypothesize about the relationship between type of murder, murder location, and disposal characteristics. It also begins to consider the types of cases that may be more likely to involve a missing murder victim. Murderers vary considerably in their disposal patterns, and those patterns depend on a complex interaction between offender, victim, and environment. The next section explores the underlying psychological processes that are thought to influence the spatial choices an offender makes during the commission of a murder, as well as the theoretical approaches that have been put forward to account for how offenders go about deciding where and when to offend.

Theoretical Approaches

A number of theoretical perspectives have been put forward to account for an offender's spatial decision-making and patterns in behaviour. These are discussed below in relation to disposal site location choice in murder.

Environmental Criminology

Environmental criminology is defined as "the scientific study of spatial patterns in crime, the perceptions and awareness spaces of potential criminals, criminal mobility patterns, and the process of target selection and decision to commit the crime" (Brantingham & Brantingham, 1981, p. 7). The theory's primary concern is with the "where and when" of the criminal event. Originating from this field of study are three theoretical approaches that are of particular relevance to understanding the spatial behaviour of offenders: routine activity theory (Cohen & Felson, 1979), crime pattern theory (Brantingham & Brantingham, 1981), and rational choice theory (Cornish & Clarke, 1986). They overlap in terms of the importance they place on the role that opportunity and familiarity play in influencing the space and time of individual criminal events (Rossmo, 2000).

Routine Activity Theory

The central proposition of routine activity theory is "the probability that a violation will occur at any specific time and place might be taken as a function of the convergence of likely offenders and suitable targets in the absence of capable guardians" (Cohen & Felson, 1979, p. 590). In other words, for a direct contact predatory offence to occur, the paths of an offender and a victim need to intersect in time and space within an environment where there are no witnesses to prevent or interrupt a criminal event (Cohen & Felson, 1979; Felson, 1992). The approach emphasizes the important overlap between the activities of offenders and victims in determining where offences take place, with crimes being viewed as opportunities taken within the awareness space—the network of places that are familiar to a person's day-to-day life (Felson, 2001). While this approach has traditionally been put forward to explain the target or victim selection stage of an offence, it can equally be applied to the body disposal stage of a murder. The focus moves from the discovery of opportunities in the form of victims and targets during non-criminal activities to suitable locations for disposing of a victim's body.

Crime Pattern Theory

Developed by Brantingham and Brantingham (1981), crime pattern theory sets out a series of propositions to explain the geographic patterns of an individual offender's criminal behaviour. In essence, they propose that offenders (like non-offenders) typically operate within an activity space, a geographical area around the home that includes a network of paths and places that are habitually used and with which they build up knowledge and familiarity over time. They propose that as offenders go about their non-criminal behaviour they will become aware of suitable opportunities and environments for criminal exploitation and it is this familiarity that shapes the locations of their criminal activity.

The theory proposed by Brantingham and Brantingham (1981) follows a distance decay function, in other words, the reduction of activity or interaction as distance from the home increases. Most offences occur close to home, with the likelihood of an offence taking place in a particular location decreasing with distance from home. There are two main explanations for this. Firstly, there are the costs of time, money, and effort in overcoming distance and if any of these factors are constrained, then close locations will have inherent advantages over distant ones. Secondly, the concentration of activity around the home is also influenced by biased information flows. In other words, more information will be available about locations close to the home base and therefore offenders are more likely to be aware of criminal opportunities in such areas.

In relation to criminal opportunities within activity spaces, Brantingham and Brantingham point out that potential targets and victims are not distributed uniformly in space, and neither are potential criminals. It is the interaction of an activity space of a motivated offender with the activity space of a potential victim that produces individual patterns of crime. Although the Brantinghams discuss the concepts of activity spaces in relation to victim selection, the same processes are just as applicable to other spatial decisions in a murder. So, just as an offender will become aware of potential victims within his activity space, so too will he become aware of suitable places for disposing of a victim's body. One important implication of crime pattern theory is the prediction of relatively short distances travelled to commit crime, bounded by the parameters of an offender's routine and familiar activity space.

While Brantingham and Brantingham (1981) proposed that offenders have the advantage of more detailed and complete knowledge about potential crime opportunities close to their home base, they also argued that a potential disadvantage to those locations would be an increased risk of recognition. Because of this, Brantingham and Brantingham proposed that there would be an area directly around the home base where little criminal activity would occur. Hodge (1998) found evidence for the existence of such a buffer zone in her study of serial murderers. She found that British serial murderers left an average minimum distance of 0.53 km between home base and disposal sites and US murderers left an average minimum distance of 3.44 km. Of course, the concept of a buffer zone does not apply to offenders who dispose of bodies in the victim's own home, although it may still apply to other locational decisions in a murder event (e.g., point of first encounter).

Rational Choice Theory

Rational choice proposes that offenders seek to benefit themselves by their criminal behaviour, making decisions and choices that exhibit a trade-off between increased opportunity and greater reward the further an offender travels from home with the costs of time, effort, and risk (Cornish & Clark, 1986). The benefits of a criminal action are the net rewards of crime and include not only material gains but also intangible benefits such as emotional satisfaction. The risks or costs of crime are those associated with formal punishment should the offender be apprehended. A murderer may place a great distance between his home and the place where he disposes of a victim's body, in order to distance himself from the offence or to reach a particular location with which he associates some emotional satisfaction (the benefit), but the risk of apprehension may increase the further he travels (the cost).

In relation to body disposal location choice, routine activity and crime pattern theory suggest that an offender's activity space would play a pivotal role in determining how far an offender would travel. The rational choice perspective places the focus on the decision-making related to the qualities of the disposal site itself, such as risk of apprehension, discovery, etc. However, these decisions would be made within the parameters of familiar environments with resulting spatial patterns that reflect the inherent logic of the choices that underlie their predatory activities.

Environmental Psychology

The environmental criminological perspectives discussed above parallel broader developments in the field of environmental psychology. This examination of how people make sense of and relate to their surroundings led to the development of the concept of "mental maps," those internal representations of the world that we all use to find our way around and make decisions about what we will do and where (Trowbridge, 1913). Like crime pattern theory, this psychological idea provides an explanation for the limitations on the geographical mobility of offenders, as well as most other people, by suggesting that it is limited mental maps that structure their activities (Canter & Hodge, 2000). From this perspective, the journey to crime is seen as an expression of a complex interaction between the offender (e.g., in terms of his background characteristics, predispositions, knowledge, and perceptions) and his location and type of target (e.g., in terms of his perceived risks, rewards, opportunities, and attractions) (Canter, 1989; Hodge, 1998).

Therefore, for investigative purposes, it may be hypothesized that the actual nature of the location selected may be indicative of the experiences of the offender. In support of this, there is substantial evidence that such offenders select disposal locations according to knowledge and familiarity of what is possible where. Nethery (2004), for example, found that 61 percent of Canadian child murderers had selected body disposal sites before committing the crime. Keppel (1997) found that the offenders had pre-selected disposal sites in the majority of sexual murders.

Each of the approaches outlined above emphasizes the local nature of spatial decision-making and leads to predictions of relatively short journey-to-crime distances in line with familiar spatial environments. Furthermore, each approach implies that offender spatial behaviour is logical, patterned, and predictable. The next section summarizes the empirical research that has been conducted to examine these possibilities.

Body Disposal Patterns in Murder

As previously stated, a relevant investigative question in relation to missing murder victims is whether the location of an unknown body disposal site can be estimated on the basis of locational information relating to either the victim or a suspect (if known). To date, the majority of empirical research in this area has examined offender residence to body recovery location, with less attention paid to the spatial relationships between other locations relevant to a murder investigation (e.g., victim residence, victim last seen site, murder site). Furthermore, most research has been conducted with serial murder samples. The horrific and brutal nature of the acts that such individuals carry out has led many researchers to suggest that they are a unique type of offender who have little in common with other types of criminals, and logical or rational behaviour is not a term typically associated with such offenders (Jenkins, 1993).

However, while serial murder is an extreme type of crime, it does not necessarily follow that spatial decision-making among serial murderers is not subject to the same underlying processes outlined above. For instance, someone whose motivation is a bizarre desire for sadistic sexual excitement is unlikely, in terms of motivation and murder actions, to share any similarities with other types of offender; however, the extreme nature of his motivation and murder actions will not necessarily be reflected in his spatial behaviour, and he will nevertheless be subject to both the external influences and internal conceptions of the larger environment, much like other offenders (Lundrigan & Canter, 2001). However, it needs to be understood that, as has been previously discussed, it may be that the serial nature of this type of murder influences the distance offenders are willing to travel to commit their crimes (Lundrigan & Canter, 2001).

Journey-to-Murder Studies

In support of the spatial familiarity hypothesis implicit in the theoretical approaches discussed, journey-to-murder studies demonstrate that typical offenders do not travel very far to offend. Table 9.2 summarizes selected journey-to-murder findings spanning the last 50 years. It is worth noting the range of different measurement methods used across these studies: in some only mean distances are reported, and in others, mean and median distances. The mean is particularly susceptible to outliers, and the inclusion of a few cases where offenders travel very long distances can be problematic. The median is a more appropriate statistic to use in research of this kind. In some studies, crime trips are expressed as a percentage occurring within different ranges of distance. These inconsistencies aside, the findings are broadly comparable and demonstrate a clear spatial bias towards an offender's home area. For example, Dern et al. (2004) showed that 58 percent of the serial sexual murders in Germany were committed within 5 km of the offender's residence, and all but one case

TABLE 9.2   Selected journey-to-murder research

Source	Crime	Location	Origin location	Destination location	Crime trip distance
Bullock (1955)	Homicide	Houston	Offender base	BRS*	40% < 1 block 57% < 0.4 miles (0.64 km) 74% < 2 miles (3.2 km)
Gabor & Gottheil (1984)	Homicide	Ottawa	Offender base	BRS	Mean = 0.54 miles (0.87 km)
Rand (1986)	Criminal homicide	Philadelphia	Offender base	BRS	53.1% within home census tract
Keppel & Weis (1994)	Single murder	Washington State	Victim last seen	BRS	76% < 200 feet (61 m)
Aitken et al. (1994)	Child sexual homicide	UK	Offender base	BRS	91.6% < 5 miles (8 km)
Godwin & Canter (1997)	Serial murder	US	Offender base	Encounter (location where perpetrator first encounters victim) BRS	Mean = 2 km Mean = 23 km
Hanfland, Keppel, & Weis (1997)	Child abduction murder	US	Victim's residence	BRS	37% cases < 2.4 km
Shaw (1998)	Sexual homicide	UK	Offender base	Encounter BRS	Mean = 2.4 miles (3.86 km) Mean = 2.2 miles (3.54 km)
Safarik, Jarvis, & Nussbaum (2000)	Sexual homicide elderly females	US	Victim's residence	BRS	56% within six blocks of victim's residence
Rossmo (2000)	Serial murder	US	Offender base	Encounter BRS	Mean = 22 km Mean = 34 km
Lundrigan & Canter (2001)	Serial murder	US	Offender base	BRS	Median = 15 km; mean = 40 km
		UK			Median = 9 km; mean = 18 km
Dern et al. (2004)	Serial murder	Germany	Offender base	BRS	58% < 5 km
Nethery (2004)	Homicide	Canada	Victim's residence	BRS	Mean: child victims = 10 km; adults = 30 km
Snook, Cullen, et al. (2005)	Serial murder	Germany	Offender base	BRS	63% < 10km, median = 6.5 km; mean = 30 km

Source	Crime	Location	Origin location	Destination location	Crime trip distance
Brown & Keppel (2007)	Child abduction murder	US	Victim last seen	BRS	46% < 1.5 miles (2.4 km)
Van Patten & Delhauer (2007)	Sexual homicide	US	Victim's residence	BRS	Median = 4.62 miles (7.4 km); mean = 56.92 miles (91.6 km)
			Offender base		Median = 2.43 miles (3.91 km); mean = 54.21 miles (87.24 km)
Santtila, Laukkanen, & Zappalá (2007)	Difficult to solve homicide	Finland	Offender base	BRS	Median = 0.85 km
Santtila et al. (2008)	Difficult to solve homicide	Italy	Offender base	BRS	Median = 0.98 km; mean = 15.98 km
Andresen, Frank, & Felson (2014)	Homicide	Canada	Offender base	BRS	Median = 0.66 km

*BRS = Body recovery site

were committed less than 20 km away from the offender's residence. Snook, Cullen, et al. (2005) showed that the median and average offender residence to body disposal site distances for German serial murderers were 6.5 and 30 km, respectively. Andresen, Frank, and Felson (2014) found that median distance travelled by homicide offenders in their Canadian sample was 0.66 km.

While most journey-to-murder studies examine offender residence to body recovery site distances, a small number of studies have examined distances between body recovery locations and other murder locations. Given that in a missing murder victim investigation, the only known locations will be related to the victim, examination of distance patterns from victim locations may be especially pertinent. Hakkanen, Hurme, and Liukkonen (2007) examined the relative distances between offender residence, victim residence, murder location, and disposal location in Finnish homicides. They found that the shortest median distance was victim residence to murder scene (3.1 km), followed by offender residence to murder scene (3.9 km), victim residence to offender residence (8.3 km), murder location to body recovery (12.9 km), and offender residence to body recovery (18.9 km). Interestingly, the longest median distance was from victim residence to body recovery site (19.8 km), although in 36 percent of cases the distance between the victim's residence and the body recovery site was less than 10 km. There was also a significant positive relationship between the distance from the victim's base to the recovery site and the offender's base to the recovery site. This study extends previous journey-to-murder research by considering the spatial relationships between a wider set of locations present in a murder and may be particularly helpful in cases where a body disposal site is unknown. Indeed, Hakkanen, Hurme, and Liukkonen suggest that their results may be of "high practical importance" (2007, p. 193) and have been utilized in a number of homicide cases in Finland. In order to fully appreciate the potential operational utility of such research, there is a need for it to be replicated in different geographical and cultural contexts.

In relation to distance patterns in cases involving child victims, Hanfland, Keppel, and Weis (1997) showed that the distance from the murder site to the body recovery site in child abduction murders in the US was less than 59 m in 72 percent of cases. Furthermore, in 37 percent of cases, the body was found less than 2.4 km from the victim's residence. Using Canadian data, Nethery (2004) showed that the average distance from a victim's residence to their body recovery site was shorter for child victims (about 10 km) than for adults (about 30 km), and the distance between the victim's and the offender's residence was, in 62 percent of the cases, shorter than 6 km.

Some studies have examined the relationship between journey-to-murder distances and other crime characteristics. Santtila, Laukkanen, and Zappalà (2007) examined the relationship between a range of crime behaviours and the distances travelled by offenders committing homicide. They found that longer distances between offender residence and body recovery were associated with those offences that took place indoors in urban areas, in the victim's home, and where the body was found at the scene of the murder. Shorter distances were associated with destroyed or hidden evidence and putting the body inside a bag. In these cases the murder scene was also sometimes the offender's home, and the murder investigation may have begun as a missing person report. Santtila, Laukkanen, and Zappalà suggest that this type of offence is more likely to involve a victim known to an offender, making it important for him to try to conceal the body, especially when committed in an offender's residence.

Disposal Site Characteristics

While journey-to-murder studies may be of utility for informing search parameters for missing victims' bodies, there is another body of research describing common characteristics of recovery locations that may be of utility in informing search strategies within a defined geographical area. As with the journey-to-murder literature, most studies examining disposal site characteristics have been conducted with serial murder, and so may be particularly relevant to investigations involving suspected serial offenders. Furthermore, such studies do not routinely distinguish between those murders where there was no attempt to conceal a victim's body (and hence no missing body) and those murders that began as missing person reports. Of interest here, of course, are common patterns and characteristics in those murders where there has been some attempt to conceal a body.

A number of studies have examined in detail the characteristics of the environments where victims' bodies are found. In a study of US serial murders, Rossmo (2000) found that 21 percent of offenders selected woods, 20 percent rivers, lakes, or marshes, 17 percent a victim's residence, and 16 percent a street. James's study (1991) on serial sexual murders in the US showed that 21 percent of the bodies were recovered in water. In a descriptive study of sexual homicide in Canada, Beauregard and Martineau (2012) found that 61 percent of offenders disposed of their victims' bodies outdoors and 10 percent in a watery location. Hakkanen, Hurme, and Liukkonen (2007) examined rural area homicides in Finland and found that 73 percent of victims were found in woods and 26 percent in water.

In studies of child victims, Nethery (2004) found that 38 percent of the bodies of abducted children were found in a forested area and most of these were either buried or covered up with twigs and branches. A further 14 percent were discovered beside a side road or path, 12 percent in water, and 10 percent on farmland. Burton (1998) showed that 20 percent of the bodies of child abduction homicide victims in the UK were recovered in water and 12 percent of the bodies of child victims had been buried. In a more recent study, Beauregard et al. (2008) compared crime characteristics of sexual murders of children with sexual murders of adult women in Canada. They found that in cases involving children 90 percent of the victims' bodies were hidden, compared to 35 percent for adult female cases.

What this research suggests is that, certainly for serial sexual murder, offenders will often select remote, rural environments to dispose of their victims' bodies. This may be motivated by a desire to delay discovery of the body and maximize the degrading of physical evidence. When a body is deliberately disposed of in these types of locations, research has identified patterns of movement that may be useful in searches in similar environments. For example, Keppel and Birnes (1997) found that a victim's body was unlikely to be carried more than 150 feet (46 m) from a murder site to a disposal site or more than 150 feet from a vehicle. In an examination of child murder in the UK, Burton (1998) found that 88 percent of the victims were found within 43 m of the road used to dispose of the victim. The above discussion on the spatial behaviour of murderers has a number of practical and investigative implications that are discussed in the final section of this chapter.

Geographic Profiling and Investigative Implications

Possibly the most significant practical application to emerge out of the above literature is the development of geographic profiling, an investigative support technique that determines the most probable location of an offender's residence based on an analysis of the crime locations linked to that offender (Canter et al., 2000; Rossmo, 2000). Geographic profiling is most often employed in murder and stranger rape investigations where there is either a series linked to one offender or a single crime but with a number of related sites. The technique involves both an objective and a subjective element. The objective element involves the application of statistical and spatial analyses to the point pattern formed by the crime sites. In recent years a number of computerized systems have been developed to carry out this stage of analysis and include Rigel (Rossmo, 2000), Dragnet (Canter et al., 2000), and CrimeStat (Levine, 2010). This method allows investigators to prioritize those areas most likely to contain an offender's residence. The subjective element involves the reconstruction and interpretation of the offender's personal geography or mental map. Specifically, factors such as the hunting style of the offender, the density of potential victims, land use, distribution of roads, and physical and psychological boundaries are taken into account to help refine a profile once the quantitative prediction has been made (Rossmo, 2000).

Geographic profiling has proven helpful in investigations, prioritizing suspects through database searches (e.g., criminal records, vehicle registration), patrol saturation, stakeouts, and door-to-door enquiries (Beauregard & Field, 2008; Rossmo, 2000). The proven operational utility of geographic profiling means that it is now offered as a specialist investigative tool in a number of police forces around the world (Canter & Youngs, 2008; Canter et al., 2013; Rossmo, 2012). However, despite its widespread use, research assessing the predictive accuracy of geographic profiling systems is somewhat limited (Paulsen, 2006a). Past research has examined accuracy in a number of ways, including the predictive accuracy of single systems (e.g., Canter & Hammond, 2006, 2007; Levine, 2010; Paulsen, 2006b; Rossmo, 2000) or comparative accuracy of systems versus human judgment methods (e.g., Paulsen, 2006a; Snook, Canter, & Bennell, 2002; Snook,

Taylor, & Bennell, 2004; Snook, Zito, et al., 2005). However, it is difficult to draw conclusions regarding relative performance because no standardized measure of accuracy has been used across studies.

Of course, in the context of the search for a missing murder victim, the utility of such systems is unknown. However, the UK police have developed a similar technique that has been successfully used in searches for the body of a missing murdered person, although only when locational information for a suspect is available. Termed Geographic Search Analysis, the process involves the application of temporal and spatial analyses that are examined in parallel with intelligence relating to the suspect's known movements, background, and lifestyle (National Centre for Policing Excellence, 2006a). The results of this analysis are used to provide a prioritized list of probable body recovery locations that, in turn, informs the search strategy within an investigation.

The systems described above rest on the underlying assumption that there is a meaningful spatial relationship between an offender and the location at which he commits a crime. Given the evidence discussed in the present chapter, there is obvious potential for utilizing such systems to predict a possible search area where an offender may have disposed of a victim's body.

Conclusion

The aim of this chapter was to review the theoretical and empirical literature on offender decision-making and spatial patterns in murder and, in so doing, explore its potential utility in informing investigations tasked with finding missing murder victims. In cases of murder where there is no information regarding the whereabouts of a victim's body, investigators are presented with the significant challenge of trying to locate this vital source of evidence. However, as has been discussed, often the only known locational information relates to the victim and their movements prior to their disappearance. In the absence of locational information relating to possible suspects or a murder location, all the more focus is placed on understanding the lifestyle and routine activities of a victim in order to try to establish the reason for their death and the likely identity of the offender. It is argued here that central to this should be a consideration of the nature and characteristics of the geographical relationship between known victim locations and the locations related to the offender, i.e., the body disposal site and home location.

The recovery of the body of a victim of murder is essential not only for investigators in the pursuit of justice but also for a victim's family and their need to understand what happened to their loved one. The research presented in this chapter has demonstrated that the locations selected by an offender in the commission of a murder are not random, but instead are based on underlying rational decisions reflecting an individual's experience and knowledge of their environment, and are therefore of potential value in revealing spatial patterns and processes in murderers' decision-making. Of course, it needs to be remembered that past research on body disposal locations is based on those cases where a body is indeed recovered, and so samples are unavoidably biased in this way. It may be that patterns of disposal for unrecovered bodies differ.

The practical potential of such research lies in search area prioritization as well as environment evaluation within a search area for likely disposal locations. Policy on search management and procedures in murder investigations empha-sizes the need for an intelligence-led approach to the deployment of resources (National Centre for Policing Excellence, 2006b). Future research needs to move beyond the journey-to-murder statistic to a more holistic examination of the locations involved in a murder event. Spatial modelling of this kind may allow for inferences to be drawn regarding the locations at which key features of murders take place, but which are unknown to investigators. It is only through such an evidence-based approach that the type of research discussed here may have the potential to be of operational use.

References

Abrahams, C., & Mungal, R. (1992). *Young runaways: Exploding the myths.* London, UK: NCH Action for Children.

Aitken, C. G. G., Connolly, T., Gammerman, A., & Zhang, G. (1994). *Statistical analysis of the CATCHEM data.* Unpublished manuscript, Police Research Group. London, UK: Home Office.

Andresen, M. A., Frank, R., & Felson, M. (2014). Age and distance to crime. *Criminology and Criminal Justice, 14,* 314–333.

Beauregard, E., & Field, J. (2008). Body disposal patterns of sexual murderers: Implications for offender profiling. *Journal of Police and Criminal Psychology, 23,* 81–89.

Beauregard, E., & Martineau, M. (2012). A descriptive study of sexual homicide in Canada: Implications for police investigation. *International Journal of Offender Therapy and Comparative Criminology, 57*(12), 1454–1476.

Beauregard, E., Stone, M. R., Proulx, J., & Michaud, P. (2008). Sexual murderers of children: Developmental, pre-crime, crime, and post-crime factors. *International Journal of Offender Therapy and Comparative Criminology, 52*(3), 253–269.

Brantingham, P. L., & Brantingham, P. J. (1981). Notes on the geometry of crime. In P. J. Brantingham & P. L. Brantingham (eds.), *Environmental criminology* (pp. 27–54). Prospect Heights, IL: Waveland Press.

Brown, K. M., & Keppel, R. (2007). Child abduction murder: An analysis of the effect of time and distance separation between murder incident sites on solvability. *Journal of Forensic Science, 39*(2), 137–145.

Bullock, H. A. (1955). Urban homicide in theory and fact. *Journal of Criminal Law, Criminology and Police Science, 45,* 565–575.

Burton, C. (1998). *The CATCHEM database: Child murder in the United Kingdom.* Presentation at the International Homicide Investigators Association Symposium, July 5–12, Zutphen, The Netherlands.

Canter, D. (1989). Offender profiles. *The Psychologist, 2*(1), 12–16.

Canter, D., Coffey, T., Huntley, M., & Missen, C. (2000). Predicting serial killers' home base using a decision support system. *Journal of Quantitative Criminology, 16*(4), 457–478.

Canter, D., & Hammond, L. (2006). A comparison of the efficacy of different decay functions in geographical profiling for a sample of US serial killers. *Journal of Investigative Psychology and Offender Profiling, 3*(2), 91–103.

Canter, D., & Hammond, L. (2007). Prioritizing burglars: Comparing the effectiveness of geographical profiling methods. *Police Practice & Research, 8*(4), 371–384.

Canter, D., Hammond, L., Youngs, D., & Juszczak, P. (2013). The efficacy of ideographic models for geographical offender profiling. *Journal of Quantitative Criminology, 29*(3), 423–446.

Canter, D., & Hodge, S. (2000). Criminals' mental maps. In L. S. Turnbull, E. Hallisey Hendrix, & B. D. Dent (eds.), *Atlas of crime: Mapping the criminal landscape* (pp. 186–191). Phoenix, AZ: Oryx Press.

Canter, D. V., & Youngs, D. (eds.). (2008). *Applications of geographical offender profiling.* Hampshire, UK: Ashgate Publishing Ltd.

Cohen, L. E., & Felson, M. (1979). Social change and crime rate trends: A routine activity approach. *American Sociological Review, 44*(4), 588–608.

Cornish, D. B., & Clarke, R. V. (eds.). (1986). *The reasoning criminal: Rational choice perspectives on offending.* New York, NY: Springer-Verlag.

Dern, H., Froend, R., Straub, U., Vick, J., & Witt, R. (2004). *Geografisches Verhalten fremder Taeter bei sexuellen Gewaltdelikten* (Spatial behaviour of stranger perpetrators in sexually violent delinquency). Weisbaden, Germany: Bundeskriminalamt.

DiBiase, T. A. (2014). *No-body homicide cases: A practical guide to investigating, prosecuting and winning cases when the victim is missing.* Boca Raton, FL: CRC Press.

Egger, S. (2003). *The need to kill: Inside the world of the serial killer.* Upper Saddle River, NJ: Prentice Hall.

Felson, M. (1992). Routine activities and crime prevention: Armchair concepts and practical action. *Studies on Crime and Crime Prevention, 1,* 30–34.

Felson, M. (2001). The routine activity approach: A very versatile theory of crime. In R. Paternoster & R. Bachman (eds.), *Explaining criminals and crime: Essays in contemporary criminological theory* (pp. 43–46). Los Angeles, CA: Roxbury Publishing.

Fox, J. A., & Levin, J. (1994). *Overkill: Mass murder and serial killing exposed.* New York, NY: Columbia University Press.

Gabor, T., & Gottheil, E. (1984). Offender characteristics and spatial mobility: An empirical study and some policy implications. *Canadian Journal of Criminology, 23*(26), 267–281.

Godwin, M., & Canter, D. (1997). Encounter and death: The spatial behaviour of US serial killers. *Policing: International Journal of Police Strategy and Management, 20*(1), 24–38.

Grice, N. (2013, May 31). April Jones: Murder trials without a body. *The Independent.* Retrieved from www.bbc.co.uk/news/uk-wales-21506482.

Hakkanen, H., Hurme, K., & Liukkonen, M. (2007). Distance patterns and disposal sites in rural area homicides committed in Finland. *Journal of Investigative Psychology and Offender Profiling, 4*(3), 181–197.

Hakkanen, H., & Laajasalo, T. (2006). Homicide crime scene actions in a Finnish sample of mentally ill offenders. *Homicide Studies, 10*(1), 33–54.

Hanfland, K. A., Keppel, R. D., & Weis, J. G. (1997). *Case management for missing children homicide investigation.* Seattle, WA: Washington State Office of the Attorney General.

Hickey, E. W. (1991). *Serial murderers and their victims.* Pacific Grove, CA: Brooks/Cole.

Hodge, S. (1998). *Spatial patterns in serial murder: A conceptual model of disposal site location choice.* Unpublished doctoral dissertation, University of Liverpool.

James. E. (1991). *Catching serial killers.* Lansing, MI: International Forensic Services.

Jenkins, P. (1993). Chance or choice? The selection of serial murder victims. In A. V. Wilson (ed.), *Homicide: The victim/offender connection* (pp. 105–118). Cincinnati: Anderson Publishing Company.

Keppel, R. (1997). Signature murders: A report of several related cases. *Journal of Forensic Sciences, 40*(4), 670–674.

Keppel, R., & Birnes, W. J. (1997). *Signature killers.* New York, NY: Simon & Schuster.

Keppel, R., & Weis, J. (1994). Time and distance as solvability factors in murder cases. *Journal of Forensic Science, 39*(2), 386–401.

Kraemer, G. W., Lord, W. D., & Heilbrun, K. (2004). Comparing single and serial homicide offences. *Behavioral Sciences and the Law, 22*(3), 325–343.

Levine, N. (2010). *CrimeStat: A spatial statistics program for the analysis of crime incident locations (v 3.3).* Houston, TX, & Washington, DC: Ned Levine & Associates & the National Institute of Justice.

Lundrigan. S., & Canter, D. (2001). Spatial patterns of serial murder: An analysis of disposal site location choice. *Behavioural Science and the Law, 19*(4), 595–610.

Mott, N. (1999). Serial murder: Patterns in unsolved cases. *Homicide Studies, 3*(3), 241–255.

National Centre for Policing Excellence. (2006a). *Murder investigation manual.* Produced on behalf of the Association of Chief Police Officers (ACPO). Bedfordshire, UK: Centrex.

National Centre for Policing Excellence. (2006b). *Practice advice on search management and procedures.* Produced on behalf of the Association of Chief Police Officers (ACPO). Bedfordshire, UK: Centrex.

Nethery, K. (2004). Non-familial abductions that end in homicide: An analysis of the distance patterns and disposal site. Unpublished master of arts thesis, School of Criminology, Simon Fraser University.

Newiss, G. (1999). *Missing presumed...? The police response to missing persons.* Police Research Series Paper 114. London, UK: Home Office.

Newiss, G. (2004). Estimating the risk faced by missing persons: A study of homicide victims as an example of an outcome-based approach. *International Journal of Police Science & Management, 6*(1), 27–36.

Newiss, G. (2006). Understanding the risk of going missing: Estimating the risk of fatal outcomes in cancelled cases. *Policing: An International Journal of Police Strategies and Management, 29*(2), 246–260. doi: 10.1108/13639510610667655

Olsen, L., & Kamb, L. (2003, February 18). Missing persons are routinely ignored. *Seattle Post Intelligencer.* Retrieved from www.seattlepi.com/news/article/Part-2-Missing-person-cases-are-routinely-ignored-1107530.php.

Paulsen, D. (2006a). Human vs. machine: A comparison of the accuracy of geographic profiling methods. *Journal of Investigative Psychology and Offender Profiling, 3*(2), 77–89.

Paulsen, D. (2006b). Connecting the dots: Assessing the accuracy of geographic profiling software. *Policing: An International Journal of Police Strategies & Management, 29*(2), 306–334.

Polk. K. (1999). Males and honour contest violence. *Homicide Studies, 3*(1), 6–29.

Quinet, K. (2007). The missing missing: Toward a quantification of serial murder victimisation in the United States. *Homicide Studies, 11*(4), 319–339.

Rand, A. (1986). Mobility triangles. In R. M. Figlio, S. Hakim, & G. F. Rengert (eds.), *Metropolitan crime patterns* (pp. 117–126). Monsey, NY: Criminal Justice Press.

Ressler, R., & Shachtman, T. (1992). *Whoever fights monsters.* New York, NY: St Martin's Press.

Rossmo, D. K. (2000). *Geographic profiling.* Boca Raton, FL: CRC Press.

Rossmo, D. K. (2012). Recent developments in geographic profiling. *Policing, 6*(2), 144–150.

Safarik, M. E., Jarvis, J. P., & Nussbaum, K. E. (2000). Elderly female serial sexual homicide: A limited empirical test of criminal investigative analysis. *Homicide Studies, 4*(3), 294–307.

Salfati, C. G. (2003). Offender interaction with victims in homicide: A multidimensional analysis of frequencies in crime scene behaviors. *Journal of Interpersonal Violence, 18*(5), 490–512.

Santtila, P., Hakkanen, H., Canter, D., & Elfgren, T. (2003). Classifying homicide offenders and predicting their characteristics from crime scene behaviour. *Scandinavian Journal of Psychology, 44*(2), 107–118.

Santtila, P., Laukkanen, M., & Zappalà, A. (2007). Crime behaviours and distance travelled in homicides and rapes. *Journal of Investigative Psychology and Offender Profiling, 4*(1), 1–15.

Santtila, P., Laukkanen, M., Zappalà, A., & Bosco, D. (2008). Distance travelled and offence characteristics in homicide, rape, and robbery against business. *Legal and Criminological Psychology, 13*(2), 345–356.

Shaw, S. (1998). *Applying environmental psychology and criminology: The relationship between crime site locations within offences of murder.* Unpublished undergraduate thesis, University of Plymouth, England.

Smith, T. B., Buniak, K., Condon, L., & Reed, L. (2005). *Children missing from care: The law enforcement response.* National Center for Missing & Exploited Children. Retrieved from www.missingkids.com/en_US/publications/NC162.pdf.

Snook, B., Canter, D., & Bennell, C. (2002). Predicting the home location of serial offenders: A preliminary comparison of the accuracy of human judges with a geographic profiling system. *Behavioral Science and the Law, 20*(1–2), 109–118.

Snook, B., Cullen, R. M., Mokros, A., & Harbort, S. (2005). Serial murderers' spatial decisions: Factors that influence crime location choice. *Journal of Investigative Psychology and Offender Profiling, 2*(3), 147–164.

Snook, B., Taylor, P., & Bennell, C. (2004). Geographic profiling: The fast, frugal, and accurate way. *Applied Cognitive Psychology, 18*(1), 105–121.

Snook, B., Zito, M., Bennell, C., &. Taylor, P. (2005). On the complexity and accuracy of geographic profiling strategies. *Journal of Quantitative Criminology, 21*(1), 1–26.

Tarling, R., & Burrows, J. (2004). The nature and outcome of going missing; The challenge of developing effective risk assessment procedures. *International Journal of Police Science and Management, 6*(1), 16–26.

Trowbridge, C. C. (1913). On fundamental methods of orientation and "imaginary maps." *Science, 38*(990), 888–897.

Van Patten, I. T., & Delhauer, P. Q. (2007). Sexual homicide: A spatial analysis of 25 years of deaths in Los Angeles. *Journal of Forensic Science, 52*(5), 1129–1141.

Wade, J., Biehal, N., Clayden, J., & Stein, M. (1998). *Going missing: Young people absent from care.* Chichester, UK: John Wiley and Sons.

Related Sources

Andresen, M. A. (2014). *Environmental criminology: Evolution, theory, and practice.* New York, NY: Routledge.

Canter, D. V. (2001) *Mapping murder: The secrets of geographic profiling.* London, UK: Virgin Books.

Rossmo, D. K. (2000). *Geographic profiling.* Boca Raton, FL: CRC Press.

Chapter 10

Mapping the Missing: A New Approach to Locating Missing Persons Burial Locations in Armed Conflict Contexts

Derek Congram (University of Toronto)
Arthur Green (Okanagan College/University of British Columbia)
Hugh Tuller (Defense POW/MIA Accounting Agency/University of Tennessee)

Introduction

In 2009, an elderly man in Spain spoke to Derek Congram, one of the authors of this chapter, about a burial of five victims of extrajudicial killing during the Spanish Civil War. On the night of August 18, 1936, five men were forcefully taken from their homes by members of the Civil Guard and a fascist militia. The next morning the witness, who was nine years old at the time, saw an arm sticking up from the ground in recently disturbed earth near a local natural spring. The place was only 2.5 km from the town where the five victims had been taken. The witness, too afraid to speak of what he had seen, had carried this knowledge of the supposed burial place for over 70 years. When asked in 2009 how confident he was about the location of the burial, the witness asserted that he was quite certain and he made reference to surrounding reference points that had not changed over the years.

Using picks and shovels, archaeologists and local volunteers began to remove the thin topsoil in the area of the alleged burial. After about an hour of excavating, one of the archaeologists quietly and excitedly whispered that she had discovered the rim of a rubber shoe sole. In fact, she had found a small tree root.

She had believed so much in the testimony of the witness, fostered by her past success at other sites in the discovery of those missing from the Civil War, that in her mind a shoe sole was a more likely find than the root of a tree in a fairly wooded area. After a few hours of fruitless hand excavation, a small mechanical excavator was brought in to expedite and expand the search. Towards the end of the day, however, no disturbance to the subsoil had been detected. The elderly witness was incredulous. He knew that he had seen an arm protruding from an unmarked grave; a grave, he was sure, that held the remains of five men who had been kidnapped and executed the night before. The witness had no reason to lie. He wanted the victims to be found, identified, and given proper burial in the local cemetery so that the families—his own neighbours—could be reunited with their loved ones after so many years of suffering.

Another man, Mr. González, was the son of one of the victims and had initiated the search. For years he had suspected that the grave was not far from the place of disappearance (as has been the case for the vast majority of the Spanish Civil War graves being discovered around the country). When Mr. González heard that his elderly neighbour had actually seen one of the partially buried bodies, he called on experts to come and help him excavate the grave. At the end of a long day of digging, after finding nothing, he was crushed, and swore he would never again try to find his father. Locals and volunteers gathered around the site for an improvised memorial for the undiscovered men. People gave short speeches, laid flowers on the ground, and someone videotaped the improvised ceremony as the summer sun set.

Motivation

This chapter presents a new approach to the problem of locating people who have gone missing during armed conflict, and who are presumed dead, using data from Bosnia and Herzegovina. Although researchers have experienced success in past work searching for missing persons in unmarked burials, this line of research is motivated by increasing frustration at having failed to find alleged graves. The search for missing people requires taking advantage of all possible tools, of which witness testimony is the primary one used in contemporary investigations. Those searching for the missing in this context need another tool that can serve as an independent test of witness testimony, because often, as the example above illustrates, that testimony fails us. Here we advocate an approach to finding unmarked burial locations that incorporates geographic and anthropological theory to interpret how those responsible for victim burial in violent conflicts navigate landscapes of physical constraints (e.g., mountains and bodies of water) and socio-political boundaries (e.g., ethnic enclaves and "friendly" neighbourhoods). The aim of this work is to inform the thinking of and provide additional methods to those who are responsible for finding missing persons, to help them be more productive in their search.

During armed conflicts people disappear. Whereas many of these people may be combatants (e.g., those who are "lost" in battle or during harried retreats, see Chapter 7, this volume), other disappeared include unintended casualties (e.g., those buried when a building collapses during bombardment). Tragically, the highest number of disappearances in many conflicts is attributable to directed killings and enforced disappearance of non-combatants (UN Working Group on Enforced or Involuntary Disappearances, 2008).

The victory of the Allies in the Second World War and the search for evidence of war crimes to take to trial at Nuremberg provided an impetus to find, identify, and better document combatants who had gone missing and were presumed to have died or been killed as prisoners of the Nazis (e.g., Mant, 1950, 1987). Cultural factors also influenced whether or not missing combatants, presumed dead, would be sought after (e.g., Chapters 7 and 14, this volume).

The same effort towards civilians missing from war came much later, necessitated by the inordinately large number of civilians that were victims of enforced disappearance during the military governments in Argentina in the 1970s and early 1980s (Bernardi & Fondebrider, 2007). Other Latin American countries, such as Guatemala and Peru, would follow the Argentine example (Fondebrider, 2009). Nevertheless, despite decades of concerted work to find and identify missing non-combatants, quantitative analysis has been limited mostly to demography of the missing (e.g., Seybolt, Aronson, & Fischhoff, 2013; Zwierchowski & Tabeau, 2010) and probability analysis of parties responsible for violence resulting in enforced disappearance (e.g., Ball et al., 2002).

While programs and projects engaged in the search for missing persons from armed conflict are sometimes supported by massive international investment (e.g., Bosnia and Herzegovina and Kosovo) and draw upon the concerted expertise of many experienced professionals, these endeavours typically rely heavily (if not exclusively) on witness testimony. Despite this reliance on oral evidence, there is great difficulty in distinguishing accurate testimonies from testimonies made in earnest but which are incorrect or contain varying degrees of inaccuracy (such as the example above, from Spain). Added to this complication, there is the problem of testimony that is deliberately false.

Errors in oral testimony are common when dealing with the complexities of space, particularly when attempting to recall traumatic events (see Chapter 8, this volume). There is also the fallibility of long-term memory, with the search for the missing often occurring years or decades after a conflict (e.g., the civil wars in Spain, Cyprus, and Guatemala). Part of this last problem is the ability of elderly witnesses to recall precise detail from events that occurred when they were children. Our collective experience in multiple countries interviewing people about traumatic events shows that there is great variation both in the amount of detail that different people remember (or claim to remember) related to a single event, but also in the details themselves. Some inaccuracies are due to cognitive biases, errors in subconscious mental reasoning and processing. At other times, testimony is deliberately skewed or false and there are many "good reasons" why people speak this way. Fujii (2010), writing about her research interviewing survivors of the Rwandan genocide, reminds us that as frustrating as false testimony can be, thinking about why people report rumours as truth and invent, deny, and evade accurate answers can tell us much about the speaker in their psychosocial context. Accurate interpretation of this metadata, however, does not necessarily bring us closer to our goal of finding the precise location of those who did not survive.

Theory

The problem of unreliable and inaccurate witness testimony inspired us to pursue a line of inquiry that examines how quantifiable, socio-spatial, and physical variables relate to disappeared person burial locations. Our work builds upon what, until now, has been only anecdotal evidence of geographic patterns of mortuary behaviour during armed conflict. Better-developed spatial-behavioural research, however, has been conducted by criminologists modelling movement of criminals, particularly those committing serial crime (e.g., Rossmo, 2000; Levine, 2000; Chapter 9, this volume). Although armed conflict contexts are different and require us to reconsider the relative value of independent variables, criminological research provides a useful framework from which to begin thinking about and testing models relevant to body disposal behaviour during war.

The typical search for missing persons follows this generalized sequence: oral testimony is collected, corroborative information may or may not be sought, and a search party goes out to follow up. This approach to the search is problematic due to its heavy reliance on witness testimony. Oral testimony is sometimes unreliable and over time has diminishing returns, as less testimony is forthcoming. This is the case in Bosnia and Herzegovina where 7,290 of the 22,427 people reported missing to the International Committee of the Red Cross are still unaccounted for (ICRC, 2014). One-third of the missing remain as such, despite 20 years having passed since the end of the war and hundreds of millions of dollars invested in the search. It is not difficult to imagine what the numbers must be like for countries devastated by conflict that are of far less geopolitical interest to wealthy countries that sponsor investigations and the identification of the missing. While witness accounts are often essential, we argue that other starting points can and should be used in the search for missing persons. Our starting point examines what we can know about the people and places that will help guide our search *before* we go "looking."

For example, one useful theoretical tool is the analysis of spatial autocorrelation. Spatial autocorrelation measures the degree of similarity between things that are clustered in space and the correlate of dissimilarity for things that are dispersed. Imagine a drop of water falling into a large body of water: the undulating waves around the point of impact are a classic example of spatial autocorrelation. In social contexts, language, income, home prices, and other demographic characteristics also often show spatial autocorrelation. A search based on spatial autocorrelation hypotheses might identify nearby areas that have physical characteristics similar to known gravesites. In addition to spatial autocorrelation, analyzing constraints to movement over space (inclusive of both physical and socio-political boundaries such as road types, political borders, ethnic enclaves, military operations, vegetation type, and land slope) also informs the search for the disappeared. From such analysis we know that the probability of finding a disappeared person decreases as one moves farther away from the place of disappearance. This is exemplified by the discovery of combatant and non-combatant victim remains at the place of their death: soldiers buried in fighting positions such as trenches (e.g., Fisk, 2005, pp. 849–853; Fraser & Brown, 2007) or civilians buried in the rubble of collapsed buildings, including their own homes (e.g., Komar, 1999; Peterson, 2002). Even when an effort is made to hide the bodies of people deliberately killed, it is not uncommon for the burial sites to be close to the place of death (e.g., Congram, 2013).

Tools

To conduct our analyses we use geo-referenced data in a Geographic Information System (GIS). While our GIS analysis was performed using Esri's ArcGIS (a proprietary software package), there are many open-source and freeware software packages (such as Quantum GIS and GeoDa), which can be used for geo-spatial analyses. In addition, for simple visualization and rapid calculations of area and distance, free programs such as Google Earth offer ease of use and access to free aerial imagery, though more complex image and spatial statistical analyses are not easily available.

Spatial Statistics for Spatial Data

Conventional statistical analysis of spatial data assumes that data is homogenously distributed over space and that statistical models that describe and predict data variation can be applied to data in different locations. While many approaches to demographic data may normalize data based on population distribution, these statistical models do not incorporate the rich diversity of spatial factors and patterns that influence events (e.g., the spatio-temporal clustering, distance from roadsides, and the modifiable areal unit problem), data collection, and analyses. These approaches assume that space has a constant, homogenous impact on data analysis, probability functions, and process modelling. Spatial data includes data referenced to geographic coordinates or virtual spatial grids. Applying non-spatial statistical approaches to model spatial phenomena, analyze spatial data, or predict spatial outcomes is problematic because these non-spatial approaches do not integrate geographic weights, or analyze spatial distributions or patterns that influence data variables. The assumptions about space made in non-spatial statistical approaches render such approaches inappropriate and misleading for modelling, and for predicting spatially dependent phenomena such as rainfall, disease spread, pollution, landscape change, and many other environmental, political, and health phenomena. The recognition of the limitations of non-spatial statistical data analysis and the rapid development of GIS and related software has led to the development of unique statistical approaches to spatial data. These approaches are framed as the growing field of "spatial statistics."

One of the first case studies that any student of spatial statistics will encounter is that of the 1854 Broad Street cholera outbreak and the research methods of Dr. John Snow. This case is also considered seminal work in health geography and epidemiology. As a severe outbreak of cholera spread through the Soho district of London, Snow mapped the geographic pattern of victims in relation to water pumps and found, through application of basic statistics to spatially bound areas, that there was a significant clustering of victims around the Broad Street pump. This led authorities to shut off the pump and to a rapid decline in the spread of the disease. As one would imagine, methods in spatial statistics have since become far more complex.

Spatial statistics includes methods for conducting exploratory spatial data analysis, spatial autocorrelation, spatial clustering (e.g., Getis G, Moran's I, and Ripley's K), geographically weighted regression, and geo-statistical approaches to interpolation of data (e.g., Kriging process regression; see Fischer & Getis, 2010). The importance of these methods for environmental and health data sets has led researchers in these fields to pilot the development of spatial statistics models through applied problem solving. Recognition of the importance of adopting spatial statistics models is now spreading across many other social science and physical science disciplines, which previously did not integrate spatial probability models for hypothesis testing with spatial data sets. As mentioned above, these techniques are also being used for criminological research and might be extended to the context of war crimes. While the application of spatial analysis techniques in political science reveals that killer behaviour in civil conflicts is spatially dependent on changing political control of territory (Kalyvas, 2006; Mikellide, 2014), there are currently no models for understanding how the spatial dependency of killer behaviour can be used to inform the search for unmarked, possibly clandestine victim graves. Below, we overview several methods that we use to explore spatial statistics approaches to locating mass graves in conflict contexts. The aim of these approaches is to use exploratory data analysis to find spatial patterns in gravesite locations and to model spatially referenced political, cultural, and environmental factors that may influence and help predict spatial patterns of killer behaviour and body disposal.

Methods

While Exploratory Spatial Data Analysis (ESDA) can include many complex statistical approaches to analyzing spatial data, at the most basic ESDA is about visualization. The advent of powerful computing systems and increased access to GIS software and sources of spatial data (including imagery) has led to an explosion in researchers' abilities to visualize different aspects of data sets. The identification of data outliers and spatial patterns for further investigation relies on both the naked eye and on algorithms that extract specific wavelength bands from imagery or that identify spatial patterns in data sets that are not evident to the naked eye. ESDA can involve running spatial statistics (e.g., regression models or spatial clustering algorithms) to determine whether there are clusters of data variables that merit further investigation. For example, metrics such as Moran's I and Local Moran's I can be used along with the Moran scatterplot to identify clusters of values in sets of spatial points and polygons that include quantitative variables. These metrics identify groups of high-high, high-low, low-high, and low-low values in data sets to reveal the spatial patterns of such things as voting patterns, crime rates, and cost of living. The use of ESDA is advantageous in contexts where little established theory can guide the formation of a hypothesis, when data gathering has not followed systematic protocols, or where "big data" data sets present opportunities to let the data guide research (adopting an inductive approach, rather than the more typical hypothetico-deductive model).

When conducting ESDA, it is important to establish statistically significant spatial distances for data sets. Ripley's K is one metric that measures deviations from spatial homogeneity (random distribution). It measures the observed versus the statistically expected distribution of a phenomenon within certain spatial ranges. In the context of the search for mass graves, we conducted Ripley's K to find out how gravesites in Bosnia and Herzegovina clustered over space. There is no existing theory to guide understanding of modern conflict grave clustering, but by using Ripley's K we were able to identify probable distances to other graves based on the distribution of known, previously excavated graves. Such ESDA allows a spatial frame to be developed around the search for graves. Though the theoretical frame developed by Ripley's K should be modified by environmental and political factors on the ground through further regression and correlation models, Ripley's K provides an initial statistical understanding of the spatial distribution of phenomena.

While the above approaches to ESDA rely on clustering, one of the most powerful implementations of spatial statistics is in developing spatially dependent regression models. One approach to these models is called Geographically Weighted Regression (GWR). While very similar to non-spatial approaches to regression, GWR recognizes that an appropriate regression model predicting, for example, crime events would need to be adjusted according to the spatial frame (this implies location as well as the modifiable areal unit problem, which changes the spatial relationships depending on where your boundaries are drawn) and that the power of specific independent variables may change among geographic locations. GWR incorporates spatial bands that weigh variables into linear, logistic, Poisson, and other regression models in order for the model's coefficients to change over space. In the context of the search for mass graves, such regression models allow for the modelling of changing political territorial control, which is spatially associated with deaths in civil conflicts, within the regression model.

Another spatial statistics approach that can be used for both ESDA and prediction is spatial interpolation. Spatial interpolation uses known values of specific locations to estimate unknown values of other locations. Interpolation is often used to model landscape-level data sets wherein cost or logistics require extrapolating from multiple collection points to model patterns over a larger area—for example, rainfall and temperature variation, mining and hydrocarbon exploration, and many other environmental data sets. The two principal approaches to spatial interpolation are deterministic and probabilistic. *Deterministic approaches* do not involve probabilistic modelling, often using a spatially weighted average of known points to predict new point values (e.g., density kernels and inverse distance weighted). Such approaches use past events to model future events, rather than using statistically probable events to module the future. *Probabilistic approaches* are more complex, as they involve developing probability models (called *semivariograms*) of data values over space and allow a quantitative estimate of the uncertainty of these data values. Semivariograms represent selected functions of distance and direction to model the spatial dependence of data values. One set of probabilistic techniques that uses semivariograms is called *Kriging*. In the simplest terms, Kriging develops a semivariogram that best represents known point variation over space. It is then used to apply this semivariogram to model rainfall, radiation, mineral deposits, and other spatial data over existing and new spatial areas. While it is a powerful method that reduces many of the problems inherent in deterministic approaches, one of the main handicaps of the Kriging approach is that it deploys a semivariogram based on known data points to areas in which the semivariogram may or may not be appropriate. In order to overcome this assumption, Bayesian analysis techniques are now being incorporated into Kriging to lead to improved models.

Bayesian analysis techniques allow new data points to change statistical models that are used to predict relationships between dependent and independent variables. In the context of spatial statistics, Empirical Bayesian Kriging (EBK) improves upon traditional Kriging techniques in that it allows new data points to modify the semivariogram model that is used to predict new data values and to quantify the uncertainty of estimates over an area. Our research is currently developing and evaluating the usefulness of EBK as a technique in the search for mass graves. While probabilistic interpolation techniques that introduce directionality (the geographic direction of spatial phenomena in a data set) and allow for the quantification of uncertainty can be used to understand how current clusters of gravesites may indicate new sites, the findings of these models have to be adjusted to individual field sites. That is, EBK and other spatial statistics techniques provide predictions that are clues to patterns of burial, though clues must be read in the context of specific field sites. Below, we introduce an applied example using some of the above methods for the search for unmarked burial locations in Bosnia and Herzegovina.

Results from Preliminary Research

In Bosnia and Herzegovina, the search for the more than 7,000 still-missing persons has slowed dramatically due to a lack of new witness information about site location (Congram, Green, & Tuller, 2015). Despite the state-of-the-art DNA laboratory that exists in the country and the anthropological expertise that has assisted with identifying those victims already discovered, the process comes to a dramatic halt when burial sites cease to be discovered. Our approach started at the U.S. Department of Defense laboratory, which searches for missing combatants from past conflicts in places like Korea, Vietnam, and Western Europe. We are currently working with the International Committee of the Red Cross in three countries to help them organize data and analyze it geographically. Our aim is to identify spatial patterns that will lead to the discovery of conflict burials. Data from multiple conflicts will help us understand the degree of consistency that exists across contexts. Is human conflict mortuary behaviour directed by universal pragmatism? How do those responsible for burying the dead process their responsibilities, taking into account limited resources and restrictive landscapes? With a study now well underway on Bosnia and Herzegovina, data collected from the Spanish Civil War, and agreements in place with organizations in several other countries, we hope to be able to answer these questions. Ultimately, we hope to be able to understand where victims of conflict are buried and why, so that their bodies can be recovered and returned to surviving families and communities for dignified funerary rites and memorialization.

The first step to using excavated burials to search for undiscovered locations is determining the environmental and human factors that characterize these sites. Using Landsat satellite images and other aerial imagery, we analyzed vegetation types, presence and size of human settlements, road types, and several environmental factors (e.g., slope and soil types). These variables were combined with knowledge of particular gravesite contents, which include number of victims, victim characteristics (e.g., age and sex), and killer identities (specific armed factions or groups). The above data was spatially referenced using public legal documentation from the International Criminal Tribunal for the former Yugoslavia, data provided by the International Commission on Missing Persons, other public sources, and first-hand knowledge from fieldwork in the region. Before conducting statistical analyses of the grave locations, a random selection of excavated gravesites was separated from the main data set so that any models developed from the data set could be tested and validated against theoretical distributions, randomly generated distributions, and this randomly selected set of known gravesites.

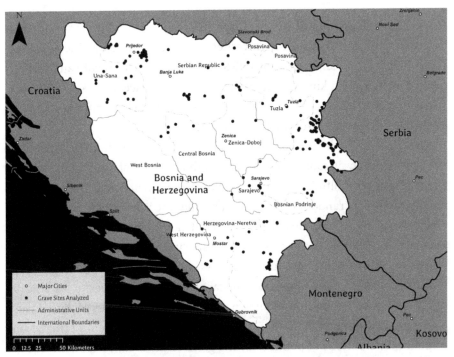

FIGURE 10.1 **Map of Bosnia and Herzegovina showing gravesite locations analyzed in this study.**
Sources: Esri, DeLorme, USGS, NPS, NOAA

One of the first models we developed examines the spatial clustering of graves. Our data set contains graves that are associated with different periods of violence between 1991 and 1995. Simple map visualization shows that these gravesites may be clustered in particular areas (see Figure 10.1). However, simple visualization does not provide a useful measure of clustering. A statistical model of how gravesites cluster during each episode of violence and during the entire conflict may provide generalizable insights into the likely distance of existing graves to undiscovered sites. As mentioned above, there are several approaches to examining spatial clustering. Below, we overview the use of Ripley's K for determining statistically significant distances in grave clusters.

Before using Ripley's K, we determined whether clustering is statistically significant using an Average Nearest Neighbour (ANN) test for burial locations that were created during 1991–93 (n=154). We eliminated 1994 and 1995 burial locations from this analysis so that these sites can be separately analyzed as distinct periods of violence (particularly because of the seeming uniqueness of the July 1995 killings and burials related to the Srebrenica massacre). The ANN test is a global clustering test that does not pinpoint specific clusters (local test) as it produces a Nearest Neighbour Ratio (NRR) that describes clustering across the entire data set. NRR measures whether the observed mean distance (Euclidean) between gravesites is more (showing dispersion) or less (showing clustering) than the expected mean distance for gravesites in a given study area. The ANN test shows highly significant clustering (NRR=0.462578, p < 0.001) with an observed mean distance of 4.2 km over an expected mean distance of 9.1 km. Ripley's K also allows us to examine the probable distance between gravesites now that we know there is spatial clustering in the data set.

Ripley's K, as implemented in ArcGIS 10.2, is called the Multi-Distance Spatial Cluster Analysis tool.[1] This tool allows the analysis of spatial dependency (clustering) over multiple predefined distance increments or spatial scales. The null hypothesis is random distribution and the test is bi-directional, in that it detects both significant clustering and significant dispersion. Understanding the scale of clustering is a necessary preliminary step for setting out study area frames for future spatial statistical tests. As well, when applied to burial locations, an understanding of probable distance can provide clues to statistically significant search areas around known graves. In order to statistically measure clustering and dispersion, the tool generates up to 999 random permutations (random distributions of points over the given study area) to compare against observed points. Using these permutations, Ripley's K transforms the data to produce an ExpectedK value and an ObservedK value at predefined distance increments. These values reflect the number of observed and expected points (given spatial randomness). When these expected and observed values reveal significant differences, this means that they detect high amounts of positive difference (clustering) or negative difference (dispersion).

We implemented Ripley's K using the following parameters. The beginning distance was set to 500 m, distance increments at 500 m, and distance bands at 100 iterations. This produced a 50 km area around graves with 100 distance increments in which expected and observed burial locations were counted. Boundary correction area and study area settings influenced the calculation of Ripley's K. We set no boundary correction method, as most boundary correction methods required making serious assumptions about the proximity of unknown graves or diminished the number of locations (n=154) too heavily. The study area was set as a minimum enclosing rectangle that included all burial locations. We generated 99 permutations, as there was no significant impact when increasing to 999 permutations.

The results show highly significant clusters peaking near 10 km from gravesites. In Figure 10.2, the expected and observed lines are displayed with a confidence interval (0.05) developed from the permutations. The positive difference between ObservedK and ExpectedK (observed minus expected) and the presence of ObservedK outside of the confidence interval shows that highly significant

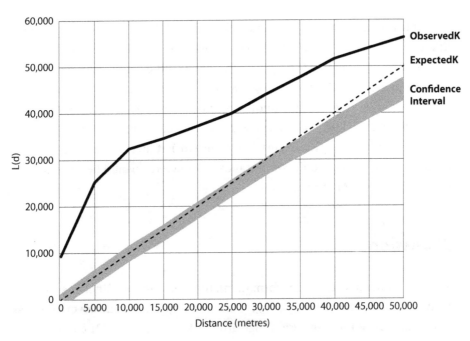

FIGURE 10.2   L(d) transformation of ExpectedK/ObservedK over distance (m).

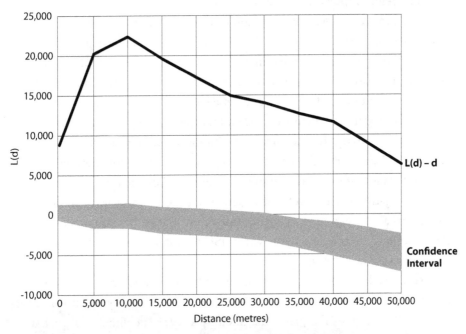

FIGURE 10.3   L(d) – d over distance (metres), showing statistical peak at 8–9.5 km.

clustering is present at all spatial scales. However, it is important to note the peak difference around 8–10 km, as it provides clues to possible clustering patterns that should be investigated. The bands that showed the highest amount of clustering were 8.5–9 km (diff. = +22,993), 8–8.5 km (diff. = +22,884), and 9–9.5 km (diff. = +22,708). The high magnitude of this difference is easily visualized in Figure 10.3, where $L(d) - d$ is displayed over distance bands ($L(d)$ = the likelihood of something (L) given a certain distance (d)). If there were no statistically significant clustering at different distances, ObservedK would be close to zero and within the confidence interval.

Discussion

Based on Ripley's K ($L(d)$ transformation), there is highly significant clustering of the graves made during 1991–93. Future searches for undiscovered graves should prioritize the 8–9.5 km range around known graves. Of course, other spatial factors need to be considered, such as soil types, road types, vegetation types, political/conflict boundaries, and the clandestinity of sites, in the process of identifying probable new site locations, but this spatial clustering exercise gives insight into the spatial frame (distance) in which such sites should be prioritized. Moreover, the results of this analysis can be used to inform spatial statistics model creation, being important factors in determining how to use spatial bands in interpolation techniques and geographically weighted regression.

Ultimately, geo-anthropological grave prospection is not expected to be a perfect solution to locating the unmarked burial place of victims of war. It does, however, have several major benefits that can be used in conjunction with traditional search methods to increase the efficiency and effectiveness of searches. Primary among these benefits is the fact that spatial analysis can be initiated as a desk-based activity. This is particularly important for places where conflict is ongoing and precludes the active, on-the-ground search for missing victims. Advance insight of potential burial locations will allow investigators to prioritize investigation place targets for windows of time when security and political conditions allow searching to begin. Among the places that could benefit from this technique are Iraq and Syria, where ISIL/Daesh has fast become notorious for its mass executions and burials.

A second advantage of spatial thinking in forensics and grave location modelling is that it can be used as a measure to test the reliability of witness information. That is, does the place identified by a witness coincide with what we know about the spatial and geographic logic of body disposal behaviour? For example, if the alleged burial place is very distant from the detention location, it casts doubt on the reliability of this testimony because of what we already know about the common spatial range of conflict mortuary behaviour. If the alleged burial location falls outside of known probable places for an individual or group of disappeared people, how should we prioritize it?

With each new conflict context assessed and with every missing person found, we have the potential to improve how we find and identify subsequent victims. To advance these searches, however, requires deliberate attention and concerted effort. We want to advocate for the importance of a forward-looking, "pre-disaster planning" approach to those who are currently missing and to those who will go missing as a result of future conflict. This research is of significant interest in various countries where non-governmental, governmental, and international organizations are finding that as there is a decline in forthcoming witnesses of killings and body disposal, the number of search options also decreases. Geo-spatial theory and techniques allow us to maintain momentum in such situations in order to continue to support bringing "home" the remains of victims to their families and communities for proper, dignified funerary rites.

In Spain, 40 years of dictatorship precluded investigation into more than 110,000 missing from the Civil War (Chapter 4, this volume). Even after the subsequent 35 years of democratic governance, the state has refused to investigate the unresolved crime of enforced disappearance. In only a few more years, all of the children of victims and all of the remaining witnesses will also be dead. The grandchildren of the victims, however, will remain, and deserve to know where their missing relatives lie. So that we might learn from the example of Spain and not leave those in other countries to suffer as they have, we ought to be exploring new ways to find the missing and account for violent pasts.

Acknowledgements

We wish to thank several people and organizations for supporting our research, particularly John Bird and Tom Holland of the Joint POW/MIA Accounting Command Central Identification Laboratory (now the Defense POW/MIA Accounting Agency), Matthew Vennemeyer, Stephen Fonseca, Maria Mikellide, Ana Maria Boza Arlotti, Pierre Guyomarc'h, Lina Milner Ennercrantz of the International Committee of the Red Cross, and the International Commission for Missing Persons.

Note

1. The particular implementation of Ripley's K in ArcGIS uses L(d) transformation. For an in-depth discussion of Ripley's K computation and its implementation in ArcGIS, see Dixon (2002), Fischer and Getis (2010), and Esri (2011).

References

Ball, P., Betts, W., Scheuren, F., Dudukovich, J., & Asher, J. (2002). *Killings and refugee flow in Kosovo: A report to the International Criminal Tribunal for the Former Yugoslavia*. New York, NY: American Association for the Advancement of Science.

Bernardi, P., & Fondebrider, L. (2007). Forensic archaeology and the scientific documentation of human rights violations: An Argentinian example from the early 1980s. In R. Ferllini (ed.), *Forensic archaeology and human rights violations* (pp. 205–232). Springfield, IL: Charles C. Thomas.

Congram, D. (2013). Deposition and dispersal of human remains as a result of criminal acts: *Homo sapiens sapiens* as a taphonomic agent. In J. T. Pokines & S. A. Symes (eds.), *Manual of forensic taphonomy* (pp. 249–285). Boca Raton, FL: CRC Press.

Congram, D., Green, A. G., & Tuller, H. (2015). Finding the graves of the missing: A study of geo-anthropological techniques in Bosnia-Herzegovina. *Proceedings of the American Academy of Forensic Sciences 67th Annual Scientific Meeting*. Colorado Springs, CO: American Academy of Forensic Sciences.

Dixon, P. M. (2002). Ripley's K function. *Encyclopedia of environmetrics*, 3 (pp. 1796–1803). Chichester, UK: John Wiley & Sons.

Esri. (2011). *ArcGIS desktop: Release 10*. Redlands, CA: Environmental Systems Research Institute.

Fischer, M., & Getis, A. (2010). *Handbook of applied spatial analysis*. Berlin: Springer-Verlag.

Fisk, R. (2005). *The great war for civilisation*. London, UK: Fourth Estate.

Fondebrider, L. (2009). The application of forensic anthropology to the investigation of cases of political violence: Perspectives from South America. In S. Blau & D. H. Ubelaker (eds.), *Handbook of forensic anthropology and archaeology* (pp. 67–75). Walnut Creek, CA: Left Coast Press.

Fraser, A. H., & Brown, M. (2007). Mud, blood and missing men: Excavations at Serre, Somme, France. *Journal of Conflict Archaeology*, 3(1), 147–171.

Fujii, L. A. (2010). Shades of truth and lies: Interpreting testimonies of war and violence. *Journal of Peace Research*, 47(2), 231–241.

ICRC (International Committee of the Red Cross). (2014, June). *Figures related to the persons missing from the Balkans Conflicts*. International Committee of the Red Cross, Regional Delegation for Serbia, Montenegro, Macedonia and Albania. Unpublished document.

Kalyvas, S. (2006). *The logic of violence in civil war*. New York, NY: Cambridge University Press.

Komar, D. (1999). *Forensic assistance project consultant report 1999-054, Foča I, Federation Commission on Missing Persons—Bosniak Side, 13 September–10 November 1999*. Boston: Physicians for Human Rights.

Levine, N. (2000). The CrimeStat program: Characteristics, use, and audience. *Geographic Analysis*, 38(1), 41–56.

Mant, A. K. (1950). *A study in exhumation data*. Unpublished MD thesis, University of London.

Mant, A. K. (1987). Knowledge acquired from post-war exhumations. In A. Boddington, A. N. Garland, & R. C. Janaway (eds.), *Death, decay and reconstruction* (pp. 65–78). Manchester, UK: Manchester University Press.

Mikellide, M. (2014). Burial patterns during times of armed conflict in Cyprus in the 1960s and 1970s. *Journal of Forensic Sciences, 59*(5), 1184–1190.

Peterson, S. (2002, October 22). "Smarter" bombs still hit civilians. *Christian Science Monitor.* Retrieved from www.csmonitor.com/2002/1022/p01s01-wosc.html.

Rossmo, D. K. (2000). *Geographic profiling.* Boca Raton, FL: CRC Press.

Seybolt, T. B., Aronson, J. D., & Fischhoff, B. (eds.). (2013). *Counting civilian casualties.* Oxford, UK: Oxford University Press.

UN Working Group on Enforced or Involuntary Disappearances. (2008). *Report to the United Nations General Assembly, Human Rights Council, A/HRC/7/2, 10 January 2008.* Retrieved from daccess-dds-ny.un.org/doc/UNDOC/GEN/G08/101/05/PDF/G0810105.pdf?OpenElement.

Zwierchowski, J., & Tabeau, E. (2010). The 1992–95 war in Bosnia and Herzegovina: Census-based multiple system estimation of casualties' undercount. Presentation at the International Research Workshop on the Global Costs of Conflict, February 1, 2010. Retrieved from www.icty.org/x/file/About/OTP/War_Demographics/en/bih_casualty_undercount_conf_paper_100201.pdf.

Related Sources

Buhaug, H., & Gates, S. (2002). The geography of civil war. *Journal of Peace Research, 39*(4), 417–433.

Mesev, V., Shirlow, P., & Downs, J. (2009). The geography of conflict and death in Belfast, Northern Ireland. *Annals of the Association of American Geographers, 99*(5), 893–903.

Chapter 11

Leading Change and Innovation in Missing Persons and Unidentified Remains Investigations in Canada

Carole Bird (Officer in Charge of the National Centre of Missing Persons and Unidentified Remains, RCMP, retired)

Policing in Canada: The Landscape

Canada is geographically vast and, since its earliest days as a country, connecting and coordinating the country has been a major challenge. As it is a federation of provinces and territories with different degrees of autonomy, the regional authorities have many of their own administrative agencies, including police services. Investigating missing persons in Canada is incredibly challenging for several reasons: because of the space that can be covered by those who go missing and those who investigate their disappearances; because of different government levels and degrees of investigation administration; because of a fairly open border with the US, the longest international border in the world; and also because of constantly changing demographics—Canada has the eighth-highest immigration in the world (United Nations, 2013). This chapter discusses very recent and ongoing changes to how Canadian investigation agencies are innovating and improving how they resolve cases of missing persons and unidentified human remains.

The Canadian Centre of Justice Statistics report titled *Policing Resources in Canada, 2010* describes policing in Canada as "the responsibility of all three levels of government: federal, provincial/territorial and municipal. While the federal government is responsible for criminal law, under the Constitution Act, each province and territory assumes responsibility for its own policing at the provincial, territorial and municipal level. Further, many First Nations communities also administer their own police service" (Burczycka, 2010). This jurisdictional mixture presents many challenges to those investigating missing persons and to ensuring a consistent standard of practice on a national level. With over 175 police services, police boundaries and activities overlap. Investigations will often cross from one jurisdiction into another. Police services may also work together in each other's area of responsibility depending on the circumstances.

The Royal Canadian Mounted Police (RCMP) is Canada's national police service providing services at multiple levels. It functions as the federal police across the country while also providing provincial or territorial policing (except in Quebec and Ontario), and municipal policing services where needed. The RCMP also provides policing services to a number of First Nations communities.

The Complexity of Missing Persons and Unidentified Remains Investigations

Missing person investigations can be very straightforward or extremely complex. The most basic investigations are instances of youths who have walked out of a youth or foster home and who are reported missing because of policies at that facility, which require police be contacted when the youth is deemed to be overdue—even, sometimes, if the youth is still in view of the individual who is calling the police!

Factors that complicate missing person investigations include the lack of information available: you have only the "who," but not the "what," "where," "when," "why," or "how" of a particular situation. For example, police may receive a report of someone who is missing, but the person reporting them missing may only be able to provide basic details such as "my friend, Ted, who is always in the park Wednesday mornings, has been missing for the past six months." The caller may not be a relative or may not know specific details regarding the individual, including their last name, their biological or cultural affinity, what they were last wearing, the person's actual age, where they live, or places they may frequent. Police also receive reports regarding individuals who have not been heard from in 20 or 30 years.

Another factor is that it is not a criminal offence to be missing; the investigator must recognize that a missing person may be someone who simply wants some time away and is entitled to that without informing others where they are. Alternatively, a missing person incident report may turn out to be the initial stage of a complex criminal investigation.

Possible reasons that people go missing include that he or she:

- is lost due to a high-risk lifestyle choice, such as hiking or camping in isolated and dangerous terrain;
- has had an accident and is unable to return;
- is in a state of crisis or at risk due to a mental health issue or disease, such as depression or Alzheimer's disease;
- has, of their own volition, left for whatever reason; or
- has been the victim of a criminal act, whether it be a parental abduction, stranger abduction, murder, forcible confinement, assault, etc.

Whatever the cause, when a report of a missing person is received the information available to police will affect the response or investigative approach that can and will be taken.

The Evolution of Missing Persons Investigations in Canada

"Change is always going to happen. The questions is: how do you manage it right?"
(Jeffrey, 2011)

The way that police investigate reports of missing persons in Canada has changed significantly over the past 30 years. In certain instances, changes were the result of cases that were later linked to a specific criminal activity or predator. Case reviews of investigations, government-mandated inquiries, and research have all resulted in new or different approaches. This also happens on an individual level as an investigator learns and may eventually become a subject matter expert, and on an organizational or even national level as agencies develop policies and procedures. An example of a national-level change is the development of a new unit in the RCMP in the 1980s to assist with missing children investigations.

New legislation, either at the provincial or federal level, has also affected investigations. For example, the addition of parental abduction offences to the Criminal Code of Canada (Greenspan, Rosenberg, & Henein, 2015) provided police with direction regarding the elements of these activities that crossed from the realm of civil matters into that of a criminal offence. Provincial legislation changes specific to missing person investigations have clarified the process by which the police can gather information to advance investigations. The complex legal landscape in Canada means that investigators must understand how various laws can interact to advance an investigation and where they may not provide for the circumstances of a particular situation. Similarly, an investigator must understand under what legal authority they are proceeding. For example, in a missing person investigation the police are usually the primary investigators. However, each Canadian province and territory has a Coroner Act or Medical Examiner Act that authorizes coroners or medical examiners to conduct investigations into sudden or suspicious deaths and unidentified remains. One of the primary goals of these agencies is to identify the deceased. Several of the provincial acts give police the mandate to assist the coroner or medical examiner (RCMP, 2013a). Therefore, investigations may have the police providing a primary investigative role or one of assistance to a coroner or medical examiner.

Changes resulting from new technologies or techniques have also affected investigative approaches. The AMBER Alert program, widely adopted in both the United States and Canada, has provided investigators with the ability to push out information to the public to assist in the rapid location of an abducted child. Though only used in very specific circumstances, AMBER Alerts have successfully assisted police in locating abducted children. Rapid-alert technologies have changed significantly in the past few decades, expanding to leverage social media and cellphone technology. Keeping pace with technological change—used both in the commission and investigation of crime—is increasingly difficult.

DNA technology is another example of an advance that has changed missing person and unidentified remains investigations. While investigators use various approaches to identify discovered human remains, including dental records and fingerprints, the evolution of DNA technology has provided investigators with an additional tool for consideration where appropriate. It is a tool that investigators apply not only to current investigations but also in re-examining older cases. For example, in 1990, a human skull was discovered in a farmer's field in Manitoba. Subsequent searches of the area located additional human remains. The partial human remains were forensically examined at the time and it was concluded that they were of a 25- to 40-year-old female. An RCMP Historical Case Unit reviewed the file in 2011 and the unidentified remains were exhumed for the purpose of re-analysis and DNA extraction. DNA analysis showed that the remains were, in fact, male. Investigators refocused on males who went missing around the time of the discovery of the remains (RCMP, 2012). The individual was subsequently identified as Patrick Lawrence Rosner, who had been reported missing in 1989. Today, investigators recognize that if the quality of the sample does not allow for a DNA profile to be derived using current technology, new advancements in DNA technologies may someday provide that information. DNA technology does not replace the need for other investigative tools; it is one of many available to investigators. As with any new tool, it must be integrated into the investigative practices where it is most effective.

Building Specialized Services on a National Level for Missing Persons Investigations

Regardless of the impetus for the change, managing change within one's own agency is difficult. Leading change or innovation across a broad community, such as the law enforcement community, brings additional challenges to be considered in order to manage the change as effectively as possible. When managing change on a national level, understanding the background and underlying issues that have led to the current state or situation is key to identifying gaps. A collaborative approach is critical to the development of this understanding, determining appropriate courses of action and ensuring stakeholder and client engagement.

Background

In the early 1980s, a number of children, male and female, were abducted and murdered in British Columbia, victims of Clifford Olson (Martin, 2011). Shortly thereafter, the Government of Canada ordered a study into the extent and nature of missing children in Canada. The study, conducted by the RCMP, concluded that the majority were runaways. A small percentage was identified as resulting from stranger abductions. Though the initial data regarding the study is no longer available, the RCMP's *Annual Report on Canada's Missing Children* for 1988 indicates that 72 percent of missing children cases reported in that year were suspected of being runaways. Of the 99 cases entered on the Canadian Police Information Centre system in 1988, three were identified as stranger abductions and all three children were safely returned home (Dalley, 1988). As a result, the Ministry of the Solicitor General of Canada initiated a multi-faceted program to assist police with the investigation of missing children (Dalley, 1988).

One aspect of the program was the creation of a Missing Children Registry. The original mandate of the Missing Children Registry (MCR), established by the RCMP, was to provide "statistical information to the public and supportive assistance to the investigating police forces in Canada as well as all international agencies through Interpol" (Dalley, 1988, preface).

By 2008, the unit, then called the National Missing Children Services, had expanded to include more active investigative support and information exchange among Canadian police, the coordination of investigations in foreign cases with Canadian implications, research on missing children, and specialized training for law enforcement personnel. Throughout this time, the work of the National Missing Children Services and the information residing in the MCR applied only to missing children investigations. By the mid-2000s, law enforcement officers in Canada were looking for options that would support investigations of missing persons inclusive of adults.

Identifying the Challenges and Gaps

With over 170 different police records management systems in existence in Canada, there was an increased recognition of the need for access to data and services across jurisdictions. This provided a great impetus for the creation of a coordinated national system to investigate missing persons in Canada. The number of police services with their own record-keeping systems and province/territory-specific death investigation agencies (coroners or medical examiners) resulted in information, or interoperability, barriers that hampered the resolution of occurrences that crossed boundaries and hindered a national view of the problem. Police investigators are often handling missing person and unidentified remains occurrences alongside many other types of cases and duties. As a result, not every unit has the expertise to conduct the most efficient and effective missing person or unidentified remains investigation, nor do they have the tools for effective analysis and information publication (RCMP, 2013a).

In 2008, the Canadian Association of Chiefs of Police passed a resolution calling for the adoption of a coordinated national approach to the development of a single analytical software program specific to missing persons and unidentified remains investigations. This led to an initial multi-provincial planning meeting (RCMP, 2013a) focusing on technical aspects to be considered in the development of the software. Out of this meeting was formed an ad hoc working group that "examined technical requirements, policy, privacy and standard operations procedures. Interested police services and coroner/medical examiner offices also participated in an effort to define a solution" (RCMP, 2013b, p. 1). Unfortunately, with no formal recognition the working group had no means to realize the strategies that they were developing.

In 2010, the Government of Canada indicated that it would "take additional action to address the disturbing number of unsolved cases of murdered and missing Aboriginal women" (Government of Canada, 2010, para. 11, sub. 4.). As part of this effort, the 2010 budget provided the RCMP with $2 million per year over a five-year period to develop a centre to support all missing person and unidentified remains investigations in Canada.

The result was the establishment of the National Centre for Missing Persons and Unidentified Remains (NCMPUR) in 2011 (Figure 11.1). Managed by the RCMP, the NCMPUR incorporated the pre-existing National Missing Children Services as the newly renamed National Missing Children Operations. Designed to provide specialized services to law enforcement, medical examiners, and chief coroners on a national level, the NCMPUR was mandated to:

- enhance specialized services available to missing persons and unidentified remains investigations;
- increase operational effectiveness and intelligence building;
- develop training for police; and
- assist in investigative comparisons involving missing persons and unidentified remains. (RCMP, 2013b, p. 1)

In support of its mandate, the NCMPUR was specifically asked to develop four key components:

1. a national public website;
2. a national database;
3. investigative best practices; and
4. training for police regarding best practices.

From the outset, the NCMPUR (herein referred to as the "National Centre," or just the "Centre") adopted a consultative and collaborative approach building on the work of the ad hoc working group.

Participants in the ad hoc working group comprised interested police and coroner/medical examiner subject matter experts in Canada, and had recognized that there were a number of existing database systems that focused on missing person or unidentified remains information, or both. However, in examining each system, the working group determined that no one system provided all of the elements needed to be included in a national database. The Canadian Police Information Centre (CPIC) database, managed by the RCMP, is the only national information-sharing system that links criminal justice and law enforcement

FIGURE 11.1   National Centre for Missing Persons and Unidentified Remains—Brand Image.
Source: Royal Canadian Mounted Police, printed by permission

partners across Canada and internationally (RCMP, 2014). However, CPIC does not capture all of the information that the working group felt necessary to support missing person and unidentified remains investigations. It also does not support the inclusion of photographs, provide sophisticated search and analysis tools, and could not support direct publishing of missing person or unidentified remains profiles to a national website. On the other hand, police agencies across Canada were already trained in the use of CPIC, had access to the system, and it was the system that had the greatest common use by investigators across Canada.

It was recognized that the development of a new national database for use by all front-line investigators would be a very costly solution, requiring completely new technical and business infrastructure as well as accompanying comprehensive training and auditing programs. The resources required to provide training on a new system to each of the 69,299 active police officers and 27,000 civilian personnel who worked with police services in Canada in 2010 (Burczycka, 2010, p. 6) made this a non-viable option.

As a result, the working group determined that the best option was to leverage the national reach of CPIC as the data input front-end system, while building a back-end system specific for missing person and unidentified remains cases with advanced searching and analysis tools that would be accessible by trained specialists.

The Business Model and Architecture of the NCMPUR

The vision for the National Centre was to build an infrastructure and services to advance investigations. The main client groups of the Centre are police services, coroners, and medical examiners in Canada, in particular missing person or unidentified remains investigators.

The Centre does not, nor was it intended to, interact directly with the families of missing persons; rather, the primary investigative agency should be the point of contact for families of missing persons. The primary investigative agency is most familiar with the community as well as geographical and situational factors vital to the appropriate response to a missing person investigation. For example, the police of primary jurisdiction will know that a particular community is prone to weather and road conditions, which when combined might indicate that the person has had an accident travelling in a particular area. Similarly, if a call is received that a person failed to check out of their hotel and others travelling with that person confirm they are overdue and will miss their return flight as a result, the police of primary jurisdiction are best positioned to respond to the call, assess the scene, and understand the information being provided by the last people to speak with the person prior to their disappearance.

In designing a new national approach and instituting change, the identification and engagement of stakeholders and indirect clients—including the involved public—was important. There were a number of stakeholders who would ultimately and indirectly benefit from the Centre's services. Accordingly, it consulted with several of them, including representatives of National Aboriginal Organizations and non-governmental organizations, in designing the business and technical infrastructure for the program. These groups, as well as primary investigators, have significant experience interacting with and supporting the families of missing persons, and provided insights to the Centre that were considered in the development of the program as well as that of the national website. For example, both groups voiced concern about producing posters in their communities for missing persons, as well as concerns about anonymity. Similarly, they identified a keen interest in updated statistical information regarding the number of reports of missing persons in Canada each year. Where possible, these ideas and many others were incorporated into the national website. For example, as of 2010, the previously titled *Annual Reports on Canada's Missing Children* were transformed into *Fast Fact Sheets* to include information on the number of reports of missing adults added to CPIC in a year, and were made available on the Centre's website, Canada's Missing. The addition of these Sheets to the website has raised awareness regarding the scope and scale of the types of missing persons reports being added to CPIC every year, highlighting statistics such as the fact that, in 2013, 66 percent of missing adult and 65 percent of missing children reports were removed from CPIC within 24 hours (RCMP, 2013c).

The Delivery Concept

The Centre had four key deliverables to develop and implement: a national database, a national website, investigative best practices, and training for police officers. As there are already a number of units in Canada specializing in missing person or unidentified remains investigations, the Centre's delivery concept includes the possibility of regional units being designated and trained as regional centres called Centres for Missing Persons and Unidentified Remains (herein referred to as Regional Centres). These Regional Centres would utilize the national infrastructure in support of investigations within a specific area, either geographical or organizational. Where no Regional Centre exists, the National Centre will provide the services. Regional Centres may include specialists from multiple agencies, similar to a Joint Forces Operations model. While a Joint Forces Operations model may be considered for adjacent areas with large populations due to the crossover of cases from one jurisdiction to another, it also allows a number of smaller agencies to work together. Regardless of the shape or span of a particular Regional Centre, their role is to offer services to assist the primary investigator and his or her agency in advancing the investigation. This can include the indication of a possible link between cases or the elimination of a possible link. The National Centre may assume primary investigator responsibilities when the police, coroner, or medical examiner of the primary jurisdiction in Canada has yet to be determined. For example, if two visitors to Canada were reported missing by family to investigators in their own country, but relatives had no information regarding their whereabouts in Canada, the National Centre would act as the primary investigative agency. Once the National Centre determines that the missing persons were last seen in a particular jurisdiction, the investigative lead would move to the primary agency for that area.

The concept that the primary investigator remains the primary investigator as it pertains to Regional Centre services is vital to effecting the changes resulting from the establishment of the National Centre and to gaining "buy-in" from investigators across the country. If investigators see that their efforts are supported by the specialized services, they are more likely to consider using the tools and technology developed by the National Centre than if they are concerned that investigational control will be lost or compromised.

The Service Model

In examining its mandate, the National Centre identified a number of specialized services as key to the advancement or the resolution of missing person and unidentified remains investigations. Some predated the establishment of the Centre but required expansion or enhancements, while others were new services required to support the new and expanded mandate.

Information Collection Service

Accurate and timely information is vital to the advancement of investigations, to supporting the publication of profiles to the national website, to complex analyses, and to research in the area of missing person or unidentified remains investigations. The Information Collection Service is a cornerstone of the Centre's program.

Activities designed to support information collection include, with very few exceptions, mandatory entry of a case on CPIC by a primary investigative agency prior to requesting and receiving National Centre or Regional Centre services. Information added into CPIC, which feeds the Missing Children/Person and Unidentified Remains database, is then used by investigative specialists in the National Centre or Regional Centres. This also ensures the front-line police officer, who does not have direct access to the Missing Children/Person and Unidentified Remains database, has access to key information regarding the report of a missing person or unidentified remains. In the event that they come across relevant information, having the data on CPIC may result in the advancement or resolution of an investigation without the use of specialized personnel. For example, there are cases where police locate a missing person while investigating unrelated matters such as a motor vehicle accident. If the information regarding the missing person is on CPIC, the investigating officer will be notified that the person has been reported as missing and can resolve the investigation.

Occurrence Publication Service

The Occurrence Publication Service pertains to the release of information on a missing person or unidentified remains with a view to soliciting tips from the public. The aim of this service is to assist the investigator in obtaining information that will advance the investigation. This function can also have a number of derivative effects, including raising public and the community awareness.

The Centre has used three main methods of publicizing cases and its work:

1. Publication to the national website.
2. Coordinating special events to focus on specific cases.
3. Publication in other venues.

The National Centre will also partner with national-level entities to highlight cases and provide additional avenues for investigators to bring attention to cases. For example, the Centre met with MSN.ca regarding the need for long-standing cases to be repeatedly brought forward in the hopes of receiving new tips. As a result of various discussions, MSN.ca advised that it would provide a "Cold Case" forum and publish articles on various types of missing persons cases (e.g., unidentified remains, persons gone missing while travelling or while engaged in high-risk activities, persons who went out for a moment and never returned).

For the "Cold Case" forum, the Centre reached out to investigative partners, providing contact information for the MSN.ca editor who they would contact directly to request their case be highlighted in the forum. MSN.ca proceeded to publish a number of articles in conjunction with the forum.

In January 2013, the Centre launched its new national website, Canada's Missing (www.canadasmissing.ca). In doing so, it implemented a number of features that allowed for a different or enhanced use of the website and provided a national focal point for the publication of case subject profiles. The website contains profiles of missing persons and unidentified remains where a primary investigator or agency has determined that the national website is a tool that could assist in advancing the investigation. Each profile contains a description of the missing individual, key factors in the case, a synopsis, photographs or facial approximations if available, and information regarding persons who might be associated with the missing person.

Each profile contains at least three contact avenues. The first is the primary investigative agency or their designate. The second is Crime Stoppers, providing an avenue to submit tips anonymously. The last option is to send an email to the Centre, which will transmit any tip received directly to the primary investigative agency or their designate for assessment and determination of next steps. Each profile also provides a "print poster" option so that family or community members wishing to print a poster in either French or English may do so and post it in their community.

In 2013 the Centre examined previous approaches to publication in conjunction with events such as National Missing Children Day, conducted annually on May 25. It was determined that these previous approaches, heavily reliant on a traditional media event press release, resulted in only localized and sometimes sporadic media coverage. With the launch of the new national website, the Centre adopted a new publication approach revolving around the website, leveraging social media and the communications capability of key partner agencies and interested media.

The new approach identified specific types of cases from across the country, for example children believed to be missing as a result of a stranger abduction, or parental abductions where the children have been taken out of Canada. The approach also called for the agencies that had cases being profiled to engage their communications personnel and social media avenues to broaden the reach of the campaign. The strategy continued to include more traditional avenues such as issuing a news release, but not as the sole focus. Online media also became engaged. One significant online media contributor provided reach to 12 million unique monthly subscribers—most of whom were located in Canada.

In May 2013 the Centre implemented this new approach with significant success. Online analytics demonstrated that public traffic to the Canada's Missing website increased from an average of 400 visits per day to 4,000 visits per day during the campaign. It also provided members of the public with opportunities to "re-tweet" or "like" the profiles of the campaign to further increase the reach of the initiative. This new approach was subsequently used to conduct a similar tailored initiative on Missing Aboriginal Women in the fall of 2013. The website approach is currently considered a communications best practice. Previous strategies that involved the Centre sending posters to partners for their office bulletin boards have been discontinued as partners can print posters directly from the website.

A key component of the Canada's Missing website is its search functionality. This feature allows users to search the profiles on the website using various descriptors. For example, users could search for and read the published profiles of all missing women with brown hair or search for all profiles published on the site pertaining to unidentified remains with tattoos. The extensive search functionality addresses a variety of needs, from the casual visitor to frequent visitors who spend time engaged in amateur sleuthing and have, as a result, provided tips. It is important to note that not all cases in Canada are published on the website.

Canada's Missing is an investigative tool, and so the primary investigator must determine whether it is appropriate to utilize, bearing in mind the unique aspects of the investigation at hand. Which cases are published, and what information about each case appears, is determined by the primary investigator.

Occurrence Analysis Service

One of the Centre's core functions is to examine potential case linkages to assist in resolving cases or to advance investigations: "An investigator may perform analysis comparing an MP [Missing Person] occurrence with unsolved UR [Unidentified Remains] occurrences, or exploring similar occurrences for potential connections or patterns. However, without access to sophisticated analysis tools and accurate information, the reach of this analysis is limited" (RCMP, 2013a, p. 32). Though the typical investigator may utilize his or her own agency's database or CPIC to assist in occurrence analysis as a starting point, he or she may now leverage the Occurrence Analysis Service provided by the National Centre or the applicable Regional Centre.

The flexible analytical tools built into the Missing Children/Person and Unidentified Remains database provide a degree of automated occurrence analysis. Specialists within the Centres can provide a more comprehensive and customized analysis upon request by a primary investigator. When receiving such a request, the national or regional analyst combines their expertise and experience, the tools in the Missing Children/Person and Unidentified Remains database, and their knowledge of investigative best practices to conduct a customized analysis to provide a primary investigator with additional investigative avenues.

If the Missing Children/Person and Unidentified Remains database identifies a potential match or link to a case assigned to an analyst, it alerts them so the information can be examined. If at any time the analyst determines that there is a possible link, they will advise the primary investigators on each investigation to communicate directly with each other to examine the possibility of a link. For example, with investigators across the country updating CPIC data on current and pre-existing cases, as well as uploading data regarding unidentified remains on behalf of coroners or medical examiners, the possibility exists that a link may be made at the initial request for analysis or later on when information on other investigations is updated resulting in the database algorithms signalling a potential match. When "introduced" to each other, the primary investigators in each case will look to identify factors that are available to support or refute the match, such as fingerprints, dental records, or DNA.

The Missing Children/Person and Unidentified Remains database and the specialized analysts consider each component in order to determine the relevance of similarities or differences in case data against other cases. An examination of the data may result in a link being made between cases, but it may also result in an exclusion. An exclusion is information that demonstrates the cases are not related. For example, when comparing a 25-year-old male with brown hair and brown eyes reported missing and last seen in 2010 to a case involving a 25-year-old unidentified male with brown hair and brown eyes whose remains were found in 2009, the similarities may result in the database alerting an analyst of a possible link. The analyst would first examine the details to confirm that there has been no error in the entry of the date information. If the time sequence is confirmed, the analyst will note that the cases are of two different individuals and will mark both records as reviewed and excluded from each other. This ensures that if another analyst receives information indicating that the two cases may be linked, they can review the exclusion to determine if it still applies or if the new information changes the factors that led to the exclusion (e.g., the primary witness who provided a date of disappearance was mistaken about the year).

The Missing Children/Person and Unidentified Remains database, which supports the aforementioned Information Collection Service, Occurrence Publication Service, and Occurrence Analysis Service, was developed utilizing a multi-phased approach. The first phase was completed in October 2014. With the implementation of the database, the support and population of the Canada's Missing website was integrated into the national database.

Best Practices and Research Service

The Best Practices and Research Service assesses investigative best practices to support a consistent approach across the country and conducts research in order to inform investigative decisions. Specifically, this service uses the knowledge and experience of Subject Matter Experts (SMEs) and takes into consideration feedback regarding community and family engagement and sensitivities. The four functions of this service are: data analysis and statistics; knowledge collection and synthesis; best practice compilation; and general publication (RCMP, 2013a, p. 37).

Of these, the greatest challenge and therefore the greatest change has been the identification of investigative best practices for missing persons and unidentified remains in Canada. The best practices were compiled by experts representing police and coroner/medical examiners (RCMP, 2013b, p. 2). The group identified effective practices that were not necessarily uniformly implemented by police agencies in Canada. Effective practices universally employed across agencies were not included in the compilation.

The "best practices do not address the local details about how an investigation is executed in an agency, which typically depends on the organization and resources available" (RCMP, 2013b, 2). Rather, the best practices were drafted utilizing a generic agency approach. For example, a best practice is that an agency engages its communications department to issue media releases at specific intervals during an investigation. However, the best practices do not advise on what each agency's communications protocols should be.

At the outset, the Centre recognized that to ensure best practices met the needs of investigative agencies, representatives of various agencies with different knowledge and experience in the actual compilation and assessment of the practices needed to be consulted. In October 2011, SMEs were brought together in Ottawa to review and discuss best practices. Drafts of the document were then circulated to various police missing person or unidentified remains agencies to solicit feedback as well as additional elements for consideration. As a result, the first Centre Best Practices compendium was published in the fall of 2012 and made available to Canadian police services, coroners, and medical examiners.

In taking a consultative and collaborative approach to developing investigative best practices, the National Centre made it a product of the "community of practice." In doing so, policing, coroner, and medical examiner partners have contributed to the best practices and have been engaged in championing the adoption of the practices.

Since the release of the Best Practices compendium, the Centre has been contacted by police agencies requesting copies and/or indicating that they are incorporating the practices into their policies or standard operating procedures. Similarly, the Centre has received requests for the document from provincial Departments of Public Safety to assist in gap or issue identification. As a result, the standardization of these investigative practices is expanding even though the Centre does not have the authority to mandate their adoption by other agencies.

Client feedback has indicated that the utilization of a generic agency approach has facilitated dialogue about the adoption of the best practices by related agencies. The document, which includes sample forms and checklists, is now utilized as a basis for the Centre's subsequently developed training for police.

The core SMEs were brought together once again in early 2014 to identify potential changes and to consider new additions. This ensures that changes in investigational tools and techniques are reflected in the document, as are applicable findings of significant reports such as the Missing Women Commission of Inquiry Report *Forsaken: The Report of the Missing Women Commission of Inquiry* (Oppal, 2013).

To lead change and innovation, you must ensure that your clients and employees understand and "buy-in" to your vision for change. To do this effectively, you need to continually reassess services and initiatives in order to ensure that your services meet the needs of your clients. This approach has enhanced the Centre's effectiveness and also ensured partner agencies feel they have contributed to the advancement of investigations in Canada, increasing future engagement.

The Multi-Discipline, Multi-Agency Missing Person Investigation Initiative

The Multi-Discipline, Multi-Agency Missing Person Investigation Initiative, referred to as the M3I2 in short form, came as a result of bilateral consultation between the National Centre and policing partners brought together to explore the development of an investigative tool. The Centre took the opportunity to speak with the policing partners about their needs. Edmonton Police Service representatives indicated an interest in brainstorming specific outstanding investigations with other agencies and SMEs to identify new investigative avenues.

National Centre personnel noted that the brainstorming approach was often used in the investigation of homicides. In these instances, consultation tended to cross areas of expertise. However, few instances could be found in Canada where the consultation expanded far beyond one's own agency or beyond a specialized national or provincial unit providing very specific services or subject matter expertise.

In the United States there are instances where consultation on outstanding cases expanded well beyond one's own agency or where non-police entities engage in similar functions. One example is the Vidocq Society, which was founded in 1990 (Vidocq Society, 2014a). The Vidocq Society is composed of forensic and investigative experts who meet monthly in Philadelphia, where law enforcement from across the US present cases and are provided with feedback (Vidocq Society, 2014b).

Inquiries by the Centre to various police agencies indicated interest in presenting outstanding cases to subject matter experts in order to advance or resolve investigations. As a result, the National Centre hosted a four-day M3I2 meeting in March 2012 in Edmonton, Alberta. The event was coordinated jointly by the National Centre, the Edmonton Police Service, and the RCMP's Project KARE (Alberta). Missing person investigators from across Canada came together to consult on outstanding case files with subject matter experts to identify additional investigative options to be pursued. Investigators were advised that only cases where all standard avenues had been exhausted would be considered for presentation.

The first M3I2 provided an opportunity for case presentation followed by round table discussions with SMEs. The SME team was composed of personnel from various police services such as Forensic Services, Behavioral Sciences (including ViCLAS, or Violent Crime Linkage Analysis System) and Criminal Profiling, Major Crime, CPIC, Missing Persons, and Cold Case Investigations. There was also an SME from a medical examiner's office as well as a forensic anthropologist.

The participants also discussed other outstanding cases with the SMEs. As a direct result of these conversations, one SME provided an expert opinion that conclusively linked an unidentified remains investigation in one agency's area with a missing person investigation in another. Once the link was confirmed the investigation continued as a homicide investigation. (Note: this offering of the M3I2 predated the establishment of the national Missing Children/Person and Unidentified Remains database).

The feedback by participants—both presenters and SMEs—on the M3I2 was overwhelmingly positive, with a clear indication that these opportunities are important to assist law enforcement agencies in resolving and/or advancing their investigations. In addition, the discussions and issues raised contributed to the assessment of the Best Practices compendium. The true value of the M3I2 was in bringing "fresh eyes" and new perspectives to investigations, as well as involving partner agencies in the planning and delivery of the event. This ensured that the event was viewed as a productive one, supported by and engaged in by practitioners from multiple jurisdictions.

Given its success, the National Centre hosted a second M3I2 in 2014. The appetite within the investigative community was high. The Centre recognized that all of the SMEs in the first M3I2 were police specialists or specialists working in some capacity with police agencies, such as constables who were also university professors.

To bring in new perspectives, the Centre reached out to research specialists and academics to gauge interest in involvement in the next M3I2. The interest was quite high. The Centre also reached out to investigators to assess any concerns in involving non-investigative personnel. Concerns were addressed through the implementation of non-disclosure agreements, thereby ensuring additional and varied new perspectives would be included in the second M3I2.

With funding from Defence Research and Development Canada, the second M3I2 was held in British Columbia. Once again, cases were presented and advice provided. However, the changes in the methods for the selection of the SMEs resulted in a noticeable change in the feedback provided to investigators. In this iteration of the M3I2, investigators with unidentified remains cases received information focused on:

- new forensic identification techniques that could be applied;
- previously applied techniques that might bear revisiting;
- investigative methods for identification utilizing artifacts (i.e., personal objects); and
- investigative methods focusing on techniques that support the solicitation of tips from the public.

As per Centre practice, participants were asked for feedback, which was again overwhelmingly positive, with participants indicating a willingness to participate in future meetings. Most investigators indicated that participating in the case presentations by other investigators gave them ideas that could also be applied to outstanding investigations of their own.

Through this unique initiative focusing specifically on missing person and unidentified remains investigations, the Centre not only advanced specific investigations but also continued to build a sense of community amongst investigators across Canada. The level of engagement of partners stemming from continually applying an "all agency," consultative, and collaborative approach has resulted in increased support for the vision for the National Centre, working in conjunction with Regional Centres to provide specialized services ultimately designed to bring closure to the families of missing persons.

Leveraging Best Practices

Throughout its development, implementation and normal operations, each National Centre service is routinely assessed to identify opportunities for improvement and enhancement in order to better meet the needs of investigators. When the Centre was established in 2011, the pre-existing training for missing children and parental child abduction investigation was determined to be out of date. Consultation with SMEs confirmed the need for and interest in training in missing children investigations. Participants pointed out that when investigators transfer into other specialized units, such as drug sections or commercial crime units, they typically receive specialized training on the types of investigations they will encounter in their new job. The same was not true for investigators transferring into missing person or unidentified remains units. Therefore, the Centre partnered with the Canadian Police College to pilot training aimed at these investigators. Specialists from across the country came as attendees, instructors, and in certain cases as both.

Overall, participants provided very positive feedback regarding the initiative. There were very popular elements, such as case reviews, although it was noted these are offered in many other venues across North America. Other elements were identified as having less immediate value and more of a "nice to know" component. For example, information regarding proposed legislative changes did not provide investigators with tools or techniques they could immediately apply to investigations, and so was deemed to be more appropriate for a conference or workshop venue. Information that was found to be of very high value was examined to determine the components that could be offered online to reach the largest number of investigators.

In reviewing the training and feedback, the Centre immediately noted two elements that could be ready as online courses in relatively short order. The first was "Child Abduction: Applicable Legislation and Charging Guidelines." The second was "Child Abduction: AMBER Alert."

Launched in January 2013, the two courses are available online in both French and English. By mid-2014, approximately 900 investigators had completed the 1.5-hour AMBER Alert course, reaching a far greater number than could have been trained individually in a classroom setting.

Next, the Centre developed a trio of courses, described as Level 1 (introductory level), specific to each of the types of investigations within the Centre's mandate:

• Missing Child Investigation
• Missing Person Investigation
• Unidentified Remains Investigation

Each online course was designed in consultation with various SMEs. The Level 1 courses were launched in June 2014. Utilizing investigative best practices throughout the training, the Centre expanded the distribution of the information directly to front line investigators.

Liaison and Coordination Service

The Liaison and Coordination Service focuses on creating links between agencies or organizations in order to advance investigations or programs. A Regional Centre, having contacts with police or other governmental agencies in their assigned geographical area and knowing specialists in relevant fields, may be in a position to introduce investigators to each other, locate an appropriate point of contact within an agency, or refer an investigator to the specialist they need. Where one of the agencies involved is international, the National Centre is notified and becomes engaged where appropriate. The National Centre also collaborates with similar services in foreign countries, such as:

- the International Center for Missing and Exploited Children (ICMEC), which coordinates the Global Missing Children Network;
- the U.S. Department of Justice's National Missing and Unidentified Persons System (NamUs);
- countries participating in the INTERPOL network; and
- countries that are signatory to The Hague Convention on the Civil Aspects of International Child Abduction.

On a national level, the networking and rapid response capabilities of the Centre and other federal government partners have been essential to the interdiction of child abductions where the abductor sought to remove the child from Canada. The success of the interdiction can be dependent on the very rapid reporting by the "left behind parent" to the police of primary jurisdiction. Similarly, rapid outreach by the police of jurisdiction impacts the effectiveness of this strategy. On an international level, this capability has been essential for the interdiction of child abductions where the abductor has already removed the child from Canada. In very specific circumstances, the Centre is able to work with police in other countries to intercept the child and abductor while in transit. With the National and the Regional Centres being involved in the liaison function, these units are also well positioned to advocate and implement investigative best practices pertaining to the identification of primary jurisdiction.

Leading the Change

While change management in one organization is complex and often mired as a result of resistance to change, the challenges can be magnified when seeking to implement change across multiple agencies on a national level, especially where there is no effective means to require compliance. The legacy of the vision of the original ad hoc working group, the forces that led to the mandate given to the National Centre, the nature of the issues, fiscal realities, and the number of interested or involved parties across Canada have meant that the Centre needed to utilize a collaborative and consultative approach. Each advancement has been attributable to the collaborative approach that has been consistently applied by the Centre, and which extends beyond the usual law enforcement community to include coroners/medical examiners, non-governmental organizations, academia, and foreign agencies. For example, the ongoing enhancement and evolution of the investigative Best Practices compendium continues to be achieved through dialogue and collaborative forums such as the M3I2, and in response to academic and government research. As police agencies discuss and incorporate these practices into their policies and investigators are educated through online courses, a level of consistency across the country is achieved. It also increases the level of engagement to one of partners who view the collaborative approach as one they can participate in, which can overcome some of the miscommunication that has taken place between investigative agencies in the past.

The services and initiatives of the Centre continue to evolve just as the manner in which investigators in Canada view and advance these investigations continues to evolve. The core concept for all services is that they must be relevant and meet the needs of investigators, utilizing a national approach as opposed to an agency-specific approach. The Centre's leadership requires lateral consultation within the RCMP as well as with other agencies on the development of each service in order to ensure that the needs of client agencies are met in the most effective way. This allows the Centre to be "intelligence led" in determining the viability and suitability of a service or initiative. It also allows the Centre to identify opportunities for enhancement, evolution, and additional engagement.

Leading the Charge

The Centre does not have the authority to mandate that external agencies implement specific operating procedures, tools, techniques, or innovations. As such, in addition to using a consultative approach, it also needed a more prescriptive approach in specific circumstances. For example, the Centre realized that not all investigators were entering their investigations on CPIC. As the entry and retention on CPIC of these reports was not mandatory, the Centre might receive requests regarding cases that had either never been on or had been removed from CPIC. This posed two problems:

1. If the information was not on CPIC, then investigators across the country did not have access to it and would not be aware that a person or child they were interacting with was a missing person.
2. It would affect the Centre's ability to link cases utilizing the Missing Children/Person and Unidentified Remains database that is fed by CPIC.

The Centre leadership adopted the position that unless a case was on CPIC, the investigator could not access Centre services or participate in case-specific initiatives. Recognizing that exigent circumstances might arise, the Officer in Charge of the Centre has the authority to provide an exemption to the policy. This is meant to apply to situations such as AMBER Alerts. It also ensures that in instances that are not urgent, the Officer in Charge is alerted to investigators or agencies that are not utilizing CPIC, and can then reach out to the appropriate senior management to address the issue.

Though there were a number of people who expressed concern that this approach would result in investigators choosing not to use Centre services, the opposite has proven to be the case. As they become aware of the services and standards, investigators seeking assistance are ensuring that their cases are entered on CPIC. In taking this stance, the Centre has effected change, raising awareness of best practices and leading investigators to take specific actions to advance their investigations.

The Road Ahead

The law enforcement community is a complex one. Investigators are often pulled in a variety of directions trying to address increasingly complex crimes while also facing growing expectations for services related to matters of a non-criminal nature, such as mental health situations and missing person reports. Their ability to respond is affected by many factors, including resources, training, funding, and the priority placed on various situations by the communities they serve. In this environment, new initiatives can find themselves competing for relevance and engagement in order to gain traction.

The National Centre has effected change at local, national, and international levels. In partnership with practitioners in the law enforcement community, including coroners and medical examiners, the Centre has enhanced and advanced missing person and unidentified remains investigations, effectively discharging each of the elements outlined in its mandate.

Directly as a result of these efforts, investigators in Canada have support from specialized investigators and analysts who leverage the Missing Children/Person and Unidentified Remains database to link cases across jurisdictions. Investigators also have access to the national website, Canada's Missing, which allows the public to search the profiles using descriptive and geographical information to locate profiles of interest and submit tips for consideration to investigators. The same website is used as a vehicle to publish *Fast Fact Sheets* providing statistical information to the public to increase awareness of the scope and scale of the issue of missing persons in Canada. Investigative agencies also have direct access to current online training based on the Best Practices Compendium supporting specific standards in these investigations.

As a result, investigators in Canada today have a much greater level of support than was available before 2010. They also have the opportunity to obtain training specific to this field and collaborate on advancing complex and outstanding investigations. In adopting best practices, agencies that did not have all of these elements in their policies and procedures can improve how they manage these investigations.

Through the National Centre for Missing Persons and Unidentified Remains and its continued dialogue with partner agencies, the road ahead entails the ongoing consideration, development, and assessment of innovative approaches to make sure that the support being provided is relevant, timely, and facilitates the advancement and successful resolution of missing persons and unidentified remains investigations. It is also vital that the Centre continues to advance the engagement of partners in various programs, as this is key to effecting change and ensuring that investigative agencies recognize that the status quo of years gone by is simply not an option.

Acknowledgements

A very special thanks to my husband, Insp. Tim Bird (ret. RCMP and WPS), an exceptional investigator whose expertise in other complex areas of policing has greatly contributed to the advancement of new or innovative approaches in policing. Aspects of these approaches have, over the past 20 years, been incorporated into a number of my national and international programs including in development of the NCMPUR. Thank you, Tim!

References

Burczycka, M. (2010). *Policing resources in Canada 2010*. Report No. 85-225-X. Ottawa, ON: Statistics Canada. Retrieved from www.statcan.gc.ca/pub/85-225-x/2010000/part-partie1-eng.htm.

Dalley, M. (1988). *Missing children's registry: Annual report on Canada's missing children 1988*. Ottawa, ON: Royal Canadian Mounted Police.

Government of Canada. (2010, March 3). *Speech from the Throne to open the third session fortieth parliament of Canada: Making Canada the best place for families*. Retrieved from www.parl.gc.ca/Parlinfo/Documents/ThroneSpeech/40-3-e.html.

Greenspan, E. L., Rosenberg, M., & Henein, M. (2015). *Martin's annual criminal code, police edition.* Toronto, ON: Canada Law Book.

Jeffrey, P. (2011, April 1). Lead change for the better. *Financial Post.* Retrieved from business.financialpost.com/2011/04/01/lead-change-for-the-better/.

Martin, S. (2011, September 30). The life and death of Clifford Olson. *Globe and Mail.* Retrieved from www.theglobeandmail.com/news/national/the-life-and-death-of-clifford-olson/article4197011/.

Oppal, W. (2013). *Forsaken: The report of the Missing Women Commission of Inquiry.* Vancouver, BC: Missing Women Commission of Inquiry. Retrieved from www.missingwomeninquiry.ca/obtain-report/.

Royal Canadian Mounted Police. (2012, August 12). *RCMP seeking the public's assistance in historical investigation.* Press release. Retrieved from www.rcmp-grc.gc.ca/mb/news-nouvelles/2012/rosner-eng.htm.

Royal Canadian Mounted Police. (2013a). *NCMPUR business architecture.* Unpublished document.

Royal Canadian Mounted Police. (2013b). *NCMPUR best practices,* Version 1.2. Unpublished document.

Royal Canadian Mounted Police. (2013c). *2013 Fast Fact Sheet.* Ottawa, ON: Royal Canadian Mounted Police. Retrieved from www.canadasmissing.ca/pubs/2013/index-eng.htm.

Royal Canadian Mounted Police. (2014). Canadian Police Information Centre. Retrieved from www.cpic-cipc.ca/about-ausujet/index-eng.htm.

Vidocq Society. (2014a). Founders. Retrieved from www.vidocq.org/founders/.

Vidocq Society. (2014b). Case acceptance. Retrieved from www.vidocq.org/case-acceptance/.

United Nations. (2013). *International migrant stock: Total.* New York, NY: United Nations Department of Economic and Social Affairs, Population Division. Retrieved from www.un.org/en/development/desa/population/migration/data/estimates2/estimatestotal.shtml.

Related Sources

Amber Alert Europe: www.amberalert.eu/

Australian Federal Police Missing Persons: www.missingpersons.gov.au/

International Center for Missing and Exploited Children: www.icmec.org/

Missing Children Society of Canada: mcsc.ca/

NCMPUR's Canada's Missing: www.canadasmissing.ca/

New Zealand Missing Persons: www.police.govt.nz/missing-persons

U.K. Home Office Missing Children and Adults Strategy: www.gov.uk/government/publications/missing-children-and-adults-strategy

U.S. DOJ NamUs System: www.namus.gov/

Chapter 12

Missing in the US-Mexico Borderlands

Robin Reineke (Colibrí Center for Human Rights)
Bruce E. Anderson (Pima County Office of the Medical Examiner)

"Migrants shine a powerful light on things that need to change."
—Father Alejandro Solalinde[1]

At the end of May 2008, a 26-year-old man named Diego[2] began the journey from his hometown in Guerrero, Mexico, to join his brothers in South Carolina. Diego was the last of his seven brothers to migrate to the US. The family had been struggling for years to make ends meet as farmworkers in southern Mexico, and many had found work in the United States. Although the pay was also low, living in the US at least provided hope for a better future for the children. In early June, Diego met a human smuggler in Altar, Sonora. The next day, he and a group of others travelled to the border town of Sasabe, Arizona, and then followed the guide over the border fence, into the desert.

On July 7 the remains of an adult male were discovered on the Tohono O'Odham Nation, near the village of Nolic. The body had been reported by a group of migrants who were apprehended by U.S. Border Patrol. The agents located the remains and contacted the Tohono O'Odham Police Department. Upon arrival at the Pima County Office of the Medical Examiner (PCOME) the body was briefly examined by a medico-legal death investigator, who noted the condition of the remains as decomposed, and the belongings as consisting of clothing, a rosary, and a religious card. The body and the items were photographed. On the back of the religious card, which was of James, the Apostle (*Santiago Apóstol*), there were words written in shaky, scrawling cursive: "Victorino," "Grande," and "Acattandela." The clothing included black Dickies pants, a blue button-up shirt, and red and black Nike sneakers.

In mid-July, Diego's eldest brother called the Medical Examiner's Office and

55

spoke with Robin Reineke (the first author). A graduate student volunteer at the time, Reineke completed a missing person report for Diego. A few weeks later, she noticed that the description of Diego's clothing—a blue shirt, black pants, and red and black shoes—matched the clothing found with the remains from July 7. With his permission, she emailed Diego's brother the photos of the clothing and items found with the body. He called back immediately, saying, "It's my brother. It's Diego. I'm certain." When she asked him how he knew, he said, "The prayer card is of Santiago Apostol, the patron saint of our hometown, Acatlan de la Cruz." The writing on the back of the card was not "Acattandela" but actually "Acatlan de la Cruz," the letters woven together tightly.

This link, while strong for the family, was not strong enough to establish a positive identification. Dr. Bruce Anderson (the second author), who had completed the forensic anthropology examination, confirmed that the biological profile of the decedent was consistent with the physical description of Diego. The family remembered that Diego had knee surgery a few years back and sent the medical radiographs. These X-ray films of Diego's left knee were then compared to the post-mortem X-rays that Dr. Anderson had taken. It was a match. Diego's body was sent to South Carolina to be buried where his brothers, his wife, and his young child, a US citizen, could visit his grave.

Introduction

Diego's body was one of 161 identified or suspected migrants discovered deceased in 2008 in southern Arizona, and one of over 2,300 discovered in the state between the years 2001 and 2014.[3] United States Border Patrol has reported that the remains of 6,330 individuals believed to be migrants were discovered on US soil between 1998 and 2014 (U.S. Customs and Border Patrol, 2014). The Pima County Office of the Medical Examiner, located in Tucson, Arizona, has been at the epicentre of this crisis, acting as the medico-legal agency for more than a third of these cases. Despite the best efforts of those at the PCOME, nearly a third of the cases examined at this facility remain unidentified to date. At the end of 2014, the Pima County public cemetery contained the remains of nearly 900 unidentified individuals believed to be migrants, and the Colibrí Center for Human Rights, a non-profit organization partnering with the PCOME, had reports for 1,476 missing persons last seen attempting to cross the Arizona portion of the US-Mexico border.[4]

This chapter will provide the basis for understanding the phenomenon of migrant deaths in southern Arizona between 2001 and 2014, the factors leading to hundreds of unidentified dead and missing persons on the US side of the border, and the efforts on the part of the PCOME and its collaborators to identify the dead and assist the families of the missing. Although the cause of death for most of those examined by the PCOME was found to be exposure to the elements, and the manner of death for most was determined to be accidental, the broader context in which these deaths occurred reveals their socially structured nature. We argue that a mass disaster has slowly unfolded along the southern border of the United States since the mid-1990s. Far from "natural," disasters always have deep roots in social structures and patterns. Anthropologically defined, a disaster is "a process/event combining a potentially destructive agent/force from the natural, modified, or built environment and a population in a socially and economically produced condition of vulnerability, resulting in a perceived disruption of the customary relative satisfactions of individual and social needs for physical survival, social order, and meaning" (Hoffman & Oliver-Smith, 2002, p. 4). Like most disasters, the crisis along the US-Mexico border has been socially engineered, rather than naturally occurring. Both the causes and the effects exist at the social level, rather than at the individual level.

The tendency to blame individual "risky" behaviour is common in both public health literature and popular discourse about disasters (Hoffman & Oliver-Smith, 2002). This individual-level framework for understanding human behaviour is also highly prevalent in conversations about migration, where the actions of migrants, such as that of crossing the border, are seen as poor individual "choices." However, when such choices are made by thousands of people each year, it is vitally important that they are seen in their proper social, cultural, and economic context. Failing to do so invites solutions that are inappropriate for solving large-scale social problems, and may in fact cause further harm. In the context of the US-Mexico border, "crossing the border is not a choice to engage in a risk behaviour but rather a process necessary to survive, to make life *less* risky" (Holmes, 2013, p. 21, emphasis in original).

Whether evidenced by the bodies or told by the families, the stories of the dead and the missing point to massive structural vulnerability and inequality in 21st-century North America. Structural vulnerability is defined as "a positionality that imposes physical/emotional suffering on specific population groups and individuals in patterned ways," (Quesada, Hart, & Bourgois, 2011, p. 340). Structurally vulnerable individuals are members of a group or class that has been disenfranchised through social processes such as economic exploitation and racial or gender-based discrimination. Importantly, the effects of structural vulnerability are felt not only emotionally or socially, but also physically, and cause increased risk of severe harm, including premature death (Friedman, 2009; Krieger, 2001).

Migrants crossing the US-Mexico border are structurally vulnerable on multiple levels. The majority of emigrants fleeing their homes in Mexico and Central America in the early 21st century have done so because of extreme poverty, racial marginalization, and/or individual persecution or threat of violence. Once in the US, "Latino migrant laborers are a population especially vulnerable to structural violence because their economic location in the lowest rungs of the US labor market is conjoined with overt xenophobia, ethnic discrimination, and scapegoating" (Quesada, Hart, & Bourgois, 2011, p. 340). Whether crossing the border for the first time, or crossing after being deported, migrants are exposed to a unique set of risks along the US-Mexico border that members of more privileged classes do not experience.

Anthropologist-physician Paul Farmer has criticized contemporary American anthropology for failing to integrate the biological with the social: "Complex biosocial phenomena are the focus of most anthropological inquires, and yet the integration of history, political economy, and biology remains lacking in contemporary anthropology or sociology" (Farmer, 2004, p. 308). The topic of this chapter readily fits into the label of "complex biosocial phenomena," as social structures and economic systems have had a direct impact on living human bodies. In turn, these bodies reveal embodied social suffering. Indeed, "there are few contexts in which the mutual constitutionality of the physical and the social are so starkly displayed as in a disaster" (Hoffman & Oliver-Smith, 2002, p. 26). Throughout nearly a decade of collaboration, the authors have taken a biosocial approach to both applied and academic work in a disaster context. That approach is represented here.

Migrant Death along the US-Mexico Border: Background and History

There has been overwhelming consensus in academic literature that the increase in migrant fatalities along the US-Mexico border beginning in the mid-1990s was brought about by a change in US border enforcement policy (Cornelius, 2001, 2005; Eschbach et al., 1999; Martínez et al., 2014; Nevins, 2005; Nevins & Aizeki, 2008; Reineke & Martínez, 2014; Rubio-Goldsmith et al., 2006). This increase was drastic. In just one year, the deaths of migrants crossing into California more than doubled, rising from 23 in 1994 to 61 in 1995 (Cornelius, 2001). Overall, between 1994 and 2000, that state saw a 509 percent increase in the fatalities of migrants (Cornelius, 2001, p. 669). In Arizona, the increase happened a few years later, but was ultimately more severe, has lasted longer, and continues to this day. From

1985 to 1998, the number of recovered migrant remains for U.S. Border Patrol's Tucson Sector in Arizona averaged 19 per year (Anderson, 2008). From 2001 through 2014, the yearly average was 170, representing a nearly tenfold increase (calculated from U.S. Customs and Border Patrol, 2014).

While there was some increase in migration during this period, it was not proportional to the escalation in migrant fatalities. As noted by Wayne Cornelius regarding California, "some portion of the increase in fatalities from 1995 to 2000 can be attributed to a rising volume of unauthorized Mexico-to-US migration during that period; however, the per-year increases in mortality are much larger than the increases in Border Patrol apprehensions" (2001, p. 670). A 2013 report released by a nonpartisan non-profit organization found that the deaths of immigrants along the entire US-Mexico border increased dramatically while the number of entrants declined: "In other words, between FY [fiscal year] 1999 and FY 2012, immigrant deaths increased by more than 80 percent at the same time apprehensions, a measure of illegal entry, declined by 77 percent" (Anderson, 2013, p. 3).

However, the nature of migration changed in the late 1990s following the effects of the North American Free Trade Agreement (NAFTA). NAFTA eliminated tariffs on several agricultural products and allowed US corporations to export cheap, mass-produced goods into the Mexican market (Nevins, 2007). In effect, NAFTA put small farmers in direct competition with large, heavily subsidized and flexible multinational corporations (Johnson, 1994; Bacon, 2004; Nevins & Aizeki, 2008). The effect on small-scale producers was devastating. An estimated 1.3 million Mexican farmers lost their jobs immediately, and another million workers who depended upon the farmers became unemployed over time (Polaski, 2004; Wise, 2010). After the effects of NAFTA, migration from Mexico to the US shifted from traditional seasonal migration from northern and central Mexico to new migrations from southern Mexico and Central America by those looking for long-term work.

The same year that NAFTA went into effect, Doris Meissner, the head of the Immigration and Naturalization Service (INS) under President Bill Clinton, signed off on the 1994 Border Patrol Strategic Plan. The strategy, known as "prevention through deterrence," rested upon the assumption that migrants would be discouraged from attempting a crossing if they recognized how difficult and dangerous it would be (Cornelius, 2001; Andreas, 2009; Ewing, 2014). Geography would be an instrumental part of the tactics deployed at the border. Through what was called "segmented enforcement," Border Patrol agents and surveillance technology were focused on urban, more easily crossed sections of the border, while the remote, arid, mountainous stretches of the border were left to act as a "natural barrier." One of the most significant effects of the new Border Patrol strategy was to push migrants into the deserts of Arizona beginning in the early 2000s. Meissner told the Arizona Republic in 2000, "We did believe that geography would be an ally to us ... it was our sense that the number of people crossing the border through Arizona would go down to a trickle, once people realized what it's like." Border Patrol's Tucson Sector quickly overtook all other sectors in both the number of apprehensions and the number of deaths (Reineke & Martínez, 2014). As would be expected, the overwhelming cause of death for these unfortunate migrants was determined by PCOME pathologists to be exposure to the natural elements.

As of 2013, the PCOME provided medico-legal death investigation over the entire southern border of U.S. Border Patrol's Tucson Sector (see Figure 12.1). Prior to 2013, the PCOME did not investigate deaths in Cochise County, and provided such services only to the western two-thirds of the Sector's border (Anderson, 2008). This still accounted for 95 percent of migrant fatalities in the state of Arizona (Reineke, 2016), and will account for the majority of the data discussed here. The PCOME is rare in the border context for the amount of detailed data the agency makes available to the public regarding the deaths of migrants each year. This, along with the agency's commitment to upholding best practices, willingness to partner with humanitarian organizations, and high identification rate has set the office apart from other jurisdictions on the US-Mexico border (Rubio-Goldsmith et al., 2006). Data from the PCOME have been widely discussed in forensic science literature, academic scholarship, and public policy reports. Only a brief summary of the demographics and the causes of death for migrant decedents will be provided here.

Data from the PCOME include both cases of individuals identified and known to be migrants crossing the border, and cases of unidentified remains believed to be migrants. With such a high number of unidentified individuals being discovered each year, the chief pathologist and forensic anthropologist at the PCOME devised a mechanism to predictively mark unidentified remains cases believed to be migrants as "Undocumented Border Crossers" or UBCs (Anderson & Parks, 2008). This was done to provide a more accurate and complete count of the number of deaths associated with attempted border crossings in southern Arizona. The authors explain, "While we readily acknowledge that this policy may serve to slightly over-report the number of undocumented border crosser deaths, to exclude the hundreds of unidentified people recovered from the Sonoran Desert would certainly *vastly* under-report the problem" (Anderson & Parks, 2008, p. 6). Indeed, without the unidentified, the complete count for this office would be reduced by a third.

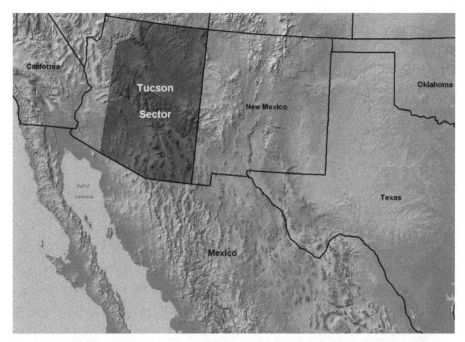

FIGURE 12.1   Tucson Sector, the area under the responsibility of the Pima County Office of the
Medical Examiner.

Source: Tucson Sector of the U.S. Border Patrol, printed by permission

The following data and demographics come from a 2014 study of PCOME data
(Martínez et al., 2014). Between fiscal year 1990 and 2013, the PCOME investigated 2,413 cases of deaths of known or suspected migrants. Out of this total,
80 percent were male, 17 percent were female, and 3 percent are currently of
undetermined sex, although DNA profiles that reveal genetic sex continue to
be received at the PCOME. Among those who were identified, which is a total
of 1,583 between 1990 and 2013, 82 percent were Mexican nationals and 14 percent were from Central American countries (most commonly Guatemala, El
Salvador, and Honduras). The other 4 percent were either from South America
or the Caribbean, or the country of origin was not recorded. The mean, median,
and modal ages were all approximately 31 years. Overall, those who have died
attempting to cross the southern border into Arizona can be characterized as
working-aged Mexican men who died from exposure to the elements.

The Unidentified

The main challenge for the PCOME has been that of identification. Arizona
now ranks third, following California and New York, for the number of cases of
unidentified remains entered into the National Missing and Unidentified Persons

System, or NamUs (Mejdrich, 2012). The PCOME was the investigating agency for the vast majority of these cases, which are believed to be migrants who died attempting to cross the border. Despite the relatively high identification rate of the PCOME, the roughly 30 to 40 percent of all cases each year who were not identified have added up over the years to approximately 800 individuals. The factors leading to such a high number of unidentified remains are both ecological and sociological. The structural vulnerability that exposes migrants to the risks associated with an undocumented crossing of the US-Mexico border also contributes to their anonymity in death. Migrants' lived experience of social marginalization impacts the work of investigators at the PCOME, who struggle without consistent access to missing persons data, investigation assistance from local law enforcement, clues based on migrants' personal effects, and other assists that are available in typical medico-legal contexts within the US. All of these challenges relate to the experience of missing migrants in life, and the experiences of their families once they begin to search. This section will explore the problem by looking at the information available to investigators upon examining the body. The following section, "The Missing," will explore the problem from the other side, the information supplied by the families about the missing.

The same conditions that lead to the deaths of migrants complicate the efforts to identify their remains. Known for its natural beauty, the Sonoran Desert is also known for its aridity and extremely high daytime temperatures, which range from 100°F to 110°F (38°C to 43°C) in the summer months. For reasons discussed above, migrants trek through some of the most remote regions of the Sonoran Desert. As was the case for Diego, those wishing to cross the border usually meet their "coyotes" (an apt and descriptive term used in Latin America for those who facilitate undocumented cross-border trafficking) and prepare for the journey in a northern Mexican town like Altar, Sonora. Groups generally cross the actual international border very quickly, and then trek for anywhere from two to five days in the desert before making it to a highway where they are picked up in motor vehicles and driven to a major city. Because coyotes lead migrants through remote areas of the desert, many bodies are not discovered or reported quickly. For those suffering the effects of hyperthermia (heat stroke), the accompanying disorientation can compel them to wander deeper into the desert, discarding their clothing and other personal belongings. If a decedent is not found and recovered on the day of death, desert conditions usually render the individual unrecognizable. Within a single summer day, the hot and arid conditions can darken and desiccate the skin so much that visual recognition of the face is no longer possible. Because some decedents are found and recovered months, years, even decades after their deaths, their bodies are reduced to skeletal remains. One estimate of the average length of time that a migrant's body can remain undiscovered in the remote desert is 6 to 11 months (Martínez et al., 2014). The ravages from scavenging animals, invading insects, intense sun and heat, and even other smugglers and migrants who happen upon a decomposing body can further reduce the skeletal remains to a few bones and teeth.

The many risks migrants experience on the journey, whether dehydration, deportation, or abuse, can also have an effect on the ability to identify them should they not survive the journey. In towns like Altar, migrants prepare for the desert trek by buying dark or camouflaged clothing, dark water bottles, and a host of other items advertised or rumoured to help them escape the eye of Border Patrol. As a result, many deceased migrants are found without distinctive clothing that would be recognizable to their families. Many do not carry identification and some carry false ID cards. Central Americans may have bogus Mexican ID so that, in the event of capture by Border Patrol, they do not provide a record of their true name and they may be deported back to Mexico, rather than all the way back to Guatemala or El Salvador. Migrants are also robbed by *bajadores* (bandits) in the desert, or are apprehended and deported by Border Patrol without their personal belongings. A survey of deported Mexican migrants found that out of those carrying identification, one in four reported that Border Patrol took their ID cards and did not return them upon deportation (Martínez & Slack, 2013). All of this means that remains are regularly found with very few material clues to help investigators locate those who knew the deceased.

The condition of UBC remains upon arrival at the PCOME often precludes identification techniques such as visual recognition by family, tattoo comparison, or fingerprint matching. It is for this reason that most UBC cases require the expertise of a forensic anthropologist to produce biometric data describing the individual's physical characteristics and approximate time of death, which then may be compared to missing person reports to identify the decedent. Forensic anthropologists at the PCOME are tasked with approximately 150 such cases per year, which is an extremely high caseload for a county medical examiner's office. Because of this high number of cases, which is in addition to the casework per-formed on US citizens, the PCOME has added a second forensic anthropologist to the staff and is in need of adding a third position.

In addition to posing challenges to medico-legal practitioners, the bodies of the dead show material evidence of the structural vulnerability of migrants in the border context. These bodies reveal a combination of biologically and socially expressed indicators of suffering ranging from short stature and poor dental health due to poverty (Anderson, 2008; Birkby, Fenton, & Anderson, 2008; Reineke & Anderson, 2010) to abrasions and blisters from the experience of travelling through remote stretches of the desert in an attempt to migrate. The environmental conditions discussed above that render bodies highly difficult to identify are another layer in this physical embodiment of social marginalization evidenced on the bodies of deceased migrants.

The Missing

Although many of the missing person reports likely match unidentified decedents, it is important to view the unidentified and the missing separately. While the problem for forensic investigators is an unidentified body, the problem for families is a missing living person. The last place that the family of a missing person would ever want to call is the morgue.

At the end of 2015, the Colibrí Center for Human Rights' database contained reports for nearly 2,700 missing people last seen attempting to cross the US-Mexico border. This number includes reports gathered between January 2007 and 2015, for people who crossed between 2000 and 2015. The vast majority were reported to have disappeared in Arizona. This is nearly double the number of unidentified remains that have been discovered in the region for the same time period. The causes behind a higher number of missing persons cases than unidentified remains cases likely include several factors. One possible cause is that there are an additional unknown number of migrants who have died in the region, but have yet to be discovered. Another explanation could be that some of the missing died in transit to the border, and are among increasingly high numbers of unidentified dead in Mexico. Finally, some of these missing persons are not dead at all, but have simply lost contact with their families. Given the circumstances reported for most missing person cases managed by Colibrí, we believe that this latter cause for missing persons represents a minimal number of cases.

Similar to the migrants themselves, the structural vulnerability of families of the missing affects their search, which in turn affects the ability of investigators to identify remains. A complex process begins for families once a loved one disappears on the border.[5] Whether due to fear, poverty, or lack of assistance, families struggle to obtain information about their missing loved ones. The most unifying challenge families of missing migrants face is the lack of a safe and centralized entity that provides support, feedback, and transparency.[6] The transnational nature of this crisis has rendered existing local, state, and national mechanisms insufficient. Simultaneously, the criminalization of migrants and their families has forced them into the shadows, afraid to report to law enforcement or government officials. Without a safe and centralized response mechanism, families report their cases to dozens of agencies, resulting in massive decentralization of data and regular exploitation and abuse of the families.

Because the bodies of migrants have been discovered throughout Mexico and in dozens of jurisdictions within the US, families of the missing find themselves in a constant and chaotic series of endless phone calls. Each call seems to reveal more possible calls, emails, or online searches to conduct. Families contact their consulates, Border Patrol, police, local medical examiner's and coroner's offices, border humanitarian groups, immigrant rights groups, journalists, private investigators, academics, churches, and many, many more. Families of missing migrants who live in Mexico or Central America usually report to local authorities, who then send case information to the Procuraduría General de la Republica (Attorney General) or its equivalent. This data is then sent to the relevant consulate in the US. The process for reporting a missing migrant by those who live in the US is often more complicated. Because many of the families living in the US are undocumented, fear of deportation often prevents them from contacting police. However, even for those who do contact police, there is no guarantee that the police will be helpful. Many families report being turned away by police who cited jurisdictional reasons for declining to take the report—that is, because the missing person was illegally crossing an international boundary, families are told to call elsewhere.

Whether living in Mexico, the United States, or Guatemala, the experiences of families searching for missing loved ones on the border expose their extreme social marginalization and vulnerability. Many families wait years before reporting, or never report at all because they are afraid of the authorities, be they Mexican police or US law enforcement. For Indigenous peoples in Mexico and Central America, there is a deep mistrust of government due to centuries of violence and exploitation at the hands of the state. Fears worsened with the increase of violence in Mexico during President Felipe Calderon's "war on drugs," in which an estimated 60,000 people were killed between 2006 and 2012 (Milenio, 2012). Such violence, often targeting poor, Indigenous people or Central American migrants, usually involves the collusion of state authorities (Human Rights Watch, 2013; Isacson, Meyer, & Morales, 2014; Pereyra, 2013). Families fear that reporting a missing migrant might bring retribution from a cartel or a corrupt police department.

For families who do report, their lived experience of poverty often means that they do not have much information about the missing person in the form of medical records, fingerprints, or dental X-rays. Some of the families who live in rural Indigenous farming communities have had no reason to track things such as exact birthdate or height, which are usually some of the first questions asked by those interviewing a family for a missing persons report. Many do not have phones or access to the Internet, and must travel or seek help from the local church to make calls. The fact that some of these families do not speak Spanish, but instead an Indigenous language such as Triqui or K'iche', can put them at a further disadvantage when searching for someone who disappeared in another country, thousands of miles away.

The desperation of families to find information about their missing loved ones adds an additional layer to their vulnerability, exposing them to risks such as exploitation or abuse. Families have reported various types of mistreatment by authorities in Mexico, Guatemala, and the US including being spoken to with racist or humiliating language, being blamed for the disappearance of the person, being denied assistance by entities tasked with providing such services, being extorted, or being threatened with physical abuse or arrest (Reineke, 2016). In addition to mistreatment by authorities, families face abuse and exploitation from non-state actors, such as human smugglers or private investigators. According to caseworkers at the Colibrí Center for Human Rights, it is exceedingly common for families to receive phone calls from people demanding ransom for the missing person, whom the caller claims to be holding captive. Families are also regularly exploited by private investigators claiming to have access to privileged information, accessible to the family for a high price. Unfortunately, many families fall victim to these schemes, often saving money for months or asking friends and relatives for help to pay for such expenses.

All of the struggles of the families affect, in turn, the ability of investigators at offices like the PCOME to find complete and accurate information about the missing. It is almost as if families and forensic practitioners are simply searching for each other, trying, often unsuccessfully, to reach across borders—geographical, linguistic, and political—to connect. But there are many efforts to help them, both governmental and nongovernmental.

Identifying the Dead

The PCOME has been recognized for adhering to best practices when it comes to forensic work in the current border context (Martínez et al., 2014; Rubio-Goldsmith et al., 2006). There is no legal imperative that forensic practitioners do everything in their power to identify unidentified remains in their jurisdiction. While certain basic criteria must be met, such as attempting to determine the cause and manner of death, the challenges discussed above demand much more investigative work if there is any hope of locating the relatives of the majority of unidentified migrant decedents. Through scientific innovation, partnerships, and local support, the PCOME has been able to maintain high-quality investigations for UBC cases. The lack of a stated legal imperative does not preclude a moral imperative.

The work of the PCOME has been innovative in several regards. One of the most crucial steps taken was the collection of missing person reports for migrants. Most coroner's or medical examiner's offices do not manage missing persons data, which is usually under the oversight of law enforcement. However, as the deaths of migrants in southern Arizona increased, families of missing migrants began to call the PCOME for information. The second author, one of two forensic anthropologists at the PCOME at the time, recognized that these families had information that was vitally important, and began to take missing person reports himself. Drawing on experience from other mass-disaster contexts, he began to create a database—three-ring binders in reality—of missing migrant reports relevant to southern Arizona. This information, previously unavailable to investigators at the PCOME, provided them with the ability to search a list of missing migrants for names, characteristics, and circumstances noted among the unidentified. This project, dubbed the Pima County Missing Migrant Project at one time, progressed until the caseload became so high that an independent effort was needed to effectively manage the data. The Colibrí Center for Human Rights was created to fill this role.

The work of the PCOME has been innovative out of necessity. Information gleaned from cases of identified migrants has allowed the comparison of these characteristics to those of the unidentified, presumed migrants. Craniometric data, non-metric cranial data, metrical analyses of the infracranial skeleton, decomposition rate data, and DNA profile analyses have been collected by more than a dozen forensic science colleagues over the past 12 years (e.g., Spradley, Anderson, & Tise, 2015; Hefner, Spradley, & Anderson, 2014; Hughes & Algee-Hewitt, 2014; Trammell et al., 2014; Reineke & Soler, 2013). The results of these scientific inquiries have allowed not only the PCOME to make more identifications and more confidently profile the unidentified as likely migrants, but also have allowed forensic scientists in other medico-legal jurisdictions who see cases of deceased migrants to incorporate what has been learned at the PCOME. These other medico-legal jurisdictions are not limited to those along the southern US border, but also include jurisdictions such as Chicago and New York, two cities with large migrant populations, where investigators draw on these results to inform some of their unidentified decedent cases. The PCOME has also created a Post-Doctoral Fellowship in Forensic Anthropology, which not only provides a significant amount of decedent casework, but also allows interaction with the Colibrí Center and missing migrant issues to provide a holistic experience for the Fellow.

Much of the success of the PCOME in identifying the remains of migrants has been achieved through working relationships with local and international entities and experts. Key among these partnerships have been those with the Tucson Office of the Mexican Consulate, the Colibrí Center for Human Rights, the Argentine Forensic Anthropology Team, NamUs, and a handful of local humanitarians, academics, and activists. The complexity and enormity of the problem described above means that no single organization or entity has the entire solution. For the PCOME, working together with organizations that are better equipped to manage missing persons data and support the needs of families has been critical. Notably, the organizations with the most comprehensive data about missing persons relevant to the border have no affiliation with US law enforcement, which in other contexts is the most common resource for medical examiners searching for missing persons data.

The longest and most instrumental partnership has been with the Tucson Office of the Mexican Consulate. Consular staff from this office visit the PCOME weekly, and even daily in the summer months when deaths in the desert peak. The consulate assists the medico-legal investigation at the PCOME by checking names found on pieces of identification against lists of missing persons, providing identification hypotheses based on circumstantial data such as tattoos or clothing, offering national or cultural insight about the significance of certain items carried by migrants, and covering the costs associated with one-to-one comparisons of DNA from unidentified remains and relatives of missing persons. When there is a probable match between a decedent and a missing Mexican national reported to the consulate, consular staff may act as a go-between, sharing photos and information between the PCOME and the family. Finally, it is the role of the consulate to assist families in the repatriation process once remains are positively identified as those of Mexican nationals.

In 2006, after several years of collecting missing migrant reports that were provided by families calling the PCOME directly, Bruce Anderson (the second author) enlisted the help of Robin Reineke (the first author), an anthropology graduate student at the time, to manage this data and search for possible matches among the unidentified dead. At that time there were about 250 reports, not only of missing Mexican nationals but also of missing migrants from Guatemala, El Salvador, Ecuador, and a handful of other Latin American countries. Reineke organized these data, and began to collect reports from all local foreign consulates, humanitarian organizations, immigrant rights groups, law enforcement, and others who had data pertaining to missing migrants last seen in southern Arizona. When the number of missing approached 1,000, it was clear that institutional support was needed to manage the casework. In July 2013, Reineke co-founded the Colibrí Center for Human Rights with William Masson to house a centralized database of all missing migrant reports relevant to not only southern Arizona, but to the entire US-Mexico border. After years of observing the challenges facing families and medico-legal investigators along the border, it was clear that a centralized mechanism was needed that was available to families regardless of nationality or citizenship status, and that had the capability to automatically compare missing persons data with unidentified persons data.

At the time of writing, Colibrí's automated system was in a pilot phase, comparing data relevant to southern Arizona. Though currently containing only circumstantial data, we plan to incorporate DNA comparison capability into the system in the near future. In the meantime, case managers at the Colibrí Center continue to work very closely with the PCOME. The PCOME has provided in-kind support to Colibrí in the form of office space and equipment, allowing the collaboration to be a regular part of the daily investigation process at the office. Colibrí supports the investigation of UBC cases at the PCOME by managing all incoming inquiries from families of missing migrants, providing detailed ante-mortem data to investigators, and producing identification hypotheses that can then be followed up scientifically.

Another important collaboration the PCOME has participated in has been with the Argentine Forensic Anthropology Team (EAAF). The internationally renowned forensic anthropology and human rights non-profit organization was founded by students of the late pre-eminent forensic anthropologist Dr. Clyde Snow following the military dictatorship in Argentina that was responsible for the disappearance of at least 9,000 people. In addition to working in Latin America, Africa, Asia, and Europe, the team now also has a Border Project focused on creating a regional system to support families of missing migrants in the Americas. The EAAF collects missing migrant reports as well as genetic Family Reference Samples (FRS) from relatives of missing migrants during the initial reporting procedure. Though the Mexican government also collects FRS, this is usually done when there is already a possible match, to facilitate a one-to-one DNA comparison between unidentified remains and the relatives of a particular missing person. Importantly, the EAAF's Border Project represents the first regional system that produces blind matches between DNA taken from the relatives of missing persons and DNA taken from unidentified human remains found on the border. The EAAF also utilizes Bode Technology for producing genetic profiles, the same DNA lab that the PCOME utilizes.

The EAAF's Border Project currently contains information on about 714 individuals reported missing primarily from El Salvador, Honduras, and the Mexican state of Chiapas. In addition to searching among unidentified remains recovered in US border states, the EAAF also works to collect information about unidentified remains discovered throughout Mexico, and in particular, just north of the Mexico-Guatemala border. The EAAF and the Colibrí Center work together closely to collaboratively develop a regional system that best supports the human rights of families of missing migrants.

The PCOME has collaborated with dozens of other individuals and groups to support the identification of discovered human remains believed to be migrants. At the University of Arizona, the PCOME has worked with researchers from the departments of Anthropology, Sociology, Geography, Mexican American Studies, and Ecology and Evolutionary Biology. Important relationships with consulates include not only that of Mexico but also of Guatemala, El Salvador, Ecuador, and Honduras. Local humanitarian and immigrant rights organizations have also assisted, including Humane Borders, Coalición de Derechos Humanos, and No More Deaths. The support from forensic anthropologists outside the PCOME, as discussed above, has been vital. The nature of the crisis of missing migrants and unidentified remains on the US-Mexico border demands collaborative, interdisciplinary, and innovative work.

Conclusion

The tragedy that has unfolded along the US-Mexico border over the last two decades has affected thousands in untold ways. Families like Diego's have gone through something deeply painful that goes beyond the normal experience of loss and grief. Anthropologists and psychologists speak of "good deaths" and "bad deaths." While all losses are individually painful experiences, good deaths are characterized by feelings that the deceased died in a particular place, time, and context, safely embedded in cultural norms. Bad deaths, on the other hand, challenge cultural structures and expectations, and often leave the bereaved to work through a more complicated grieving process. Families of those who have died on the border are usually experiencing the psychosocial pain of a bad death. Whether it is the knowledge that their loved one suffered, alone in the desert, left to be consumed by wild animals, or the stigma that often comes with border deaths, these families suffer complicated grief. For relatives of the missing, the pain is amplified by the ambiguity of the disappearance. The ripple effects of such trauma and loss will undoubtedly leave a footprint in the social memory of immigrants in the United States for generations to come.

Recognizing the significance of the loss of life on the border is an important step towards saving lives. The predominant social lens through which migration is viewed sees migrants as individual actors making choices that are deemed irresponsible, illegal, or morally reprehensible. As anthropologist-physician Seth Holmes has stated, "this framing is used regularly to justify a lack of grief for those who die and a lack of action to achieve meaningful equality and change" (Holmes, 2013, p. 21).

Those caring for the dead and the missing provide an alternate way of viewing the migrant. At important stages in its journey, Diego's body was treated with care. From the migrants who reported seeing his body to Border Patrol while they were being apprehended and deported, to the forensic investigators at the medical examiner's office who went above and beyond their official roles, decisions were made to honour the humanity of another person first. This recognition of shared humanity was prioritized above actions that come out of fear, disgust, anger, or resentment. Although the socio-political context for migrant death and disappearance on the border reveals that individual migrants are not "at fault" for their fates, this need not be the truth for there to be humane treatment of migrants and their families.

Notes

1. Words of Father Alejandro Solalinde, who is a Mexican Catholic Priest and champion of human rights for migrants throughout Mexico, from the documentary film *Who Is Dayani Cristal?* (2013).

2. Name changed to protect privacy.

3. These numbers are taken from the database of the Pima County Office of the Medical Examiner, and represent the number of recovered remains examined at the facility for the calendar years 2001–14.

4. This number was reported by the Colibrí Center for Human Rights, and includes missing person reports for southern Arizona for the calendar years 1998–2014.

5. The impetus for families to begin searching for a missing person is either a phone call from a coyote or a fellow traveller, notifying the family that the person was left behind, or a period of time without contact from the person that is deemed unusual or significant by the family.

6. Observations about the experiences of families of missing migrants are taken from Robin Reineke's (2016) article, "Missing Persons and Unidentified Remains at the United States–Mexico Border."

References

Anderson, B. E. (2008). Identifying the dead: Methods utilized by the Pima County (Arizona) Office of the Medical Examiner for undocumented border crossers: 2001–2006. *Journal of Forensic Sciences, 53*(1), 8–15.

Anderson, B. E., & Parks, B. O. (2008). Symposium on border crossing deaths: Introduction. *Journal of Forensic Sciences, 53*(1), 6–7.

Anderson, S. (2013). *How many more deaths? The moral case for a temporary worker program*. Policy Brief. Arlington, VA: National Foundation for American Policy.

Andreas, P. (2009). *Border games: Policing the U.S.-Mexico divide*. Ithaca, NY: Cornell University Press.

Bacon, D. (2004). *The children of NAFTA*. Berkeley, CA: University of California Press.

Benski, T., & Silver, M. (2013). *Who is Dayani Cristal?* [Film]. UK/Mexico: Pulse Films, Canana; Canana USA; Candescent Films; & Rise Films. Retrieved from whoisdayanicristal.com.

Birkby, W. H., Fenton, T. W., & Anderson, B. E. (2008). Identifying Southwest Hispanics using nonmetric traits and the cultural profile. *Journal of Forensic Sciences, 53*(1), 29–33.

Cornelius, W. A. (2001). Death at the border: Efficacy and unintended consequences of US immigration control policy. *Population and Development Review, 27*(4), 661–685.

Cornelius, W. A. (2005). Controlling "unwanted" immigration: Lessons from the United States, 1993–2004. *Journal of Ethnic and Migration Studies, 31*(4), 775–794.

Eschbach, K., Hagan, J., Rodriguez, N., Hernandez-Leon, R., & Bailey, S. (1999). Death at the Border. *International Migration Review, 33*(2), 430–454.

Ewing, W. (2014). "Enemy territory:" Immigration enforcement in the US-Mexico borderlands. *Journal on Migration and Human Security, 2*(3), 198–222.

Farmer, P. (2004). An anthropology of structural violence. *Current Anthropology, 45*(3), 305–325.

Friedman, S. (2009). Globalization and interacting large-scale processes and how they may affect the HIV-AIDS epidemic. In C. Pope, R. White, & R. Malow (eds.), *HIV-AIDS: Global frontiers in prevention-intervention* (pp. 491–500). New York, NY: Routledge.

Hefner, J. T., Spradley, M. K., & Anderson, B. (2014). Ancestry assessment using random forest modeling. *Journal of Forensic Sciences, 59*(3), 583–589.

Hoffman, S. M., & Oliver-Smith, A. (2002). *Catastrophe & culture: The anthropology of disaster*. Santa Fe, NM: School for Advanced Research Press.

Holmes, S. (2013). *Fresh fruit, broken bodies: Migrant farmworkers in the United States* (1st Ed.). Berkeley, CA: University of California Press.

Hughes, C., & Algee-Hewitt, F. B. (2014). *A structured approach to assessing morphogenetic variation in Mexico: Tests of method informedness for improved identifications*. Paper presented at the American Academy of Forensic Sciences, February 21, Seattle, Washington.

Human Rights Watch. (2013). *Mexico's disappeared: The enduring cost of a crisis ignored*. Retrieved from www.hrw.org/node/113706.

Isacson, A., Meyer, M., & Morales, G. (2014, June 17). Mexico's other border: Security, migration, and the humanitarian crisis at the line with Central America. Press release, Washington Office on Latin America. Retrieved from www.wola.org/news/new_wola_report_mexicos_other_border.

Johnson, K. R. (1994). Free trade and closed borders: NAFTA and Mexican immigration to the United States. *U.C. Davis Law Review, 27*, 937–978.

Krieger, N. (2001). Theories for social epidemiology in the 21st century: An ecosocial perspective. *International Journal of Epidemiology, 30*(4), 668–677.

Martínez, D. E., Reineke, R. C., Rubio-Goldsmith, R., & Parks, B. O. (2014). Structural violence and migrant deaths in southern Arizona: Data from the Pima County Office of the Medical Examiner, 1990–2013. *Journal on Migration and Human Security, 2*(4), 257–286.

Martínez, D. E., & Slack, J. (2013). *Bordering on criminal: The routine abuse of migrants in the removal system, Part II: Possessions taken and not returned.* Washington, DC: Immigration Policy Center. Retrieved from www.immigrationpolicy.org/sites/default/files/docs/ipc/Border%20-%20 Possessions%20FINAL.pdf.

Mejdrich, K. (2012, July 7). Arizona ranked 3rd in U.S. for unidentified human remains. *The Arizona Republic.* Retrieved from www.azcentral.com/news/articles/20120708arizona-unidentified-human-remains.html.

Milenio. (2012, November 1). Guerrero repite como el estado más violento. *Milenio.*

Nevins, J. (2005). A beating worse than death: Imagining and contesting violence in the U.S.-Mexico borderlands. *AmeriQuests, 2*(1). Retrieved from ejournals.library.vanderbilt.edu/index.php/ ameriquests/article/viewFile/64/61.

Nevins, J. (2007). Dying for a cup of coffee? Migrant deaths in the US-Mexico border region in a neoliberal age. *Geopolitics, 12*(2), 228–247.

Nevins, J., & Aizeki, M. (2008). *Dying to live.* San Francisco, CA: Open Media/City Lights Books.

Pereyra, A. J. L. (2013). México, una moneda al aire: informe sobre las y los migrantes no localizados, desaparecidos y restos no identificados en México. In *Diagnóstico de derechos humanos en la frontera sur de México: Migración territorio mujeres defensores y defensoras de derechos humanos* (pp. 11–44). San Cristobal de las Casas and Morelia: Iniciativas para la Identidad y la Inclusión A. C.

Polaski, S. (2004). Jobs, wages, and household income. In J. J. Audley, D. G. Papademetriou, S. Polaski, & S. Vaughan, *NAFTA's promise and reality: Lessons from Mexico for the Hemisphere* (pp. 11–37). Washington, DC: Carnegie Endowment for International Peace. Retrieved from carnegieendowment.org/files/nafta1.pdf.

Quesada, J., Hart, L. K., & Bourgois, P. (2011). Structural vulnerability and health: Latino migrant laborers in the United States. *Medical Anthropology, 30*(4), 339–362.

Reineke, R. (2016). Missing persons and unidentified remains at the United States–Mexico border. In *Global Report on Missing Migrants and Unidentified Remains.* Geneva, Switzerland: International Organization for Migration.

Reineke, R. C., & Anderson, B. E. (2010). *Sociocultural factors in the identification of undocumented migrants.* Poster presented at the American Academy of Forensic Sciences, February 25, Seattle, WA.

Reineke, R., & Martínez, D. (2014). Migrant deaths in the Americas (United States and Mexico). In T. Brian & F. Laczko, *Fatal journeys: Tracking lives lost during migration* (pp. 45–75). Geneva, Switzerland: International Organization for Migration (IOM). Retrieved from publications.iom. int/bookstore/free/FatalJourneys_CountingtheUncounted.pdf.

Reineke, R. C., & Soler, A. (2013). *Dental ornamentation among southwest Hispanic border crossers at the Pima County Office of the Medical Examiner.* Paper presented at the American Academy of Forensic Sciences, February 23, Washington, DC.

Rubio-Goldsmith, R., McCormick, M., Martínez, D., & Magdalena Duarte, I. (2006). *The "funnel effect" and recovered bodies of unauthorized migrants processed by the Pima County Office of the Medical Examiner, 1990–2005.* Report submitted to the Pima County Board Of Supervisors. Tucson, AZ: Binational Migration Institute.

Spradley, M. K., Anderson, B. E., & Tise, M. L. (2015). Postcranial sex estimation criteria for Mexican Hispanics. *Journal of Forensic Sciences, 60*(Suppl. 1), S27–S31.

Trammell, L. H., Soler, A., Milligan, C. F., & Reineke, R. C. (2014). *The postmortem interval: A retrospective study in desert open-air environments.* Paper presented at the American Academy of Forensic Sciences, February 21, Seattle, WA.

U.S. Border Patrol. (1994). *Border Patrol strategic plan: 1994 and beyond*. U.S. Border Patrol.

U.S. Customs and Border Patrol. (2014). U.S. Border Patrol fiscal year Southwest Border Sector deaths (FY 1998–FY 2014). Retrieved from www.cbp.gov/newsroom/media-resources/stats.

Wise, T. A. (2010). *Agricultural dumping under NAFTA: Estimating the costs of U.S. agricultural policies to Mexican producers*. Report of the Woodrow Wilson International Center for Scholars. Retrieved from www.ase.tufts.edu/gdae/Pubs/rp/AgricDumpingWoodrowWilsonCenter.pdf.

Related Sources

Benski, T., & Silver, M. (2013). *Who is Dayani Cristal?* [Film]. UK/Mexico: Pulse Films, Canana; Canana USA; Candescent Films; & Rise Films. Retrieved from whoisdayanicristal.com.

Brian, T. & Laczko, F. (2014). *Fatal journeys: Tracking lives lost during migration*. Geneva, Switzerland: International Organization for Migration. Retrieved from publications.iom.int/system/files/pdf/fataljourneys_countingtheuncounted.pdf.

British Broadcasting Corporation (BBC). (2014, March 30). *The missing migrants* [Film]. Retrieved from www.bbc.co.uk//programmes/p01v5sq8.

Colibrí Center for Human Rights: www.colibricenter.org/about-us/

Martínez, D. E., Reineke, R. C., Rubio-Goldsmith, R., Anderson, B. E., Hess, G. L., & Parks, B. O. (2013). *A continued humanitarian crisis at the border: Undocumented border crosser deaths recorded by the Pima County Office of the Medical Examiner, 1990–2012*. Tuscan, AZ: Binational Migration Institute, University of Arizona. Retrieved from bmi.arizona.edu/sites/default/files/border_deaths_final_web.pdf.

Silver, M. (2013, August 17). *Bodies on the border* [Film]. *New York Times*. Retrieved from www.nytimes.com/video/opinion/100000002390527/bodies-on-the-border.html.

Chapter 13

The Evidentiary Value of Cultural Objects from Mass Graves: Methods of Analysis, Interpretation, and Limitations

Ariana Fernández Muñoz and Derek Congram
(University of Toronto)

Introduction

Investigations of multiple victims in mass graves are complex for many reasons. The graves often hold victims of armed conflict and the bodies may be those of people who were internally displaced, combatants stationed far from their home base, prisoners held in detention centres, or civilian victims taken long distances from their homes to a place of execution and burial. In this chapter we discuss the analysis of cultural objects and how it contributes to personal and group identification, often in a way that can be much more individualizing than other forms of physical evidence such as skeletal remains. We also make recommendations for the organization and interpretation of objects recovered from disturbed mass gravesites with an aim to re-association with individual victims and preparation for their repatriation to surviving families and communities.

The primary rationale for de-commingling and re-associating objects (both pieces to the whole and the whole to the person to whom it belongs) is to return them to the state that they presumably were in at the time of the person's death. This reconstruction has four goals:

1. To allow the analyst to have a "complete" object or garment to examine for possible defects (e.g., from bullets, sharp objects, blood stains), which might be related to the circumstances of disappearance and death;
2. To maximize information about cultural affiliation attributes of the clothing;
3. To observe other, non-cultural characteristics of a person associated with it (e.g., gender, age, or size of clothing), which can individualize or at least reduce the number of potentially associated individuals; and
4. To recover/reconstruct objects that might be recognized by families as having belonged to a missing member.

In our experience, the cleaning and analysis of personal objects is often sidelined, considered by some as a less valuable and less interesting form of evidence. Our experience has shown that hired labourers with no forensic expertise have been used to clean clothing separated from bodies at autopsy, effectively giving the workers control over evidence and with no mandate to observe or document potentially useful information. During cleaning, it is not unusual to discover items such as jewellery, money, ballistic fragments, and even bone, all of which can contribute to establishing who a person was and how they died. Beyond the value of these objects as evidence for criminal investigation, however, they often hold tremendous social (and possibly economic) worth to the next of kin.

The Value and Meaning of Personal Objects as Evidence of Crimes and Identification

Personal effects, including clothing, can tell us different things about the people who chose, created, altered, and carried them. Most importantly, they might reveal who an individual was and how they died. Archaeologists are very familiar with the analysis and value of personal objects for identifying anonymous remains (e.g., Janaway, 2002, p. 380), but increasingly forensic anthropologists—who are first and foremost biological anthropologists working with skeletal remains—are acknowledging the importance of material markers of identity as ancillary or even primary evidence. This is especially true in contexts where DNA family reference samples are not available, as with undocumented border crossers (e.g., Anderson, 2008; Birkby, Fenton, & Anderson, 2008; Chapter 12, this volume) or when DNA technology is not available (e.g., Baraybar, 2008). Although DNA analysis is becoming cheaper and more ubiquitous, places that are most prone to large-scale killings and disappearance are also often those that lack advanced infrastructure and resources for genetic identification analysis. In addition, countries with limited resources may consider the expenditure of identification of the dead to be a lower priority when compared with other needs, such as the security and health of the survivor population (cf. Jessee, 2012).

In some contexts, particularly those with tropical or semi-tropical climates, only sparse biological remains (e.g., dental crowns) may be present because of destructive environmental conditions including acidic soil, high temperatures, insect and animal scavenging, and seasonal waterlogging. In such instances, synthetic clothing and objects, such as rubber shoe soles, may be very well preserved. In these environments it is the objects—especially if their positions still represent where and how bodies were deposited—that best tell us the minimum number of people who died and about the circumstances of their death.

Objects as Evidence of Cause of Death

Damage to clothing may be the only remaining indication of cause of death (e.g., multiple gunshots to the torso as evidenced by holes in the clothing). This is true not only in cases of sparse skeletal remains but also considering that only a proportion of people shot demonstrate trauma to the skeleton, even when bones are very well preserved (Lorin de la Grandmaison, Brion, & Durigon, 2001; Langley, 2007). To properly interpret these items, however, de-commingling is often necessary: of objects from as few as two individuals (or the remains of one person from extraneous objects) and up to hundreds of individuals whose bodies are in mass graves or scattered across the ground surface. This is particularly the case for mass graves that have been disturbed, as in Bosnia and Herzegovina (see Chapter 2, this volume).

Chacón et al. (2008) discuss a case from Guatemala of commingled and dismembered remains of nine people in two mass graves. A comparison of cut marks to clothing and peri-mortem cut mark injuries to bone allowed the re-association of body parts and clothing to a single person, as well as the attribution of clothing to seven more of the nine victims.

Group and Individual Identity through Material Culture

Objects can work as identifiers in the investigation of crimes of disappearance because our individual and social group identities are sometimes expressed through objects (Wobst, 1977). We all know this and see it on a daily basis: a man with a button saying "kiss me, I'm Irish," police in uniforms, a man in a kilt, or a women wearing an *abaya*. These identifiers matter also because they may be the basis of victimization (Komar, 2008a).

The identification of an ethnic group is of critical importance to investigations of genocide. The 1951 United Nations Convention for the Prevention and Punishment of the Crime of Genocide states in Article 2 that genocide is any of a number of acts committed with the intent to destroy, in whole or in part, a national, ethnical, racial, or religious group. The basis upon which a person's nation, ethnicity, race (a now outdated term that most people agree has no biological basis), or religion can be determined is largely seen in material culture. Religion and ethnicity (these things not being mutually exclusive) cannot be known by analyzing a person's skeleton or DNA. Biological evidence can only (sometimes) lead us to a surviving family member or records that tell us what a person's ethnicity or religion might have been.

In a report to the defence for a trial at the International Criminal Tribunal for the former Yugoslavia (ICTY), Debra Komar, a biological anthropologist, declared that in her expert opinion ICTY investigator Dean Manning was unqualified to comment on cultural objects because he was neither an anthropologist nor trained in religious studies (Komar, 2008b). She was criticizing Manning's deduction that victims in a mass grave were Muslims based on copies of the Quran and prayer beads found with victim bodies.

Beyond the investigation of violations of international criminal law, however, group affiliation as evidenced by material objects can be the basis of community repatriation (e.g., Chapter 6, this volume), or even be the basis of familial repatriation (e.g., an engraved wedding band). We study cultural objects during medico-legal and humanitarian investigations, first, to try to determine a specific cultural, national, and religious affiliation, and second, to try to individuate a victim. The objects found could have been made in traditional fashion and could tell us where the object comes from. Weaving patterns, fabric types, and colour schemes are sometimes important and distinguishing features of clothing that can and do change from region to region, village to village, or ethnic group to ethnic group. Examples of this include *huipil* (traditional Mayan embroidered blouse) and hair sashes in Guatemala. By helping to identify an ethnic or religious group we might also be uncovering evidence of an international crime.

Sex identification in biological anthropology is fairly straightforward if remains are complete and well preserved. If they are not, something as simple as shoe soles (which typically preserve remarkably well) can be very indicative of sex (so far as they coincide with gender, which they often do, particularly in more traditional societies). In general, establishing if a victim is male or female will decrease by half the number of potential identification candidates. However, in many mass burials in armed conflict contexts most victims are male, so sex/gender identification is of limited value.

An object in the pocket of a pair of pants, a watch, or a handmade sweater (especially stitching to repair a tear) could help identify someone at the individual level. "I'd recognize even the buttons on my son's clothes, for it was me who gave them to him," said Valeri Sergeevic Lagvilava, a father whose son went missing in March 1993 in Georgia (Miranda, 2003). Despite this and other assertions, however, the recognition of clothing by relatives and friends has had mixed success in the identification of disappeared persons in Rwanda, Kosovo, and Bosnia (e.g., see Wagner, 2008, pp. 123–150).

Some authors warn of placing too much weight on material culture for identification purposes: "Reliance on external indicators, such as clothing, is often overemphasized. Such physical characteristics survive and are recognizable postmortem. In situations such as late twentieth-century Bosnia, in which there was remarkable uniformity of material culture among all three ethnic groups, artefact and clothing styles provided little evidentiary value" (Komar & Buikstra, 2008, p. 244). Despite this statement, in Komar's report to the defence mentioned previously, she disputed not the validity or significance of objects as identifiers; rather, she argued that the investigator was not qualified to make such a determination.

In an effort to refine determinations, Komar and Lathrop (2008) devised a method for categorizing and weighing the value of material culture as indicators of ethnicity. Their study demonstrated that personal objects and clothing had an 81.5 percent success rate in distinguishing "ethnic Whites" (presumably people of European ancestry) and "ethnic Hispanics" (generally people living in the United States with Latin American ancestry) in New Mexico. There are multiple problems with their study, including the ambiguous boundaries of cultural labels such as "White" and "Hispanic" as well as differences between how these labels are applied to oneself and how people of a different ethnic group apply them. Nevertheless, their study illustrates how material objects and clothing carry meaning and reflect different aspects of identity.

Commingling

Commingled remains are those that have been mixed and are not in the normal order or position. In the context of mass burials, bones could be from one or multiple people or a mix of human and non-human remains. Images abound on the Internet and we need not include one here. The integrity of mass graves, their contents and associations between bodies and objects, is often negatively affected by natural and cultural events: flooding; decomposition of soft tissues; human activity around the time of or following death and burial, which may be accidental (e.g., building construction) or deliberate and criminal (see Congram, 2013); or animal activity (e.g., Pokines, 2013; Pokines & Baker, 2013). At times, commingling occurs as a result of deliberate actions with good intentions, such as the inexpert excavation of human remains during sometimes desperate attempts to recover bodies by family members of the missing or personnel who lack training in controlled exhumation (e.g., Bouckaert, 2003). Commingling also occurs during formal and professional investigations after bodies have been removed from the grave because of inappropriate storage, transportation, and even analytical or processing protocols (Ubelaker, 2002).

Beyond the causes of damage to and commingling of objects, the rate at which certain materials degrade is highly variable. With clothing, sometimes synthetic fibres are stitched with organic (e.g., cotton) thread. Over time, the natural thread degrades, causing the components of a garment to detach. This separation is exacerbated with any subsequent disturbance to a burial site or surface deposition. Clothing and objects are disturbed by scavengers that must go beyond clothing to get what they are really after. Damage from scavenger activity can complicate the assessment of damage related to a person's death; however, the comparison of types of scavenger damage between clothing and related parts of human remains—just as with damage associated with a cause of death—can serve as a basis for re-association (e.g., the displacement of both a hand and shirt cuff from an arm with an incomplete shirt sleeve).

Baraybar, Brasey, and Zadel emphasize the purpose of de-commingling:

> The individualization of victims from mass atrocities is of importance for the healing of psychological wounds resulting from a conflict and destabilizing the society it imbalanced ... a general social benefit can often derive from individual identification. Often a single, definitive identification of a person can trigger an emotional release and acceptance of loss from an entire community, allowing the healing process to begin. (2006, p. 21)

Remains—biological and material—that are commingled defy a norm and we are naturally inclined to counter this effect, for judicial-analytical and cultural reasons. Wagner expresses it this way:

> ... commingling frequently forces scientists, religious leaders, and
> surviving kin to deviate from accepted social practice surrounding
> proper funereal and burial ritual. Their resolution necessarily inter-
> sects with the demands of tradition and exigencies of the physical
> remnants of the deceased, prompting negotiations especially
> among surviving relatives. In this sense, exceptions prove the rules
> in how societies respond to death, even in the most jarring and
> unconventional contexts. (2014, pp. 491–492)

Until recently, little attention has been paid to de-commingling human remains in forensic anthropology (Ubelaker, 2002). Two recent volumes, however, address this with a focus on methods of individuating skeletal remains (Adams & Byrd, 2008, 2014). Much less attention has been paid to the personal effects of the mixed remains, themselves commingled.

The de-commingling of objects and personal effects, if not done as part of judicial inquiries, should be done for humanitarian reasons. At the conclusions of investigations, once all the human remains have been identified and bodies have been repatriated, what is one to do with bags of clothing that belong to one or many of the victims? If it is impossible to analyze or individuate personal effects, then at least this should be made known to the families of the victims. We must not underestimate the value of these objects, not just as potential evidence, but as meaningful parts of the lives of victim families and communities (e.g., Renshaw, 2012, pp. 457–458).

Advice for De-commingling Personal Effects

We have briefly explained how the analysis of material objects can help us discover who a person was or how they died, and how commingling of objects occurs. Below, we propose steps for de-commingling and analyzing these objects, which we have developed throughout investigations in multiple countries.

Recovery Site Procedures

Associations between objects or body parts are best determined during careful excavation of a burial site while items are still *in situ*. Useful conclusions about relatedness follow from the thorough recording of object/body part location, better in the field than in the lab, because at the latter objects or parts will have

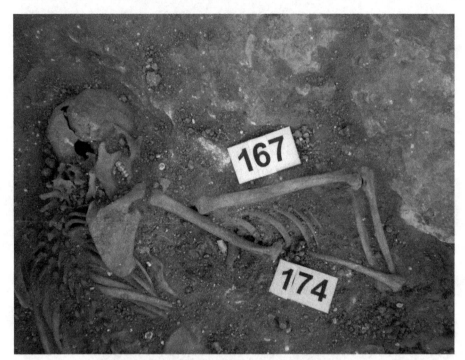

FIGURE 13.1   The right wrist of skeleton 174 and left wrist of skeleton 167 are overlapping, suggesting that the two people were bound to one another at the wrists when they were shot and buried. Woven rope had been found in other graves at the site, the burial grounds of a Spanish prison where hundreds were executed in a postwar purge.
Photo credit: D. Congram

been excavated, handled, packaged, transported, and unpacked, making spatial and relational associations much less obvious. Associations can easily be lost once the exhumation of bodies begins.

Associations that might be made with different degrees of confidence include a ring around a carpal phalange (finger bone), a necklace or a scarf around cervical vertebrae, or a head wrap on the hair or still present on the skull. If found on the human remains or in a pocket within a garment worn by a set of human remains, these objects should be considered "personal effects" of the individual—although there are some limitations to this approach, which are discussed below.

At primary mass burials (original burial locations) that are also execution sites one must consider the effects of the circumstances of death (e.g., people panicking/moving). Did people survive the initial executions and affect the location of other bodies or objects? Similarly, burial by heavy machinery shifting large amounts of soil (infilling) will cause bodies to shift, and clothing to be torn, moved, etc. Decomposition and bioturbation (i.e., animal and insect activity) will also affect post-mortem positions. In situations where hands have been bound, especially with natural fibres that might degrade, the position and relationship of left and right hand bones is extremely important (Figure 13.1), as is the relationship between these bones and rings or objects that might have been held in arms and hands (including young children).

Of course, one must be very careful about making definitive associations. This is especially true in cases of disturbed mass graves or mass fatality incidents, such as aircraft crashes, where high-energy events can displace, disperse, and disassociate body parts and objects. Likewise, remains that are on the ground surface are much more prone to post-mortem movement (e.g., animal scavenging). In these contexts, a hand near an arm does not guarantee that they belong to the same person. Taking into account contextual information will inform the confidence that can be given towards drawing associations. Recent innovative research by Tuller and Hofmeister (2014) demonstrates that even in cases where deliberate, concerted efforts are made to commingle and destroy bodies, many spatial associations still hold.

Although spatial relationships should be recorded, and relationships deduced, conclusions about the significance of relationships must be cautious. If there are uncertainties, these should be noted (e.g., with wording such as "apparent" or "probable"), and judgments should be conservative. The moment when things are seen *in situ* is the only moment that they will be seen in that way, and so careful documentation is important for subsequent interpretation. This documentation (e.g., video, photography, scale drawings) can be used to support associations if there is commingling during transport, storage, or analysis. Observations about relationships might come well after excavation, but will be stronger if supported by an accurate record from the excavation.

When buried bodies and objects are exposed, the change of environment can and often does have detrimental effects. Changes in temperature and humidity, and the effects of sunlight and oxygen, can destroy fragile items such as paper. The authors have seen rope ligatures disintegrate from the skeletonized wrists of Spanish Civil War execution victims during their excavation and exhumation. Cognizant of the potential to find partially or fully degraded ligatures at the same site, recording the juxtaposition of wrists was important because it was suggestive of them having been bound to one another, presumably prior to being shot and buried (Figure 13.1). Likewise, it made the excavators aware of the possible commingling of objects, which could have belonged to one of several persons buried together (e.g., a ring discovered below the overlapping hands of two people). Recording the precise location of such a ring and potential associations can provide corroborative evidence of identification when, for example, skeletal analysis is not discriminating (e.g., all of the bodies are of males aged 18–24). Initials on a ring can lead to directed DNA sampling, which will limit costs.

Laboratory Analysis of Personal Objects

Above all, de-commingling is a sorting problem (Stewart, 1979) and the criteria to de-commingle personal effects that we advocate here is generally the same for the de-commingling of human remains. The process follows a morphological approach and sorts by element type, side (if applicable), and size to extrapolate along typological and morphological lines. An intimate knowledge of human anatomy is necessary for a biological anthropologist to piece together sometimes fragmented and out-of-order skeletal remains. Likewise, although perhaps more challenging because of the range of materials that one could encounter, those responsible for piecing together and analyzing cultural objects need to know (or be able to infer) what things looked like before they became broken, mixed, scattered, and degraded.

Before starting with the analysis of objects, cultural analysts should clean (but not necessarily wash because of the potentially negative effects of water and rough handling), photograph, and catalogue. Traditionally, isolated objects and clothing are photographed lying on a flat surface. Once clothing has been reassembled, however, we advise photographing on a mannequin (Figure 13.2). This will help provide more accurate and precise estimations of how clothing was being worn, as evidenced by marks from creases, habitual folds, and related wear (e.g., fading). Photographs of clothing on mannequins also provide a much more realistic and humanistic image of victims. It might also demonstrate peri-mortem damage to the clothing that better corresponds with skeletal injury.

Once facing the commingled evidence in a controlled environment, the analyst should approach the objects as part of a puzzle. She or he should work with the premise (although possibly mistaken) that every one of the objects or remains thereof were intact before the death and burial, and that they were separated because of peri- or post-mortem events. The puzzle might, and often will be, incomplete, but the assumption of completeness is a good starting point towards the most complete re-association possible.

Cultural object analysts should be looking at materials, conditions, textures, and colours to relate pieces to other objects recovered from the same area. We recommend first doing what is possible without making reference to records of the recovery site. This initial separation of information can help make a final conclusion more robust, similar to the effect of using a holdout sample in statistical analysis. In other words, conclusions drawn about potential associations in the laboratory that are independent of information from the recovery site will be seen as more secure than conclusions made after referencing site information, which might bias an analyst's decisions.

FIGURE 13.2 **Author Ariana Fernández Muñoz pointing out possible bullet holes on the clothing of a child exhumed from a mass grave.**
Source: Max Becherer/Polaris, printed with permission

As with skeletal remains, matching together damaged pieces (e.g., along fracture lines) is very useful, although some less robust materials such as clothing can stretch and degrade, making a match less obvious. In order to confirm a hypothesis about association based on laboratory analysis of objects, the analyst should then take into consideration site provenance of the respective objects (or pieces thereof), mindful of potential post-deposition displacement, inclusion, and spurious relationship. For example, one might identify a possible match of two pieces of torn fabric based on similar weave and material, but which have different hues and which do not mirror one another precisely along the tears. Subsequent reference to excavation records might show that the piece of fabric with a lighter hue was recovered from the ground surface near a disturbed area at the edge of a grave. The darker piece of fabric might have been found still buried, lying around a set of remains against the wall of the grave and by the disturbed area. The physical closeness of the two pieces of fabric makes their association possible. Weathering explains why the fabric found outside the grave is a lighter shade as well as why the line along the tear has started to become unwoven, not exactly matching the corresponding tear line of the fabric piece that was excavated from the grave. Multiple lines of evidence and reasoning support a direct association, and careful recovery site observations including post-burial disturbance at the edge of the grave offer a reasonable explanation for the physical space between the two pieces, as well as their different states of preservation. Just as the study by Tuller and Hofmeister's (2014) demonstration that body parts closer in space in mass graves are most likely of the same person—even when subjected to violent killings, burial, mechanized exhumation, transport (across international boundaries), re-deposition, burning, and reburial—should also apply to objects in similar circumstances.

Steps of Analysis of Objects and Clothing
1. Objects should be photographed upon receipt in the laboratory, prior to cleaning. This might occur in a criminal investigation, as part of a transfer of custody, and the analyst should confirm that images also exist of the objects from the recovery site. In this way, any changes to the objects between recovery and laboratory analysis have been documented.
2. Clean, photograph, and catalogue the personal effects, fragments, or any object found individually. Often cleaning will only involve brushing soil off, as water and rough handling can damage objects.
3. Ideally, the analyst will have ample secure space for displaying and documenting all of the material evidence at once. When the analyst has looked at the entirety of the remains one by one, she should go back and revisit each of them. One technique could be to look back at the pictures taken (if there are dozens of fragments) or the actual objects and start to segregate them by pattern, colour, texture, and material. The basis for this is that garments are generally made of homogenous patterns, colors, and textures within themselves. The first look at material remains will familiarize the analyst with all that is available. A second look can trigger recognition of now familiar and potentially associated objects.
4. Look at sizes, shapes, and sides to segregate objects. For example, are all blue sleeves the same size, shape, or side? "Pair matching" (comparing possible sets of opposite sides, as with buttoned shirt sleeves) might not produce definitive matches, but can be very useful for eliminating those that do not match (i.e., exclusions). While de-commingling human remains, the variation in size of the long bones of the upper and lower limbs is much greater between individuals than the asymmetry within individuals (Hamre, 2005), and therefore the pairing of elements should follow this base. The same applies for material remains that are potentially bilateral (e.g., fabric that appears to be from a pair of trousers).

Re-Associating and Reassembling Commingled Personal Effects, Particularly Clothing

When comparing object shapes, bear in mind that colour may have faded or have been affected by staining. Staining can occur on a very micro level and can be caused by minerals in soil, by other objects (e.g., oxidization and leaching of certain metals), or by bodily decomposition fluids. Objects or parts thereof might also change shape under pressure from the body or bodies on top of them and overlying soil. Also, one must not assume that the clothes or items were new and in their original condition when buried. The effects of wear, laundering, the type and the quality of the dyes, and the material used to make the thread stitching the seams together all respond differently to burial conditions. Therefore, when looking at personal effects, one must consider a range of intrinsic and extrinsic taphonomic factors affecting changes on objects.

In order to make a whole object from smaller component pieces, cross-reference with partial, broken, or tattered objects in other assemblages. Once this is done, put the objects side by side to see if there is a match. After cross-referencing every individual fragment of clothing, assign it a category (e.g., clothing vs. shroud), a type of clothing (e.g., a shirt vs. dress), and a cultural description (e.g., Kurdish *shikak* motif).

Try to match all the elements with the largest object/garment recovered. Success develops from testing a hypothesis and having a result that is beyond doubt. By starting with the largest piece first, you are working with the element that, by virtue of being the largest, is the most likely to reflect the uniqueness of the object and related detail that can contribute to its individualization, association, and other information. The labelling of garments and the reattachment of fragments to matrices are not a coincidence, but stem from the thoughtful exercise of trial, error, and success.

This work is based on the usually accurate premise (which has almost always been true in our experience) that individuals were wearing different types of clothing or uniforms when buried (although mass killings by the Nazis often deviated from this, in part to facilitate looting). With clothing, we begin with the knowledge that just as people are bilateral, so will there also be a right and a left of most components of their garments. In matching reconstructed clothing to bodies, however, there are problems of specificity: with uniforms, dress greens are typically custom made, whereas battle dress often comes in standardized sizes. Further, in less organized or formal armed conflict where fighters are not wearing uniforms, there is less consistency in dress (and in some circumstances no particular uniform at all). There is general correspondence in clothing to bodies (tall people wear longer trousers and shirts with longer sleeves than short people). Nevertheless, the lack of specificity of clothing to a person's size and the significant overlap in peoples' sizes have a similar effect to that observed by Hamre with osseous remains: "in a sample of individuals of similar size more bones than expected will be classed as possible matches" (2005, p. 66). In addition, we want to remind readers that when there are disparities between clothing and body (part) size, it is logically far more common for clothing to be too large rather than too small. Younger siblings who grew up with hand-me-downs are acutely aware of this axiom.

Prior to analysis, it is important to have information on customary and contemporary clothing, objects, and any other material culture of the missing. This presupposes identity, and so is somewhat problematic, but can be used for refutation as well as confirmation, mindful of the fluidity of cultural representation in clothing and objects. A context-specific (broadly speaking) vocabulary will result in a more accurate description of the items and will also allow one to identify particular cultural and gender attributes of clothing. In Iraq, investigators working with the US authorities used a catalogue of clothing images and descriptions that had been prepared by Kurdish authorities. Other reference materials included published ethnographies and catalogues of fabric types and patterns that were created by the manager of the cultural objects laboratory (author AF). Collaboration with victim populations on object description and cataloguing will not only support more accurate and precise determinations, but will work towards a more open, inclusive, and trustworthy (in the eyes of victim communities) process.

Some Limitations of Material Culture Analysis

Having discussed the potential of material object and clothing analysis in investigations of unidentified remains, we must now acknowledge some of the more significant limitations. Only by acknowledging potential problems of this type of evidence and analysis can we best serve the missing, their families, and communities.

The specificity or precision of objects as evidence varies greatly. A man in a kilt might identify himself not only with a national group but also with a family group that uses a specific tartan, and one might assume the man's surname. However, culture is far more complex than this. Derek Congram, one of this chapter's authors, wears a wool tartan scarf. If his remains were found during an investigation, one might conclude that he died and was buried when the weather was cold and that he was a member of the Clan Farquharson (because of the specific colours and pattern of the scarf). The author's Scottish heritage, however, is on the maternal line, and belonging to a patriarchal society the author's surname in official documentation does not reflect his mother's heritage. Further, warm clothing as indicative of season can be misleading: people flee their homes during conflict and take more clothing than they might normally wear, or perhaps they are planning to flee along a safer route through high-altitude mountains. Alternatively, the scarf could have been found on the ground, stolen, or traded. The tartan scarf wearer may not know the familial significance of the pattern—they may simply like the colours (just imagine how many members of the Clan Burberry might be supposed to live along the strikingly warm Rodeo Drive in Beverly Hills).

Ariana Fernández Muñoz, the other author of this paper, is Latin American and normally uses two surnames, in keeping with practice in her native country: that of her father and her mother. Contrary to (changing) convention, she did not adopt the surname of her North American husband when she married. When she moved to North America, however, she registered at university under only her father's surname because her full name did not fit into the boxes of the registration form, and because her mother's surname had a letter that does not exist in English (ñ). Social (and biological) identification gets filtered, and in examining material culture we get a skewed, limited vision that is open to competing interpretations of who a person is or was. Physical evidence is often presented as factual and something that "cannot lie or be forgotten" (Blau, 2014), but in fact we must acknowledge that physical objects do not necessarily speak for themselves—they always require *interpretation*. In identifying and understanding objects much can get lost in translation; nuance and context can be critical.

In the case of potential gunshot damage to clothing it is presumptuous to conclude that the damage corresponds with the person's death. It is, of course, possible (albeit remotely) that someone was previously shot, survived, and continued to wear the shirt as a badge of honour. There is also the possibility that a projectile passed through loose-fitting clothing and did not touch the body of the person wearing the clothing. During one investigation, author Derek Congram challenged a ballistics expert to prove that the holes in clothing that he was examining were from bullets. The author told him that a more objective approach would be to document all holes in the clothing first, then separate those that he considered to be from bullets from the others. Then we could compare these with injuries to the skeleton to see if there was a correlation. Perhaps resenting the challenge to his expertise, the ballistics expert (who was Colombian and who has a tremendous amount of experience in multiple conflict contexts analyzing this type of evidence) kindly and quietly began calling the author over to his desk to observe holes in clothing under the microscope. As he photographed the damage for his report, he talked the author through the characteristics of woven fabric damaged by ballistics. He also showed several cases where a high-energy, fast-moving projectile penetrated a couple of layers of folded cloth, which was something far less likely to occur if, for example, the cloth had been caught on a nail. Just to reinforce his point, he also pointed out that these holes in the clothing corresponded to skeletal injuries (upon completion of his own analysis, so as not to be unduly influenced by evidence that was not within his professional remit). Although this true expert was keenly aware of how to identify what was and was not damage due to projectiles, there are very few with his level of experience. The reliability of objects as evidence must be judged on a case-by-case basis, is context dependent, and confidence of conclusions should reflect the relative expertise of the analyst.

Individualizing victims based on clothing and personal objects can sometimes be challenging or impossible, as when these types of evidence are sparse and relatively generic. Komar (2003) claimed that clothing could not be individualized amongst the more than 7,000 mostly men and boys from Srebrenica, Bosnia, and Herzegovina, who were massacred over four days in July 1995. There may likewise be very few distinguishing features among the clothing of thousands of young-to-middle-aged Kurdish and Shi'a males who were victims of mass detention and killing under the Ba'ath Party regime in Iraq. The same is most likely true for many of the hundreds of thousands of victims who were forced at gunpoint to work and live far from their homes in simple black uniforms under the murderous Khmer Rouge government in Cambodia.

Finally, there is the problem of vocabulary. A visit to many North American supermarkets will reveal an aisle ambiguously labelled "ethnic" foods. Troublesome clothing descriptors such as *western* can refer to something worn by Clint Eastwood in *Pale Rider* or to commonly seen clothing in the geopolitical "West" (usually North America and Western Europe). Often several different words refer to the same or very similar things (e.g., *shemagh, kuffiyeh,* and *ghutra*). As noted earlier, having local analysts and input from victim populations can help distinguish terms that might be very unfamiliar to those working in a country or region that is not their own (e.g., the differences between *dish-dasha, khimar, hijab,* and *abaya*). Among vocabulary problems are the somewhat relative nature of garment sizes: a small to a Samoan may be an extra large in Bolivia.

Conclusions

Earlier in this chapter, we made reference to a forensic anthropologist's ICTY court report, which asserted that only those trained and educated in culture and religion are qualified to comment on such topics. Questions of ethnical, racial, or religious identity are critical to human rights investigations of crimes such as genocide. We agree with the anthropologist's stress on the importance of approaching cultural material in an informed, cautious, and systematic way. However, we do not share her elitist approach that insists a police investigator is necessarily unqualified to do this work. In her report, she goes further by asserting that there is no scientific basis or precedent to infer group identity from the direct association of material culture with select individuals (all recovered from the same mass grave, the product of a war largely fought along ethnic lines). This is simply false: sampling is a basic tenet in all scientific research, including anthropology.

In this chapter we emphasized the social and evidentiary value of clothing and personal possessions. We also explained the circumstances in which those objects can and do become commingled. We made basic recommendations on how to resolve commingling, so that material objects including clothing can be individualized for evidentiary purposes and with the goal of repatriating these things to victim families and communities. Wagner says, "The story of these partial, highly commingled remains remind us of the dynamic interplay between scientific knowledge and social meaning, defying facile claims of 'closure' at the same time as they expose the necessarily improvisational side of caring for the dead whose bodies have undergone repeated dislocation and disruption" (2014, p. 505).

Lewis Binford (1964) urged the coordination of work of archaeologists and social anthropologists towards the solution of anthropological problems. This certainly applies in the context of missing persons investigations where the missing, like all of us, are a complex combination of biology and culture, both of which manifest in personal and group identities as well as others' perceptions of these identities. We work to "correct" the commingling and disassociation of objects from bodies in order to restore what our cultures consider a natural order.

References

Adams, B. J., & Byrd, J. E. (eds.) (2008). *Recovery, analysis, and identification of commingled human remains*. Totowa, NJ: Humana Press.

Adams, B. J., & Byrd, J. E. (eds.) (2014). *Commingled human remains: Methods in recovery, analysis, and identification*. San Diego, CA: Academic Press.

Anderson, B. E. (2008). Identifying the dead: Methods utilized by the Pima County (Arizona) Office of the Medical Examiner for undocumented border crossers: 2001–2006. *Journal of Forensic Sciences, 53*(1), 8–15.

Baraybar, J. P. (2008). When DNA is not available, can we still identify people? Recommendations for best practice. *Journal of Forensic Sciences, 53*(3), 533–540.

Baraybar, J. P., Brasey, V., & Zadel, A. (2006). The need for a centralized and humanitarian-based approach to missing persons in Iraq: An example from Kosovo. *The International Journal of Human Rights, 11*(3), 247–265.

Binford, L. (1964). A consideration of archaeological research design. *American Antiquity, 29*(4), 425–441.

Birkby, W. H., Fenton, T. W., & Anderson, B. E. (2008). Identifying southwest Hispanics using nonmetric traits and the cultural profile. *Journal of Forensic Sciences, 53*(1), 29–33.

Blau, S. (2014). Working as a forensic archaeologist and/or anthropologist in post-conflict contexts: A consideration of professional responsibilities to the missing, the dead and their relatives. In A. González-Ruibal & G. Moshenska (eds.), *Ethics and the archaeology of violence* (pp. 215–228). New York, NY: Springer.

Bouckaert, P. (2003). The mass graves of al-Mahawil: The truth uncovered. *Human Rights Watch, 15*(5) E, 1–15. Retrieved from www.hrw.org/reports/2003/iraq0503/iraq0503.pdf.

Chacón, S., Peccerelli, F. A., Paíz Díez, L., & Rivera Fernández, C. (2008). Case study 6.1: Disappearance, torture and murder of nine individuals in a community of Nebaj, Guatemala. In E. Kimmerle & J. P. Baraybar (eds.), *Skeletal trauma: Identification of injuries resulting from human rights abuse and armed conflict*. Boca Raton, FL: CRC Press.

Congram, D. (2013). Deposition and dispersal of human remains as a result of criminal acts: *Homo sapiens sapiens* as a taphonomic agent. In J. T. Pokines & S. A. Symes (eds.), *Manual of forensic taphonomy* (pp. 249–285). Boca Raton, FL: CRC Press.

Hamre, S. (2005). Bilateral asymmetry as a means of reassembling commingled human remains: A study of the long bones of the upper and lower limbs. *Scandinavian Journal of Forensic Science, 2*, 54–62.

Janaway, R. C. (2002). Degradation of clothing and other dress materials associated with buried bodies of archaeological and forensic interest. In W. D. Haglund & M. H. Sorg (eds.), *Advances in forensic taphonomy: Method, theory and archaeological perspectives* (pp. 379–402). Boca Raton, FL: CRC Press.

Jessee, E. (2012). Promoting reconciliation through exhuming and identifying victims in the 1994 Rwandan genocide. Centre for International Governance Innovation Africa Initiative Policy Brief, No. 4, 1–9.

Komar, D. (2003). Lessons from Srebrenica: The contribution and limitations of physical anthropology in identifying victims of war crimes. *Journal of Forensic Sciences, 48*(4), 1–4.

Komar, D. (2008a). Variables influencing victim selection in genocide. *Journal of Forensic Sciences, 53*(1), 172–177.

Komar, D. (2008b). *Expert witness report dated 28 February 2008. Exhibit 2D00534*. The Hague, The Netherlands: International Criminal Tribunal for the former Yugoslavia.

Komar, D. A., & Buikstra, J. E. (2008). *Forensic anthropology*. New York, NY: Oxford University Press.

Komar, D. A., & Lathrop, S. (2008). The use of material culture to establish the ethnic identity of victims in genocide investigations: A validation study from the American Southwest. *Journal of Forensic Sciences, 53*(5), 1035–1039.

Langley, N. R. (2007). An anthropological analysis of gunshot wounds to the chest. *Journal of Forensic Sciences, 52*(3), 532–537.

Lorin de la Grandmaison, G., Brion, F., & Durigon, M. (2001). Frequency of bone lesions: An inadequate criterion for gunshot wound diagnosis in skeletal remains. *Journal of Forensic Sciences, 46*(3), 593–595.

Miranda, V. (2003). The missing: The right to know. *The Magazine of the International Red Cross and Red Crescent Movement.* Retrieved from www.redcross.int/EN/mag/magazine2003_1/22-23.html.

Pokines, J. T. (2013). Faunal dispersal, reconcentration, and gnawing damage to bone in terrestrial environments. In J. T. Pokines & S. A. Symes (eds.), *Manual of forensic taphonomy* (pp. 201–248). Boca Raton, FL: CRC Press.

Pokines, J. T., & Baker, S. E. (2013). Avian taphonomy. In J. T. Pokines & S. A. Symes (eds.), *Manual of forensic taphonomy* (pp. 427–446). Boca Raton, FL: CRC Press.

Renshaw, L. (2012). The scientific and affective identification of Republican civilian victims from the Spanish Civil War. *Journal of Material Culture, 15*(4), 449–463.

Stewart, T. D. (1979). *Essentials of forensic anthropology.* Springfield, IL: Charles C. Thomas.

Tuller, H., & Hofmeister, U. (2014). Spatial analysis of mass grave mapping data to assist in the reassociation of disarticulated and commingled human remains. In B. J. Adams & J. E. Byrd (eds.), *Commingled remains: Methods in recovery, analysis, and identification* (pp. 7–32). San Diego, CA: Academic Press.

Ubelaker, D. H. (2002). Approaches to the study of commingling in human skeletal biology. In W. D. Haglund & M. H. Sorg (eds.), *Advances in forensic taphonomy: Method, theory and archaeological perspectives* (pp. 331–352). Boca Raton, FL: CRC Press.

Wagner, S. (2008). *To know where he lies.* Oakland, CA: University of California Press.

Wagner, S. (2014). The social complexities of commingled remains. In B. J. Adams & J. E. Byrd (eds.), *Commingled human remains: Methods in recovery, analysis, and identification* (pp. 491–506). San Diego, CA: Academic Press.

Wobst, H. M. (1977). Stylistic behaviour and information exchange. In C. E. Cleland (ed.), *For the director: Research essays in honor of James B. Griffin* (pp. 317–342). Anthropological Papers 61. Ann Arbor, MI: Museum of Anthropology, University of Michigan.

Related Sources

Heilen, M. P. (ed.). (2012). *Uncovering identity in mortuary analysis.* Walnut Creek, CA: Left Coast Press.

Renshaw, L. (2013). The archaeology and material culture of modern military death. In S. Tarlow & L. Nilsson Stutz (eds.), *The Oxford handbook of the archaeology of death and burial* (pp. 781–800). Oxford, UK: Oxford University Press.

Renshaw, L. (2011). *Exhuming loss: Memory, materiality and mass graves of the Spanish Civil War.* Walnut Creek, CA: Left Coast Press.

Simon Fraser University Museum of Archaeology and Ethnology, Investigating Forensics Identification videos, Virtual Museum of Canada: www.sfu.museum/forensics/eng/pg_media-media_pg/identification.

Chapter 14

Farm to France: The Identification of Canada's Missing Winnipeg Soldiers from the Amiens Battlefield

Laurel Clegg (Former Casualty Identification Coordinator, National Defence Canada)

Introduction

Private Sidney Halliday and his fellow soldiers were exhausted, and had been holding the village of Hallu, France, with few if any reinforcements, supplies, or water for nearly 19 hours. As a member of the 78th Battalion of the Canadian Expeditionary Force, also known as the Winnipeg Grenadiers, he and his fellow soldiers led a rapid attack on the German lines during the final days of what was later called the Battle of Amiens (Nicholson, 1962). Their advance had moved quickly until they reached the village of Hallu, where the German Alpine Corps launched a counterattack. It was mid-morning on August 11, 1918, and the Canadians had been hemmed in from the north, east, and south, holding the village, but barely. A series of strong counterattacks on their position eventually forced them to retreat and, by the afternoon of the 11th, the battalion had lost the village. They were never to return to the area for the duration of the war. Between August 10 and 11, 46 soldiers of the 78th Battalion were killed in and around the village of Hallu, of whom the bodies of 35 could not be recovered for burial (Canadian Expeditionary Force, 1918d). Private Halliday's fiancée received a telegram in the late autumn of 1918 explaining the circumstances of his death and stating that his body remained missing.

Private Halliday is one of the over 19,000 Canadian soldiers whose remains were not recovered following the end of the First World War, 11,245 of whom went missing in France (Commonwealth War Graves Commission, 2015). Every year the remains of Canada's missing service personnel are discovered by chance throughout the former battle and training fields from the First and Second World War.

In 2006, three sets of skeletal remains were discovered on the property of the Demeusere family by the son, Fabien, in Hallu, Somme, France. Fabien had been digging in his parents' garden when he discovered a button from the 78th Battalion. The following year, another five sets of remains were recovered from the same area—all remains were those of Canadian soldiers from the First World War and from the 78th Battalion (Caux, 2007; Gauthier, 2006). The Canadian Department of National Defence sought to identify the eight soldiers as part of their overall program of Casualty Identification. This chapter explores the challenges of identification of Canada's missing that died and were not recovered during and following the end of the First World War.

Historical Background

The Battle of Amiens involved the clandestine mass movement of the 4th Division of the Canadian Expeditionary Force, part of a strategy of surprise whereby the division was moved in secret from one part of the Western Front to the region west of Amiens, France. At the same time, they continued preparations for "fake" attacks to divert the attention of the German army (Nicholson, 1962). The Allies were covered by artillery fire and tanks and they moved an astonishing 13 km on August 8 alone (Canadian War Museum, 2015; Canadian Expeditionary Force, 1918d). The high numbers of killed-in-action combined with the high speed of troop movement is one possible explanation for the inability to inter deceased soldiers or to accurately record grave locations.

In the second phase of the Battle of Amiens (Figure 14.1), the 78th Battalion were ordered to move towards the village of Hallu on the morning of August 10 and hold the line. By 3 p.m., the battalion had managed to cross the difficult terrain of old British trenches and barbed wire and settled into Hallu and were waiting for the 72nd Battalion (British Columbia) and the 38th Battalion (Ottawa) to the north and south of Hallu to join them. At the same time, the German army had recovered from the initial surprise and, on the morning of the 10th, countered with multiple attacks, including reinforcements. This included two battalions between the villages of Hallu and Hattencourt (Nicholson, 1962).

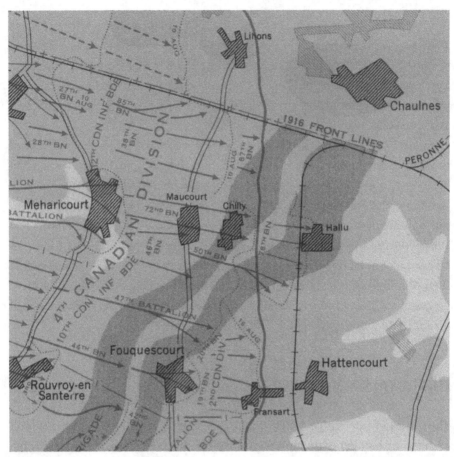

FIGURE 14.1   Map of troop movements during the Battle of Amiens, August 8–18, 1918.
Source: Nicholson, 1962, Map 11

Subjected to sweeping machine-gun fire, together with the division's own artillery falling short all around them, the Canadians became trapped in the village
with no reinforcements or supplies until 6 a.m. the next morning. The battalion's
request to retreat was denied over and over throughout the 10th and the early
morning of the 11th, until finally permission to fall back came shortly after noon
(Canadian Expeditionary Force, 1918d).

The battalion never regained the territory lost at Hallu, and the remains of
those soldiers killed in the village were never recovered following the end of the
war. It is likely that they were interred quickly by German troops in the nearest
available trench and covered over (Loe, Barker, & Wright, 2014). "Hallu, which
marked the most easterly point reached by any formation of the Fourth Army,
was given up. During the previous night (10th) and on the morning of the 11th
the 4th Canadian Division had beaten off three counterattacks launched against
the village by the [German] Alpine Corps" (Nicholson, 1962, p. 418).

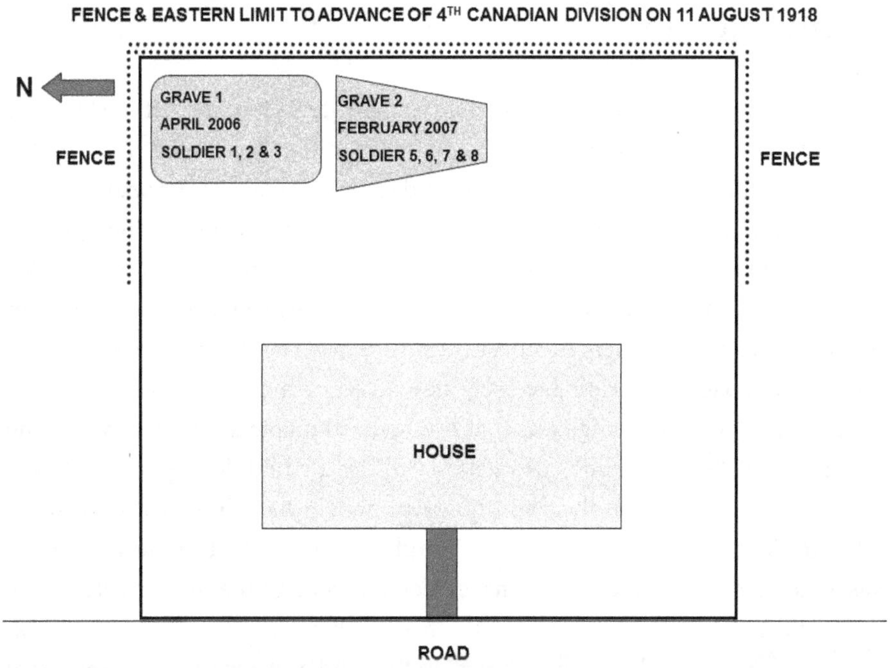

FENCE & EASTERN LIMIT TO ADVANCE OF 4TH CANADIAN DIVISION ON 11 AUGUST 1918

N ←

GRAVE 1
APRIL 2006
SOLDIER 1, 2 & 3

GRAVE 2
FEBRUARY 2007
SOLDIER 5, 6, 7 & 8

FENCE

FENCE

HOUSE

ROAD

FIGURE 14.2 Diagram of the approximate distribution of the eight soldiers in the Demeusere
yard based on discussions with the Demeusere family and the Commonwealth War
Graves Commission.

Analysis

In 2007, the fledgling historic forensic identification program at the Canadian
Department of National Defence was notified by the Commonwealth War Graves
Commission of the location of graves in the Demeusere backyard (Figure 14.2).

Like other accidentally discovered and unnamed soldiers from the First World
War, identification of the eight soldiers from Hallu required a combination of
historical and biological analysis. Historical analysis provided an important
context, a list of potentially missing personnel, and their physical and medical
profiles. Osteological analysis provided a physical and dental profile of each of
the decedents, which eliminated potential candidates from the list of the missing
based on height and age. Genetic analysis eliminated further candidates based
on mitochondrial (maternal) or Y-STR (paternal) DNA profiles. Finally, oxygen
isotope analyses provided geo-chemical maps of where the unknown soldiers
lived during their lifetimes.[1] When combined, such analyses can ultimately lead
to identification.

Material Evidence

With thousands of missing soldiers in France, any items found on or next to a set of remains can be important in determining the nationality, and thus the country responsible for undertaking the process and expense of identification. Members of the 78th Battalion headed into battle loaded with canteens, webbing, heavy leather boots, metal helmets, bayonets, rifles, and ammunition. Importantly for identification, their uniforms were also laden with the insignia of their battalion and of their country. Even in the most catastrophic of war deaths, there is usually a button or a badge remaining, closely associated with the deceased.

The 78th Battalion's badge was that of a stylized maple leaf with a "78" in the middle, as well as a grenade, also with a "78" in the middle (Figure 14.3). Not all of those fighting with the 78th, however, would have been with the same battalion for the entirety of the war. Found next to the first unknown soldier was a metallic "221," which would have been attached to the soldier's cloth cap. This indicates that it is possible that the first soldier was a member of the 221st Battalion (Canada), which, upon arrival in England, was broken up to reinforce other battalions that had suffered losses. Only four of the 35 men who had gone missing on August 10–11, 1918, had served both with the 221st and the 78th (Reynolds, 2007), serving as a potentially powerful tool for narrowing the field of candidates. There were also badges from the 203rd and 14th Battalions, providing equally important indicators of potential identity. Such powerful clues can also be problematic, however, as lying next to one of the soldiers was the badge of a Scots Fusilier and Australian shoulder flashes (Figure 14.3). Considerable research was undertaken to clarify whether it would be remotely possible for a British or Australian soldier to have become so badly lost that he would have ended up fighting with the Winnipeg Grenadiers, miles from where he should have been. Although the Canadians were bordered to the north by the Australian Corps and sometimes shared resources such as the field ambulances, only the 78th was in Hallu during the Battle of Amiens (Nicholson, 1962). It was thought more likely that the handsome insignia of the other Commonwealth battalions would have been an attractive collectible (Reynolds, 2007). It is possible that one of the soldiers had collected several insignia from different battalions throughout the war, somewhat negating the power of the earlier, singular badges. As the majority of the badges found were from the 78th Battalion Winnipeg Grenadiers, however, we can assume that the majority of the soldiers, if not all, derived from that same battalion (Reynolds, 2007).

Although rare, personal items are also sometimes found next to First World War casualties. In this case, a metallic identification tag was found next to the

FIGURE 14.3 **Insignia of the 78th Battalion and other battalions associated with those who died in Hallu. Also found were insignia of Australia and the Scots Fusiliers.**
Photo credit: L. Clegg

fourth set of remains, a gold-plated, heart-shaped locket was found in between the second and third set of remains, and two rings were found in the bottom of the graves of the second groupings of remains (soldiers 5 to 8). While the identification tag clearly indicates by name one of the soldiers who went missing in Hallu on August 10–11, it could not be assumed that it belonged to the soldier nearest to the item. It was later discovered that the identification tag belonged not to the fourth soldier, but the fifth, highlighting the importance of biological versus material evidence in identification. It is also important to note that the spatial relationships of objects with remains could shift between the time of burial and discovery, and that the recovery process itself was neither carefully documented nor performed by an expert (e.g., an archaeologist).

Correctly associated with body 3, however, was a "sweetheart" locket found enclosing two lengths of human hair divided by a small piece of card.[2] A name and address was scribbled on the card in pencil, but it could not be clearly read until returned to Canada for professional conservation (following the outcome of biological testing). As a result of the cleaning, a name could be read, which corresponded to a family that was well-known in Winnipeg, Canada, during the turn of the last century. The discovery of the locket supported the belief that the deceased soldiers were members of the 78th Battalion from Winnipeg, and that one of them had had a tie to the family.

Anthropological Evidence

Despite the compelling evidentiary weight of identification tags and jewellery, the legal identification of the remains of soldiers, regardless of their time since death, still requires biological evidence. For the eight soldiers in Hallu, a biological link was sought through the creation of an anthropological, genetic, and isotopic profile to which medical records, familial DNA, and geo-physical history could be compared.

The anthropological analysis of human skeletal remains includes the determination of whether the remains are human or non-human, the sex of the individual, the decedent's height and age at the time of death, their ancestry, their overall health and past (healed) injuries, as well as any indicators of what injuries or illnesses may have contributed to their death (İşcan & Kennedy, 1989). In April 2007, the Casualty Identification program was presented with the remains in eight separate boxes at the Commonwealth War Graves Commission mortuary in Beaurains, France. When analyzing the remains found in Hallu, the primary difficulty lay in the fact that the remains had been removed from their location with no record of their initial provenance (the practice has since improved slightly to include the GPS coordinates and photographs of the remains in place prior to their exhumation). All eight were cleaned and laid out anatomically. Even at the time, there was a clear mal-association between bones of the upper and lower bodies of multiple individuals, in particular soldiers 5 to 8, who appear to have originally been placed in the grave in a more haphazard manner than the soldiers in the first grave.

The state of preservation of the bone was very poor in comparison with other First World War soldiers' remains that had been analyzed from neighbouring regions of France. This was possibly due to microbes in the soil that attack the surfaces of bone. Most of the earlier cases analyzed were interred in the Pas-de-Calais region, where the soil is very chalky and the bone surfaces are well protected. The degree of erosion of the bones of the eight soldiers made it difficult to fully assess degenerative changes in some of the joints (which could help with age determination) or determine the nature of some traumatic injuries (Nicholson, 1996).

Human vs. Non-Human

Non-human remains are frequently found intermingled with the remains of soldiers from the First World War. This particular trench, though used only for two days in 1918, had been in long-standing use by the British Army in 1915 (Nicholson, 1962), and it would have contained food waste from meals. In addition, the battlefields were farmland before and after the war, and trenches were used as places to dispose of both battlefield and farm waste. From personal experience, sheep and pig tend to be the most frequently found faunal remains co-associated with human remains. Despite the potential of having human and non-human remains mixed together, all bone recovered from these graves was verified as human.

Minimum Number of Individuals

British, Canadian, Australian, French, and German soldiers alike fought on the land—all of whom sustained many numbers of missing—so it could not be immediately assumed that the recovered remains were necessarily members of the 78th Battalion. Before the Department of National Defence was contacted, the local police first eliminated the likelihood of the remains being civilian (e.g., unmarked village cemetery), archaeological, or even criminal in nature. A considerable problem with such sites is also the likelihood of finding active ordnance, such as hand grenades and unexploded gas shells, which are removed by experts and the police.

As an expert had not conducted the recovery in 2006 and 2007, it could not be assumed that all remains had been recovered from the site. In 2008, the backyard of the Demeusere family was revisited and what was left of the trench was surveyed (Figure 14.4).

Unfortunately, as Canada does not actively search for its missing soldiers, the Casualty Identification section was not authorized to conduct more than a brief scan of the edges and depth of the trench. It was enough to confirm that all soil had been turned over to the level of the initial depth, and that what could have been recovered had been transferred to the Commonwealth War Graves Commission. What had not been recovered at the time of exhumation was unlikely to be recoverable in 2008, as the soil had since been dispersed. The remnants of the trench extended to the north and south, along the eastern property limit of the Demeusere's neighbours. It is possible that more soldiers from the 78th remain interred in the trench outside the property limits of the Demeusere family; but in

FIGURE 14.4 The remains of the trench on the Demeusere property in 2008, facing northeast.
Photo credit: L. Clegg

this part of France the discovery of war dead is a possibility on most properties.

The recovery site visit was also an opportunity to view any artifacts retained by the family, as those items not relating to any particular individual were left with them. After removal of the skeletal remains, the Commonwealth War Graves Commission attempted to collect personal items linked with a soldier, such as jewellery or identifying objects like badges and buttons, and retain their association with the soldier. As the collection of the young Demeusere later confirmed, multiple badges from at least four countries indicated that the trench had been occupied by more than one battalion, and that one or more of the deceased had traded or collected the badges of fellow soldiers during the war. One particular problem, which cautioned against leaning too heavily on regimental badges as viable evidence, was the fact that while three badges, one locket, and one identification tag were provided as identifiers for those among the eight sets of remains, other identifiers such as a fountain pen and several rings had been found afterwards and were retained at the site.

Physical Profiles of the Unknown Soldiers

The overwhelming majority of Canadian First World War fatalities were Caucasian males under the age of 40 (Commonwealth War Graves Commission, 2015). Morphological methods used in anthropological analysis to determine age at death (Buikstra & Ubelaker, 1994) were used to profile the eight individuals, using primarily the pelvis, the cranium, dental wear, and long bones such as the femur. In cases where the pelvis or cranium had been badly damaged, other characteristics of the skeleton (e.g., overall robusticity, angle of the femur, and features of the lower jaw) indicated that all individuals were, unsurprisingly, males between the ages of 20 and 35 at the time of death. Of the eight soldiers, five of them displayed Caucasian (of European ancestry) facial features, while the ancestry of the remaining three could not be determined with confidence due to severe trauma. The stature of each soldier was calculated using a common equation that uses the length of one of the long bones, in this case the femur, to estimate overall height (Klepinger, 2006). Of the five soldiers eventually identified, the average age at the time of death was 27 years, with the youngest at 22 and the eldest 33 years of age, and the average estimated height from those identified was 167 cm (approximately 5'5"), with a range of 162 cm (5'3") to 173 cm (5'8") (Klepinger, 2006).[3]

Trauma

Although the purpose of human remains analysis in this context is to find a name for the deceased, the manner in which they died can be an important part of the overall analysis. Trauma assessment can also provide more information for those families who wish to know as much as possible about a long-dead relative, and importantly it contributes to a more accurate historical record about the nature of wartime skeletal injuries (Loe, Barker & Wright, 2014). It should be noted, however, that skeletal analysis is more likely to underestimate the number and severity of traumas to an individual than they actually experienced, depending on the state of the remains when found. The activity of soil microbes, the expertise used in recovery, and the storage conditions affect the rate of decomposition and fragmentation of remains—often muddling the distinction between peri-mortem (around the time of death) trauma and post-mortem deterioration (Holland, Anderson, & Mann, 1997). In the case of the eight soldiers, some of the skeletal elements had been badly eroded due to the soil and level of moisture, making it difficult to determine if damage to a hip or long bone was due to a traumatic injury or to natural decomposition.

From war diaries, we know that the soldiers at Hallu were exposed to heavy machine-gun fire, which would have been directed cross-wise to the advancing battalion (Canadian Expeditionary Force, 1918d) and at leg level (Loe, Barker, & Wright, 2014). Presuming that those who reached Hallu did so in spite of the machine guns, they would also have had to survive long-range machine-gun fire, field guns (Canadian Expeditionary Force, 1918d), and heavy artillery from the east of their attack. Upon arriving in Hallu, just before 4 p.m., they were hit with explosive munitions (shelling) and became cut off from the battalions to the left and right of the line (Nicholson, 1962).

Amongst the remains of the eight soldiers, the most common skeletal injury noted during analysis was ballistic trauma to the cranium and mandible. Bullet or shrapnel trauma to the skull occurred to seven of the eight soldiers, with six of the eight demonstrating more than one injury to the cranium or face. For two of the eight soldiers, metal fragments were embedded in both the side and front of the cranium or at the cranium's base, with one soldier demonstrating possible gunshot wounds with an entry at the rear of the skull. Some of the soldiers' crania demonstrated more than two points of trauma to the same area, deforming or even shattering the skull. Three of the eight decedents demonstrated a gunshot or shrapnel injury to the hip, but due to the poor preservation of the pelvis it is possible this number is much higher (Author field notes, 2007 and 2008).

Of course, analysis is limited by the fact that only skeletal injuries are observable. More recent studies from the 1990s war in the Balkans found that blast injuries were a significant cause of death, followed by hemorrhage from a traumatic amputation (Cernak et al., 1999). Symptoms of blast injury can include damage to air-containing organs, such as ears, lungs, and the bowels. It is possible that the soldiers in Hallu would have experienced burst eardrums, pulmonary edema, and a blast concussion (Cernak et al., 1999).

Overall Health

We know from their medical records that many of the soldiers lost in Hallu had possibly suffered from earlier blast trauma. In Cernak et al.'s study (1999), a major but seemingly under-detected symptom of blast trauma was damage to the central nervous system—an injury that could take up to a year to completely heal. Several of those who went missing in Hallu have "shell shock" listed in their medical files.

It is important to recognize that not only were the soldiers enduring terrible living conditions while attempting to survive artillery and machine-gun fire; they were doing so under a general malaise related to poor dental health, osteoarthritis, and, as noted above, possible damage to their central nervous system. As bone carries markers of nutritional, physical, and pathological stress (Klepinger, 2006), it can provide an idea of what each soldier may have experienced prior to their death. In some cases, such as a non-disabling deformity or a recently healed gunshot wound, it may provide yet another means of identification.

All but one of the soldiers' remains demonstrated that they had lived physically demanding lives leading up to their subsequent role in the infantry, with strong muscle attachment sites in their bones. They would also have been prone to stress fractures from repetitive and demanding tasks (Klepinger, 2006), as seen by signs of joint inflammation in the hips and shoulders of several of the soldiers. From analysis of remains from both the First and Second World Wars, soldiers from the First World War tend to show more pronounced muscle attachment sites, and more severe signs of osteoarthritis—even in men in their mid- to late 20s (as compared to soldiers who died in the Second World War) (Author field notes, 2008). Conditions seen in soldiers from this time period, normally seen in older individuals, may give an overall indication of just how physical their lives were leading up to and during the war.

Previous traumatic injuries that did not hinder physical ability were also evident in one particular soldier. He had sustained a mid-shaft femur fracture in his right leg several years before death, which had healed but was badly misaligned and may have forced him to limp. Accommodating the shorter and rotated right leg, the bony structure of the right hip had grown to compensate, and showed evidence of an inflammatory response. Considering the physical nature of the infantry, he may have been living with chronic pain (Klepinger, 2006). One of the missing soldiers who remained a strong candidate for identification had a severe leg wound listed on his medical file, later helping to confirm his identity. Another unidentified soldier had sustained a mid-shaft fracture to his upper left arm that, based on healing in the bone, may have healed several years before he died. The left shoulder healed in a slightly rotated position, which would have forced his arm to be slightly turned away from his body (Ortner, 2003). Unfortunately, there was no record of this injury in the files of the candidates, so it is possible that it occurred before the person joined the military, but did not hinder his chances of joining. Alternatively, the remains could have been of another, as-yet-undiscovered candidate for identification.

Three of the soldiers displayed evidence of nutritional stress during child-hood (e.g., enamel hypoplasia, horizontal lines demonstrating interruption in the normal growth of dental enamel) (Ortner, 2003), and almost all had some form of mild-to-severe dental disease. All eight had dental caries and at least one amalgam or gold filling. The resulting overall health of the dentition varied, with some having severe antemortem tooth loss from periodontal disease caused by poor dental hygiene or nutrition-related defects. Two of the eight had an upper denture to ameliorate loss of teeth, but for those with severe antemortem tooth loss, there was evidence that parts of the jaw were being resorbed and, in one individual, the disease was very progressive and his jaw resembled that of a much older man. The two recovered dentures were made by the Canadian Dental Corps (Colonel Dwayne Lemon [Canadian Armed Forces Dentist], personal communi-cation, May 2014), and although sufficient to allow the soldier to eat, did not appear to be well fitted. All eight soldiers had evidence of tobacco staining on their teeth, either through smoking or chewing. One individual showed evidence of heterotopic dentition, where the third upper right molar never erupted from the gums, and instead was visible in the bone of the upper jaw (Ortner, 2003).

In 1916, Private Halliday was admitted to hospital for diphtheria, and in 1917 for rubella. He was later listed as wounded in 1918, but remained on duty (Can-adian Expeditionary Force, 1918b, 1918c). Private Halliday is also listed under the Circumstances of Death Registers for the First World War (Canadian Exped-itionary Force, 1918a, 1918b), indicating that he was killed by an exploding shell that landed in a neighbouring trench (Figure 14.5).

Genetic Analysis

Historical analysis and anthropological analysis allow for the narrowing of can-didates for identification based on height, age, and injuries at death, but a bio-logical link is still required for a formal identification. Analyzing DNA profiles has been a tool in human remains identification since 1992 (Goodwin & Hadi, 2007), and it is the most important tool used in the identification of Canada's First World War missing soldiers. Certain types of DNA, such as mitochondrial

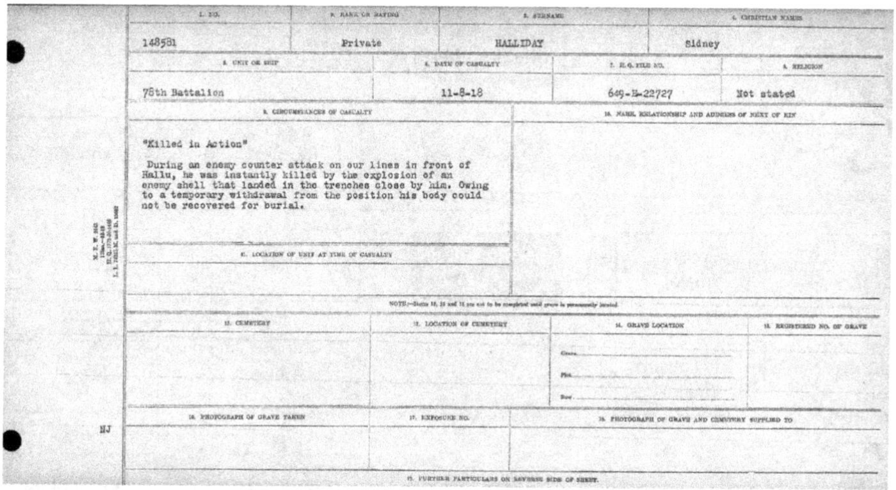

No.	Rank or Rating	Surname	Christian Names
148581	Private	HALLIDAY	Sidney

Unit or Ship	Date of Casualty	H.Q. File No.	Religion
78th Battalion	11-8-18	649-H-22727	Not stated

Circumstances of Casualty

"Killed in Action"

During an enemy counter attack on our lines in front of Hallu, he was instantly killed by the explosion of an enemy shell that landed in the trenches close by him. Owing to a temporary withdrawal from the position his body could not be recovered for burial.

Location of Unit at Time of Casualty

Name, Relationship and Address of Next of Kin

Cemetery	Location of Cemetery	Grave Location	Registered No. of Grave

Photograph of Grave Taken	Exposure No.	Photograph of Grave and Cemetery Supplied To

Further particulars on reverse side of sheet.

FIGURE 14.5 Private Sidney Halliday, Circumstances of death register, First World War.

Source: Library and Archives Canada, Record No. B016684-00296

(or mtDNA, which is derived from the energy-producing organelle of the cell), is more easily analyzed in skeletal remains as there are many more copies of mtDNA per cell than nuclear DNA. This increases the likelihood that a profile can be extracted successfully when most biological tissue has deteriorated over the 90 years since the soldiers' deaths. MtDNA is also useful in that it passes unchanged from mother to son and daughter, and again from daughter to grandson and granddaughter (Goodwin & Hadi, 2007), and so is useful in historical cases where locating a surviving close blood relative is unlikely.

While extraction of DNA from skeletal remains becomes increasingly common with improvements in modern technology, the profiles extracted from the unknown soldiers must still be compared with profiles of their genetic descendants. For historical investigations, mtDNA is also useful in that it is compared against a descendant through the maternal line—a line, unlike paternity, that can be verified through birth records.

The accuracy of the genetic line is as important as the accuracy of the genetic testing, so much so that a professional genealogist was hired by National Defence to verify the birth order through a family's maternal line. This ended up being the lengthiest portion of the identification process. While the rate is unknown, it was not uncommon for those signing up to fight to lie or be ignorant of their date of birth or the location of their next of kin, and oftentimes surnames were changed for ease of assimilation and pronunciation. In the end, even the most professional and complex tracing cannot eliminate the problem of having a soldier with no surviving or traceable mtDNA donors, such as sisters or maternal aunts[4] (see Figure 14.6). Yet another problem is the reality of life in Canada at

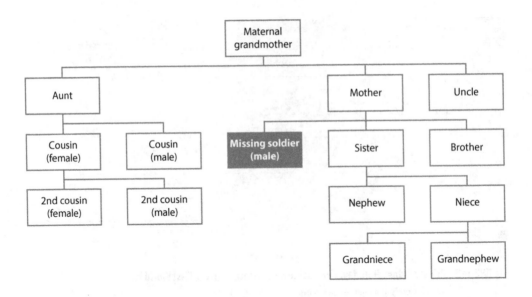

FIGURE 14.6 MtDNA testing chart outlining the eligible donors for a missing soldier based on mitochondrial DNA inheritance.

the turn of the century. One of the candidate soldiers turned out to be a home child—that is, a child brought from Britain to work on Canadian farms as extra household labour. Tracing his genetic descendants took almost two years and, even then, the outcome of any genetic exclusion could not be weighted with much certainty, as it was not possible to verify his maternal descendants.

As an example, the height and age ranges derived from study of the skeleton of soldier 2 coincided with known information for at least four of the soldiers from the 78th Battalion who were listed as missing from the Commonwealth War Graves Commission records. We sought maternal descendants of each of the four candidates and requested that they help us with genetic testing by giving a sample. These samples were then profiled for mtDNA and compared against the mtDNA profile of the deceased soldiers and against a database of profiles from the general population. The database is required to create a probability value and put a DNA match in context: if the mtDNA profile is very common in the general population, then the DNA from the descendant of a soldier and the DNA from the soldier may have matched just because they are not rare and not because the two are distantly related. If a match is made with a common profile, further testing would be required. In the case of soldier 2, however, the mtDNA profile sequence was uncommon in the Canadian population and thus it was very likely that the match between the relative and the remains was not due to chance. The DNA profiles, together with all other circumstantial factors indicated that the remains of soldier 2 were those of Clifford Abraham Neelands.

TABLE 14.1 Mitochondrial DNA testing results[5]

	Soldier								
Candidates	**1**	**2**	**3**	**4**	**5**	**6**	**7**	**8**	**Notes**
Ahmed	■		■						
Anderson	■		■						
Andrews	■		■						
Bunch									No donor found
Cousans									No donor found
Giles									Excluded
Halliday			■						
Hockin	■		■						
Lindell				■					
MacKinnon							■		
Neelands		■							
Simms						■			

In 2007 and 2008, a dental sample was taken from all eight sets of remains and returned to Canada for testing.[6] From the original 35 missing soldiers, 12 were selected for descendant tracing and mitochondrial DNA testing because they were strong candidates based on height and age at death. Of the 12, genetic donors could not be traced for two, while the mtDNA profile of one descendant of a missing soldier failed to match any of the profiles of the sampled skeletons, and thus was excluded.

A full mtDNA profile could be extracted from soldiers 1, 2, 4, 5, 6, 7, and 8, while only a partial profile could be extracted from soldier 3. A partial profile is still informative in that it can still exclude some candidates while including those who are a likely match. It is not as discriminatory, however, as a full profile, and as a result soldier 3 had many matches against those tested (up to five)—rendering the DNA testing only moderately helpful for identification.

Table 14.1 outlines the outcome of the mtDNA testing at the time of writing. The names in the descending column are those missing soldiers from the 78th Battalion who were strong matches for the found eight soldiers based on height and age at death. Each of the soldiers in the left column, except for two (Privates Bunch and Cousans), had a genetic profile donated by one of their maternal descendants. Despite a considerable effort, descendants for Bunch could not be found, while the search for the descendants of Cousans is ongoing. The shading in the table indicates a full or partial mtDNA profile match.

Even when an mtDNA donor is found and agrees to testing, it does not guarantee that the profile is rare enough to be exclusionary. In the cases of soldiers

1 and 3, their profiles were common enough, when compared to a representative population, to bring up more than one match. What makes mtDNA useful (i.e., that it is carried within families) can also make it problematic, because a particular profile can be relatively common, carried in more than one family (i.e., distantly related families) (Goodwin & Hadi, 2007).

For those soldiers who demonstrated only one match against the profiles of the donor samples, the profiles were checked for probability—that is, the profile had to be sufficiently rare to guarantee that the match was based on a direct familial link, rather than a random match. The identifications of soldiers 2, 4, 5, and 7 were checked with the genetic scientists conducting the testing and were judged to be a strong match.[7] The remains of these soldiers were also re-analyzed for height and age, to ensure that these criteria matched the purported identification.

For those soldiers whose mtDNA matched multiple donors, or for whom we could not find a donor, further analysis was required. In these cases, stable isotope testing was chosen as a means to provide an additional method of identifying candidates.

Oxygen Isotope Analysis

Stable isotope profiles were first used as a tool towards identification of First World War dead in December 2010 (Clegg, 2012), differentiating two candidates for a set of First World War remains based on oxygen isotope compositions in dentition. Although still a relatively new technique and not to be relied upon as the sole source for identification (Meier-Augenstein, 2010), stable isotope signatures derived from human skeletal and dental tissue can provide a map of where a person lived at different stages of their life, and thus can narrow a pool of candidates for identification through their geographic history (Evans, Chenery, & Montgomery, 2012). Soldiers with similar physical composition and genetic partial profiles could be differentiated through a general knowledge of their birthplace, where they lived during the first decade of life, and where they spent the last decade of their lives.

Oxygen isotope analysis is based on the $^{18}O/^{16}O$ ratio in bone mineral (bioapatite), which is reflective of the isotopic makeup of precipitation (e.g., drinking water from rain and snow) (Luz & Kolodny, 1985). The ratio of the two isotopes are expressed as $\delta^{18}O$ values in per mil (‰) relative to international standards, and varies in drinking water geographically as a function of temperature, elevation, humidity, and distance from the ocean. In perhaps overly simplistic terms, "we are where we drink." As an individual takes in precipitation through drinking water and food consumption, the $\delta^{18}O$ value of the ingested water of that region is taken up into dental and bone mineral structure (Daux et al., 2008). Depending on the tooth and timing for the mineralization of the elements of the tooth, the $\delta^{18}O$ values extracted from the phosphate of dental enamel reflect the values and thus the location of the drinking water ingested at the time of development (while still being relatively safe from post-mortem depositional change). While dentition retains its structure after development, and thus maintains its $\delta^{18}O$ values, bone remodels over time and as such the mandible provides a $\delta^{18}O$ value reflecting water consumption spanning approximately the last 10 to 20 years of a person's life (Lamb et al., 2014; Longstaffe, personal communication, 2015). By measuring along the dental arcade and bone, we can gain a general history of where an unidentified soldier was raised during the first several years of his life and where he spent the last several years of his life, and then compare this with the known life histories of the candidates.

In order to determine the geographic location of the drinking water for each of the still unidentified soldiers, stable isotope analyses were performed on mandibular bone and dental enamel for soldiers 3, 6, 8, and, as a control, soldier 2. Soldier 2, identified through DNA testing as Clifford Abraham Neelands, had a well-documented geographic history, so the isotopic ratios derived from his remains could be anticipated. By comparing the results of isotopic analysis of soldier 2 against the unknown soldiers (3, 6, and 8), the possibility of contamination of samples could be assessed (Longstaffe, White, & Yau, 2014). For each of the soldiers tested, incisors, premolars, and molars were extracted, as well as a sample of the mandible, and processed to determine the $\delta^{18}O$ values in the bioapatite (Longstaffe, White, & Yau, 2014). All samples were tested per the industry standards, including controls for any post-mortem effects that can alter the profile, such as microbial attack (Meier-Augenstein, 2007).

Isotope profiles for each of the individuals were compared against verifiable life histories, which helped narrow the potential candidates for soldiers 3, 6, and 8. Analysis showed that soldier 3 had lived in a location with the same isotopic signature as the British Isles for much of his youth before moving to the Canadian prairies. This profile helped eliminate those who could not be eliminated earlier through mtDNA, including Privates Anderson, Hockin, and Ahmed. It could not exclude Privates Bunch, Cousans, Andrews, and Halliday, as all had grown up in England and emigrated to Alberta or Manitoba for work in their late adolescence or early twenties (Longstaffe, White, & Yau, 2014).

Establishing Identification

Unlike the identification of persons who have gone missing more recently, the identification of Canada's First World War dead does not include biological reference samples from the deceased, or a close relative such as the decedent's mother, from which to gather genetic information. For those from the First World War, there are no X-rays, and rarely dental records—only distant relatives from which to pull genetic information. Identification is approached slowly by building up overlapping evidence, creating a profile of the decedent that can hopefully be matched to one of the still-missing soldiers.

In the case of Private Sidney Halliday, his identification rested on four major overlapping pieces: the historical record of those who went missing, the physical profiles of the deceased, comparison of mtDNA profiles of the deceased and distant relatives, and finally oxygen isotope profiles of the deceased compared against known life histories. Historical research provided the circumstances of Private Halliday's death and his record of injury and height and age. Anthropological analysis matched the physical profiles of the deceased with that of the military medical record, while mtDNA and stable isotope analysis could not exclude two of the soldiers (1 and 3) as a possible match for Halliday. Eventually Privates Cousans and Andrews could be excluded as being soldier 3 based on a re-evaluation of height and age, whereas Bunch and Halliday remained potential candidates due to consistencies between their heights, ages, and isotopic histories, and those of soldier 3. DNA analysis would have differentiated Bunch from Halliday for comparison with soldier 3; however, no genetic descendant for Bunch could be located and so he could not be excluded. The identification of soldier 3 appeared stalled again.

In the summer of 2014, while providing an update to the families of missing soldiers, the Casualty Identification section was contacted by the nephew of Private Halliday. The nephew shared what he had been told as a child, remembering that Sidney had a fiancée before the war, and that she had stayed in touch with Sidney's sister following his death. Apparently his fiancée eventually remarried and returned to his family the rings that Sidney had given her. Before ending the call, Mr. Halliday was asked about the name of Sidney's fiancée. He replied that it was Miss Elizabeth "Lizzie" Walmsley (Figure 14.7). The locket found near the remains of soldier 3 belonged to Miss Walmsley. She had given it to Private Halliday as a keepsake. The close spatial relationship between soldier 3 and the locket, combined with consistencies in height, age, and isotopic history, provided circumstantial evidence that identified soldier 3 as Private Sidney Halliday.

FIGURE 14.7   Locket found alongside the remains of Private Sidney Halliday, open. Written inside is the address of Elizabeth Walmsley in Winnipeg.

Photo credit: E. Marchand, printed by permission

At the time of writing this chapter, five of the eight soldiers have been identified, primarily using mitochondrial DNA and isotopic comparison. Of the remaining three, one has had multiple genetic links with the other soldiers tested, and it is possible that further testing using paternally inherited DNA will provide the exclusion required. The remaining two soldiers, 6 and 8, however, will require a re-examination of possible candidates and what assumptions were made about soldiers of the First World War that can no longer be sustained. As these soldiers have had to wait 96 years to be found, I trust that they will not have to wait much longer to have a name.

Notes

1.   Isoscapes are maps setting out measured or calculated spatial distribution of $\delta^{18}O$ values throughout a geographic area, which can be used to calculate the predicted $\delta^{18}O$ values in human tissue, or a geo-chemical map of where they lived (Meier-Augenstein, 2010).

2.   Sweetheart jewellery was produced by commercial companies during the war and was worn by female relatives of soldiers as a symbol of support (Rutherford, 2014).

3.   For the purposes of identification, proof of age and name was based off of baptismal and birth records and not the attestation paper. It should be noted, however, that for some of the soldiers, their birthdates may have simply been what they were told, or what was recorded on the day

of their baptism, which could have been months or years after their physical birth. One soldier who was a strong candidate for at least two of the identifications, Private Albert Edward Ahmed, listed his birthdate as November 26, 1888. His actual birth date was the same date, but four years earlier; a considerable difference when determining age of skeletal remains. Furthermore, while he fought under the name of Albert Edward, his birth name was actually William L'Hadji Abdullah Ahmed.

4.   When a missing soldier is determined to be a strong candidate for a match to a set of unidentified human remains (based on physical profile and circumstantial evidence), his maternal descendants are sought through genealogical research. Those descendants are then contacted by the Casualty Identification Coordinator or another member of National Defence, and asked if they wish to participate in the process of identification. For the maternal descendants, the fact that they had a relative who fought, died, and went missing in the First World War is frequently a surprise. Most descendent families agree to participate in genetic testing, which is of no cost to them, and must be on a voluntary basis. The contracted lab then sends them a test kit. The actual profile of the donor is never shared with National Defence, and the only information that is shared is whether the donor DNA profile is a match to the DNA of the decedents and, if so, the strength of that match.

5.   Confirmed results as of January 2015.

6.   Canada, together with the other Commonwealth nations who fought, agreed to an approach for the treatment of their deceased service personnel during and then following the end of the First World War. This agreement, made in December 1918, set out several major tenets—the most important being the tenet of equality. Regardless of rank, social position, or location of death, all fatalities would be cared for in equality and in perpetuity. In practice, this meant that if a soldier died in France, his remains would not be returned to Canada or England for burial (even if the family were willing to pay for the transfer). Instead, he or she would be interred nearest to where he or she died, together with those with whom he or she served. Whether he was the rank of private or general, he would be buried in a Commonwealth War Graves Commission cemetery, which contained uniform headstones and markings (Imperial War Graves Commission, 1918). Canada is a member nation of the Commonwealth War Graves Commission, and still abides by the central tenets of equality, and thus non-repatriation and non-exhumation. For modern identifications, there is some flexibility in that Canada is permitted to bring a small sample back for testing, but any aliquot or unused bone must be returned to the rest of the remains at the time of interment. When seeking a sample for genetic or isotopic testing, though permitted to temporarily remove a sample, it has to be sufficiently small to be easily transported from France to Canada. As DNA is weighted most heavily for identification, it is preferred to take samples of both DNA and stable isotopes from the same location in the remains, making the mandible the ideal shippable sample.

7.   Although the mtDNA profile of a maternal descendant and that of an unknown soldier may match, its strength must be assessed statistically. Variation in the mtDNA genome changes frequency within certain populations, and, as such, the sequence must be compared against a database of known samples. The sample donated by the maternal descendants of the lost soldier and the sample extracted from a set of unidentified remains can match (1) from chance (i.e., the profile is common in families from western England) or (2) from familial relationship (i.e., the profile matches because the descendants and the decedent are maternally related to each other). The more unlikely that the match is because of luck (only 1/4,000 in a comparative database share the same genetic profile as the decedent and donor), the more likely that the match is an indicator of identification. Unfortunately, in testing of Hallu, three of the decedents shared a commonly found genetic profile, so common that when compared against a database, it was found in 1/10 profiles. In some cases, up to five different soldiers could not be genetically excluded from matching soldiers 1 and 3 (Goodwin & Hadi, 2007).

References

Buikstra, J. E., & Ubelaker, D. H. (1994). *Standards for data collection from human skeletal remains.* Fayetteville, AR: Arkansas Archaeological Survey.

Canadian Expeditionary Force. (1918a). *Circumstances of death registers, First World War. Private Sidney Halliday.* Volume 31829_BO16684 (pp. 296–297). Ottawa, ON: Library and Archives Canada.

Canadian Expeditionary Force. (1918b). *Commonwealth war graves registers, First World War. Private Sidney Halliday.* Volume 31830_B016610 (p. 675). Ottawa, ON: Library and Archives Canada.

Canadian Expeditionary Force. (1918c). *Service files of the First World War, 1914–1918. Private Sidney Halliday.* RG 150, Accession 1992-93/166, Box 3961-19. Ottawa, ON: Library and Archives Canada.

Canadian Expeditionary Force. (1918d). *War diary of the 78th Canadian Infantry Battalion, August, 1918, Appendix V.* Ottawa, ON: Library and Archives Canada.

Canadian War Museum. (2015). Canada and the First World War. Retrieved from www.warmuseum.ca/firstworldwar/.

Caux, L. A. (2007). *Documentary package addressed to Dr. Stephen Harris, DHH2, from Lieutenant-Colonel L. A. Caux, Assistant Defence Attaché, Paris, 27 June.* Directorate of History and Heritage—Section 6. Department of National Defence, File number 5090-10-10 (Avion).

Cernak, I., Savic, J., Ignjatovic, D., & Jevtic, M. (1999). Blast injury from explosive munitions. *The Journal of Trauma: Injury, Infection, and Critical Care, 47*(1), 96–104.

Clegg, L. (2012). *Report for the Department of National Defence: Identification of First World War soldier from the 49th battalion, Canadian Expeditionary Force, found in Avion, France, 31 October 2003.* Ottawa, ON: Directorate of History and Heritage.

Commonwealth War Graves Commission. (2015). Commonwealth War Graves Commission. Retrieved from www.cwgc.org.

Daux, V., Lécuyer, C., Héran, M, Amiot, R., Simonk L., Fourel, F., Martineau, F., Lynnerup, N., Reychler, H., & Escarguel, G. (2008). Oxygen isotope fractionation between human phosphate and water revisited. *Journal of Human Evolution, 55*(6), 1138–1147.

Evans, J. A., Chenery, C. A., & Montgomery, J. (2012). A summary of strontium and oxygen isotope variation in archaeological human tooth enamel excavated from Britain. *Journal of Analytical Atomic Spectrometry, 27,* 754–764.

Gauthier, C. (2006). *Documentary package addressed to Major James McKillip, DHH3 from Commander Claude Gauthier, Assistant Defence Attaché, Paris, 10 August.* Directorate of History and Heritage—Section 6. Department of National Defence, File number 5090-10-10 (Avion).

Goodwin, W., & Hadi, S. (2007). DNA. In T. Thompson & S. Black (eds.), *Forensic human identification: An introduction* (pp. 5–27). Boca Raton, FL: Taylor & Francis Group.

Holland, T. D., Anderson, B. E., & Mann, R. W. (1997). Human variables in the postmortem alteration of human bone: Examples from U.S. war casualties. In W. D. Haglund & M. H. Sorg (eds.), *Forensic taphonomy: The postmortem fate of human remains* (pp. 263–274). Boca Raton, FL: Taylor & Francis Group.

Imperial War Graves Commission. (1918). *Report.* London, UK: Imperial War Graves Commission.

İşcan, M. Y., & Kennedy, K. (1989). Reconstruction of life from the skeleton: An introduction. In M. Y. İşcan & K. Kennedy (eds.), *Reconstruction of life from the skeleton* (pp. 1–10). New York, NY: Alan R. Liss.

Klepinger, L. L. (2006). *Fundamentals of forensic anthropology.* Hoboken, NJ: John Wiley & Sons.

Lamb, A. L., Evans, J. E., Buckley, R., & Appelby, J. (2014). Multi-isotope analysis demonstrates significant lifestyle changes in King Richard III. *Jounral of Archaeological Science, 50,* 559–565.

Loe, L., Barker, C., & Wright, R. (2014). An osteological profile of trench warfare: Peri-mortem trauma sustained by soldiers who fought and died in the Battle of Fromelles, 1916. In C. Knüsel and M. J. Smith (eds.), *The Routledge handbook of the bioarchaeology of human conflict* (pp. 575–601). London, UK: Routledge, Taylor & Francis Group.

Longstaffe, F. J., White, C. D., & Yau, G. (2014). *Report for the Department of National Defence: Oxygen isotope analysis of human bioapatitie CMP/DHH-14-001.* London, ON: Department of Earth Sciences, The University of Western Ontario.

Luz, B., & Kolodny, Y. (1985). Oxygen isotope variations in phosphate of biogenic apatites, IV. Mammal teeth and bones. *Earth and Planetary Science Letters, 75*(1), 29–36.

Meier-Augenstein, W. (2007). Stable isotope fingerprinting—chemical element "DNA"? In T. Thompson & S. Black (eds.), *Forensic human identification: An introduction* (pp. 29–53). Boca Raton, FL: Taylor & Francis Group.

Meier-Augenstein, W. (2010). *Stable isotope forensics.* Chippenham, UK: Wiley-Blackwell.

Nicholson, G. W. L. (1962). *Official history of the Canadian Army in the First World War: Canadian Expeditionary Force, 1914–1919.* Ottawa, ON: Roger Duhamel, Queen's Printer and Controller of Stationery.

Nicholson, R. (1996). Bone degradation, burial medium and species representation: Debunking the myths; an experimental approach. *Journal of Archaeological Science, 23*(4), 513–533.

Ortner, D. J. (2003). *Identification of pathological conditions in human skeletal remains* (2nd Ed.). San Diego, CA: Elsevier.

Reynolds, K. (2007, July). *Memorandum 2nd re: Hallu remains.* Department of History and Heritage—Section 6. Department of National Defence, File number 5090-10-10 (Avion).

Rutherford, D. (2014, August 4). Commercial sweetheart jewellery. *Australian War Memorial.* Retrieved from www.awm.gov.au/blog/2014/08/04/commercial-sweetheart-jewellery/.

Related Sources

Bartelink, E. J., Berg, G. E., Beasley, M. M., & Chesson, L. A. (2014). Application of stable isotope forensics for predicting region of origin of human remains from past wars and conflicts. *Annals of Anthropological Practice, 38*(1), 124–136.

Commonwealth War Graves Commission: www.cwgc.org

Department of National Defence, Casualty Identification: www.cmp-cpm.forces.gc.ca/dhh-dhp/dc-tc/hci-idp-eng.asp.

Library and Archives Canada, Military Heritage: www.bac-lac.gc.ca/eng/discover/military-heritage/Pages/military-heritage.aspx.

Loe, L., Barker, C., & Wright, R. (2014). An osteological profile of trench warfare: Peri-mortem trauma sustained by soldiers who fought and died in the Battle of Fromelles, 1916. In C. Knüsel & M. J. Smith (eds.), *The Routledge handbook of the bioarchaeology of human conflict* (pp. 575–601). London, UK: Routledge, Taylor & Francis Group.

Summers, J., Loe, L., & Steel, N. (2010). *Remembering Fromelles: A new cemetery for a new century.* Berkshire, UK: Common Wealth War Graves Commission.

Afterword

The Interconnectedness of Missing Persons as a Problem and as a Solution

Derek Congram (University of Toronto)
Luis Fondebrider (Argentine Forensic Anthropology Team)
Eleonor Fernández (United Nations, Extraordinary Chambers at the Courts of Cambodia)

Interconnectedness

This book highlights how "missing persons" as a subject, despite the absence of a person or persons, is about interconnectedness. People go missing everywhere and by definition are missed by others. The problem is ubiquitous, but the presence of those who can resolve the problem is still limited. In the search for the missing, governments and international organizations often call upon the help of those who became experts in the search for the missing in their native countries. The best example of this is the staff of the Argentine Forensic Anthropology Team (Equipo Argentino de Antropología Forense, or EAAF), who have worked in over 50 countries. In turn, the EAAF has taught many others (including author Derek Congram and other contributors to this book) how to best approach the problem.

Each context, however, has its particularities. Finding the disappeared in a way that is truly helpful and in the interests of the families is unique to each context (legally, culturally, politically), just as each family is distinct in their needs and desires. We can learn from fellow experts in different disciplines and locations, but the legitimacy of our work is rooted in our connectedness with these families. Although states hold the responsibility to investigate the whereabouts of missing persons and inform families of their fates, individual experts enact this responsibility. The work is sometimes on behalf of national or international institutions such as a court, truth commission, or a United Nations inquiry; other times this work is at a much more local level, as when acting directly on behalf of victim families. In any case, it is through the collective sharing of our expertise, particularly as it relates to our interactions with the families of the missing, that we will be most effective.

That most contributors to this volume are anthropologists is not coincidental. The editor (who is also the first author of this chapter) is an anthropologist and so knows, has worked with, and has called on his colleagues to contribute to the book (such as the second author of this chapter). In this sense, the sample of authors here is biased towards anthropology. In their academic and professional formation, anthropologists explore the intersection of culture and biology and assess a person or group's bio-cultural history and identity. Well before specializing in forensics, anthropologists have as a primary goal the understanding of wider cultural and social processes. By virtue of this, they are often better placed to operate in the many culturally nuanced contexts where forensic expertise is required for the search and identification of disappeared victims of violence. The science is a critical aspect of forensic work, but we operate within a cultural and political milieu that anthropologists are keenly adept at understanding. Many chapters in this book demonstrate how these two skills intersect. Anthropologists engage with people and cultures, both living and dead. In most settings where long periods of time separate the disappearance of people and the discovery of their mortal remains, what is left to analyze are their personal objects, which reflect their social identity, and their skeletal remains, which largely reflect their biological identity. Thus, other disciplines are not as commonly involved in the search for, identification, and return of the missing to their families.

Despite this possibly prejudiced representation of the role of anthropologists, this book demonstrates the critical roles of other disciplines: historians, geographers, pathologists, criminologists, psychologists, lawyers, and police personnel (and in many instances these people are expected to play multiple roles at once). In well-funded and well-planned investigations, there is a division of labour and expertise. In many situations, however, any one of these experts will be doing historical investigation, witness interviewing, testifying in court, advocating on behalf of victims, and consoling those who feel the loss most acutely. This is, of course, inappropriate because none of us is truly qualified or capable of doing all of these things. The great variation of circumstances of disappearance (e.g., optional, forced/criminal, accidental, due to natural disasters) means that no single discipline or agency can effectively resolve these cases. The burden that is sometimes placed upon an investigator to play multiple roles is a reflection of the lack of resources and attention given to missing persons. This was exemplified in Argentina following the start of civilian government, when firefighters and cemetery workers were being asked to conduct judicial exhumations (Bernardi & Fondebrider, 2007).

In many ways the term "disappeared" is a terrible euphemism. Strictly speaking, people are dead or alive.[1] It is not by coincidence, however, that (as we learned in Chapter 11) special police agencies are formed to deal with both "missing persons" as well as "unidentified remains." Until the bodies of the disappeared are found or other evidence of their fate leads us to deduce their death, we cannot with certainty distinguish those who were forced to disappear from those who chose to do so. In some cases, such as natural disasters or terrorist attacks like 9/11, the presumption of death is well founded, at least after a few days have passed.

In many other instances it is clear that people are victims of illegal detention or kidnapping and non-judicial execution. This is especially the case in contexts of armed conflict, authoritarian governance, and political repression. In instances of forced, criminal disappearances, not knowing is a further injustice against the families of the disappeared—that they must go, sometimes for decades, sometimes forever, without being able to know and call a crime by its name. They are instead forced to live with uncertainty and avoid declaring what much circumstantial evidence suggests to be true. For victims of state-sponsored political violence, families are victimized further by their presumption that the state will not investigate, or at least will not tell the truth that derives from an investigation.

This ambiguity of a missing person's status is why those who operate in the political and legal sphere are so critical: as advocates and drivers of the process of discovery. Often other specialists, the social and forensic scientists, only become productively involved when politico-legal demands create a position (and budget) for them. Increasingly, internationalized courts are incorporating representation and the voices of the families as active participants in legal proceedings. This is the case currently before the Special Tribunal for Lebanon, the Extraordinary African Chambers within the courts of Senegal, and at the Extraordinary Chambers in the Courts of Cambodia (ECCC). Remarkably, on August 7, 2014, at the ECCC, the judgment rendered against the two most senior surviving leaders of the Khmer Rouge regime declared them guilty of the crime of enforced disappearance.[2] The Trial Chamber found that enforced disappearances may be of similar gravity to the other crimes against humanity enumerated in the ECCC law and thus fall within the ambit of other inhuman acts. The components that constitute crimes were enumerated following the International Criminal Court

Elements of Crimes, which recognized the crime of enforced disappearance as a standalone crime (International Criminal Court, 2011). This is an important legal precedent and step forward because it gave the victim families, who had been waiting for 40 years for such a judgment, a measure of justice. However, the victim families have requested, as reparation, the chance to bury their loved ones, or to know precisely what happened to their relatives. Given the scale of the killings and the time passed since their deaths, this wish will remain unfulfilled.

More recently, in the International Court of Justice's case *Croatia vs Serbia*, the government of Croatia asked the court to declare Serbia's obligation to take all steps possible to provide an immediate and full account of the whereabouts of missing persons from their war in the 1990s.[3] Croatia contends that one of the remedies it seeks is the return of the mortal remains of the deceased to their families. Croatia claims that Serbia has not been providing the assistance required to carry out the search for those remains and for their identification. In a dissenting opinion (when one judge disagrees with the other judges on a panel), Judge Cançado Trindade underlined that "The contending parties' identification and return of all the mortal remains to each other is yet another relevant step in the path towards reconciliation."[4] The fight against impunity for the crime of enforced disappearances is slowly but firmly starting to become part of international and national jurisprudence.

Interconnectedness and Knowledge Transfer Responsible for the Missing

Unfortunately, although the authors in this book demonstrate geographic and disciplinary interconnections in the resolution of the missing, there are also apparent cases of experts, or at least expertise (i.e., knowledge transfer) responsible for the opposite. One apparent example of this transfer is the *"ley de fugas,"* mentioned by Pinzón González, which was enacted in Guatemala in the early 1930s and which allowed people fleeing to avoid detention to be shot (or in more extreme circumstances, victims were told by the authorities to run away and were then shot for "resisting arrest"). An unofficial law of the same name was applied by Franco's army and government in Spain a few years later. The tactics of repression often employed in Francoist Spain and later by death squads in Argentina very much resembled the Nazi Nacht und Nebel ("Night and Fog") directive that aimed to quash dissent by making people simply disappear. Is it coincidence that many Nazi Germans fled to Argentina following the Second World War and that a couple of decades later a military government with fascist

The 'tree of subversion': the genealogy of political opposition as seen by instructors at the Air Force Academy in Buenos Aires *(see page 263).*

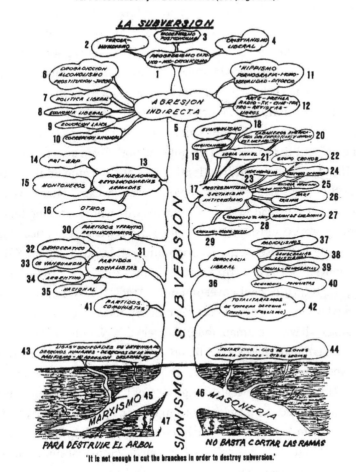

1 Progressive Catholicism –	16 Others	33 Vanguard party
Neo-Catholicism	17 Protestants – Sects –	34 Argentine party
2 Third worldism	Anti-Christians	35 National party
3 Modern Catholicism	18 Evangelism	**36 Liberal Democracy**
(post-Vatican II)	19 Anglicanism	37 Radicals
4 Liberal Christianity	20 American Knights of Fire(?)	38 Christian democrats
5 Indirect Aggression	Union of Argentinian	39 Social democrats
Drug addiction, Alcoholism	Cultural Establishments(?)	40 Popular demagoguery
Prostitution – Gambling	21 Anael Lodge(?)	**41 Communist Parties**
7 Political liberalism	22 Cronos Group(?)	**42 Extreme Right-Wing**
8 Economic liberalism	23 Mormonism	Totalitarian Systems –
9 Lay education	24 Jehovah's Witnesses	(Nazism – Fascism)
10 Trade union corruption	25 International School of	43 Human rights leagues –
11 'Hippie-ness', Pornography –	the New Acropolis	Women's rights – Pacifism –
Homosexuality – Divorce	26 Hare Krishna	Non-aggression – Disarmament
12 Art – Newspapers –	27 Divine Light Mission	44 Rotary club – Lions club
Radio – TV – Cinema –	28 Brotherhood of the Ark	Junior chambers – Other clubs
Theatre – Magazines – Books	29 Snobbery (elitism) – Youth Power	**45 Marxism**
13 Revolutionary Armed Organisations	**30 Revolutionary Front Parties**	**46 Masons**
14 Popular Revolutionary Army	**31 Socialist Parties**	**47 Zionism**
15 Montoneros	32 Democratic party	

FIGURE 15.1 An illustration used in training Air Force cadets during the most recent military rule in Argentina. Subversion in Argentina was being attributed to the same groups (Marxists, Zionists, and Masons) as in Francoist Spain.

Source: Simpson & Bennett (1985, p. 225), printed by permission

tendencies would round up and execute thousands? The 1976 coup in Argentina coincided with the end of the Franco era in Spain—the latter also having started with a military uprising against a democratic government pursuing leftist reforms. In the Argentine Air Force, academy recruits were taught that the roots of subversion in the country were Marxism, Zionism, and Masons (Simpson & Bennett, 1985; Figure 15.1), the same trifecta that the Franco Nationalists claimed were threatening Spain and justified their coup (Beevor, 2006, pp. 23, 96; Thomas, 2003, p. 253). There were also the thousands of forced adoptions of babies taken from "the enemy" and given to military families in both Spain and, decades later, Argentina. These babies, raised by adoptive parents, became adults without realizing that they were also "missing persons." Only decades later have many come to realize that they had biological relatives who were searching for them (Beevor, 2006, p. 407; Gandsman, 2012). Of course the fascist political right is not unique in its use of these methods. Communist states such as the USSR and the Cambodian Khmer Rouge were experts at en masse enforced disappearance.

Following the return of civil government in Argentina, Argentine military advisors worked in Guatemala to assist with military government actions during their continuing civil war (Feldman, 1985). Guatemalan National Police archives reveal how now familiar tactics of kidnapping and extrajudicial execution by state agents were employed (Weld, 2014). The interference of the United States (and the USSR) in Latin America during the Cold War, in particular, is well established and included the provision of supplies and police/military training during the worst state-led violence in many countries including Guatemala. The US International Criminal Investigations Training Program that supported Guatemalan police during their repression would later be used, ironically, to train state employees in the investigation of victims of enforced disappearance from the conflict in Colombia (personal experience of author Congram).

Multidisciplinary, Humane, and Forward-Thinking Resolution of the Missing

At a forensic science conference in South Korea in October 2014 there was some debate about how to best identify victims of mass disasters. The principal problem, as seen by those in the room, was this: marginalized communities that are most susceptible to mass fatalities such as natural disasters are the least likely people to have antemortem records (e.g., dental charts, X-rays), which can be used to compare with physical features of the dead to aid in identification. One colleague, thinking "outside the box," excitedly suggested that given the increasingly low cost of high-tech material, microchips could be implanted into the bodies of susceptible populations, which could be used for identification purposes in the case of their unfortunate deaths (similar to when microchips are implanted into dogs to identify them when they become lost). Tragically, these highly specialized and very accomplished scientists failed to explore the possibility of making marginalized people less susceptible to disaster, which would negate the necessity of implanting them with microchips.

This book illustrates the innovative and coordinated work of many scientists, academics, and other professionals in the resolution of cases of missing persons. Beyond bringing a measure of peace to families of the missing, there is also the hope that those responsible for acts that cause people to go missing will be held accountable for their actions. Further, there is the hope that others will be deterred from similar actions. These include acts of commission, such as criminal homicides, domestic violence, politically motivated murders, and targeted killings during armed conflict. Others go missing due to acts of omission, often related to structural violence, as with wanton neglect of minority populations and the places where they live, and the subsequent disrespect for the disposition of their bodies when they die. When a massive earthquake struck Haiti in 2010, both wealthy tourists and poor local residents died and were buried in the rubble of buildings. It was only the bodies of the latter group, however, that would be loaded onto trucks and dumped into large, unmarked pits outside the capital of Port-au-Prince in the days that followed.

The authors who have written in this book have dedicated their lives to resolving cases of missing people, but we do not do it for the dead. We do it for those who remain: so that the survivors closest to the victims can honour the dead, seek justice for their loss, deter those who are in positions of authority from ordering the deaths of others, and see that governments create conditions that reduce the chances of people becoming missing in the future.

Notes

1. As the chapters by Young and Pinzón González demonstrate, however, there are varying cultural beliefs that defy the biological dichotomy of "alive" or "dead."

2. Extraordinary Chambers in the Courts of Cambodia, Trial Chamber Judgment in Case 002/01 against Nuon Chea and Khieu Samphan, August 7, 2014.

3. International Court of Justice, Case Concerning Application of the Convention on the Prevention and Punishnment of the Crime of Genocide, February 3, 2015.

4. International Court of Justice, Case Concerning Application of the Convention on the Prevention and Punishment of the Crime of Genocide, February 3, 2015, Dissenting Opinion of Judge A.A. Cançado Trindade, para. 493.

References

Beevor, A. (2006). *The battle for Spain*. London, UK: Penguin.

Bernardi, P., & Fondebrider, L. (2007). Forensic archaeology and the scientific documentation of human rights violations: An Argentinian example from the early 1980s. In R. Ferllini (ed.), *Forensic archaeology and human rights violations* (pp. 205–232). Springfield, IL: Charles C. Thomas.

Feldman, D. L. (1985). The United States' role in the Malvinas crisis, 1982: Misguidance and misperception in Argentina's decision to go to war. *Journal of Interamerican Studies and World Affairs, 27*(2), 1–22.

Gandsman, A. E. (2012). Retributive justice, public intimacies and the micropolitics of the restitution of kidnapped children of the disappeared in Argentine. *The International Journal of Transitional Justice, 6*(1), 423–443.

International Criminal Court. (2011). *Elements of crimes*. The Hague, The Netherlands: International Criminal Court. Retrieved from www.icc-cpi.int/NR/rdonlyres/336923D8-A6AD-40EC-AD7B-45BF9DE73D56/0/ElementsOfCrimesEng.pdf.

Simpson, J., & Bennett, J. (1985). *The disappeared*. London, UK: Robson Books.

Thomas, H. (2003). *The Spanish Civil War*. London, UK: Penguin.

Weld, K. (2014). *Paper cadavers*. Durham, NC: Duke University Press.

Contributor Biographies

Bruce E. Anderson is the Forensic Anthropologist for the Pima County Office of the Medical Examiner (PCOME), in Tucson, Arizona. He received his PhD in 1998 from the University of Arizona, where he is an Adjunct Assistant Professor of Anthropology. He has served as Senior Anthropologist for the US Army's Central Identification Laboratory in Hawaii (CILHI) where he conducted the field recovery and laboratory analyses of remains of missing personnel from past US military conflicts. Dr. Anderson currently mentors anthropology students in the Forensic Anthropology Internship Program at the PCOME and works with post-doctoral fellows as part of the PCOME's Forensic Anthropology Fellowship Program. He is certified as a Diplomate by the American Board of Forensic Anthropology (ABFA), is a Fellow in the American Academy of Forensic Sciences (AAFS), is a founding member of the Scientific Working Group in Forensic Anthropology (SWGANTH), and served as a Forensic Anthropologist during the development and initial launch of the National Missing and Unidentified Persons System (NamUs) project.

Carole Bird worked approximately 27 years with the Royal Canadian Mounted Police, specializing in leading change and innovation in policing. She began her career providing policing to First Nations communities and later worked in highway patrol, federal, and rural policing. She commissioned as the first Officer in Charge of Business Continuity Planning, subsequently leading the RCMP's Technological Crime Program Management Services and the Strategic Partnership and Heritage Program. In 2011, she was asked to lead the National Centre for Missing Persons and Unidentified Remains. In this role, she spearheaded the implementation of the National Centre and the development of specialized services for police, medical examiners, and coroners. She has presented as a keynote speaker at both national and international forums. She sits on the Board of Directors of the Missing Children Society of Canada and AMBER Alert Europe. In 2015, Insp. Bird was appointed a Member of the Order of Merit of Police Forces.

Laurel Clegg is an anthropologist who served as the Historical Casualty Identification Coordinator for Canada's Department of National Defence and Canadian Armed Forces, creating the program in 2006 and running it until 2015. The program seeks to actively recover, identify, and inter its formerly missing military service personnel. Laurel is currently on secondment with the Identification and Disaster Response Unit at the British Columbia Coroner's Service, Vancouver, working to resolve cases of unidentified human remains for the province.

Derek Congram has a PhD in archaeology with a focus on bioarchaeology (the analysis of skeletal remains in archaeological contexts). He has worked as a forensic archaeologist and forensic anthropologist since 1999 in 20 countries for organizations including the United Nations, International Committee of the Red Cross, the International Criminal Court, the Argentine Forensic Anthropology Team, and the United States Departments of Justice and Defense. His primary research interest is the development of Geographic Information Science methods in the search for and identification of missing persons in armed conflict contexts. His other interests include professional ethics, Spanish Civil War archaeology/anthropology, and transitional justice, particularly from the perspective of marginalized communities.

Michael R. Dolski earned a PhD in history from Temple University in 2012. His first book, an edited collection titled *D-Day in History and Memory: Comparative Perspectives of the Normandy Invasion* (2014), focuses on international commemoration of the D-Day battles, and his second, *D-Day Remembered: The Normandy Landings in American Collective Memory* (2016), highlights American remembrance of that invasion. Over the past four years, Dr. Dolski has researched the Korean War, particularly the Chosin Reservoir campaign. He works as a US government historian involved in accounting for unresolved casualties from previous military conflicts, with a focus on the identification of soldiers at war cemeteries who are buried as "unknowns."

Shuala M. Drawdy is a Regional Forensic Coordinator for South Asia for the International Committee of the Red Cross, based in Colombo, Sri Lanka. She has worked at the ICRC's headquarters in Geneva, Switzerland, and has served as the ICRC's Regional Forensic Adviser for the Caucasus and Balkans, based in Tbilisi, Republic of Georgia. A forensic anthropologist by training, she received her education at the University of Florida, where she worked at the C. A. Pound Human Identification Laboratory. She began working internationally as a forensic specialist in 1996 for the International Criminal Tribunal for the former

Yugoslavia. Since that time, she has participated in various activities related to the humanitarian identification or legal investigation of victims of conflict or disaster in over 25 countries.

Ariana Fernández Muñoz is a cultural anthropologist. She has graduate degrees in social anthropology, human rights, and international politics. She has worked for the United Nations International Criminal Tribunal for the former Yugoslavia in Bosnia and Herzegovina, Croatia, and Kosovo, and she managed a cultural objects laboratory during forensic investigations for the Iraq High Tribunal, documenting and analyzing cultural objects recovered from mass graves. She has also worked as a volunteer for exhumations and analyses of victims of the Spanish Civil War and postwar repression.

Eleonor Fernández has worked in different capacities for the Civil Parties (victims participating in the criminal proceedings) at the Extraordinary Chambers in the Courts of Cambodia since 2009. She is currently the Senior Legal Consultant of the Civil Party Lead Co-Lawyers Section. She previously worked at the International Criminal Court and the Inter-American Court of Human Rights. Eleonor is a Costa Rican jurist who graduated from the Université Catholique de Louvain, Belgium, and has graduate diplomas in Human Rights Law (Coimbra) and Criminal Law (Köln).

Francisco Ferrándiz is tenured researcher at the Spanish National Research Council (CSIC). He has a PhD in anthropology from the University of California, Berkeley, funded by a Fulbright Scholarship. Since 2002, he has conducted research on the politics of memory in contemporary Spain through the analysis of the exhumations of mass graves from the Civil War (1936–39). On this topic, he has recently published *El pasado bajo tierra: Exhumaciones contemporáneas de la Guerra Civil* (Anthropos/Siglo XXI, 2014), and co-edited (with Antonius C. G. M. Robben) *Necropolitics: Mass Graves and Exhumations in the Age of Human Rights* (University of Pennsylvania Press, 2015). He has also published his research in journals such as *American Ethnologist, Anthropology Today, Critique of Anthropology, Journal of Spanish Cultural Studies,* and *Ethnography.*

Luis Fondebrider is a forensic anthropologist, co-founder and current Director of the Equipo Argentino de Antropologia Forense (EAAF, or Argentine Forensic Anthropology Team). As a member of EAAF, he has participated in forensic investigations in 35 different countries. He has worked as a consultant for: Truth Commissions in Argentina, El Salvador, Haiti, Peru, and South Africa; the UN

International Tribunal for the former Yugoslavia; the Committee of Missing Persons of Cyprus; UN Secretary General Investigation Team for the Democratic Republic of Congo; UN Commission of Inquiry on Darfur; the Special Commission search for the remains of Ernesto "Che" Guevara; a Panel of Experts for Chile; Special Prosecutor Office of the Transitional Government of Ethiopia; International Committee of the Red Cross for the project "The Missing"; and the Medical Legal Institute of Colombia, among others. In 2014 he was awarded a PhD (*honoris causa*) by the University of Buenos Aires.

Arthur Green is a post-doctoral fellow in the Department of Geography at the University of British Columbia, where he also teaches courses in Geographic Information Science. His doctoral research at McGill University focused on post-conflict property management in Aceh, Indonesia, and has been featured in several international conferences including an official event at the 2012 Rio+20 United Nations Conference on Sustainable Development. Before receiving his doctorate, he taught as a college professor and was Chair of the Department of Geography, Earth and Environmental Sciences at Okanagan College in British Columbia. Dr. Green has extensive experience as a researcher and consultant in sub-Saharan Africa and Southeast Asia. His most recent research focuses on advancing applied spatial statistics for humanitarian issues, public participation in agricultural land governance in British Columbia, and the ways in which models of property impact political movements (particularly in post-conflict settings).

Cheryl Katzmarzyk is a Regional Forensic Coordinator for the International Committee of the Red Cross (ICRC), an independent and neutral organization ensuring humanitarian protection and assistance for victims of war and armed violence. Her work involves assisting authorities to develop capacities and best practices in handling the dead, promoting policy development on the proper and dignified management of the dead, and facilitating local and regional networking/cooperation of emergency responders and forensic experts in response to emergency situations. She develops and delivers national and international training courses in the Asia region and is currently developing a resource centre dedicated to best practices in the Management of the Dead in Emergencies in Islamabad. Prior to joining the ICRC, she was the Head of Anthropological Examinations/Mortuary Manager for the International Commission on Missing Persons (ICMP) and an anthropologist serving various missions with the United Nations International Criminal Tribunal for the former Yugoslavia.

Rifat Kešetović is an Assistant Professor in the Medical School of the University of Tuzla, Bosnia and Herzegovina. Dr. Kešetović has been the Head of the Podrinje Identification Project (PIP), Exhumation and Examination Department of the Scientific Program, International Commission on Missing Persons since 1999. To date, PIP has completed the identification of almost 7,000 of the victims of the July 1995 Srebrenica genocide. He co-authored, with Laura Yazedjian, "The Application of Traditional Anthropological Methods in a DNA-Led Identification Process" in *Recovery, Analysis, and Identification of Commingled Human Remains*, edited by Bradley J. Adams and John E. Byrd (2008).

Samantha Lundrigan, PhD, is a criminal psychologist with more than 15 years' experience of teaching and researching issues relating to crime and criminal justice. Currently employed as a Principal Lecturer at Anglia Ruskin University in Cambridge, UK, she teaches both undergraduate and postgraduate courses in criminology and investigative psychology. Previously she was a Research Fellow at the Institute of Criminology at Cambridge University and, before that, a Lecturer in Criminology at the University of Wellington in New Zealand. She has conducted research with a number of police forces and national policing bodies. She is particularly interested in understanding the spatial behaviour of stranger violent offenders. Other research interests include male sexual victimization and jury decision-making. She has provided offender and geographic profiles to serious crime investigations in the UK, US, and New Zealand, and is regularly asked to provide expert opinion for crime news stories and documentaries.

Alex Maass was the Research Project Manager for the Indian Residential Schools Truth and Reconciliation Commission of Canada from 2009 to 2013, where she managed the Commission's Missing Children Project team. Prior to joining the Commission, she worked as a consulting archaeologist and cultural resource manager for First Nations and resource development firms in Canada and the American Pacific Northwest. She has 15 years' experience in ethnographic and archaeological research and has directed archaeological impact assessment and inventory studies, cultural heritage overviews, and traditional use studies. Her research interests include historical archaeology, heritage conservation, and contact-period material culture studies, most recently in relation to residential schooling for Indigenous children in Canada and the other colonial countries where similar assimilationist schemes were pursued. Currently she works in Ottawa for the Department of Aboriginal Affairs and Northern Development Canada in the areas of First Nation governance and community development.

Vedrana Mladina, PhD in Clinical Psychology, is a Licensed Clinical and Health Psychologist. She is a Clinical Psychologist/Wellness Counsellor at the Health and Wellness Center at NYU in Abu Dhabi. Previously, she worked for the past 12 years as Associate Victims Expert at the International Criminal Court (ICC) in The Hague providing psychosocial care for victims of sexual crimes and children affected by conflict worldwide. Since 2008, she has also been a part-time member of the faculty at Webster University in Leiden. Prior to her work at the ICC, Dr. Mladina worked for almost three years with victims and witnesses at the International Criminal Tribunal for the former Yugoslavia (ICTY). Dr. Mladina specializes in the treatment of PTSD, anxiety, depression, burnout, and work-related stress.

Mónica Esmeralda Pinzón González has a master's degree in social psychology and political violence (Universidad de San Carlos de Guatemala), with an ethno-psychology focus. She has a specialist degree in gender studies from the Autonomous University of Mexico (UNAM). She has worked in Guatemala on the defence of Indigenous peoples' rights and with female survivors of forced disappearance, torture, and sexual violence. She is a Professor at the Universidad de San Carlos de Guatemala, and is registered as an expert in international gender crimes by Justice Rapid Response, UN Women, and the Institute for International Criminal Investigations. She has consulted in 23 countries with civil society organizations, governments, universities, and the United Nations Population Fund. Her principal interest is the development of investigations from Indigenous peoples and gender perspectives, and the reform of social institutions to create access to justice and equity for Indigenous women and children.

Robin Reineke is co-founder and Executive Director of the Colibrí Center for Human Rights (www.colibricenter.org), a family advocacy organization working to end death and suffering on the US-Mexico border by partnering with families of the dead and the missing. Originally from Seattle, Washington, she received a BA in anthropology from Bryn Mawr College and an MA in anthropology from the University of Arizona, where she is currently a doctoral candidate in the School of Anthropology, completing her dissertation titled "Naming the Dead: Identification and Ambiguity along the U.S.-Mexico Border." She was awarded the Institute for Policy Studies' Letelier-Moffitt Human Rights Award in 2014, and is an Echoing Green Global Fellow.

Emilio Silva Barrera is a journalist with a BA in sociology and political science and postgraduate studies in the sociology of consumerism (both from the Universidad Complutense, Madrid). In 2000, he organized the first scientific excavation of a Spanish Civil War mass grave, an unmarked grave of 13 men—including his grandfather—who were extrajudicially executed. Responding to calls for help from other families of missing persons from the war and postwar repression, he founded the non-governmental group Asociación para la Recuperación de la Memoria Histórica (ARMH, or the Association for the Recovery of Historical Memory). He has authored many works on the subject of historic memory and missing persons from the Spanish Civil War, including *Las fosas del Franco* (Franco's graves) (2003), with S. Macías, and *La memoria de los olvidados* (The memory of the forgotten ones) (2004). In 2015, ARMH and Silva were awarded the Abraham Lincoln Brigade Archives/Puffin Award for Human Rights Activism.

Mark Skinner received his doctorate in palaeoanthropology from University of Cambridge in 1978. In 1982, he became the first Canadian board-certified Diplomate of the American Board of Forensic Anthropology. He has consulted on hundreds of forensic cases in multiple countries. He has worked for various agencies investigating missing persons and unidentified remains in Afghanistan (1997), Bosnia (1998–2001), East Timor (1999), Serbia (2001–02), and Kosovo (2006). In 2002 he received the Bora Laskin National Fellowship in Human Rights Research. He was Director of the International Commission on Missing Persons from 2004–05. In 2011, he retired from his teaching career at Simon Fraser University in Canada. He is currently an Honorary Visiting Fellow in the Department of Archaeology at the University of York (UK) and he consults with families and agencies working for the wrongfully convicted.

Hugh Tuller is a forensic anthropologist/archaeologist with experience working in post-conflict contexts. He has worked for the United Nations International Criminal Tribunal for the former Yugoslavia (ICTY), the Sarajevo-based International Commission on Missing Persons (ICMP), and with the Committee on Missing Persons (CMP) in Cyprus. For the past 10 years he has worked at the Defense POW/MIA Accounting Agency (DPAA, formally the Joint POW/MIA Accounting Command, or JPAC), the United States government's effort to search for and identify missing servicemen from America's past wars. He is currently on leave from the DPAA to pursue his PhD at the University of Tennessee, exploring the nexus of forensic science and transitional justice.

Sarah Wagner is an Associate Professor of Anthropology at George Washington University and author of *To Know Where He Lies: DNA Technology and the Search for Srebrenica's Missing* (University of California Press, 2008), and *Srebrenica in the Aftermath of Genocide* (co-authored with Lara Nettelfield, Cambridge University Press, 2014). Her research has explored connections between the destructive and creative forces of war, focusing on the identification of missing persons in Bosnia and Herzegovina, specifically victims of the Srebrenica genocide, and the United States military's attempts to recover and identify service members Missing In Action (MIA) from the past century's conflicts.

Marie Wilson has over 30 years of experience as a journalist, teacher, senior executive manager of Crown Corporations, and project manager. Much of her time has been spent working in Canada's north, particularly on issues of interest to First Nations and Inuit communities. This experience led to her involvement in journalism training in South Africa during the transition to democracy and covering the post-apartheid Truth and Reconciliation Commission. Since 2009, Dr. Wilson has been one of three Commissioners leading the Truth and Reconciliation Commission of Canada, which investigated Indian Residential Schools. She has received a lifetime CBC North achievement award, a Northerner of the Year Award, a Queen's Diamond Jubilee Medal, and Honorary Doctorates of Law from St. Thomas University (2012) and the University of Manitoba (2015).

Janet Young holds an honours BA in archaeology and ancient history from the University of Ottawa, an MSc in human osteology, palaeopathology and funerary archaeology from the University of Bradford, England, and a PhD in population health from the University of Ottawa. She has been working at the Canadian Museum of History since 1994 and is currently Curator of Physical Anthropology. Dr. Young is responsible for the creation, implementation, and coordination of the Human Remains Repatriation Program, whose goal is to document human remains prior to repatriation. Her research interests include biomechanical and pathological changes in the human skeleton as they relate to activity patterns and the general health outcomes of past and present populations.

Index

National Memorial Cemetery of the Pacific
  (NMCP, Hawaii)
  disinterment project, 145
  Korean War unknowns, 142–44, 157–58,
    167nn6–7, 167n14
National Missing and Unidentified Persons
  System (NamUs), 244
  collaboration with PCOME, 262
  unidentified remains cases, 255–56
Native American Graves Protection
  and Repatriation Act (US), 2–3
Native Americans. *See also* First Nations peoples
  multi-generational respect of the dead, 120
natural disasters
  ICRC training initiatives for first responders,
    65–66
  management strategies, development of,
    66–67
  political sensitivities, 70
  socio-economic support, 69
NCMPUR. *See* National Centre for Missing
  Persons and Unidentified Remains
  (NCMPUR)
Neacappo, David, 30
Neelands, Clifford Abraham, 302, 305
Nethery, K., 194, 198, 199
New York, unidentified remains cases, 255
New Zealand, assimilationist residential
  schooling, 35
Newiss, G., 185, 186
Nicaragua, 34
No More Deaths, 264
non-governmental organizations (NGOs),
  and governmental partnerships, 6
non-judicial execution, 313
non-Western cultures
  humanitarian obligations, interpretation
    of, 63
North American Free Trade Agreement
  (NAFTA)
  economic impact on Mexican farmers, 253
North Korea. *See* Korean War
nuclear DNA, 49, 301
Nuremberg Statute
  crimes of illegal detention, 79

Olson, Clifford, 228
Operation Glory
  anthropological comparisons, 145–46

forensic odontology, 145–46
Korean War unknowns, identification of,
  142–44
provenance of remains, 144–45, 167n8
oral testimony
  diminishing returns over time, 210
  fallability of, 207–8, 208–10
  in identification of residential school burial
    sites, 19, 27
  use of in investigations, 7
Organization of American States
  Inter-American Court of Human Rights, 77
ortho-maps, 27
osteology
  physical/dental profile of human remains, 291
  in Srebrenica identification process, 47
oxygen isotope analysis, 291, 304–5, 307n1

PCOME. *See* Pima County Office of the Medical
  Examiner (PCOME)
Pérez Esquivel, Adolfo, 91
perpetrator behaviour
  disposal sites, 7–8
  withholding of knowledge, 52
personal effects
  advice for de-commingling, 275–82
  bilateral asymmetry, 282
  clothing, 257, 262, 270
  cultural analysts, role of, 278–82
  de-commingling of objects, 269–70, 271
  definitive associations, care in making, 277
  documentation of spatial associations, 277
  as evidence of cause of death, 271
  experience level of investigators, 284, 285
  filtering of social/biological identification,
    282–83
  First World War items, 292–94
  gunshot damage to clothing, 283–84
  as identifiers of group identities, 271–72
  laboratory analysis of, 278–82
  limitations of analysis, 282–84
  as markers of identity, 270–71, 292–94
  pair matching, 280
  problem of vocabulary, 284
  problems of specificity, 281–82
  re-associating/reassembling clothing, 281–82
  recognition of clothing by relatives, 273
  recovery site procedures, 275–77
  reference materials, 282

Missing Persons: Multidisciplinary Perspectives on the Disappeared

social/evidentiary value of, 285
steps in analysis of, 280
"sweetheart" locket, 293–94, 306–7, 307n2
tattoos, 262
use of in gender identification, 272–73
value of to next of kin, 270
personhood of archaeological skeletal
    remains, 131
Peru
    ICRC investigations of conflict-related
        missing persons, 62
    transitional justice initiatives, 34
physical anthropology
    collection of human remains, defined, 124
    in Srebrenica identification process, 48
Physicians for Human Rights (PHR)
    antemortem database, 48–49, 177
    Srebrenica identification, role in, 48
Pichinao, J., 111
Pickton, Robert William, 7
Piehler, Kurt, 147
Pima County Missing Migrant Project, 261
Pima County Office of the Medical Examiner
    (PCOME)
    consular relationships, 264
    craniometric data, 261
    data collection and analysis, 254–55, 261
    decomposition rate data, 261
    DNA profile analyses, 261
    forensic anthropology caseload, 257
    identification process, 260–61
    infracranial skeleton, metrical analyses of, 261
    migrant deaths, 249, 250–51, 265nn3–4
    non-metric cranial data, 261
    Post-Doctoral Fellowship in Forensic
        Anthropology, 261–62
    unidentified remains cases, 255–56
    working relationships with other
        organizations, 262, 263–64
Pinzón González, Mónica Esmeralda, 6, 102–18,
    314, 317n1
Podrinje Identification Project (PIP)
    Srebrenica identification process, 46–47,
        49–50, 58nn1–2
police, as facilitators, 122
Policing Resources in Canada, 2010 (Canadian
    Centre of Justice Statistics), 224–25

political violence
    cover-up of Franco regime crimes, 91
    of forced disappearance, 84–85, 98n14, 313
    international forms of parallelism, 88
post-conflict societies
    timely resolution of absence, 52
Post-Doctoral Fellowship in Forensic
    Anthropology (PCOME), 261–62
poverty
    as cause of migration, 252, 257–58
    lack of formal medical records, 259–60
practitioners, 178–81
    burnout, and work-related stress, 178–80
    interview concerns, 7, 171–72
    interview risks, 178
    professionalism of self-compassion, 181
    PTSD risk, 178
    secondary traumatization, 180
Pradera, Javier, 81
    on category of missing persons, 86–87, 98n18
Prentice, James, 16–17
primary actor/action model
    the missing, 121
    seekers and facilitators, 121–22
primary mass graves, 42
    Bosnia and Herzegovina, 48
    complexities of identification, 47
    decomposition, affect on post-mortem
        positions, 276–77
    interconnection with secondary mass
        graves, 50
privacy, and professional discretion, 9
probability models, 215
processuality, of Maya people, 103
PTSD, and interview practitioners, 178
public sphere, and theories of interaction, 146
Puller, Lewis "Chesty", 153

Quantum GIS, 211
Quinet, K., 186

Rarick, Pfc Warren Jackson, 153
RCMP. See Royal Canadian Mounted Police
    (RCMP)
Recovery of Historical Memory (REMHI), 107,
    116n2
Red Crescent Movement, 60, 61. See also
    International Committee of the Red Cross
    (ICRC)

CPSIA information can be obtained
at www.ICGtesting.com
Printed in the USA
BVHW012144130120
569471BV00005B/124/P

9 781551 309309